Java Gently

INTERNATIONAL COMPUTER SCIENCE SERIES
Consulting Editor A D McGettrick University of Strathclyde

SELECTED TITLES IN THE SERIES
Programming in Ada 95 (2nd edn) *J G P Barnes*
Ada from the Beginning (3rd edn) *J Skansholm*
Programmming Language Essentials *H E Bal and D Grune*
Human–Computer Interaction *J Preece et al.*
Fortran 90 Programming *T M R Ellis, I R Philips and T M Lahey*
Principles of Object-Oriented Software Development *A Eliens*
Object-Oriented Programming in Eiffel (2nd edn) *P Thomas and R Weedon*
Miranda: The Craft of Functional Programming *S Thompson*
Software Engineering (5th edn) *I Sommerville*
Haskell: The Craft of Functional Programming *S Thompson*
Functional C *P Hartel and H Muller*
C++ from the Beginning *J Skansholm*

OTHER RELATED ADDISON-WESLEY TITLES
The Java Programming Language *K Arnold and J Gosling*
Java Essentials for C and C++ Programmers *B Boone*
Learn Java on the Macintosh *B Boone and D Mark*
The Java Tutorial *M Campione and K Walrath*
The Java Class Libraries *P Chan and R Lee*
Active Java *A Freeman* and *D Ince*
The Java Application Programming Interface *J Gosling, F Yellin, and the Java Team*
The Java Language Specification *J Gosling, B Joy and G Steele*
Hooked on Java *A Van Hoff, S Shaio and O Starbuck*
Internet Programming *D Ince and A Freeman*
The Java FAQ (Frequently Asked Questions) *J Kanevra*
The Concise SGML Companion *N Bradley*
SGML and HTML Explained *M Bryan*
How to Write Better HTML with Style Sheets *H Lie and B Bos*
Learn HTML on the Macintosh *D Mark and D Lawrence*
HTML 4 *D Raggett, J Lam, I Alexander and M Kmiec*
JDBC Database Access with Java *G Hamilton, R Cattell and M Fisher*
Concurrent Programming in Java *D Lea*
Programming the Internet with Java *D Ince and A Freeman*
Java Software Solutions *J Lewis and W Loftus*

OTHER TITLES BY THE SAME AUTHOR
Pascal Precisely (3rd edn) *J Bishop*
Turbo Pascal Precisely *J Bishop*
Pascal Precisely for Scientists and Engineers *J Bishop and N Bishop*

Java Gently

2nd edition

Judy M. Bishop
Computer Science Department
University of Pretoria

 **Addison-Wesley**

Harlow, England • Reading, Massachusetts • Menlo Park, California • New York
Don Mills, Ontario • Amsterdam • Bonn • Sydney • Singapore • Tokyo • Madrid •
San Juan • Milan • Mexico City • Seoul • Taipei

Pearson Education Limited
Edinburgh Gate
Harlow
Essex CM20 2JE
England

and Associated Companies around the World.

Visit us on the World Wide Web at:
www.pearsoned-ema.com

First published 1997
Second edition 1998

© Pearson Education Limited 1998

ISBN 0-201-342979

British Library Cataloguing-in-Publication Data
A catalogue record for this book is available from the British Library

10 9 8 7 6 5
04 03 02 01 00

Cover designed by Od B Design and Communication, Reading
Typeset by 30
Printed in Great Britain by Henry Ling Ltd., at the Dorset Press, Dorchester, Dorset.

To my parents, Tom and Pat,
with love and admiration

Contents

List of examples and case studies

Preface to the second edition

Java Gently is a first programming text. It aims to teach students, as well as those fascinated by the possibilities of their desktop computers, how to program, and how to do it in the best possible style in the Java programming language. In the process, *Java Gently* covers all of the Java 1.1 language, most of its core libraries and utilities and the prospects it offers for the future. In terms of programming, it covers object-orientation, software design, structured programming, graphical user interfacing, event-driven programming, networking and an introduction to data structures.

A philosophy of teaching Java

When this book began in 1996, the way to teach Java as a first programming language was still uncharted. My experience since then in teaching Java courses many times, and in the overwhelmingly favourable reaction to the first edition, has reinforced my belief that teaching Java requires a different model from previous languages. Java is different from its predecessor first languages (Pascal, C++, Ada) in the following ways:

1   It is small, yet object-oriented.
2   It has no built-in data structure types other than the array.
3   It provides for full graphical user interface (GUI) and multimedia (sound, image and animation) facilities, and promotes GUI programs as applets associated with web browsers.
4   It provides built-in multi-threading features and facilitates programming on the network in a variety of ways.

Given this list there seem to be two possible approaches to presenting Java as a first teaching language. The first is immediately attractive: start at point 3; go straight into GUI, multimedia, applets and the whole network environment, thereby catching the students' interest and showing them how modern and different Java really is. The second approach is to start at the beginning, laying a sound foundation of basic concepts, and then moving on to the newer aspects.

Java Gently does **some of both**, as they both have advantages. Starting with applets and GUI is exciting, but requires so much underlying knowledge of objects that even if students learn the outer shell of programs parrot-fashion, they may never fully understand what they are doing. On the other hand, proceeding at a steady pace through all the background first is a sound policy, but can be both boring and overwhelming.

Java Gently's approach

The approach we have devised is a middle ground, which hinges on Java's two main selling points: it is network-enabled but it is small. So we start off with programs that show how the web is used, but then move straight into covering the basic concepts. Because Java has a smaller number of constructs than Pascal or C++, we can spend *less time* here, and therefore can *get back* to the GUI and network aspects sooner, certainly within the first half of a course. Then applets, multimedia, graphics and so on can be introduced properly, to students who have already encountered classes, objects, instantiation and inheritance, and know how to handle them.

Approach is not everything, however, and *Java Gently* uses three other tried and tested teaching techniques:

- diagrams everywhere,
- explanation by example,
- self-check quizzes and problems after every chapter.

There are also three kinds of diagrams used throughout the book:

- **Algorithm** diagrams, which show the flow of small programs, and also serve to illustrate new concepts such as exceptions and multi-threading.
- **Class** diagrams, which show the structure of the program at the class level, while still revealing the basic components such as methods and variables and the interaction between them.
- **Form** diagrams, which show the syntax of each new Java construct in a way that mirrors its usage in practice.

There are over 80 complete fully worked examples, together with test data and output. Each example has been carefully chosen so that it both illustrates the feature that has just been introduced, and also solves a real problem in the best possible Java style. Most of the examples have a 'real world' flavour, which reinforces the need for a programmer to understand the user's problem, and to write programs in a user-friendly way. As soon as a new feature is introduced, it becomes part of the repertoire of the programmer, and will re-emerge in subsequent examples when needed. As the book progresses, the examples get longer and more challenging.

The book subscribes to the belief that Java is, and will be for many years in the future, an excellent first teaching language, and that it is in a different class from its competitors, C++, Pascal and Ada. For that reason, we teach Java properly, with the web, objects and exceptions coming in right at the beginning.

Teaching programming vs teaching Java

For a first-year course, it is no longer sufficient just to teach a language. The expectation of today's computer users is that the whole computing milieu will assist in the solution of day-to-day problems. In addition to explaining syntax and the construction of a well-formed program, a programming textbook for the next century has to include techniques for problem solving.

Java Gently is indeed such a modern textbook. Each worked problem is introduced with a typically inexact statement. This is then refined in the process of devising a solution. Where applicable, the appropriate technique is selected from those previously discussed, and then we proceed to algorithm development. As an additional aid, algorithms are illustrated with structured diagrams, and important techniques are discussed, highlighted and identified for reuse later on. The important programming paradigms of:

- structured programming,
- object-oriented programming,
- class design,
- abstraction,
- software reuse, and
- generality

all receive attention, and examples are carefully chosen to show how these techniques can encourage correctness and efficiency. For example, there are discussions on guidelines for class design, on the relationship between arrays and classes, on the interplay between loops and exceptions, and on the different ways of implementing data structures, to mention just a few.

Order of topics

The topics are grouped into chapters to enable an easy introduction to programming right at the beginning. The order of statements as covered is: output, assignment, for, input, if, while, do, switch. This grouping does not follow that of the Java reference manual, nor of a book intended for someone who already knows programming. It is a pedagogically tried and tested order, which gets the student through the fundamentals of Java, gently, but without undue delay and fuss.

Most of the chapters contain an even mix of control, data structure and input-output issues, plus some Java specialities. My experience has shown that this integrated approach to the order of topics has tremendous benefits for motivation and understanding, and that students are able to get ahead and accomplish more in a shorter time, without compromising their assimilation of the principles of Java and programming. The key points of the order of all the material are:

- rapid entry to genuine programming problems;
- the power of object-oriented programming presented with realistic examples from the start;
- exceptions introduced early on and explained as a natural way to control flow between classes;
- 'no fuss' discussion of features that are simple in Java (such as class structure) but in-depth treatment of potentially difficult topics (such as casting and cloning);
- hash tables grouped with arrays to show their efficacy in providing for non-integer indices;
- a custom-made input package, which is used from Chapter 4, and explained in full in Chapter 7 once string tokenizers have been covered;
- introduction to object references and their implications through the development of a linked list class;
- almost full coverage of the awt (abstract windowing toolkit) facilities, but geared towards examples;
- applets presented through a viewer and a browser, and the differences between applets and applications explained once the student can genuinely appreciate the issues;
- multi-threading done before socket programming, so that the socket programs can illustrate multiple client–server operations.

Full coverage

In terms of full coverage, *Java Gently* ensures that the reader is presented with **all** the language. Applets and graphics are covered, as are threads, networking, database connectivity and remote objects. Ample use is made of images and colour, in the modern idiom, as illustrated in the colour plate section.

Java Gently aims to excite students and to keep them interested in programming, so the Web aspects of Java are covered, but they are not allowed to overshadow the primary purpose of the book, which is to teach good principles of programming. So much of programming-in-the-web is knowing the correct library method to call, and there is a great deal of repetitive setting of fonts and so on, the details of which can be easily left to a second course.

Because object-oriented programming lends itself to presenting data structures, Part II has a thorough treatment of classical data structures, with mention of sorting and searching algorithms. There is discussion of the standard Java data structures as well as several written especially for the book. *Java Gently* gives its readers a direct entry into a second course syllabus.

What's new in the second edition

Most importantly *Java Gently* second edition has been thoroughly modernized to take full advantage of the new facilities in Java 1.1. Specifically, these include:

- the new event model of multiple events, listeners and event handlers;
- internationalization of formatting for dates, currencies and numbers;
- inner classes;
- Java Database Connectivity for accessing databases from Java;
- Java Remote Invocation for linking up programs on different machines.

One might wonder whether these new topics are applicable for the first programming text. My view is that students stumble on them anyway, and the role of *Java Gently* is to present them in a manner that is easy to understand and assimilate, and yet is **correct**. They are also 'fun' topics, as the examples in Chapters 7 and 14 show. In keeping with the book's approach, the new topics are not introduced in isolation, but are carried through in later examples as they fit in.

In addition, there are new sections throughout the book, some based on suggestions from adopters. Particular attention has been paid to adding more diagrams to explain the structure and semantics of the language:

- how to acquire the Java Development Kit and get Java up at home;
- where to find assistance on Java, including more prominent mention of the web site;
- parameter passing for objects;
- package creation and accessing (several utilities such as opening a file, sorting and the list class are added to a 'myutilities' package as the book progresses);
- protection modifiers, what they mean and how inheritance affects things;
- greater emphasis on the common Java libraries, and careful assistance for learners to find their way around them easily (specifically `java.text`, `java.util` and `java.awt`);
- more on graphics and how to draw a graph.

Finally, the usual additions for a second edition include in this case:

- a standardized programming presentation, with comments everywhere;
- more emphasis on screen dumps, with a special colour section to show the full effect of Java in action on the web;

- over 30 new examples and case studies, bringing the total to over 70;

- many more exercises, accounting for 120 altogether;

- index to syntax forms for easier access.

Coping with Java development in the future

The Java community is in the fortunate position of entering a period of relative stability. In assessing Sun's proposals for Java 1.2 as of January 1998, it would seem that there are minimal language changes now. Specifically, input methods (which the *Java Gently* Text class addresses) will be added, as well as collections and weak references (one is not sure whether these are a good idea!). Some changes are envisaged to the remote method invocation (RMI), but the remainder of the enhancements in Java 1.2 affect performance and the application programming interfaces (APIs) not directly covered by this book, such as Java Beans and Java Foundation Classes. Java 1.2 is due only in mid-1998, and will take at least six months to mature, if past experience is anything to go by. Moreover, the browsers will have another task of converting, and this may take up to a year.

The net result is that we can now relax and work with a language (Java 1.1) which covers all our needs, is stable and supported and, of course, is the basis for *Java Gently* 2nd edition.

Teaching aids and the web site

Java Gently contains:

- over 70 fully worked examples and case studies;

- summaries after each chapter;

- ten-point quizzes at the end of each chapter, with solutions;

- over 100 exercises;

- an active web site;

- special Text class for augmenting Java's input from the keyboard;

- notations for algorithms and classes resulting in over 70 diagrams;

- a unique way of presenting Java syntax to the novice programmer.

All examples have been tested and run and are available on a web site which is actively maintained and updated. The web site at

www.cs.up.ac.za/javagently

also contains

- web pages which introduce the book;
- all the examples for downloading, either individually, in chapters or in one go;
- frequently asked questions, with answers;
- error list;
- discussion board;
- future plans for the book;
- e-mail contact with the author and the *Java Gently* team.

Who is the book for?

The book is intended for students learning to program for the first time in Java, and who have access to the Java Development Kit from Sun, running on PCs, Macs or Unix. There is no reliance in the book on any of the myriad of development environments that are becoming available. Students would normally be in their first year at a university or college, and could be in the science, engineering, commerce or liberal arts faculties: the examples are sufficiently wide-ranging to cater for all. The book does not require mathematical experience, and would certainly be accessible for school pupils taking computer science in senior years. Because there is an emphasis on facts and examples, rather than long discussions, the book would also be suitable for experienced programmers or hobbyists who wish to pick up Java quickly.

The book is based on many courses given in Java since 1996, and on courses in other languages presented to science and engineering students at first year university level since 1980. Included are many of the class-tested examples and exercises from these courses. All examples have been tested on JDK 1.1.4 on a Sun (Unix) and PC (Windows 95 or NT). The browser used for applets was HotJava, with NetScape Communicator and Internet Explorer for the earlier programs.

Because technology, and especially Java, is advancing at a rapid rate, it may be that a new version of the Java library is available simultaneously with this book. Consult our web site for the latest information and for program updates.

Acknowledgements

This second edition of *Java Gently* has been greatly influenced and improved by the many people from all round the world who took the trouble to write in and share their experiences and ideas. In particular, I would like to acknowledge the input of Hanspeter Amend, Sonia Berman, Alexander Lawrence, Yehiel Jake Milman, Monica Schraefel, Ian Wilson and Darrell Wick.

Once again I am grateful to the technical staff and research students in the department who continued to help solve numerous problems of a rapidly moving Java on multiple platforms: Tony Abbott, John Botha, Louis Botha, Alywn Moolman. This team has also kept the *Java Gently* programs and web site up to date and running, answering questions and queries from all over the world on a daily basis with me. Louis' amazing enquiring mind proved a ready source of accurate answers to arcane Java questions at all hours. I am grateful also for his contribution to the programs in Chapter 14.

Addison-Wesley Longman has once again provided outstanding professional service in the editorial and production departments in getting this book to print on time; my gratitude to Emma Mitchell, Michael Strang, Martin Klopstock, Elaine Richardson and their teams.

Finally, as always, my love and thanks to Nigel, William and Michael for yet again having to put up with me writing a book over the summer holiday, and beyond.

Judith M Bishop
Pretoria, South Africa
February 1998

A Companion Web Site accompanies *Java Gently*, *2e* by Judy Bishop

Visit the Companion Web Site for *Java Gently* at www.booksites.net/bishop_jg
Here you will find valuable teaching and learning material including:

General:
- Information about the book
- Errata

For Students:
- Links to the individual examples specified in the book
- Downloads of the programs referred to in the book
- A discussion board
- Frequently asked questions

For Lecturers:
- A complete set of answers to the exercises at the end of each chapter will be made available.

Chapter summary

The book is divided into two parts – Part I introduces Java and covers the fundamentals of object-oriented programming (OOP) and programming-in-the-small. By the end of Chapter 7, you will be able to write complete Java applications consisting of several classes interacting via data and method accesses. Part II builds on this foundation by extending the coverage of objects and introducing GUI, applets, networks, Java's connection mechanisms to databases and data structures.

Chapter 1   **Introduction**

All about Java on the web using a multimedia presentation on nature conservation with images and applets. A description of how Java software is developed via the software components of a typical computer (editor, compiler and so on) plus an introduction to the diagrammatic notations used in the book and how to use the Java Development System, which is available free from Sun.

Chapter 2   **Simple programs**

Introduction to Java via two starter programs; fundamentals of classes and objects; all about printing and assignment. Examples involving output and the use of some Java classes such as `Locale`.

Chapter 3   **Structuring**

The objective of this chapter is to reach a point where programs can be written which do more than a human would be prepared to do! The areas covered are: Java primitive types, counting loops, methods and parameters. Either side of these, there are sections on how to design good programs, and an introduction to the class diagram notation which is used extensively hereafter. A case study that uses multiple classes and objects is used to bring all these points together and to illustrate the class notation in action.

Chapter 4   **Changing the state**

Following naturally on from Chapters 2 and 3, we add facilities to read data, and to make decisions that change the path of a program, either by means of selection statements or by means of exceptions. Exceptions have to be done at this point, because they are intimately bound up with the way input is handled in Java. Facilities developed in this chapter are put into packages, and the way to create and access user-definded packages, such as `javagently` and `myutilities`, is carefully explained.

Chapter 5   **Controlling the flow**

The last two control structures are discussed – conditional loops and switching. Conditional looping is one of the areas of programming that can be profitably studied at length, and two sections are devoted to loop design. The chapter ends with an interactive game case study which illustrates most of which has gone before.

Chapter 6   **Arrays and tables**

To complete Java's programming-in-the-small capabilities, we consider arrays and their applications. A generalization of arrays to dictionaries, using Java's hashtable facility, is introduced, and used extensively in the chapters that follow. There is an explanation of sorting, with an application in a student marker system.

Chapter 7   **Formatting**

This chapter brings together all aspects of presenting input and output, which in Java has far-reaching possiblities, including the ability to operate in different languages, depending on where in the world a program is running. This is the chapter that finally discusses what the `String` class is all about (although strings have been used since Chapter 2), as well as the `Text` class written for this book. `Text` makes use of envelopes and tokenizers, two concepts useful for input in Java.

Chapter 8   **Objects at work**

This chapter centres around a case study of an inventory program, looking at dynamically created objects, linked lists and the rules about objects which Java's strict classing enforces. Opportunities for protecting objects are discussed, as well as the advanced ways of structuring programs with inner classes.

Chapter 9   **Abstraction and inheritance**

Java's approach to inheritance is covered with genuine working examples. The chapter discusses interfaces as a really useful alternative to multiple inheritance, and shows how abstract classes are used. Potentially difficult subjects of references and cloning are covered in detail, with diagrams.

Chapter 10   **Graphical user interfaces**

We assume that the student has not encountered GUI programming before and therefore needs to be introduced gently to the different components such as buttons, text fields, frames and canvases. Each new feature is introduced with an example. Graphics drawing and colour are also covered.

Chapter 11   **Event-driven programming**

Event-driven programming is treated seriously as a separate topic, with a detailed discussion of Java's event model, listeners and handlers. The programming techniques needed to handle sequences of events are explained and the chapter winds up with a case study of a supermarket till.

Chapter 12   **Applets in action**

The transition from applications to applets can now be smoothly achieved. The steps for converting applications are given, as well as guidelines for developing applets from scratch. How to add multimedia excitement of sound and images is covered, and the nature conservation system shown in Chapter 1 can now be dissected and explained.

Chapter 13   **Multi-threading**

To be truly active on the web, programs must be able to attend to different tasks seemingly simultaneously. Threads are built into Java and this chapter shows how they can be used in a variety of ways, from independently running identical versions of objects, to synchronizing tasks with different functions.

Chapter 14   **Networking**

Java's networking facilities are extensive and novel. This chapter starts by looking at simple web connections for text and images, discusses socket programming in detail with a case study, and then goes on to two of Java's most important application programming interfaces: database connectivity (JDBC) and remote method invocation (RMI). The final case study of an airport announcer system is an extensive one, bringing together RMI, applets, threads and more.

Chapter 15   **Algorithms and data structures**

This looks at two searching and two sorting algorithms (including Quicksort) and gives an introduction to performance estimation. Classes for stacks (from Java), queues, linked lists and bit sets (from Java again) are then presented with in-depth examples.

Review board for the first edition

PART I

Fundamentals

CHAPTER 1

Introduction

1.1 Welcome to Java

Java is unlike any other language that has gone before. It is designed to work easily within the World Wide Web of computers through commonly available, user-friendly software called **browsers**. All computers these days have a browser – be it Netscape, Explorer or Mosaic – and all browsers are now **Java-enabled**. This means that you can scan through documents stored all around the world and, at the click of a link, activate a Java program that will come across the network and run on your own computer. You do not even have to know that it is a Java program that is running.

The key advantage of being Java-enabled is that instead of just passive text and images appearing on your screen, calculations and interaction can take place as well. You can send back information to the **host** site, get more Java programs, more documents, and generally perform in a very effective way. Figure 1.1 sums up the circle of activity that takes place with a Java-enabled browser. Java programs that run on the web are actually called **applets** (short for 'little applications'), and we shall use this term from now on.

Another important property of Java is that it is **platform-independent**. This means that it is independent of the kind of computer you are using. You may have a

Macintosh, or a Pentium, a Silicon Graphics or a Sun JavaStation. Java applets do not mind. They are stored on a **host site** in such a way they can run on any computer that has a Java-enabled browser.

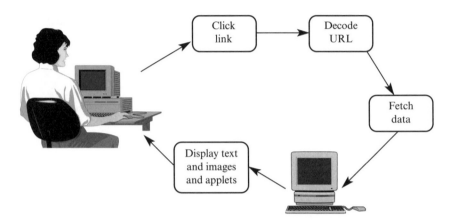

Figure 1.1 *Browsing the World Wide Web with Java applets.*

So what does Java-enabled mean? It means that inside the browser there is a program known as a **Java Virtual Machine** (JVM) which can run Java for that particular computer. The Java that comes over the net is in a standard form known as **byte-code**. Your JVM can understand the applet in bytecode and make it work properly on your particular computer. That is why if you get an applet when running under Windows, it will have a Windows 'look and feel' to its buttons and layout. If you pull the same applet down to a Macintosh, it will look like a typical Mac program. Figure 1.2 sums up this process.

Enough of theory. What are applets actually good for, and what would one really look like? Let us now consider an example especially set up on *Java Gently's* web site. This site can be found at the URL[1] http://www.cs.up.ac.za/javagently.

The Nature Conservation project

As part of its international outreach programme, the country of Savanna (situated on the grasslands of Africa) is funding a project to make information about nature available on the web. Rather than just finding an electronic book, visitors to the web site will be able to make enquiries about animals, birds or trees that they have spotted, and even to contribute interactively to the information on the site. Consider the web pages from the first version of the site, shown in Figures 1.3 to 1.6 and colour plates 1 to 4. It all looks pretty interesting, and even impressive, but where is the Java?

---

[1] The term URL, also referred to in Figure 1.1, stands for Universal Resource Locator. It is a unique reference to a document on the web, usually consisting of a protocol such as http and the name of the site or computer where the item is stored, followed by some subdirectory information.

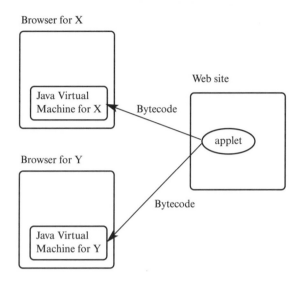

Figure 1.2 *A Java applet going to two different computer types X and Y.*

Figure 1.3 *The first page of the web site, showing two links to animals and trees. (See Plate 1.)*

Figure 1.4 *The second web page, showing images and text. (See Plate 2.)*

The fact that it is not obvious is a tribute to Java's usefulness and power. The first web page (Figure 1.3) announces the project and gives the links to the three proposed sections. The birds section is not yet ready, so the link is not enabled. If we click on the animals link, we get Figure 1.4. The animal section is just pictures at the moment, but the section on trees (Figure 1.5) has a table showing how to codify a tree according to its leaf appearance. You are then invited to enter in three values related to your tree. This is the applet at work, running quietly on your machine should you want it. Once it has three values, it calculates a tree code and then asks the browser to bring down from the web site information about that specific tree. For the information as entered, the web page would contain a picture of a boabab tree, plus information about its seeds, flowers and habitat as shown in Figure 1.6. There is more about this applet in Section 12.4.

Should the applet not recognize the combination of leaf appearance and size that you entered, it will give you the opportunity of entering these as a problem for the resident botanists, who will come back to you via e-mail in a few days with whatever information they can glean.

Of course, Java is not just a means for moving information around on the web: it is a real programming language, of the stature of C++, Pascal, Ada and Modula-3. Learning to use Java is what this book is all about, but it also serves as a general introduction to the principles of programming. By the end of the book, you will be

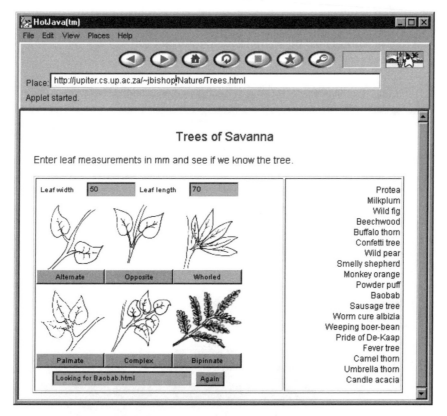

Figure 1.5 *The Trees web page with an applet at the bottom. (See Plate 3.)*

able to program Java applications and applets to perform such diverse tasks as inventory control, averaging and sorting marks, computer games and competitions and of course web 'surfing'.

1.2 Software development

Computers consist of hardware and software. When one buys a computer, or uses it in the laboratory, the tendency is to focus on the hardware: the amount of memory, the speed of the processor and so on. These are factors in using a computer, but they are not the most important. It is of course annoying if, for example, one runs out of disk space, but at least a plan can be made to store some of the information somewhere else, or even to delete it, to make room.

We would claim that the software that the computer comes with is what really determines its quality. In this section, we shall briefly run through the software components that are necessary for programming in Java, and show how they interact.

The description is intended to be a general one, not specific to any particular make or supplier of software. Then we shall outline the stages of software development. The next section shows how these are tackled in this book.

Figure 1.6 *The result of the applet's deduction of your tree. (See Plate 4.)*

The programming process

The programming process is the activity whereby programs are written in order to be stored and made ready for execution or running. The programs can be run on the same computer on which they were written, or they can be fetched over the web in the manner we have already described. Programming these days needs the support of many software packages, themselves programs developed by others. Some of the software comes with the computer you buy, some you can purchase later, and some you can get as freeware, shareware or applets over the web. In order to develop your own programs, you will need at least an operating system, an editor and a compiler.

Operating systems

The core software loaded onto a computer is its **operating system**. Some operating systems are specific to certain types of computers – for example Windows runs on Intel processors – and others are designed to run on a variety of different designs. Unix and its derivative, Linux, are examples here. The operating system provides the necessary interfaces to the hardware: reading from disk, writing to the screen, swapping between tasks and so on. It also looks after files and provides commands for the user to move files, change their names, etc. Through the operating system, we activate the next level of software.

Editors and compilers

The programming process involves creating a sequence of instructions to the computer, which are written down in the particular programming language. The creative process is expressed through an **editor**, of which there are many on the market. Once ready, the program is submitted to a **compiler**. The function of the compiler is two-fold. In the first instance, it makes a thorough check on the validity of what has been written. If there are any errors (called compilation or syntax errors) then these must be corrected and the program resubmitted for compilation. Activating the Java compiler can be done at a simple level by typing in the following to the operating system, where Trees.java is the file we created through the editor:

```
javac Trees.java
```

Once the program is free of compilation errors, the compiler enters a second phase and translates the program into a form that can run on a computer. For compilers for most other languages this form will be the native machine instructions of the particular computer's processor. For Java, though, it is the Java virtual machine that is the target of compilation, no matter what the computer is that will ultimately run the translated program.

Although the compiler checks the grammar of the program and can look for quite a range of potential errors, it cannot detect errors in the logic. For example, in the applet shown in action in Figure 1.5, it would be quite possible for a careless programmer to read the width value as the length and the length as the width by mistake. These are known as **logic** errors (also known as **execution** errors).

Logic errors can be avoided by

- carefully structuring the program in the first place,
- following good programming guidelines, and
- actually reusing existing pieces of program instead of rewriting everything from scratch each time.

However, sometimes the only way to detect a logic error is to run the program and see what happens. This is the second last stage of the software development process. The program is **executed** or **run** by activating it through the operating system. In Java we would activate an ordinary program by a command such as `java Trees`

Some logic errors can be detected by carefully testing the program with well-chosen test data. After finding and correcting an error, the test should be re-run because it is very easy to introduce some other error while fixing the first. All of these topics are covered in this book. The programming process is summed up in Figure 1.7.

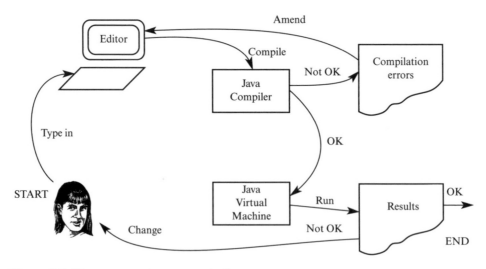

Figure 1.7 *The programming process in Java.*

Development environments

Because the edit–compile cycle repeats itself over and over again in the programming process, software exists that combines editing and compiling and enables one to switch between them at the touch of a button. Examples of such Java systems are Java Workshop, Visual J++, Kawa and Symantec Café. An integrated development environment (IDE) also includes facilities for managing large projects, perhaps involving several programmers. Another feature is an enhanced editor for creating user interfaces by designing them on the screen. See Section 1.4 for more on IDEs.

An advantage of some Java IDEs is that, like Java itself, they are platform-independent, so that you can continue working in the same environment even if you change computers. A disadvantage of IDEs is that they are not always intuitive and sometimes take a while to learn to operate effectively.

Maintenance

It is suprising, but true, that Figure 1.7 represents in industry terms only about 30% of the programming process. The real hard programming starts after the product has been delivered and it begins its useful life. Then it has to be **maintained**, an activity that is similar to the maintenance on an airplane: essential and sometimes costly. Maintenance for software includes fixing errors, making user-required changes and adding enhancements. A primary aim of a programmer even when learning to program should be to make maintenance as easy as possible. Throughout the book we shall mention ways of achieving this goal.

1.3 The approach of this book

Java Gently teaches programming by example. There is a tried and tested progression of examples which leads you from first principles through to the more complex constructs in the language. Each example is carefully chosen so as to use only those features that have been covered, and each example uses the features correctly. Achieving this balance means that the order of topics covered has to be precise. While it is possible to dip into the later chapters of the book, the first five should be covered sequentially. They form the core and are closely interlinked.

Each example follows a sequence of steps which is usually:

- problem
- solution
- algorithm
- class design
- example
- program
- testing

The problem is a short statement in the user's terms of what needs to be done. The solution starts to give an idea as to what approach should be followed to solve the problem, including what software can be reused from elsewhere. The algorithm forms the nub of the problem-solving process. The program is a complete, running Java program and each program can be found on our web site given on page xxii. The example and testing help to make the programs realistic.

Algorithms

An **algorithm** is a precise, unambiguous statement of steps to follow to solve a problem. Algorithms can be expressed in a variety of ways and we shall use a mixture of English and lines and arrows to express the concepts of decision making and repetition. The resulting diagrams are formal enough to show the structure of the program yet informal enough to be written down with the minimum of fuss. For example, in the trees applet, there are three values to be entered. The

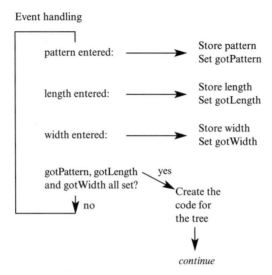

Figure 1.8 *A sample algorithm.*

algorithm for getting all three in, in any order, before proceeding, would be represented as in Figure 1.8.

In general the flow of the algorithm is downwards. Sideways arrows indicate action to be taken if the condition is true. Often, the algorithm will need to be repeated, and the line from the bottom and up the left joins around the top again to show that this should happen.

Class design

Java is an object-oriented language, which means that a program in Java is composed of interrelated objects. *Java Gently* describes programs in terms of their objects and the relationships between them using a simple set of blocks and lines. The notation used is based on OMT (object modelling technique), with additions to make it more suitable for the level of programming that we are tackling, and to make visible all of Java's interesting features. For example, there are symbols for simple methods and variables, as well as for interfaces and listeners. An example of a class diagram related to the Nature project would be as in Figure 1.9.

Nature is a class with a name and a means of displaying it. Animals, Birds and Trees are all derived from Nature. Herbivore is a class which, among other things, records the amount of grass needed by such an animal. All of these classes are shown as dotted oblongs because they are only descriptions of what could exist. Elephant is our only real object, and it is instantiated from Herbivore. There is much more about this notation in Section 3.6.

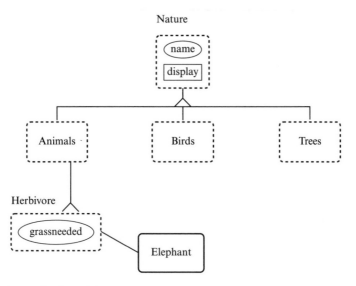

Figure 1.9 *A sample class diagram.*

Programs

Programs are written in programming languages. There are many such languages, but relatively few are available on all kinds of computers. Those that have achieved more or less universal use include Pascal, Ada, FORTRAN, COBOL, BASIC, C++, LISP, PROLOG, Modula and now, of course, Java. Java was developed in 1993 under the name of Oak, and achieved popularity in 1996 when Sun Microsystems launched their Java compilers free on the web.

Java programs look like stylized English, and examples can be found on any page of this book. The form of a program is important: any mistakes will cause the compiler to reject your efforts. It is therefore necessary to learn the syntax of the language precisely. To assist you in this endeavour, *Java Gently* has a unique approach. When a new construct is introduced, its syntax is shown precisely in a **form** that not only explains how a feature is constructed, but also gives an indication of how it should be laid out in a regular way. An example of a simple form is:

if-statement
| ```
if (condition)
    then-part;
else
    else-part;
``` |

The meaning of the bold face and italics will become clear as we start introducing Java statements.
```

1.4 Getting started with Java

If you do not have Java development facilities where you are studying or working, then you will want to set them up for yourself. The Java Development Kit (JDK) is Sun's free gift to the Java programming community. You can download, install and us it as freeware. The JDK gives you a full reference compiler and interpreter for the very latest version of Java. There is also a directory on documention for all the Java libraries (known as APIs or application programming interfaces) and a directory called the Java tutorial. Both of these are worth downloading if you have time and space. The JDK, the API documentation and the tutorial each occupy about 10 MBytes on disk, so you are looking at about 30Mbytes all together.

The following instructions regarding acquiring and installing the JDK are correct at time of writing.

Downloading the JDK

To download the JDK, first don't. Find out whether it is available locally on your server or on CDROM form in your organization. Only if you cannot get the system you want nearby, go to Sun's site:

www.javasoft.com

Here, choose the 'Products and APIs' from the list of options, and then look from there for the JDK. You will be asked about your machine and operating system, and then you can download. You should also print out the web page associated with the download, which tells you how to install and test the system.

Once you have got the JDK, you will need to install it. Follow the instructions given on the site carefully, especially such things as setting classpaths.

Testing the system

To test whether you have installed the system correctly, use a simple text editor of your choice to type in the first Java program shown in Example 2.1 and save it in a file called Welcome.java. Keep your editor open while opening up a command line window as well (Unix or MS-Dos). Here type in

javac Welcome.java

The JDK compiler will take the file and compile it. If you made no typing errors, the command prompt will be returned. If there are error messages, go back to the edit window, fix the Java program acordingly, then recompile.

Once you have a clean compilation, the compiler will have created a file called Welcome.class. To run the program, type in

java Welcome

(Note: do not add the word 'class' here.) The program should produce output on the next line in the command window.

The `javagently` package

Once you get started with Java, you will encounter the need to interact with your program, and an easy way to do this is provided by a special Text class in the `javagently` package written for this book. Details about the package and how to install it are given in Sections 4.1 and 4.5 and there is a full listing of the package (which is not very long) in Section 7.2. You do not have to type the package in if you can fetch it from the web (as described in Section 4.5).

The documentation and tutorial

The additional information supplied with the JDK is invaluable. The documentation gives a hypertext view of all Java's libraries, with detailed descriptions and examples of each method. This is the Java programmer's 'help'. The tutorial consists of a collection of articles written by different people at different times and at different levels. It is not comprehensive, in that it is not intended to cover all of Java or to replace textbooks, but it does give insight into how and why certain parts of Java were developed, and the sample programs form a good addition to those in a book.

Java integrated development systems

Although the JDK is free and many people use it solely, there are more elaborate systems on the market. These IDEs fall into two classes: those that come with their own built-in Java compiler, and those that make use of the JDK for compilation.

The first kind includes Sun's Java Workshop, MicroSoft's Visual J++, Symantec's Café, Borland's JBuilder and Metrowerks' CodeWarrior (available from your local computer store or computer representative). The advantage of these systems is that some of the compilers can outperform the JDK in speed. The disadvantage is that when the Java language is upgraded, as it is at intervals, you have to upgrade your IDE (at a cost) as well.

All the above are available for PC platforms using Windows 95 or NT or later. In addition, Java Workshop runs under Solaris on Suns and CodeWarrior is available for the Macintosh.

The second kind of system includes Tek-Tools' Kawa system, which we have found to be really very user-friendly, with good performance. Kawa is available electronically from kawa@tek-tools.com at reasonable cost. It runs only on PC platforms. Once you have Kawa, you can continue to download new versions of the JDK and link them into your IDE immediately. Thus you are able to take advantage of new Java features in the latest release.

Web sites for Java

Java is a web language and there are several excellent sites which discuss Java issues, have Java articles and Java resources for downloading. Four in particular are worth watching:

- www.javasoft.com – Sun's Java site, regularly updated with topical articles and news about Java products and use.

- www.gamelan.com – incredible collection of Java resources, information and applets.

- www.javaworld.com – a monthly on-line magazine devoted to Java.

- www.cs.up.ac.za/javagently – the web site for this book.

1.5 The *Java Gently* web site

The first edition of *Java Gently* came out with a web site whose initial purpose was to be a repository for the programs in the book. Since May 1997, the site has grown into an active web site, with readers from all over the world contributing to the discussions, making suggestions, and informing us of their ideas about Java and the book. The number of hits is 14 000 and growing daily.

On the web site, you can find the following:

- About the book

- Summary of the chapters

- List of institutions using *Java Gently* for teaching

- All the examples for individual viewing or downloading in bulk

- Answers to frequently asked questions

- A discussion board, watched over by the author and the JG team

- Messages about Java of immediate interest

- Other material available from the author on Java

- List of known errors in the book

- Plans and dates for future versions and editions of *Java Gently*

- Link to the publisher's site

In addition to providing a great deal of information, the web site can be used in two innovative ways. Firstly, for lecturers with access to online facilities in the classroom, the programs can be displayed and viewed directly from the site. I have used this method in teaching, and have found it more effective than copying the programs onto transparencies first. The ability to move rapidly between programs, to save, compile and run very quickly, makes for a dynamic teaching environment. Figure 1.10 shows a typical screen from the web page with one of the examples displayed.

The second innovation of active web sites such as *Java Gently*'s is that you can interact with a team who can answer questions and discuss Java issues. This team starts at the author's institution, the University of Pretoria, but ultimately includes all the *Java Gently* readers who access the web site and are prepared to share their expertise. In other words, you are not alone out there.

The web site is updated regularly and comments and suggestions are always welcome. All queries are answered and contributions acknowledged.

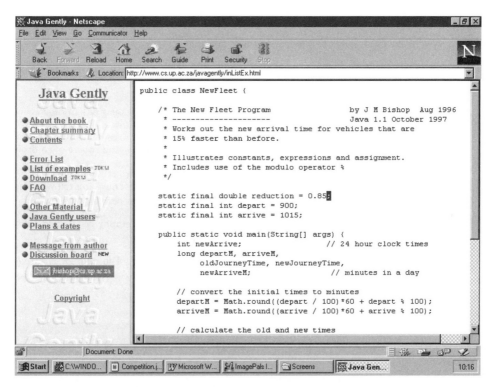

Figure 1.10 *An example program on the Java Gently web site.*

SUMMARY

It is often said that programming is fun. It certainly can be, and *Java Gently* tries to make it so. Support is available from many sources around the world, and also from the *Java Gently* web site. However, no matter how much you enjoy learning to program – and I sincerely hope you do – I hope that you will also remember the following, adapted from the immortal words of Rudyard Kipling:

If you can keep your head when all about you
Are losing theirs and blaming it on you,
If you can trust yourself when all men doubt you,
But make allowance for their doubting too;
If you can wait and not be tired by waiting, . . .
If you can fill the unforgiving minute
With sixty seconds' worth of Java run,
Yours is the Web and everything that's in it,
And – which is more – you'll be a programmer, thank SUN!

QUIZ: TO GET YOU STARTED

1.1   What does a compiler do?

1.2   What is the difference between a compilation error and a logic error?

1.3   What is the clock speed of the computer you are using?

1.4   How much memory does your computer have?

1.5   What is the capacity of the disks you are using?

1.6   Would this textbook (including all the spaces) fit on your disk, assuming one printed character per byte of memory?

1.7   List all the computer applications that you come into contact with in the course of an ordinary week.

1.8   Have you ever been on the wrong end of a computer error? If so, could you tell whether the mistake was in the program or was caused by the data that was read in?

1.9   Find out the name, version and creation date of the computer, operating system and compiler that you will be using.

1.10   Get into *Java Gently's* web site and try out the Nature system. The address is http://www.cs.up.ac.za/javagently.

CHAPTER 2

Simple programs

2.1 Two starter programs

To start this chapter we shall look at two small programs. The first is a simple text-based program, and the second uses drawing and colours. We shall not go into the details of the programs, but just use them as a starting point for introducing programming in Java, and for enabling you to start using the computer straight away. There are several amendments you can make to the programs, which will give you a reason to get to grips with your programming environment.

EXAMPLE 2.1 Welcome

The aim of our first program is to display the message Welcome to Java!. The program is:

```
class Welcome {

  /* Welcome to Java! program        by J M Bishop Dec 1996
   * -----------------------
     Illustrates a simple program displaying a message.
  */
```

```
public static void main (String [ ] args) {
  System.out.println("Welcome to Java!");
}
}
```

and it does indeed, if run, display the required message on the screen as follows:

Welcome to Java!

At this stage we shall note only a few points about the program. Firstly, the text between /* and */ is called a **comment** and is there to help explain to the reader what the program does. It is not **executed** (or **run**) by the computer. Secondly the text in quotes in the third last line is known as a **string** and is what is actually displayed. The rest of the lines and the closing curly brackets are part of the outline that always accompanies a Java program. We shall learn more about them soon.

Exercise: Run the Welcome program. Change it so that it includes your name in the message, e.g. Welcome to Java, Peter! Change it again so that it prints out more than one line of greeting, or underlines the greeting using hyphens. Experiment and use the opportunity to become familiar with your programming environment.

EXAMPLE 2.2 Olympic rings

One of the advantages of Java is its built-in facilities for graphics, colour, animation, sound and so on. Here is a very simple program to display the five Olympic rings in a window:

```
import java.awt.*;
import java.awt.
    event.*;
class Rings extends Frame {

  /* Ring drawing program           J M Bishop Dec 1996
   * --------------------           Java 1.1 version Dec 1997
   * Illustrates colour and simple graphic output
   */

  public Rings ( ) {
    setTitle ("Olympics Rings");
  }

  public static void main (String [ ] args) {
    // Create a graphics frame
    Frame f = new Rings ();

    // Enable the window to be closed
    f.addWindowListener(new WindowAdapter () {
      public void windowClosing(WindowEvent e) {
        System.exit(0);
      }
    });
```

```
        // Set the frame's size and show the drawing
        // outlined in the paint method.
        f.setSize (300, 200);
        f.setVisible (true);
    }

    public void paint (Graphics g) {
        // Draw five interlocking rings
        // of different colours.

        g.setColor (Color.red);
        g.drawOval (90,80,30,30);
        g.setColor (Color.blue);
        g.drawOval (115,80,30,30);
        g.setColor (Color.green);
        g.drawOval (140,80,30,30);
        g.setColor (Color.yellow);
        g.drawOval (165,80,30,30);
        g.setColor (Color.black);
        g.drawOval (190,80,30,30);

        // Label the drawing
        g.drawString("Olympic Rings", 120,40);
    }

}
```

The output produced by the program is shown (not in colour, unfortunately) in Figure 2.1.

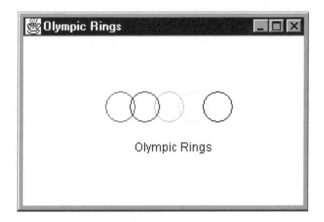

Figure 2.1 *Graphical output from the Rings program.*

Rings is a much longer program than Welcome but, if you look carefully, you will see that the real substance of the program – drawing the rings – occurs in the paint method. Each of the lines such as

```
g.drawOval (35,30,30,30);
```

draws one of the circles. The numbers in brackets are measurements in pixels (screens can have 600 or more pixels across). In order, the numbers represent:

- x-coordinate of the top left of the oval,
- y-coordinate of the top left of the oval,
- width of the oval,
- height of the oval.

Of course, circles are a special case of ovals, with the width and height the same. We can therefore see that the instructions to draw the circles progress across in the *x* direction, but keep the *y* values the same.

The rest of the program can be described as 'baggage': necessary Java instructions that give us access to the graphics facilities, but that are not particular to our problem. In brief, these are:

- enabling the window to be closed (at the start of the main method),
- creating a graphics window of a particular size (using setSize and setVisible),
- giving the window a name using setTitle.

The program in Example 2.2 also illustrates the use of Java's second type of comment: the one-liner, introduced by //. Either kind of comment is acceptable. The advantage of // is that it is automatically ended by the end of a line. On the other hand, many programmers regard the /* */ pair as more elegant. The convention for using the paired comment symbols is to have the closing */ underneath the /*, as shown in these programs.

Being able to program in a graphics environment is an essential skill for today's programmers, but there is a lot of detail to learn, much of which is repetitive and can be looked up when needed. We therefore leave graphics to Part II and will concentrate on text programs while we learn the fundamentals of programming, and of how to do this well in Java.

Exercises: Run the Rings program and check that the rings come out in the right colour and in the right order for the Olympic emblem. In fact, the emblem does not have the rings in a straight line as in Figure 2.1, but the second and fourth are set lower down. Change the program to fix this. Also experiment with making the rings bigger and positioning them in the centre of the screen.

2.2 Fundamentals of object-oriented programming

In this section we give a broad overview of the different parts of a Java program and how they fit together. The rest of the chapter will concentrate on a few of the essential components so that by the end, we shall be able to create and run simple programs that have tangible results. These results will be in text form rather than diagrams and pictures as producing the latter requires specialized programming techniques which are best left to Part II.

A Java **program** consists of a set of one or more inter-dependent classes as shown in Figure 2.2. **Classes** are a means for describing the properties and capabilities of the objects in real life that the program has to deal with. For example, the Nature Conservation program described in Chapter 1 could well have classes for trees, animals and birds. Once we have a class, we can create many objects of that same class. Not every class is related to every other, and the kinds of relationship vary, as we shall see later. The notation used to illustrate object-oriented programs shows the different relationships with arrows, diamonds and triangles. Their significance will become clear as early as Section 3.6.

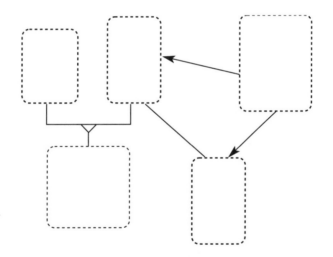

Figure 2.2 *A program consisting of interrelated classes.*

An **object** is a concrete realization of a class description. It is usually associated with a noun, such as a tree or a book, a student or a map. The process of generating new objects for a program is referred to as creating an **instance** of a class. For example, suppose we have defined a `Trees` class:[1] then we could create three instances of the class as follows:

---

[1] From now on, Java programs and parts of them, are shown in Courier font.

```
Trees acacia= new Trees ();
Trees willow= new Trees ();
Trees palm  = new Trees ();
```

The first occurrence of the class name `Trees` indicates that the object is of this class. Then the '= new' is the signal to create a new instance of the class and we once again say that we want the storage to be for items of the size of the `Trees` class, as shown in Figure 2.3. The class is shown as a dotted oblong and the objects are solid, to emphasize that they are the concrete instantiations of the class, which serves as a description and does not physically exist in the computer.

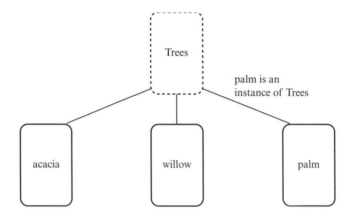

Figure 2.3 *An example of creating objects as instances of classes.*

Each of the new objects will have all the properties and capabilities of the `Trees` class. Although in most cases the class used for declaring the object is the same as the one for creating the instance, there are occasions when they need not be, and these will be explained in Section 2.5.

The properties and capabilities of a class are called **fields** and **methods**, respectively, in Java, and are jointly known as **members** of the class. Thus following on from Figure 2.2, the next level of decomposition for a Java program is shown in Figure 2.4. There are several ways of **declaring** fields and methods, and we shall touch on some of them here. The topic is revisited in later chapters.

Notice that although the diagram in Figure 2.4 might indicate that the class is laid out with the fields first and then the methods, this is not the case: individual fields and methods can be interleaved as required to make the class easier to read.

Declarations

The properties of a class are given by means of **declarations** of the data items or fields that its objects can use to store information. An example of such a data item would be the number of times people enquire about a particular tree. Declarations in Java indi-

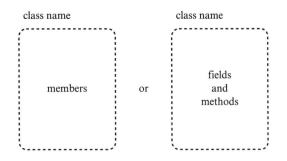

Figure 2.4 *The structure of a class.*

cate both the name of the data item and its **type**. The simplest type is an integer number. In Java terms, we refer to an integer as int. Therefore, as part of the Trees class, we would have the declaration:

```
int noOfEnquiries;
```

Names in computer languages are called identifiers. An **identifier** in Java consists of letters, underscores and digits, but must start with a letter. Spaces are not allowed, and capital and small letters are considered to be different so that noOfEnquiries is not the same as noofenquiries. Unlike Trees, noOfEnquiries consists of more than one word, so to make it easier to read, the convention is to use capitals for the inner words.

The declaration sets aside storage in the computer's memory for this field, and the amount of storage will depend on the type. An integer, for example, occupies four bytes. There is more about storage in Section 3.2.

The correct Java term for the data item we have defined is a **variable**. When making declarations, we can also declare other **objects**. The term **field** encompasses both data items, and we shall use it whenever either is meant. Strictly speaking, variables have types and objects have classes, but the term **type** is usually used when referring to fields in general. Figure 2.5 summarizes the structure of a program so far in terms of the words used for its different parts.

We shall now look at methods, and come back to declarations before the end of this section.

Methods

The capabilities of a class are expressed in one or more methods. A **method** is a named sequence of instructions to the computer, written out in the language we are using, in this case Java. The instructions are properly called **statements,** and fall into the following categories:

- **invocation** – causing a method to be performed;
- **assignment** – changing the state of a field by using another value of the same kind;

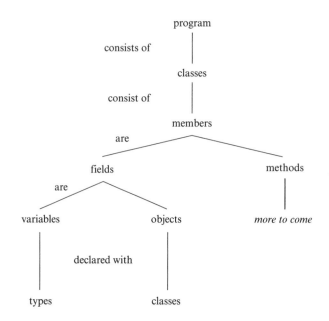

Figure 2.5 *Terms used so far in exploring the structure of a program.*

- **repetition** – performing certain statements over and over again;
- **selection** – deciding whether to perform certain statements or not;
- **exception** – detecting and reacting to unusual circumstances.

Most languages have a similar set of options.

In addition, a method can also declare its own fields which are said to be **local** to it, and therefore not accessible to other methods, even those in the same class. On the other hand, the fields declared in the class (see Figure 2.4) are accessible to all the methods in that class. Methods may also have **inner classes**, declared for a specific purpose (full details in Chapter 8) but may not have their own local methods, a concept known as **nesting** in other languages such as Pascal. Finally, a method can declare at its start a set of **parameters** that enable it to be customized when it is invoked.

Figure 2.6 follows Figures 2.2 and 2.4 with the third level of decomposition – from a program to a class to a method. Notice that once again, the diagram is not meant to imply that groups of fields come before all statements and so on: they can be intermingled.

In the Trees class, a probable method would be one to increase the count of the number of enquiries by one. In Java, such a method would be written as:

```
void enquiry () {
   noOfEnquiries ++;
}
```

method name

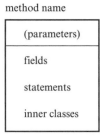

Figure 2.6 *The structure of a method.*

The term void indicates that in this method all the activity takes place within its statements, and that is the end of it. It does not return anything when it is finished. Methods that are not void, but have a type instead, can return values as well.

The name of the method is enquiry, and it does not have any parameters, as indicated by the pair of brackets. The curly brackets indicate the start and end of the statements in the method. In this case there is only one statement. It is of the assignment type, and adds one to our data item, noOfEnquiries, by using the special operator ++.

Invoking a method

At this point, we wish to examine how we cause the method to perform its statements. In simple terms, when we mention the name of a method, control within the program is transferred to that method, which then progresses through its statements until it reaches the end. The method then passes control back to where it was called from. This process is called method invocation, and we talk about **invoking** a method.[2] In object-oriented parlance, calling a method is also sometimes referred to as passing a message; this is not usual in Java.

The methods in a class define its capabilities, which are then available for every object created from that class. However, there has to be a way of indicating *which* object we want a method to act on. Therefore, when we refer to a method, we prefix it with the name of the object whose fields we wish to access. Recalling that willow is an object, if we invoke

```
willow.enquiry ();
```

the enquiry method gains access to the noOfEnquiries variable in the willow object, not the noOfEnquiries in either of the other trees.

---

[2] *Invoke* is the formal and correct term for causing statements of a method to be performed. It is a rather unusual word derived from the Latin *vocare* to call. We shall therefore adopt (as many other books do) the more gentle English term *call*.

Constructors

An object is created when its declaration is reached in the program. Upon creation, a special kind of method, a **constructor**, is automatically called by the Java system. The programmer writing the class can set up one or more constructors which have different numbers of parameters, and will be matched against those supplied at creation. Constructors have the name of the class itself. Thus we could have the following two constructors in the `Trees` class:

```
Trees () {
  noOfEnquiries = 0;
}

Trees (int n) {
  noOfEnquiries = n;
}
```

In the first constructor, there is no parameter, and so we initialize the variable to zero. In the second, we take the value given at creation as the number of enquiries so far. Thus the following are both valid object creations:

```
Trees willow = new Trees ( );
Trees acacia = new Trees (55);
```

The first creates `willow` as a tree with zero enquiries. The second creates `acacia` as a tree with 55 enquiries already.

We can now extend Figure 2.5 and add to it all we have learnt about the terminology for methods, as shown in Figure 2.7.

Class members

We explained above that each time an object is created as an instance of a class, a completely new instance of all fields that the class declared is created for this object. It is not always desirable to have all the fields distinct. We may not always want a new copy of every field for each object: we may want to have some that are common to all objects of the class.

For example, the variable `noOfEnquiries` will tally the enquiries for each tree object, i.e. there will be a separate tally kept for acacias, willows and palms. Suppose we also want to keep track of the total enquiries for all trees (as opposed to animals and birds, which have their own classes). What we need here is a **class variable**, as opposed to an **instance variable**. To distinguish such fields, Java uses a **modifier** before the kind name. There is a whole selection of modifiers that we shall introduce as they are required, but the one we need here is called **static**. Using the modifier `static` indicates that storage for the field is to be created once only for the class, and not each time a new object is created. So, for example, the counter for the total number of enquiries would be declared as:

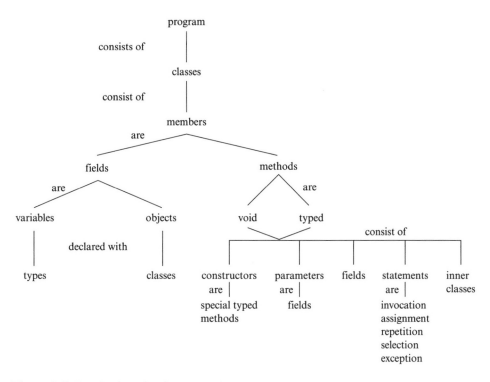

Figure 2.7 *Terminology for the parts of a program.*

```
static int totalEnquiries;
```

Now the method to increment the original variable will be expanded to:

```
void enquiry () {
  noOfEnquiries ++;
  totalEnquiries ++;
}
```

To illustrate the difference between class and instance variables, Figure 2.8 shows how the three sample tree objects will look once some queries have come in. In earlier figures, we used a rounded rectangle for a class and a squared off rectangle for a method. Here an oval represents a variable. From the diagram we can see clearly that each of the objects has its own version of the instance variable noOfEnquiries, even though the variables all have the same name.

Suppose now that we would like to get a record of the number of enquiries to date. How would we refer to these variables? The rule is simple:

- Within their class, fields can be referred to by their names alone.
- When used from another class or object, the fields with the name of their class (for class fields) or its object (for instance fields).

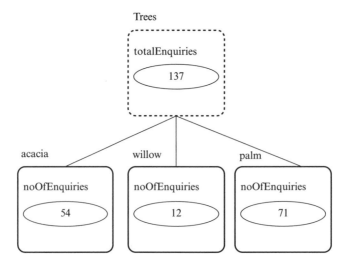

Figure 2.8 *The tree objects after a number of enquiries.*

So, at the point where these objects were created, we could refer to the following variables:

```
acacia.noOfEnquiries
willow.noOfEnquiries
palm.noOfEnquiries
Trees.totalEnquiries
```

In the same way as for variables, there can be class or instance objects and methods. Collectively, these are referred to as class and instance members.

Class and instance methods

The enquiry method is an **instance method**. It relies on being told which particular object it must access. In the same way as there may be fields common to all objects in a class, so there may be methods that do not depend on a particular object for their operation.

An example within the Trees class might be a method to issue a report after every 100 enquiries. This method would not be called by user's object, but would be activated from within the enquiries method, say. **Class methods** will be further discussed in the last section of this chapter. What we do note here, for completeness, is that, following the convention for class fields, a class method is defined with the modifier static and is called with the class name as a prefix.

The form of a program

Before leaving this section, we note precisely how to write down the instructions that introduce a Java program. The following pattern gives the format we must use for a simple program. Java is a language and as such has a syntax. In this book, Java's syntax is explained by means of **forms** and examples.

Simple program

```
class classname {
  public static void main (String [] argname) {
    declarations and statements
  }
}
```

The top line of the form gives the name of the Java concept being defined. The contents of the box gives the syntax of the concept, in the usual layout that would be used for it.

There are three kinds of words in a form, with the following meanings:

- bold text – Java keywords that must be there, e.g. **class** or **void**;

- italics – identifiers and other parts that we fill in, e.g. *classname*;

- plain words – words that have to be in these positions but are not keywords, e.g. main and String.

Keywords are those identifiers that are reserved for Java's use and may not be used by the programmer for anything else. Thus we cannot call a variable 'static'.

The curly brackets of a program must match for each class and method. In the form, the outer set refers to the class and the inner set refers to the main method. The words in italics describe parts of the program that must be supplied by the programmer. The class name is compulsory, but the declarations and statements are optional. Thus the following is a valid Java program that does nothing:

```
class DoNothing {
  public static void main (String [] args) {
  }
}
```

When there are statements, each ends with a semicolon. In this way, there can be several statements to a line, but most of the time Java programmers stick to one statement per line.

Following on from the discussion in this section, we can interpret what is meant by each of the lines of the program. The introduction of the class name is clear. Thereafter, we have a single method called main. It is a void method, and also has a static modifier, indicating that it is a class method and will be called by the outside world as DoNothing.main. Who calls it? When the Java virtual machine is activated, as described in Chapter 1, it must be given the name of a class. It then looks for a method called `main` in the class of that name, and starts running the program from there.

Because the method has to be accessed by the virtual machine, it must have an additional modifier, `public`. The rest of our methods for the moment do not need this modifier, nor its opposite, `private`, and we shall discuss the need for them in more detail in Chapter 8.

Finally, the parameter in the form is there so that information can be transmitted to the program when it starts up. The square brackets indicate that the parameter is going to be an array – a computer term used for several fields, all with the same name and indexed by numbers. Arrays are fully covered in Chapter 6. Often we do not use the `main` method's parameter, but it is still necessary to include it when the method is defined.

2.3 Beginning with output

Having covered the fundamental structure of a Java program in terms of its most important constituents – classes and objects – we can now consider how to write a simple program that displays something on the screen. In programming parlance, what goes to the screen is called **output**, but programmers often use the terms write, print, output and display interchangeably. If we refer to the previous section, we shall see that there is no special statement group for output in Java. All input and output is handled by methods in classes supplied by the language. Thus in order to print, we have to know *which* methods to call: we already know *how* to call them from Section 2.2.

The methods we are looking for are called `println` and `print`. They are found in a built-in Java class called `PrintStream`. They are instance methods, so there must be an object through which we call them. Within the special, universally available class called `System`, there is already such an object defined, called `out`. The object `out` is automatically connected by Java to the screen of your computer. Therefore from these three components:

- the class `System`,
- the object `out`, and
- the methods `print` and `println`,

we can construct the correct method call statements for displaying output. Because these method calls will be used so often, we refer to them as output statements as a shorthand. The simple form of Java statements to display a piece of text is:

Output statements

```
System.out.println (items);
System.out.println ();
System.out.print (items);
```

The first kinds of item we consider for printing are string literals. A **string literal** is any sequence of characters enclosed in quotes, for example

```
"London"
"USA"
"$5.95 per lot"
```

Although string literal is the correct term, much of the time we just use the word string. If a quote itself is needed in the string then a backslash \ precedes it. The backslash is called an **escape character**: it does not form part of the string, but enables the next character to do so. An example is:

```
"He said \"No\""
```

which is the string *He said "No"*. Calling the `println` method displays the string given as a parameter and ends the line of printing. (The '-ln' in `println` is short for 'line'). Thus, the statements

```
System.out.println("$5.95 per lot");
System.out.println("He said \"No\"");
```

will cause the following to be displayed:

$5.95 per lot
He said "No"

(In examples from now on, Java statements are given in plain type, and the corresponding output is shown in bold.)

The `print` method works in a similar way except that it does not end the line, so that a subsequent `print` or `println` will continue on the same line from the last point reached.

The string is optional for the `println` method. If `println` is called on its own, then it will finish the current line. This facility can also be used to obtain a blank line, as in:

```
System.out.println ("$5.95 per lot");
System.out.println ();
System.out.println ("He said \"No\"");
```

which would give as output:

$5.95 per lot

He said "No"

Note that any Java method call that does not provide parameters (the items in brackets) must still have the brackets. To obtain several blank lines, we can use several `println` calls in a row, as in:

```
System.out.println();
System.out.println();
System.out.println();
```

Alternatively, we can make use of another escape character, \n, standing for 'new line', as in:

```
System.out.println ("\n\n\n");
```

One final point about strings and printing. What happens should a string be too long to fit on a single line of a screen when we are writing a program? We cannot go on to the next line. We have to end the string and start a new one, joining the two together with a plus operator. This is known formally as **concatenation**. An example of concatenation would be:

```
System.out.println ("Your tree is not known to us. Would "+
    "you like to submit details of it by WWW or " +
    "courier?");
```

There are many more examples of long strings in the programs that follow.

EXAMPLE 2.3   Displaying a warning

Problem   Display a warning message on the screen that the computer might have a virus.[3]

Program   This program is very simple, and similar to that in Example 2.1. It has a class and a main method, followed by several output statements which when executed will display the box shown below.

```
class DisplayWarning {

    /* Displaying a warning program        by J M Bishop  Aug 1996
     * ---------------------------          Java 1.1 October 1997
     * Illustrates the form of a program and the use of println.
     */

    public static void main(String[] args) {
        System.out.println("------------------------------");
        System.out.println("|                            |");
        System.out.println("|         W A R N I N G       |");
        System.out.println("|   Possible virus detected   |");
        System.out.println("|     Reboot and run virus    |");
        System.out.println("|       remover software      |");
        System.out.println("|                            |");
        System.out.println("------------------------------");
    }
}
```

---

[3] A virus is a program that can infect your computer and cause damage to fields on the disk and so on. This program does not itself detect a virus; it just prints out the warning message.

Testing The output produced by this program would be:

```
------------------------------
|                            |
|        W A R N I N G        |
|   Possible virus detected   |
|     Reboot and run virus    |
|       remover software      |
|                            |
------------------------------
```

Here we use dashes and bars for effect, but in Part II we shall see how to make use of the graphics facilities of a computer screen to obtain smarter-looking output.

Layout

How the program is written down, in terms of lines and spaces, does not have an effect on how the output appears. Only what is inside the quotes is actually displayed when the program executes.When the output statements display strings, there is no gap in the output if the string in the program had to be split into different pieces joined by +. In the same way, blank lines or comments in the program do not have any effect on the output. Therefore, the following statements will cause the same output to be displayed as before:

```
System.out.println("$5.95 " + "per lot");

                    System.out.println();
   System.out.println("He " +
"said \"No\"");
```

The point is that the instructions given to the computer do not *have* to be in any special layout. We usually write them neatly one underneath each other, and we also use **indenting** to make groups of statements stand out, but there is no formal rule that says this should be so. Other points about the layout of the program are:

- more than one statement can be written on a line;
- statements can be split over several lines (but strings cannot);
- statements are ended by semicolons.

2.4 All about assignment

Assignment is the first real statement that we shall consider from the five groups mentioned in Section 2.2. An assignment statement is used to give a value to a variable or object. There is quite a lot involved in getting ready for an assignment, and we shall tackle it in the following steps:

1. What is type?
2. How to declare a variable and a constant.
3. How to compute values from expressions.
4. Assignment itself.
5. How to print variables and expressions.
6. An example.

Types

Java, like most modern languages, is what is known as **strictly typed** and also **strictly classed**. This means that every field and expression has a type or a class, and only those of the same types or classes can be used together. Put in simple terms, this means that we cannot mix strings and numbers, nor could we mix trees and birds. Java has eight built-in types, known as the **primitive types**, but the three that are commonly used in calculations are:

- `int` for ordinary positive and negative integer numbers in a range extending over two thousand million;

- `long` for even longer integer numbers or for the results of any integer calculations;

- `double` for numbers with fractional parts (i.e. real numbers) or for the results of calculations involving at least one real number.

The other types are `boolean`, `byte`, `char`, `float` and `short`, and we shall introduce them as they are needed in the following chapters.

A type governs how much storage is made available for the values that are stored in variables of that type. Thus an `int` uses 32 bits (4 bytes), and `long` and `double` each 64 bits (8 bytes). The full table of numeric types and their storage is given in Section 3.2.

Declarations of variables

We have already mentioned in Section 2.2 that objects store their data in fields. Fields may be declared anywhere in a Java class or method, but most of them are grouped at the start or end. The form of a variable declaration is one of the following:

Variable declaration

```
type name;
type name1, name2, name3;
type name = value;
```

The declaration introduces one or more variables of the given type. The last form can be used to initialize a variable at the same time as declaring it. Examples of declarations of variables are:

```
int temperature;         // in degrees Celsius
int oldWeight, newWeight;  // in kilograms
double salary;
double tax = 14;         // per cent
long k, m, n;            // integer unknowns
double x, y, z;          // real unknowns
```

It is worth while keeping declarations neat and tidy, with the identifiers and types lined up. It is also a useful habit to indicate what the variables are to be used for, if this is not immediately obvious from their identifiers, as well as to give some supporting information regarding the units that are intended, as shown in the first two examples.

In the real world, many values acquire names. For example, 3.141592 is known as *pi*, and a *decade* is 10. Giving names to quantities makes them easier to remember and use. In Java, named entities whose values are not going to change are known as **constants**. They are declared in declarations of the form:

Constant declaration
static final *type name = value*;

Examples of constant declarations are:

```
static final int speedLimit = 120;
static final int retirementAge = 65;
static final double kmperMile = 1.609;
```

We have already seen that the declaration modifier `static` makes the item into a class field. Thus constant declarations can occur only at the class level, and not inside methods, even inside `main`. The second modifier, `final`, indicates that the contents of the field cannot be changed during the program: in other words, it is constant.

When variables are declared we have the option of specifying an initial value or of receiving a **default initialization**. For the numeric types, the default is zero. For this reason, initialization is seldom used in Java programs. The third form of declaration is more common when we are declaring constant values. How does such an initialization differ from a constant declaration? The fundamental difference is that once constants are set, they cannot be changed again. With variables, the values can change through assignment.

Expressions

Expression is the term given to formulae in programming languages. The way in which expressions are written in programming languages is somewhat different from the normal way of writing them. The main differences are that:

- multiplication is indicated by an asterisk *;
- division is indicated by a slash /;
- denominators follow numerators on the same line.

For example, consider some simple formulae and their Java equivalents:

$$\frac{1}{2.5} \qquad => \qquad 1 / 2.5$$

$$6\ (7-3) \qquad => \qquad 6 * (7-3)$$

The implication of the last point – writing on one line – is that we use more brackets in Java expressions than we would in ordinary arithmetic or mathematics. Division that would usually be written as a fraction has to be split into two bracketed parts separated by a slash. For example, consider the following:

$$\frac{100 - 9.99}{15 + 0.1} \qquad => \qquad (100 - 9.99) / (15 + 0.1)$$

As another example, to print 15 °C converted to Fahrenheit, using the formula

$$\frac{9t}{5} + 32$$

where t is the temperature, we would say

```
System.out.println (9 * 15 / 5 + 32);
```

which would print out

    59

An important consideration is that in Java the **division operator** / works at two levels: integer and real. If both the values are integer, it performs integer division, otherwise it performs real division. Integer division is not usually what one wants so that often one of the values must be made real explicitly. For example 1/2 will produce 0, whereas 1.0/2 will give 0.5. However, integer division does have its uses, as shown in Example 2.5 later on in this section.

As well as the usual four operators (or five, if we regard / as having two meanings), use is often made in programming of finding the remainder after integer division. The operator used to represent this **modulus** is %. Examples of its use are:

```
23 % 2    → 1
6 % 6     → 0
81 % 11   → 4
```

In Java, the normal **precedence** rules apply, with brackets coming before division and multiplication, which are performed before addition and subtraction. The precedence groups for arithmetic operators are therefore:

```
group 0:   ( )
group 1:   ++   -- + (unary) - (unary)
group 2:   * / %
group 3:   + - + (concatenation)
```

While we are on the subject of writing out formulae, we note for the mathematically minded that the trigonometric functions are called like this:

```
sin x    → Math.sin(x)
```

`Math` is a built-in class which supplies methods for trigonometry, exponentiation and other operations. Going back to the 'all on one line' restriction, we see that to raise to a power, we have to call a method, as in

$$x^2 \quad \rightarrow \quad \texttt{Math.pow(x,2)}$$

Another useful method in the `Math` class is that for rounding a real[4] number to an integer in the usual way. Examples are

```
Math.round (6.6)→7
Math.round (6.3)→6
```

There is more to expressions than this short introduction reveals, but the more advanced features will be added as we need them in the next few chapters.

Assignment

Having declared a variable, we can now use an assignment to give it the value of an expression. The assignment statement has the form:

Assignment statement
`variable = expression;`

The effect of an **assignment statement** is to evaluate the expression and to assign the resulting value to the variable indicated by the identifier. The equal sign which indicates the assignment is read 'becomes'. Thus we can write:

```
temperature = 24;
```

---

[4] The term real number has its usual meaning in this book, and includes both the `double` and `float` types that Java provides for expressing real numbers.

and read it 'temperature becomes 24'. The value of the expression is 24, and this is assigned to the variable temperature. In the next sequence:

```
oldWeight = 65;
newWeight = oldWeight - 5;
```

oldWeight is assigned the value 65, and is then used to calculate the value for the variable newWeight which is 60.

Assignment requires that the types of the expression and the variable are the same. Thus we cannot assign something of type int to a Tree, or even a double variable to an int variable. However, bearing in mind that even in mathematics the real numbers encompass the integers, we *can* assign integers to reals. So the following is permissible:

```
double rate;
rate = 10;
```

Printing expressions and variables

The examples so far have used calls to the print and println methods to print **strings**. It is also possible to print **numbers** and, indeed, to print the results of calculations. For example, to print 4 times 5 less 2 we would have

```
System.out.println (4 * 5 - 2);
```

which would print out

```
18
```

Similarly, we can print out the values of expressions involving variables or constants, for example,

```
static final double kmperMile = 1.609;
System.out.println (1000 * kmperMile);
```

which would print

```
1609
```

What if we want to print more than one value out, or a mixture of numbers and strings? We said in the previous section that several strings can be printed out in one print call if they are joined by a plus operator. The same applies here. However, now we have to understand what is going on behind the scenes.

The concatenate operator joins strings. When it finds something else to its left or right – for example, a number – it looks for a toString method defined by the class, which can convert that value to a string. All the built-in types have toString methods. The + operator can then perform the concatenation and the printing proceeds. For example, we can say:

```
System.out.println (1000 + " miles is "
              + (1000 * kmperMile) + " kilometres");
```

which would print

```
1000 miles is 1609 kilometres
```

The number and the expression were converted to strings and joined up with the other two strings to make the full message. Notice that it is important to include spaces in a string that is adjacent to a number, since such spaces are not otherwise inserted.

EXAMPLE 2.4 Calculating interest

Problem The bank in the country of Savanna – called SavBank – quite often changes its interest rate for savings accounts. We would like to know what difference the change will make to the interest we may receive for the rest of the year.

Solution In this, our first real problem, we have to start by asking:

- What do we know?
- What do we want to know?
- How are we going to get there?

We know that the formula used for calculating interest, I, is the usual one of

$$I = \frac{PTR}{100}$$

where P is the principal, T is the time in years and R is the rate per annum. In this case, we know our principal – let us suppose it is G1000. (The unit of currency in Savanna is the graz, abbreviated to G.) The time is going to be $(12 - M)/12$ where M is the month we are currently in. So if we are in April, the time left will be 8/12. Finally, we must know the old rate and the new rate, for example 12.5% and 13%.

What we want to know is whether we are better off or worse off under the new rate, and by how much. We find that out by calculating the interest under both rates and finding the difference.

Algorithm The algorithm includes the names of all the values we have just been discussing.

Print out the difference between
$$(P * (12 - M)/12) * \text{newRate}) / 100$$
and
$$(P * (12 - M)/12) * \text{oldRate}) / 100$$

Program The program does just that! It initializes all the values we know, and uses expressions in the final `println` statement for the answer. Since both the expressions are the same except for the rates, we can simplify things by creating a variable which holds the value of the common part and then using this twice in the final calculation.

```java
public class InterestIncrease {

    /* Interest Increase Program                by J M Bishop Aug 1996
     * ------------------------                  Java 1.1 Oct 1997
     * Calculates the difference in simple interest for two interest
     * rates for the remainder of the year from a given month.
     *
     * Illustrates declarations, assignment, constants,
     * expressions and printing.
     */

    static final double p = 1000;          // in graz
    static final int    m = 4;             // for April
    static final double oldRate = 12.5;    // %
    static final double newRate = 13.00;   // %

    public static void main(String[] args) {
      // Start with a title
        System.out.println("SavBank Interest Calculation");
        System.out.println("============================");

      // perform the preliminary calculation
        double ptOver100 = p * (12 - m) / 12 / 100;

      // print out the results
        System.out.println("Given a change of interest rate from "+
                oldRate+"% to "+newRate+"% in month "+m+",");
        System.out.println("on a principal of G"+p+
                " the interest for the rest of the year");
        System.out.print("will change by graz and cents: ");
        System.out.println(ptOver100 * newRate - ptOver100 * oldRate);
    }
}
```

Testing If we run the program, the output will be:

```
SavBank Interest Calculation
============================
Given a change of interest rate from 12.5% to 13.0% in month 4,
on a principal of G1000.0 the interest for the rest of the year
will change by graz and cents: 3.3333333333333286
```

The output is actually a bit of a surprise. Why was the last number printed with such a long fractional part? The short answer is because that is how it is stored. When the calculation was done, the result was $3\frac{1}{3}$. Real numbers are not stored as fractions, but as decimals and there is a great deal of space to store them. In this case, there were 17 digits. So the second question is, why did Java print all of them? Let us consider the answer in detail.

More on printing integers and reals

As we have said earlier, when a number is to be printed, Java calls its `toString` method which returns the string version, and this is passed to the `print` method. `toString` has no information about how many digits it should produce, so it gives all of them. `long` integers may yield as many as 10 digits and `double` real numbers up to 17 as we have seen above. If the real number's value lies outside the significance of 17 digits, Java resorts to printing the number as a fraction and an exponent raised to the power of 10. There is one digit before the point and between an additional one and 16 (as required) after it. The resulting required decimal exponent comes after an E. This format is known as **scientific format**, or **E-format**. So, how would Java print the following numeric expressions?

```
Number              Printed as
10                  10
650                 650
2001                2001
14.75               14.75
1.6213              1.6213
1/1.6213            0.6167889964843027
123456789           123456789
0.000000001         1.0E-9
1.0/2               0.5
1/2                 0
```

Only the last one is surprising, but remember that Java regards / as a integer operator if both the values are integers. In integer terms, the result of 1 divided by 2 is 0.

Clearly, the problem with the above scheme is the long real numbers. In order to achieve finer control, we shall have to delve into Java's large range of formatting classes in the `java.text` package. We leave this to Chapter 4. The next example relies on integer arithmetic only.

EXAMPLE 2.5 Fleet timetables

Problem Savanna Deliveries Inc. has acquired new vehicles which are able to travel faster than the old vehicles (while still staying within the speed limit). They would like to know how this will affect journeys.

Solution Times are represented in a 24 hour clock, such as 0930 or 1755. We need to find out how an arrival time will change, based on an average reduction in the total journey time of 15%. Therefore, we need to be able to subtract times to find the journey time and multiply the result by 0.85, representing a 15% reduction. The question is how to do arithmetic on times.

Algorithm Times consist of two parts – hours and minutes. In order to do subtraction and multiplication on times, we have to convert them to minutes first, perform the calculation, then convert back. Assuming we can do this, the overall algorithm is:

> **New fleet**
> > Read in the departure and arrival times
> > Calculate journey time
> > Reduce journey time by 15%
> > Add to the departure time to get the new arrival time
> > Print out new journey time and arrival time.

The first conversion involves splitting an integer into two parts. To do this, we need to divide by 100, giving the hours, and get the minutes by taking the remainder. The algorithm is:

> **Convert to minutes**
> > Time is   0715
> > Find hours from time / 100   7
> > Find minutes from time modulo 100   15
> > Set minutes to hours * 60 + minutes   435

Converting back is similar. The algorithm is:

> **Convert to hours and minutes**
> > Minutes are   435
> > Set hours to minutes / 60   7
> > Set minutes from minutes modulo 60   15
> > Set time to hours*100+minutes   715

Program The program to handle one journey is quite simple. The departure and arrival times of a particular vehicle are set as constants. In Chapter 4 we shall see how to read them in from the keyboard instead. Remember that division of integer values yields an integer result, so that the algorithms above have a direct translation into Java.

```
public class NewFleet {

    /* The New Fleet Program          by J M Bishop  Aug 1996
     * --------------------           Java 1.1 October 1997
     * Works out the new arrival time for vehicles that are
     * 15% faster than before.
     *
     * Illustrates constants, expressions and assignment.
     * Includes use of the modulo operator %
     */
```

```
static final double reduction = 0.85;
static final int depart = 900;
static final int arrive = 1015;

public static void main(String[] args) {

    long newArrive;             // 24 hour clock times
    int  departM,
         arriveM,
         oldJourneyTime;
    long newJourneyTime,
         newArriveM;            // in minutes in a day

// convert the initial times to minutes
    departM = (depart / 100)*60 + depart % 100;
    arriveM = (arrive / 100)*60 + arrive % 100;

// calculate the old and new times
    oldJourneyTime = arriveM - departM;
    newJourneyTime = Math.round(oldJourneyTime*reduction);

// create the new arrival time in minutes and
// then in a 24 hour clock time
    newArriveM = departM + newJourneyTime;
    newArrive = (newArriveM / 60)*100 + newArriveM % 60;

// Report on the findings
    System.out.println("Departure time is "+depart);
    System.out.println("Old arrival time is "+arrive);
    System.out.println("Old journey time is "+oldJourneyTime+" minutes");
    System.out.println("New journey time is "+newJourneyTime+" minutes");
    System.out.println("New arrival time is "+newArrive);
    }
}
```

Notice that we use six different variables to keep all the values relevant at any one time. They are also given names that indicate their meaning well.

An interesting point in the above program is why some of the variables were declared as long. Java uses long and double as the default types for the result of integer and real expressions respectively. Thus the expression

```
oldJourneyTime*reduction
```

which involves a real number will produce a double result. The version of Math.round that takes a double parameter produces a long result. In order to keep the types the same across the assignment, newJourneyTime must be declared as long. There is actually a way of changing from one type to another, but we shall delay the discussion of this to the next chapters.

Testing Testing the program gives:

```
Departure time is 900
Old arrival time is 1015
Old journey time is 75 mins
New journey time is 64 mins
New arrival time is 1004
```

2.5 Using packages, classes and objects

Having introduced classes and objects in Section 2.2, we can now look at how to use them. Since we are not yet far enough ahead to be able to define our own classes, we shall make use of a class already defined in Java. In so doing we shall see how:

- to import a Java package;
- to declare objects with initial values;
- to call methods from our objects.

Using packages

Java is a relatively simple language in itself (with fewer features than C++, say) but it makes up for its brevity by having a substantial number (24 in fact) of core packages which can be used by any program. A **package** is a collection of classes which logically fit together, and which may interact between themselves. Some of the main Java packages in the order in which they are encountered in this book are:

- lang – for routine language functions;
- util – for additional useful utilities;
- io – for input and output;
- text – for specialized formatting
- awt – for graphics and graphical user interfacing;
- awt.event – for handling events from the keyboard, mouse and so on;
- applet – for creating Java programs to run on the Web;
- net – for networking.

To gain access to any of these packages, except lang which is always available, we use the following form:

Accessing a package
`import java.package.*;`

The asterix indicates that all classes in the package are made available. We can be more selective and choose just the ones we want by having several individual imports, one for each class. For example, `Date` and `Random` are classes in the `java.util` package. If we say

```
import java.util.Random;
import java.util.Date;
```

we shall just gain access to only those two classes. If we say

```
import java.util.*;
```

and only use `Random` and `Date`, the effect is the same. Java is careful enough to distinguish between `import` meaning 'I may want to access' and actual use in the program. Since there is no performance degradation associated with mentioning the whole package for import, most programmers do use the .*.

There is more to know about packages when we actually want to declare our own ones. This important part of Java is discussed in Chapter 4.

Object declarations

Once we have access to classes, we can declare objects of that class. The forms for object declarations are:

Object declaration

```
modifier classname objectname = new classname (parameters);
modifier classname objectname = classname.getInstance (parameters)
```

An example of the first form that we have already seen for an object declaration is:

```
Trees palm = new Trees ( );
```

An example of a modifier is `static`, indicating a class object. Other modifiers are covered later, especially in Chapter 8. In the form, the class name is mentioned twice. While in most cases it will be the same class name, on rare occasions we might use a different name. There was an example of this in the main method of the second starter program in Example 2.2:

```
Frame f = new Rings ();
```

In the class header, `Rings` is declared to extend `Frame`, so there is a clear connection between the two, which is exploited when the object is declared. Using two related classes in this way is the realm of object inheritance, which is discussed fully in Chapter 9.

In any case, the object is defined to be of the class given at the start of the declaration, and it is a new object, so new storage is created for it. When an object is instantiated, the class often gives the opportunity for it to be customized by providing some initial parameters. Examples of such customization are given in the example that follows.

When working with Java's built-in packages, there are some classes that we cannot instantiate in this way. The reason why will become clear in Chapter 9. Meanwhile we note here that all is not lost: these classes provide a special class method (usually called `getInstance` or `getDefault`) which can be called to create the instance we need. This facility is exploited in the next example.

The computer's locale

Java is very much an international language, and it provides for internationalization in numerous ways. The idea is that as programs move around the world on the Internet, they can present themselves in local parlance to users. For example, in the United States, dates are written with the month first, whereas in other countries either the year or the day comes first. If you are using an operating system such as MS Windows, you can access the regional settings in the control panel and see where your computer thinks it is. Computers come set by default for English (United States), so you could experiment and change the setting. Notice that if you change the country, other settings change automatically, such as the currency symbol and the date format.

Java provides a class in the `java.util` package which enables a program to interrogate the computer's settings and print them out. The class is called `Locale`, and its full definition is:

```
public final class Locale extends Object
                        implements Cloneable, Serializable {
// constructors
    public Locale (String language, String Country, String variant);
    public Locale (String language, String Country);

// Constants
    public static final Locale CANADA;
    public static final Locale CANADA_FRENCH;
    public static final Locale CHINA;
    public static final Locale CHINESE;
    public static final Locale ENGLISH;
    public static final Locale FRANCE;
    public static final Locale FRENCH;
    public static final Locale GERMAN;
    public static final Locale GERMANY;
    public static final Locale ITALIAN;
    public static final Locale ITALY;
    public static final Locale JAPAN;
    public static final Locale JAPANESE;
    public static final Locale KOREA;
    public static final Locale KOREAN;
    public static final Locale PRC;
```

```
    public static final Locale SIMPLIFIED_CHINESE;
    public static final Locale TAIWAN;
    public static final Locale TRADITIONAL_CHINESE;
    public static final Locale UK;
    public static final Locale US;

// class methods
    public static synchronized Locale getDefault();
    public static synchronized void setDefault(Locale newLocale);

// instance methods
    public Object          clone ();
    public boolean         equals (Object obj);
    public String          getCountry();
    public final String    getDisplayCountry();
    public String          getDisplayCountry(Locale inLocale);
    public String          getLanguage();
    public String          getDisplayLanguage(Locale inLocale);
    public final String    getDisplayLanguage();
    public String          getName();
    public String          getDisplayName(Locale inLocale);
    public final String    getDisplayName();
    public String          getVariant();
    public String          getDisplayVariant(Locale inLocale);
    public final String    getDisplayVariant();
    public String          getISO3Country()
                                 throws MissingResourceException;
    public String          getISO3Language()
                                 throws MissingResourceException;
    public synchronized int hashCode ();
    public final String    toString ();
}
```

The purpose of including the full specification is not to overwhelm you with detail, but to give you an example of what a standard class in Java looks like. As you can see, it starts off with two constructors. We can create a new locale if we know the language and country we want. Thereafter, there are two class methods, one of which provides the other option: a locale object can be created from the default setting in the machine. The second class method is used in conjunction with regular object declarations to set up one of the locales which follow as constants. The constants include only a limited number of locales, but Java is not restricted to these, as it can and will fetch other information from the machine, as shown in the example following.

The bulk of the class is made up of instance methods, and as is usual, there are several variations on each theme. Let us explore these practically.

EXAMPLE 2.6 Where am I?

Problem Find out which geographical region and which language the computer running a program uses.

Solution The obvious solution is to pull in the `Locale` class and find out the necessary information. Once we have done that, we shall extend the specification slightly and create another locale to see the effect on the various properties that are returned when interrogated.

Program The program looks at the local machine's locale, and then creates a locale for Germany.

```
import java.util.*;

class WhereAmI {

    /*  The program for finding Where Am I?    by J M Bishop Dec 1997
     *  -----------------------------------
     *  Illustrates the use of classes in Java packages
     *  and the facility of changing locales.
     */

    public static void main (String [ ] args) {
        Locale here = Locale.getDefault();

        System.out.println("My Locale is " + here);
        System.out.println("Country:  " + here.getCountry());
        System.out.println("Language: " + here.getLanguage());
        System.out.println("Country:  " + here.getDisplayCountry());
        System.out.println("Language: " + here.getDisplayLanguage());
        System.out.println();


        Locale there = new Locale("GERMAN","GERMANY");
        there.setDefault(Locale.GERMANY);
        System.out.println("New Locale is " + there);
        System.out.println("Country:  " + there.getCountry());
        System.out.println("Language: " + there.getLanguage());
        System.out.println("Country:  " + there.getDisplayCountry());
        System.out.println("Language: " + there.getDisplayLanguage());

    }
}
```

Testing The output when run on my Windows computer was:

```
My Locale is en_SOUTH AFRICA
Country:  SOUTH AFRICA
Language: en
Country:  United States
Language: English

New Locale is german_GERMANY
Country:  GERMANY
Language: german
Country:  Deutschland
Language: Deutsch
```

What this says is that the computer detects that it is in South Africa and the main language is English ('en'). However, for display purposes, it will use the conventions of the United States, as South Africa is not currently one of the options in its list. If we then create a new locale and declare it as Germany, we see that the country and language will in fact be completely localized.

SUMMARY

This chapter looked at programming from two levels. On the higher level, a program is composed of classes, which are composed of fields and methods, and methods are composed of parameters, fields and statements. Creating objects as instances of a given class led to the idea that some declarations would belong to the class, and some to each instance of it. This treatment of classes and objects was rounded off in a practical way in the last section, where we used an existing class, `Locale`, to create and manipulate objects.

On a lower level, there are several options for fields in the form of variables or constants. Two statements for early programming are assignment and output calls. There are eight types in Java, of which three – `int`, `long` and `double` – were discussed. How to write expressions within the restrictions of a single line was followed by two examples that made use of the features learnt so far. Details regarding how Java writes numbers were given. We also learnt that the output statements, strictly speaking, output only strings but that other types, such as numbers and dates, are converted into strings behind the scenes. Any data item for which the `toString` method is defined can be used in a `println`, and concatenation is a very useful facility for joining several items in a single output call.

QUIZ

2.1   Give a Java method call to draw a blue circle in the centre of a window 300 by 300 pixels.

2.2   Give a Java declaration for a `Tree` object called `marula`.

2.3   If we wanted to store the names of trees, would these be declared as class variables or instance variables? Why?

2.4   Give two ways of printing your name and address in a neat label (a) using only one statement, and (b) using several statements. Explain why concatenation will almost certainly be necessary in (a).

2.5   What would be printed out on your computer from the following expressions?

```
52 % 10
9000009
Math.pow(4,3)
21 / 7
22 / 7
4 - 3 / 4 - 2
```

2.6   The `Math` class has a `sqrt` method. Give a statement to assign to x the value of

$$\sqrt{\frac{b^2 - 4ac}{2a}}$$

2.7   In Example 2.6, why were the `here` and `there` objects declared in different ways?

2.8   Set up suitable declarations for the following variables: a distance in track events in the Olympics, the mass of bags of flour sold in a supermarket, the age of a child in a school, minutes in a hour, a bank balance in graz.

2.9   Referring to Example 2.5, classify each of the following as a keyword, variable, constant, method, object, class or package.

```
main       newArrive   Math      round
final      NewFleet    class     100
System     out         println   arrive
```

2.10   Given the following declarations in the same class, which ones would cause the compiler to report errors and why?

```
integer i, j, k;
max = 10;
double x = 1;
double K = 1,000;
static int 2ndPrize = G25;
static double x = 6;
```

PROBLEMS

2.1   **Singing snowman**. Using the program in Example 2.2 as a template, construct a program to draw a singing snowman on the screen like this:

2.2   **Percentage change**. Consider the program in Example 2.4. The old rate and new rate are given as constants. Instead, define a percentage change in the rate and calculate the new rate from that. For example, if the change is −20% on an old rate of 10%, then the new rate is 8%. Adapt the program and run it again.

2.3   **Weighted averages**. A computer science course has three parts to it: a test, an assignment and an examination, which are weighted at 20%, 30% and 50% respectively. Write a program that will set marks for the three components (out of 100) and print the final mark using the weightings.

2.4   **Fuel consumption**. A motor car uses 8 litres of fuel per 100km on normal roads and 15% more fuel on rough roads. Write a program to print out the distance the car can travel on a full tank of 40 litres of fuel on both normal and rough roads.

CHAPTER 3

Structuring

3.1 Properties of a good program

The structure of a program indicates how its parts are connected together, and how sound those connections are. One can think of the structure of a bridge: each strut and rivet plays its role, and the whole performs a defined function efficiently. Bridges can even look pleasing. So it is with programs. When we create them we aim to achieve a structure that in the first instance achieves the required purpose, but then which is also readable, reusable and efficient. These are the properties of a good program.

Correctness

It seems obvious that a program when complete should be correct but we all know that the two properties can diverge widely. Much software these days is released to the world with errors remaining (called bugs). In defence of such software, one must say that programming is one of the most complex engineering tasks that we know, and it is also one of the newest (genetic engineering is perhaps more recent). It is only since the mid-1980s that codified books on software engineering started to appear, and standards of software reliability began to be set by international bodies. So how do we program to achieve correct software? There are two golden rules:

- Follow good programming practice while writing a program.

- Test the program thoroughly once it is done.

This book aims to instil good practice by example, and by motivating guidelines that can be followed in any programming activity. Interestingly enough, these are frequently not Java-specific.

Testing is very important, as no matter how hard we try, we cannot always imagine all possibilities that might occur when the program starts running. With simple programs, we can read through the logic and reason about what will happen. With more complex programs (extending over more than two pages, say) and, in particular, programs where the user can alter the course by supplying data, the task is very much harder. Here the careful design of test data pays off.

Readability

In order to reason about a program, we have to be able to read it, and perhaps even discuss it with others. Some of the factors that aid readability are:

- use of meaningful identifiers, e.g. `noOfEnquiries` instead of `e`;

- careful layout, especially indenting and blank lines;

- comments to explain the function of statements that follow.

One can also take readability further by starting to develop a **style** of writing that enables you to find what you are looking for quickly, and to communicate effectively within a group of programmers. For example, you may organize your methods so that their declarations always appear before the statements, at the front. Another suggestion is to arrange the methods of a large class alphabetically by name (as shown in the `Locale` class in Section 2.5). Software organizations will often set up such guidelines – and expect them to be followed by employees.

Reusability

While some might say that the inaccuracy of software is a major crisis in the industry, of equal concern is the inability of firms to produce software on time. One of the ways in which we aim to alleviate this position is to reuse software that has been tried and tested before. Java's packages are a classic example of reusability: instead of each of us writing a class to store and manipulate locales, one is provided.

Reusability works both ways: when writing a new program, we look around for existing classes that can be used or even adapted, and at the same time, we try to write our own classes so that they have a general appeal, without compromising their efficiency or readability in their primary program. Java has specific class constructs which aim to assist with reusability, and these are covered in Part II.

Efficiency

There is nothing more frustrating than a program that is too slow or too big. Of course, a complex task might require time, memory and disk space, but simple tasks should not. There are many small ways in which we can start out by programming thriftily, while once again not compromising our other goals. Just a few ideas for keeping a program compact are:

- declare variables as needed, do not overdo it;
- maximize the use of methods, thus avoiding copies of common statements;
- do common calculations once and store the result.

As we progress in programming maturity, more of these will be mentioned.

About what follows

This discussion has introduced the rest of the chapter well. Section 3.2 looks at some more types in Java. By choosing a type to fit the items we are dealing with, readability is considerably enhanced. Efficiency is also a factor, since by selecting different numeric types, we can obtain storage correctly suited to our needs.

The next sections show different ways in which we can group statements to aid readability, reusability and efficiency. The main one is the definition of classes and their use, and considerable time is spent in Section 3.6 and the case study that follows clarifying the design principles for classes and objects.

3.2 Talking about types

Having examined integer and real numbers in Section 2.4, we now complete our discussion of types. The three Java types for numbers – `int`, `long` and `double` – are augmented by `byte`, `short` and `float`. Then there are the two special types, called `boolean` and `char`. We shall look at these first. When considering the numeric types again, we raise the issue of how to convert from one to the other, so that assignments can be made between variables of different types.

Booleans

Conditions govern the decisions made in programs as to alternative paths to follow. A condition yields a value **true** or **false**. Another name for a condition is a **boolean expression**.[1] Boolean expressions use the six comparison operators to compare the results of numeric expressions. The operators are:

==	equal to
!=	not equal to
>	greater than
<	less than
>=	greater than or equal to
<=	less than or equal to

The result of such an expression can be stored in a **boolean variable**. For example, given the declarations:

```
boolean isaMinor, isaPensioner;
int age;
```

we can store various facts about the age of someone as:

```
isaMinor = age < 18;
isaPensioner = age >=65;
```

and display these later using:

```
System.out.println ("Driver's licence denied:" + isaMinor);
```

If your age is 15, then `isaMinor` would be true so the statement would print:

Driver's licence denied: true

As another example,

```
System.out.println ("It is " + isaPensioner +
            " that you can ride the bus for free.");
```

will for a 15-year-old display:

It is false that you can ride the bus for free.

There are also the boolean operators:

&	and
|	or
^	xor, the exclusive or
!	not

---

[1] Booleans are named after the nineteenth century mathematician George Boole.

For the expression (x & y) to be true, both x and y must be true; for the expression (x | y) to be true, either x or y or both can be true. There is also a precedence between the operators, so that in the absence of brackets, & will always be evaluated before |. The results of the operators are summarized in Figure 3.1.

and &	false	true
false	false	false
true	false	true

xor ^	false	true
false	false	true
true	true	false

or |	false	true
false	false	true
true	true	true

not !	
false	true
true	false

Figure 3.1 *Boolean operator tables.*

Referring back to the earlier example with the minor and pensioner conditions, suppose we make the declarations:[2]

```
boolean isEmployed, isaYoungWorker, isaVoter, isaTaxpayer;
```

Then further facts can be deduced as follows:

```
isaYoungWorker = isaMinor & isEmployed;
isaVoter = ! isaMinor;
isaTaxpayer = isaVoter | isEmployed;
```

Boolean operators can be combined to express more complex conditions. For example, if both minors and pensioners can go free on the buses provided they are not working, then we have:

```
boolean freeBus = (isaPensioner | isaMinor) & !isEmployed;
```

The brackets are needed so that the | is evaluated first whereas normally & would be.

Boolean operators are very useful in conjunction with the comparison operators in establishing detailed conditions. An example is an expression for deciding whether school should be cancelled because it is too cold or too hot, that is:

```
goHome = temperature > 40 | temperature < 0;
```

In Java, the precedence between the comparison operators and the boolean ones is such that the comparisons will always be executed first (that is, they have higher

[2] It is a useful habit to preface Boolean variables with 'is' or 'isa' so that statements that use them read more naturally.

precedence). In other languages, the reverse is true, and many programmers are used to putting brackets around conditions. You might often see an expression such as the go home test written as:

```
goHome = (temperature > 40) | (temperature < 0);
```

On the other hand the concatenation operator does take precedence over & and |. To print out a&b and a|b, we cannot use:

```
println(a&b + a|b);
```

because + will try to operate on the central b + a, and will report an error. Instead, we introduce brackets:

```
println((a&b) + (a|b));
```

Java also has 'short circuit' versions of *and* and *or* which are the && and || operators respectively. In the case of

```
c&&d
```

d will only be evaluated if c is true. Similarly, for ||, once c has been established as true, d is ignored. A nice example of such operators is establishing whether one date (comprising three integers) is earlier than another. The statement – quite long – would be:

```
boolean earlier = y1 < y2 ||
                  (y1 == y2 && m1 < m2) ||
                  (y1 == y2 && m1 == m2 && d1 < d2);
```

To summarize, the precedence of the boolean operators and comparisons is:

```
group 0:    ()
group 1:    !
group 2:    &
group 3:    |
group 4:    &&
group 5:    ||
```

Characters

We have already looked informally at strings in Java. They are covered more formally in Chapter 6 when we deal with arrays. A string in Java is an object, and a single character in quotes, e.g. "a", is also a string. Java provides a more simple type for single characters called **char**. The char type encompasses all the letters, digits and symbols that appear on a keyboard, typically:

A to Z
a to z
! @ # $ % ^ & * ( ) _ + - = { } [ ] : " | ; ' ~ ` ? /

In addition, we can represent some other keyboard characters with the escape prefix:

\b   backspace
\t   tab[3]
\n   new line
\f   new page (i.e. form feed)
\r   return to the start of the line

Notice that these particular keyboard keys cannot otherwise appear on the screen: they cause special effects when pressed.

Characters in Java are written with a single quote, e.g. 'a' and the following operations are automatically valid for them:

- assignment,

- comparison (all the six comparison operators described above),

- input and output.

The result of a comparison for less or greater depends on the order of the characters as set up in Java. What we need to know is that the letters are in order so that 'g' < 'z' , for example.

Finally, Java also provides, through the escape charater \u, space for an additional 10000 additional characters that are not available on the usual keyboards. These are called Unicode characters and enable Java to be truly international: there are Unicode sequences for letters in Greek, Cyrillic, Hebrew, Arabic, Tibetan and so on, conforming to international standards where they exist. However, we do not need to be concerned with these while we are dealing in what is called the Latin alphabet.

Numeric types

The six numeric types are shown with their properties in Table 3.1. byte is typically used in programs that are dealing with data at the level of the machine. short can be a way of saving space, but is not often used in Java. int is the usual type for declaring integers, but long also frequently appears as it is the default for the result of an integer expression. float would be the natural choice for real numbers, except that double is the default type for the result of real expressions. That is why we introduced int, long and double in the previous chapter.

The numeric types have access to all the operations mentioned already, and can be output as explained in Section 2.4. In addition, there are some new and interesting operators which will be useful almost immediately. In programming, a common operation is to add one to a counter. For example, we might have the assignment:

---

[3] There is a sequence of fixed positions across a line on a screen, usually eight characters apart, known as **tabs**. Pressing the tab key on the keyboard or displaying the tab character via a program moves the output to the next tab position.

Table 3.1 *Details of the numeric types*

Type	Representation	Initial value	Storage	Maximum value
byte	signed integer	0	8 bits	127
short	signed integer	0	16 bits	32767
int	signed integer	0	32 bits	2147483647
long	signed integer	0	64 bits	over 10^{18}
float	floating-point	0.0	32 bits	over 10^{38}
double	floating point	0.0	64 bits	over 10^{308}

```
int total;
total = total + 1;
```

Since this is such a common kind of assignment, it seems wasteful to have to type the variable's name twice in every case. Thus there are four special assignments defined to abbreviate common increments and decrements. These are shown in the next form.

Increment and decrement assignments

```
variable ++;        // add one to variable
variable --;        // subtract one from variable
variable += exp;    // add exp to variable
variable -= exp;    // subtract exp from variable
```

---

i++ or i+=1 mean the same thing: 'add 1 to i', whereas 'i+=2' means 'add 2 to i', and so on. Thus the example above becomes:

```
total++;
```

If we were always adding five, then we would use

```
total += 5;
```

One way to remember that the increment operator is += and not =+ is that the latter, in an assignment, could be misinterpreted as assigning a positive value, not adding it. That is,

```
total =+ 5;
```

would treat +5 as a constant and assign it to total.

Conversions between types

We have hinted on several occasions that it is possible to convert between numeric types. Why would we wish to do this? A common example is that of calculations which result in real values, but that then should be displayed as integers for ease of understanding. So far, two specific conversions have been discussed:

- Rounding a double number up to a long using Math.round.

- Assigning an int to a double number.

Another kind of conversion applies across the board to the numeric types in order of size, which means we can assign

```
byte => short => int => long => float => double
```

or any combination of these in the same direction. For example, byte to long is allowed, and short to double. But what about the other direction? Suppose we want to 'down-size' a double to a float. In this case we have to use a **type cast**. The type cast takes the form:

Type cast
(type) expression

For example,

```
float kilograms;
double estimate = 45;
kilograms = (float) (estimate * 1.2);
```

The proviso is that the value of the expression must be applicable to the values that can be stored by the type. Referring to Table 3.1, we could not cast a short value of 1000 into a byte, since it would not fit. Java will report a compilation error (if the value is deducible at compile time) or otherwise a run-time error. In the case of real to integer type casts, however, any fractional part is discarded. For example,

```
(int) 6.3 gives 6
(int) 6.8 gives 6
```

Finally, we note that type casting is allowed only between numeric types. Unlike other languages, there is no facility in Java for converting characters and booleans into numbers and vice versa.

3.3 Repetition with for-loops

Computers, like all machines, are very good at doing the same thing over and over again. In a program, such repetition can be formulated as a **loop**. There are two kinds of loops possible in Java, as in most languages – **for-loops** and **conditional loops**. In this section we look at for-loops; the conditional ones are introduced in Chapter 5.

The form of a for-loop

A basic Java for-loop is specified in the following form:

Simple for-statement

```
for (start; check; update) {
    body
}
```

The `for`, brackets and curly brackets form the compulsory structure of the loop, and the italicized parts have to be expanded. The **start** part introduces one or more **loop variables** which are to be tested and updated. If there is more than one loop variable then their starting statements are separated by commas.

The **check** is a comparison which gives the condition for the loop to end, based on the current value of the loop variables. The **update** part consists of assignments to change the values of the loop variables each time round the loop. The **body** of the loop consists of statements. If there is only one statement, then the curly brackets can be omitted.

Usually, there is only one loop variable. Loop variables must be numbers, and by convention they are usually integers. It is possible, but is considered bad practice, to have a loop variable that is a real number. The reason is that a comparison on real numbers is inexact at the limits, and a loop may execute for one more or less than the number of times expected.

Now consider the following example to print out five rows of stars

```
for (int i=0; i<5; i++)
    System.out.println("**********");
```

Are we sure that five and not six rows are printed? Once the initialization has been completed (and it happens only once) the sequence in which the other three parts of the loop are executed is:

- check
- body
- update

Taking it slowly, i starts at 0. It is checked against 5, a line of stars is printed and i is incremented to 1. When i gets to 3, the stars are printed, i is incremented to 4, checked against 5, more stars are printed, and *i* is incremented to 5. Now it is checked that it is *less than* 5 and fails. The loop then ends and control continues after the final brace. We can therefore verify that five rows are printed for values of i from 0 to 4.

It is good practice to have a standard way of writing simple for-loops. If we want to run a loop *n* times, we can choose between:

```
for (int i=1; i<=n; i++)
for (int i=0; i<n; i++)
```

The first version is perhaps easier to understand. However, many related sequences in Java, especially arrays (as discussed in Chapter 6), use zero as a starting point. It has therefore become conventional to start loops at zero, and the second form is therefore preferred.

EXAMPLE 3.1 Multiple labels

Problem Ms Mary Brown of 33 Charles Street, Brooklyn, would like to print out several return addresses which she is going to photocopy onto sticky labels.

Solution We checked with Ms Brown and confirmed that for the time being, she is happy to have the labels one underneath each other. (Later on we shall see how to fill a page with labels.) The solution is to take the body of the DisplayWarning program in Example 2.1 as a model and put it in a loop.

Program The program follows on quite easily. Note that we follow each label by two blank lines to separate them, and use a constant, nLabels, to specify how many labels there must be.

```
class lotsaLabels {

    /* The Lots of Labels program        by J M Bishop July 1996
     * -------------------------          Java 1.1
     * Prints labels one underneath each other.
     * Illustrates a simple for-loop.
     */

static final int nLabels = 8;

    public static void main (String [] args) {

        for (int i=0; i<nLabels; i++) {
            System.out.println ("---------------------");
            System.out.println ("|                    |");
            System.out.println ("| Ms Mary Brown      |");
            System.out.println ("| 33 Charles Street  |");
            System.out.println ("| Brooklyn           |");
            System.out.println ("|                    |");
            System.out.println ("---------------------");
```

```
        System.out.println ("\n\n");
    }
  }
}
```

Using the loop variable

The loop variable serves to record the current iteration of a loop and its values can be used in various ways, some of which are:

- in an output statement;
- in simple arithmetic;
- as part of the bounds of another loop.

Together, these three facilities make looping much more interesting. Take the first use. We can number the star lines printed earlier as follows:

```
for (int i=0; i<5; i++) {
  System.out.print((i+1));
  System.out.println(" **********");
}
```

which would print

```
1 **********
2 **********
3 **********
4 **********
5 **********
```

Notice that the loop variable, i, runs from 0 to 4, but we print out $(i+1)$, giving 1 to 5. If we had not put the $i+1$ in parentheses, then it would have been misinterpreted as the value of i plus a string concatenation with the value 1, giving 01 11 21 31 41. Check it to see.

Now consider how to print out the first 10 even numbers. There are actually two ways. We can have a loop from 0 up to and not including 10 and write out double the loop variable, as in:

```
for (int number = 0; number < 10; number++)
   System.out.print ((number * 2)+" ");
System.out.println ();
```

which will produce:

```
0 2 4 6 8 10 12 14 16 18
```

The other way is to do the doubling in the update-part, which would be:

```
for (int number = 0; number < 20; number+=2)
   System.out.print (number+" ");
System.out.println ();
```

To print the first 10 odd numbers requires a bit of thought. If `number*2` is an even number, then `number*2+1` or `number*2-1` is an odd number. Choosing one of these expressions, we have:

```
for (int number = 0; number < 10; number++)
   System.out.print ((number * 2 + 1)+" ");
System.out.println ();
```

which will produce:

```
1 3 5 7 9 11 13 15 17 19
```

EXAMPLE 3.2 Conversion table

Problem An oceanography laboratory measures temperatures of lakes in Celsius, but some of the technicians want the values in Fahrenheit. For the time being, the managers have agreed to put up conversion tables around the laboratory. You have to write the program to generate the conversion table.

Solution Use a loop to go through the range of temperatures required, writing out the one temperature and then its conversion.

Algorithm The algorithm for a conversion table needs a heading, and then a sequence-printing loop, as described in the discussion above. Figure 3.2 shows the algorithm in diagrammatic form. What will the required range of C values be? Well, if these are water temperatures, they could range from 5 to 20.

Program The program follows on easily. Notice that we type cast the real value produced by the expression to get the answers out as integers. To get reasonable layout, we use the escape character \t for tab.

```
class TemperatureTable {

    /* The Temperature Conversion Program    by J M Bishop Aug 1996
     * -------------------------------        Java 1.1
     * Displays a simple table converting Celsius
     * to Fahrenheit for a given range.
     *
     * Illustrates using the loop variable
     * in expressions in the loop
     */
```

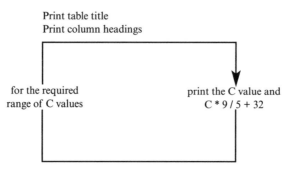

Figure 3.2 *Algorithm for a conversion table.*

```
public static void main(String[] args) {
   System.out.println("Temperature Conversion Table");
   System.out.println("=============================");
   System.out.println();
   System.out.println("C          F");
   for (int c = 5; c <= 20; c++) {
      System.out.print(c+"\t");
      System.out.println(Math.round(c*9/5 + 32));
   }
}
}
```

Testing The program output follows. We could redirect the output to a file, print the file and pin the table up on the wall.

```
Temperature Conversion Table
=============================
C    F
5    41
6    42
7    44
8    46
9    48
10   50
11   51
12   53
13   55
14   57
15   59
16   60
17   62
18   64
19   66
20   68
```

We note that loops can also count backwards using -- or -=. Thus, to print the sequence

```
10 9 8 7 6 5 4 3 2 1 0 -1 -2 -3 -4 -5 -6
```

we could say

```
for (int n = 10; n >=-6; n--)
   System.out.print(n+" ");
System.out.println();
```

A nice example of counting backwards is found in the song 'One man went to mow', which is discussed in the next example.

In addition, we can have loops within loops, which is also illustrated in Example 3.3. The rule here is that the loop variables of the loops must have different identifiers to avoid confusion. Such loops are called **nested loops**.

EXAMPLE 3.3   Campfire song

Problem A popular campfire song goes like this:

> 1 man went to mow, went to mow a meadow,
> 1 man and his dog, went to mow a meadow.
>
> 2 men went to mow, went to mow a meadow,
> 2 men, 1 man and his dog, went to mow a meadow.
>
> 3 men went to mow, went to mow a meadow,
> 3 men, 2 men, 1 man and his dog, went to mow a meadow.

We would like to print out the words up to a given number of men.

Solution The way of tackling this problem is to take a verse from the output and underline those parts that change each time, that is:

> <u>3</u> men went to mow, went to mow a meadow,
> <u>3</u> men, <u>2</u> men, <u>1</u> man and his dog, went to mow a meadow.

We have carefully used digits rather than words for the numbers, to make programming easier.

Algorithm We set up one loop for the verses, based on how many men there are, and one loop to repeat all the men in reverse order.

Program A first attempt at a program for five men is:

```
class Mow {

    /* The Song Printing program        by J M Bishop    Aug 1996
     * ------------------------                Java 1.1
     * Displays the "One man went to Mow" song
     *
     * Illustrates nested and backward counting for-loops
     */

  public static void main (String [] args) {

    System.out.println("****** One man went to mow ******");
    for (int man = 1; man<=5; man++) {
      System.out.println(man +
          " men went to mow, went to mow a meadow,");
      for (int companions=man; companions>=2; companions --)
          System.out.print(companions + " men, ");
      System.out.println("1 man and his dog, " +
          "went to mow a meadow. ");
      System.out.println();
    }
  }
}
```

Testing The program will produce:

```
****** One man went to mow ******
1 men went to mow, went to mow a meadow,
1 man and his dog, went to mow a meadow.

2 men went to mow, went to mow a meadow,
2 men, 1 man and his dog, went to mow a meadow.

3 men went to mow, went to mow a meadow,
3 men, 2 men, 1 man and his dog, went to mow a meadow.

4 men went to mow, went to mow a meadow,
4 men, 3 men, 2 men, 1 man and his dog, went to mow a meadow.

5 men went to mow, went to mow a meadow,
5 men, 4 men, 3 men, 2 men, 1 man and his dog, went to mow a meadow.
```

The output has one defect: the first line is written as '1 men ...' rather than '1 man ...'. To correct the program, we need to know about if-statements, covered in the next chapter.

Skipping the body of a loop

It may happen with a loop that the starting condition may already exceed the finishing one. In this case, the loop body is not executed at all. In the above example, the statement

```
for (int companions = man; companions >=2; companions --)
```

will be in this situation when man is 1. No 'men' phrases are written out for this verse, which is exactly what was intended.

3.4 Making methods

The concept of a method was introduced in Section 2.2 and used extensively in the previous chapter, where we became familiar with using methods from packages (such as `println` and `getCountry`), and writing programs with a main method. We now look at how to declare our own methods.

Declaring a method

A **method** is a group of declarations and statements that is given a name and may be called upon by this name to perform a particular action. The form of a method declaration is:

Method declaration

```
modifiers kind name (parameters) {
   fields and statements
   return expression;   // typed methods only
}
```

As before, the parts in italics are intended to be filled in. The modifiers that we have encountered so far include `public`, `static` and `final`. These can be used with their same meanings. The kind can be one of:

- void,

- a type,

- a class.

`void` indicates that the method can be called to perform an action in a self-standing way, for example `println`. In contrast, methods that have a type (one of the eight above, for example `int`) or a class (for example `Locale`) will return a value and are called in a different way. These methods must have a return-statement somewhere which is executed to assign to the method a final value. The brackets after the identifier are compulsory and introduce the parameters, about which there is more in Section 3.5. An example of a simple void method without parameters is:

```
static void box () {
   System.out.println ("-------------");
   System.out.println ("|           |");
   System.out.println ("|           |");
   System.out.println ("|           |");
   System.out.println ("-------------");
}
```

Creating a method like this is a **declaration**. The name box is declared to introduce the performing of the given statements.

As an example of a typed method, consider the conversion from Celsius to Fahrenheit. If this operation is to be performed frequently, we could create a method for it as follows:

```
static int Fahrenheit (int Celsius) {
   return Celsius * 9/5 + 32;
}
```

Calling a method

If a method is declared as void, it is called by mentioning its name and parameters (if any). For example, to display a box, all we need to say is:

```
box();
```

the effect of which will be to print:

```
-------------
|           |
|           |
|           |
-------------
```

If it has a type or class (known generally as a **typed method**), then a call to it constitutes an expression and can be used wherever an expression of that type is permitted. Typically, typed methods would be called in assignments, as parts of expressions, or in output statements.

For example, referring back to the Locale class discussed in Section 2.5, there is a method defined as

```
public String getLanguage ( );
```

Within our main method we declare an object:

```
Locale special = new Locale ("Finnish","Finland");
```

and then we can find out the language by calling:

```
System.out.println (special.getLanguage ( ));
```

Let us go through this example very carefully. `getLanguage` is an instance method; in other words it is available for each object declared as a `Locale`. It is also a typed method as opposed to a void method in that it is declared as `String`. This means that it will return an string object when called. The method has no parameters. When we call `getLanguage`, we preface it with the object we are using, and it will return the relevant information for that object, in this case the language of, say, Finnish.

Calling the conversion method defined above would be similar:

```
System.out.println (30 + "C is " + Fahrenheit (30) + "F");
```

which would print out

```
30C is 86F
```

A nuance of method calls that we have already mentioned in Section 2.2 is that the prefix depends on the method's modifiers and where it is defined relative to the call.

Method calls

```
method (parameters);              // declared static in this class
object.method (parameters);       // declared in another object
classname.method (parameters);    // declared static in another class
```

Specific examples of these different calls will arise in Section 3.6 as we get into the design of classes.

Defining methods, whether they are static as part of small programs, or subdivisions of a class's operation, enables us to cut down on repetition. It provides a means of creating a structure for a program, since the name of a method can be carefully chosen to reflect the action it performs. Readability is also enhanced.

3.5 Passing parameters

Methods can be made more powerful by allowing their effect to differ each time the method is called. For example, if we have a method that prints a 5 by 5 box, it would be useful if it were able to print a 10 by 10 box, or a 12 by 16 box, or whatever. In other words, the action of printing a box by means of `println` methods should appear to be independent of the number of `println`s that are actually needed. This is called **generalizing** or **parameterizing** a method and the values that are going to be different are known as **parameters**.

What we are aiming at is a means of being able to write:

```
box (5,5);
box (10,10);
box (12,16);
```

We achieve this goal by declaring the method with parameters that are given names and receive their values at the time the method is called. For the box, the declaration would become:

```
static void box (int width, int depth)
```

Although we refer to the items in the declaration and the call as parameters, strictly speaking the declaration introduces **formal** parameters, and the call provides **actual** parameters. The form for a list of formal parameters is:

Formal parameter declarations
`(type field, type field ...)`

whereas the form for actual parameters is:

Actual parameters
`(expression, expression, ...)`

The number, types and order of the formal and actual parameters must match exactly. For example, the box method can be called with:

```
int size = 60;
box (size, (int) size/2);
```

but not with any of

```
box(100);
box ("very wide");
box (12.5, 10);
```

Although we are concentrating on variables here, we note that objects can also be formal parameters, in which case the matching actual parameter must also be an object.

To understand how parameters work, study Figure 3.3 carefully.

EXAMPLE 3.4   A large conversion table

Problem The oceanography laboratory was so pleased with the table we produced (Example 3.2) that it has asked us to do one for a larger range of temperatures, but to arrange it so that the whole table fits nicely on the screen or on a page.

Solution We know how to do the conversion, so what we need to think about is how to arrange the layout of the table. A standard computer screen has lines 80 characters wide. Each pair of temperatures will occupy no more than 16 characters. We can

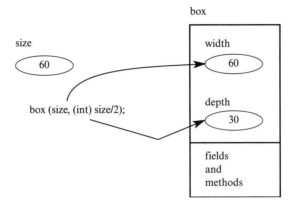

Figure 3.3 *An example of parameter passing.*

therefore fit five columns on the screen. For temperatures from 0 to 99, this gives 20 lines, which will fit nicely on a screen or a page. We can then use nested loops to get the desired effect.

Algorithm We can tackle the solution from the top. We know how to print one line because we did it in Example 3.2. It is:

```
System.out.println (C + "\t" + Math.round(C * 9 / 5 + 32));
```

We can therefore set up a loop to print 20 such lines. The printing of the lines can go in a typed method.

Program Let us define the following constants:

```
static final int colsperline = 5;
static final int maxlineno = 20;
```

The lines will be numbered by the loop from 0 to 19 (that is, up to but not including 20) with a loop variable `line`. Printing one line can be put in a method, `outaLine`, with its own loop and loop variable, say `col`. Then the expression for the Celsius value on a given line and column will be:

```
thisline * colsperline + col
```

In order to clarify the program, we make some improvements at the point where the above expression would appear. Firstly, we create a typed method to perform the conversion from Celsius to Fahrenheit. Then because the Celsius value appears twice – once when it is printed out and once when it is used for the conversion – we assign it to a local variable, c.

Finally, tabs are set so that the columns line up, for both the headings and the values. However, notice that the numbers will be left-justified by Java, rather than lined up on the right, as would be more natural. The full program has plenty of comments to explain what is happening.

```java
class LargeTemperatureTable {

    /* Large Temperature Table Program by JM Bishop September 1996
     * ----------------------------      Java 1.1
     *
     * Produces a conversion table from Celsius to Fahrenheit
     * for values from 0 to 99.
     *
     * Illustrates static methods for structuring, as well as
     * typed methods and parameters.
     */

    static final int colsPerLine = 5;
    static final int maxLineNo = 20;
    static final String gap = "\t\t";

    public static void main(String[] args) {
        System.out.println("\t\tTemperature Conversion Table");
        System.out.println("\t\t=============================");
        System.out.println();

        for (int col = 0; col < colsPerLine; col++)
            System.out.print("C    F"+gap);
        System.out.println();

        /* for each of the lines required, the outaLine
         * method is called with the line number as a
         * parameter.
         */
        for (int r = 0; r < maxLineNo; r++)
            outaLine(r);
    }

    static void outaLine(int thisline) {
        /* Using the information given by the parameter as
         * to which line this is, the method calculates the
         * celsius values for that line and displays them with
         * their Fahrenheit equivalents
         */

        for (int col = 0; col < colsPerLine; col++) {
            int c = thisline * colsPerLine + col;
            System.out.print(c+"   ");
            System.out.print(fahrenheit(c)+gap);
        }
        System.out.println();
    }
```

```
// a simple conversion function
static int fahrenheit(int Celsius) {
   return Math.round(Celsius*9/5+32);
}
}
```

Testing Running the program confirms that it does produce the required effect, and the right answers.

```
Temperature Conversion Table
===============================
```

C	F	C	F	C	F	C	F	C	F
0	32	1	33	2	35	3	37	4	39
5	41	6	42	7	44	8	46	9	48
10	50	11	51	12	53	13	55	14	57
15	59	16	60	17	62	18	64	19	66
20	68	21	69	22	71	23	73	24	75
25	77	26	78	27	80	28	82	29	84
30	86	31	87	32	89	33	91	34	93
35	95	36	96	37	98	38	100	39	102
40	104	41	105	42	107	43	109	44	111
45	113	46	114	47	116	48	118	49	120
50	122	51	123	52	125	53	127	54	129
55	131	56	132	57	134	58	136	59	138
60	140	61	141	62	143	63	145	64	147
65	149	66	150	67	152	68	154	69	156
70	158	71	159	72	161	73	163	74	165
75	167	76	168	77	170	78	172	79	174
80	176	81	177	82	179	83	181	84	183
85	185	86	186	87	188	88	190	89	192
90	194	91	195	92	197	93	199	94	201
95	203	96	204	97	206	98	208	99	210

Example 3.4 illustrated methods and parameters well. However, the call to outaLine used just a single variable, r, each time. Methods and parameters become more interesting when the actual expression passed to the formal parameter is computed from several values, as shown in the next example.

EXAMPLE 3.5 Financial modelling

Problem SavBank has a growth plan for savings that gives interest based on a novel formula. If the money is invested for a fixed period (say 10 years), then the interest is calculated as:

$$\frac{P \times (T + 20\%) \times R}{100}$$

where P is the principal invested, T is the number of years and R is the rate of interest. We would like to produce a diagram of how the principal will grow, given different investment periods, say from 5 to 15 years.

Solution We could write a program similar to the temperature conversion one, listing the years versus the final principal. However, it would be much clearer for customers if the growth was shown in a graph. How do we draw a graph?

For financial modelling, a histogram is usually a good idea. We can show the number of years down the vertical axis, and draw the histogram going outwards, with graz (the currency) on the *x*-axis. Here is what we would hope to achieve.

```
SavBank Growth Plan
===================
Principal of 1000 at rate 12.5

Years
 5  |**************** 1750
 6  |****************** 1900
 7  |******************** 2050
 8  |********************** 2200
 9  |*********************** 2350
10 |************************* 2500
11 |************************** 2650
12 |**************************** 2800
13 |***************************** 2950
14 |******************************* 3100
15 |******************************** 3250
    ==================================================
    +        +        +        +        +        +
    0       1000     2000     3000     4000     5000
                        graz
```

In order to write a program to do this, we draw on all the techniques we have explored so far, and set up the following plan:

1. Decide how to print a single histogram bar for a given value *h*, including scaling *h* to fit on one line. This function is given to the bar method. It has an additional parameter for the *y*-axis label (the year).

2. Express the interest formula in proper Java.

3. Set up a call to the bar method with the formula as a parameter.

4. Put the call to bar in a loop over the number of possible investment periods (years).

5. Design the println statements for the heading and final axis using loops.

Program Put all together, the program is quite long, but the comments help to explain it. Notice that we have placed the main method first, and followed it by the bar and axis methods which it calls. Unlike some other languages, Java does not mind in which order methods are declared.

```java
class GrowthPlan {

    /**
     * Financial Modelling Program         by J M Bishop Aug 1996
     * -------------------------           Java 1.1
     * Displays a histogram of simple interest * 1.2
     * for a given principal and rate for 5 to 15 years.
     *
     * Illustrates parameter passing of variables
     * and for-loops.
     */

    static final double p = 1000;
    static final double rate = 12.5;

    public static void main(String[] args) {
    // The headings
        System.out.println("SavBank Growth Plan");
        System.out.println("===================");
        System.out.println("Principal of "+p+" at rate "+rate);
        System.out.println();
        System.out.println("Years");

    // Display a bar for each year and then the final axis
        for (int year = 5; year <= 15; year++)
            bar(year, p*1.2*year*rate/100 + p);
        axis();
    }

    static void bar(int label, double h) {
    // Draws a single histogram bar labelled
    // with the years and consisting of h/100 stars

        System.out.print(label+"\t|");
        int stop = (int)(h/100);
        for (int star = 0; star < stop; star++)
            System.out.print('*');
        System.out.println(" "+(long)h);
    }

    static void axis () {
    // Draws a horizontal axis with ticks+1 divisions
    // labelled in steps of 1000. Each division is 10
    // characters wide.

        int ticks = 5;

    // Print the line
        System.out.print('\t');
        for (int line = 0; line < ticks*10; line++)
            System.out.print('=');
        System.out.println('=');

    //Print the ticks
        System.out.print('\t');
        for (int n = 0; n < ticks; n++)
            System.out.print("+         ");
        System.out.println('+');
```

```
    // Label the ticks, including the last one
        System.out.print('\t');
        for (int n = 0; n <= ticks; n++)
        System.out.print(n*1000+"        ");
        System.out.println();

    // Label the whole axis
        System.out.println("\t\t\t\tgraz");
    }
}
```

Testing The output has already been shown. This example is extended in the problems at the end of the chapter.

Returning values from a method

Now we note a very subtle point. Although many other languages have in and out parameter passing techniques, in Java, parameter passing goes in only one direction. Values can be passed into methods via parameters, but not out of them. To get a value out of a method, we use the return process of typed methods, as described above. This is not a Java restriction: it is the essence of object-oriented programming. But what happens if we want more than one value to be returned? Typed methods do not help here. Instead, there are other options which all enable the changes to fields to be reflected in an object x of class Obj declared outside the method as

```
class Obj {
    int fields1;
    double field3;
}

Obj x = new Obj();
```

1. Pass the object as a parameter, and alter its fields via its formal parameter name, as in:

    ```
        static void m1 (Obj formalpar) {
           formalpar.field1 = value1;
           formalpar.field3 = value3;
        }

        // called by
        m1(x);
    ```

    x becomes formalpar inside m1, but it still refers back to its original space. Thus changes to formalpar are actually changes to x.

2. If x is accessible from m (and probably declared as static), do away with the parameter and just access the fields via x itself. Thus we have a new m2:

```
static void m2 ( ) {
   x.field1 = value1;
   x.field3 = value3;
}

// called by
m2 ();
```

3.   If there are no initial values in x, we can redeclare m as a typed method, create a new object, set up the values required in it, and then return it as the result of the method:

```
static Obj m3 ( ) {
   Obj local = new Obj ();
      local.field1 = value1;
      local.field3 = value3;
      return local;
}


   // called by
   x = m3 ( );
```

4.   Use individual set methods to change the fields. These methods are defined in the Obj class, and can therefore be better protectors of the fields.

```
class Obj {

   int field1;
   double fields2;

   void setField1(int v) {
      field1 = v;
   }

   void setField3(int v) {
      field3 = v;
   }
}

static void m4 (Obj formalpar) {
   formalpar.setField1(value1);
   formalpar.setField3(value3)
}

// called by
m4 (x);
```

Which of these methods is the best? It really depends since not all are applicable in all circumstances. The next section takes up the issue of how to design classes, and in the process covers parameter passing for objects again.

3.6 Guidelines for designing classes

Methods are a means of grouping statements. At the next level, classes are a means of grouping methods. Specifically, we group together methods that serve a common purpose. For example, the Math class in Java provides trigonometrical methods, and the PrintStream class provides printing methods.

In a class, we can do more than just group methods. We can also include data items. The design of the class in terms of the methods and data it provides is the cornerstone of object-oriented programming, and central to the way Java is intended to be used. We therefore consider some guiding principles for design here and follow this with an example and a case study, both of which make good use of classes and objects.

Guidelines for class design

1. **Coherence**. A class should be concerned with a single physical entity or a set of similar operations. For example, the Locale class defines and manipulates locales; the Math class provides operations of a trigonometric and exponential nature.

2. **Separation of concerns**. Even for a single entity, one can have several related classes rather than one class. For example, Locale does not provide any output for locales, but we could imagine settting up quite a useful class which could provide nicely formatted output for the fields, much as we did in Example 2.6.

3. **Information hiding**. A class should reveal to the user only that which has to be revealed and no more. In this way data can be protected from misuse, and the class can operate on a more secure basis. There is also a case to be made for methods to be hidden if they are not relevant to users, but are needed only by the class itself. The modifier for hiding declarations is private. By default, all declarations are accessible.

4. **Data access via methods**. Following on from 3, a guideline that is followed in all of Java's standard classes is that most data is hidden from the user, but made accessible via appropriate methods. In this way the data is protected from inappropriate changes. For example, the Locale class does not reveal the country and language fields of any Locale instance. To access them, one uses an appropriate get or set method.

5. **Object initialization**. When an object is created, it is efficient to copy in values for all its initial values, so that these can be used later. This is in preference to supplying the values repeatedly as parameters. For example, with the Locale class, we set up the initial values for there, and unless we changed them, they are always available. Of course, some values must change, but the aim is to keep method calls as simple as possible. This guideline is tested to the full in the Case Study that follows in Section 3.7.

Other guidelines will be mentioned as the need arises.

Design notation

There are many diagrammatic notations for representing classes and objects. Some of these are quite complex and become languages in their own right. In order to keep the notation gentle, we have tried to use very simple blocks and lines here, with the meanings as laid out in Figures 3.4 and 3.5.

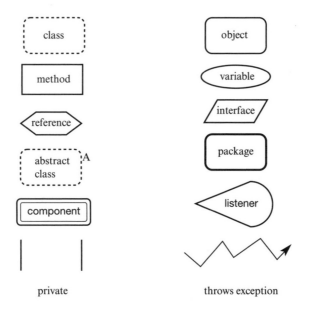

Figure 3.4 *The components in a notation for class diagrams.*

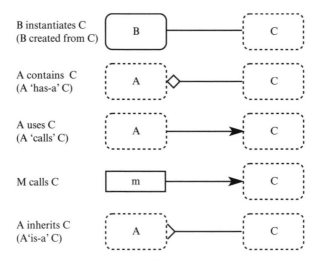

Figure 3.5 *Relationships in a notation for class diagrams.*

The method described is based on one of the most popular – Rumbaugh's OMT (object modelling technique) – but has been slightly adapted for use in *Java Gently*, forming what we might call JMT. The adaptations are as follows:

- Methods, variables and other detailed items have symbols, so that programs can be fully depicted with JMT.

- The class symbol is a dotted oblong, not a rectangle, as a rectangle is used for a method. This symbol is similar to that used in the Booch notation.

- The indicator for instantiating an object from a class does not necessarily have to have an arrow, since it is obvious which symbol is instantiating the other (that is, a class cannot be an instantiation of an object). Arrows tend to clutter a diagram.

- There are additional symbols for Java entities not envisaged by OMT: reference, component, private, exception, and so on.

An alternative to the diamond in the contains relationship is a circle. The private lines apply to most of the other symbols, or they can be used down the side of a whole section of a class. The usage of the rest of the different symbols and lines will be explained as we go along.

Constructors

Every class that is going to be used for instantiating objects should have at least one constructor, which is called when an object of the class is declared. If the class is merely a wrapper for a main method, then it does not need a constructor, and if it only has static methods in it (which means there is no point instantiating it), it also does not need a constructor.

We saw how to use the `Locale` class constructor in Section 2.5. How do we create constructors for new classes? The form is:

Constructor

`modifiers classname (parameters) {`
`    statements`
`}`

In other words, a constructor is a method with the name of the class itself. A class can have several different constructors with different lists of parameters, including, often, one with no parameters at all. A constructor from the next example is:

```
Labels (int a) {
   across = a;
}
```

which has the function of storing an initial value given in a parameter into a private class variable, in accordance with guideline 5 above.

Modifiers may include only the ones used on the class itself. For simple user classes, there will be no modifiers, but for standard packages, the `public` modifier is needed, as we saw in the `Locale` class (Section 2.5).

The next example shows how a system can be built up from two classes. It uses the JMT notation to describe their interaction.

EXAMPLE 3.6 Labels with class

Problem We wish to print out blank labels side by side, with suitable gaps between them.

Solution There exists a method to print a rectangle, that is:

```
static void box () {
   System.out.println ("--------------------");
   System.out.println ("|                  |");
   System.out.println ("|                  |");
   System.out.println ("|                  |");
   System.out.println ("--------------------");
}
```

but if we call

```
box(); box(); box();
```

the labels will come out one underneath each other. The Java `println` method regards the output file as consisting of lines that are written in sequence. The contents of each line have to be composed and written out before going on to the next line. This model corresponds very closely to a screen in text mode or printer. It is also possible to create a model whereby the screen or page can be drawn on freely, going up and down, back and forth, and this is discussed in Part II.

However, given the sequential nature of ordinary output, the way to get the labels side by side is to have the outer loop being concerned with rows, then for each row, consider each label across the page.

Class design At this point we must consider the design of the classes. Clearly labels are potential objects. The question is, what operations do they need? We notice that there are two kinds of rows in a label: the one with the dashes, and the one with the uprights and spaces. The printing of these could be offered as methods by the labels class. The controlling class could then call them in loops as required.

What information should be supplied when this label class is instantiated? Since it is going to print several labels across the page, the number of labels could be set up at initialization. This number must remain the same for all the calls for a particular

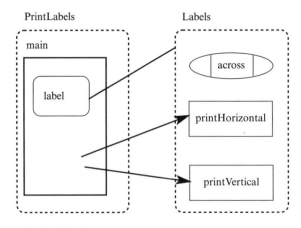

Figure 3.6 *Design for the label printing program.*

size of label, so it is quite correct that it be a constructor parameter, and not one for
the methods themselves. The design of the program is shown in Figure 3.6.

PrintLabels is a class that has one method, main. main has an object, label,
instantiated from the Labels class. For each label there is a private variable, across,
and two methods, printHorizontal and printVertical, both called by main.

Program First we look at the labels class.

```
class Labels {

    /* A class to provide services for printing
     * a given number of labels across.
     * This figure is supplied as a parameter to the
     * constructor when a label object is instantiated.
     * All labels have the same width, but
     * the depth of the labels is not known in this class.
     */

    Labels (int a) {
        across = a;
    }

    void printHorizontals () {
        for (int box = 0; box < across; box++)
            System.out.print ("-------------      ");
        System.out.println();
    }


    void printVerticals () {
```

```
      for (int box=0; box < across; box++)
        System.out.print("|              |       ");
      System.out.println();
   }

   private int across;
}
```

The class is neat and easy to read. Notice that the constructor parameter is copied into a private variable, which can be used by the class's methods but not seen by anyone who uses the class.

Now consider the program:

```
class PrintLabels {

    /*
     * The Label Printing program.     by J M Bishop
     * -----------------------         revised December 1996
     *                                 Java 1.1
     *
     * Displays labels across the screen of a certain depth.
     * Illustrates the use of a class, the use of instance
     * methods and parameter passing.
     */

    static final int nLabels = 4;
    static final int depth = 5;

    public static void main(String[] args) {

      //Create an instance of the class that will do the printing,
      //and say how many labels are needed

      Labels label = new Labels(nLabels);

      // Print the two horizontal lines around the
      // required number of vertical ones.

      label.printHorizontals();
      for (int row = 2; row < depth; row++)
        label.printVerticals();
      label.printHorizontals();
    }
}
```

Testing Running the program will produce:

```
 ----------      ----------      ----------      ----------
|          |    |          |    |          |    |          |
|          |    |          |    |          |    |          |
|          |    |          |    |          |    |          |
 ----------      ----------      ----------      ----------
```

To change the number of labels across, all we need do is change the `nLabels` constant in the main program. Notice that the use of methods has helped in two ways:

- **Repetition** – the horizontal loop is not repeated, as it is packaged up in a method;

- **Understanding** – the nested loops are separated out, making the program easier to read.

In the exercises, we look at how to print more than one size of label in one run of the program. In the case study, we take this further by looking at different instantiations of the same object, based on variations in the constructor.

3.7 Case Study 1: Price tickets

The solution to the following problem exploits classes, objects, constructors, loops, methods and parameters, showing their power fully.

Problem

Savanna High School is having a fête and has set all food and drink at prices of one, two, five or eight graz. The students would like to design suitable price tickets on the computer. The G5 and G8 tickets should be bigger and more impressive than the G1 and G2 ones. Some suggestions are:

```
------------          ==============
|2222222222|          =5555555555555=
|2222222222|          =5555555555555=
|2222222222|          =5555555555555=
------------          =5555555555555=
                      =5555555555555=
                      ==============
```

Solution

We need a method that can print a box of any size, up to a maximum of 80 wide and 20 deep. Parameters should help here, and so certainly will classes. Let us first simplify the problem by considering only the smaller tickets with a standard hyphen and bar border. Then the only variable parts are the width and depth of the ticket, and the price.

In Example 3.6, we treated the 'horizontal' and 'vertical' lines of the box separately. In fact, by using generalization, we can regard them as the same, but with different left, centre and right symbols. In other words, we have:

Line type	Left	Centre	Right
Horizontal	—	—	—
Vertical	|	price	|

Now we can define a further method to print a line with the symbols as parameters, and call it the required number of times.

Algorithm

Let us assume that the *width* and *depth* are the given measurements. Then each line consists of the following sequence:

aLine (left, centre, right)
> Draw the left symbol
> Draw width-2 centre symbols
> Draw the right symbol

The box itself consists of:

varyBox (price)
> Draw a line with arguments (-, -, -)
> Draw depth-2 lines with arguments (\|, price, \|)
> Draw a line with arguments (-, -, -)

The two methods to print the smaller tickets are:

```
void aLine (char left, char centre, char right) {
  System.out.print(left);
  for (int w=2; w < width; w++)
    System.out.print (centre);
  System.out.println (right);
}

void varyBox (char price) {
  aLine('-','-','-');
  for (int d=2; d<depth; d++)
    aLine('|',price,'|');
  aLine('-','-','-');
  System.out.println();
}
```

Class design

Clearly the two methods fit together. In fact they are the basis for a `Tickets` class. What we still need to establish is the constructor. What should it contain? It must have the values for the depth and width. And at this stage we can generalize to the other kind of ticket design and let the horizontal and vertical characters be supplied as well. We do not, however, supply the price, since this could change with the same object, which encapsulates a certain design. For example, G1 and G2 tickets have everything in common except the price. The new `Tickets` class is:

```
class Tickets {

    /* The Ticket Class      by J M Bishop Dec 1996
     * ----------------      Java 1.1
     * Creates and prints a label for a ticket
     * of given size, style and value.
     *
     * Illustrates the declaration of a class.
     */

    private char hori, verti;
    private int depth, width;

    Tickets(char h, char v, int d, int w) {
        hori = h;
        verti = v;
        depth = d;
        width = w;
    }

    void varyBox(char price) {
        aLine(hori, hori, hori);
        for (int d = 2; d < depth; d++)
            aLine(verti, price, verti);
        aLine(hori, hori, hori);
        System.out.println();
    }

    private void aLine(char left, char centre, char right) {
        System.out.print(left);
        for (int w = 2; w < width; w++)
            System.out.print(centre);
        System.out.println(right);
    }

}
```

Everything that can be declared private, is. Only `varyBox` and the constructor are available. Notice the clustering of the private method and variables at the end of the class: this helps to remove them from the eye of the reader. At this point we can envisage the class diagram, as in Figure 3.7.

And now for the program. It is very simple, declaring two objects and then using each of these twice to print different valued tickets. In so doing, it very clearly shows the difference between objects and method calls on those objects.

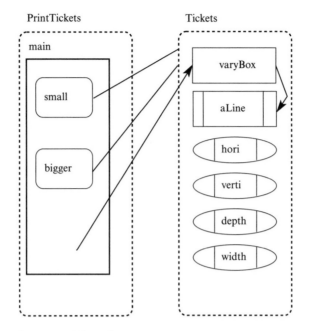

Figure 3.7 *Class diagram of the ticket printing program.*

```
class PrintTickets {

    /*
     * The Ticket printing program          by J M Bishop Sept 1996
     *                                       revised Dec 1996
     *
     * Prints out four tickets from two different designs.
     */

    public static void main(String[] args) {

        System.out.println
            ("Suggested Price Tickets for the fete");

        Tickets small = new Tickets('-','|',5,11);
        small.varyBox('2');
        small.varyBox('1');

        Tickets bigger = new Tickets('=','=',7,15);
        bigger.varyBox('5');
        bigger.varyBox('8');
    }
}
```

Testing

The output from the program above is:

```
Suggested Price Tickets for the fete
-----------
|222222222|
|222222222|
|222222222|
-----------


-----------
|111111111|
|111111111|
|111111111|
-----------


===============
=5555555555555=
=5555555555555=
=5555555555555=
=5555555555555=
=5555555555555=
===============


===============
=8888888888888=
=8888888888888=
=8888888888888=
=8888888888888=
=8888888888888=
===============
```

SUMMARY

Programs need to be properly structured to achieve correctness, readability, reusability and efficiency. Contributing to proper structure are types (for data items), methods and parameters (for grouping statements) and classes (for modelling objects and grouping methods).

Apart from the numeric types, Java has types for `boolean` and `char`. The numeric types can be converted into each other. Methods fall into two kinds: typed and void. Typed methods return values and are used in expressions. Methods can be prefaced with modifiers such as `static` and `private` which govern how they may be called. Parameters generalize methods, with values being able to be passed in but not out again.

For-loops provide repeated execution of statements. The loop variables can be used in the loop, and loops can be nested inside each other as well as run 'backwards': that is, from a higher number to a lower one.

The design of classes is a crucial part of programming, and a simple notation for describing the design is useful. Guidelines for design included coherence, separation of concerns, information hiding, and careful access to and initialization of data.

QUIZ

3.1   How many stars would the following loop print out?

```
for (int star = 9; star<0; star++){
  System.out.print('*');
}
```

3.2   The following statements are meant to print a sequence consisting of a number and then that many equal signs followed by a plus, each on a new line. For example:

```
4====+
```

Can you work out what they actually print, and how to fix them?

```
int number;
for (number = 1; number < 5; number++) {
    System.out.println(number);
}
for (int sign = 1; sign < number; sign++) {
    System.out.println(sign);
}
System.out.println('+');
```

3.3   Under what circumstances does a class not need a constructor?

3.4   Write a loop to print out the decades of the 20th century (e.g. 1900, 1910 . . .).

3.5   Write declarations of boolean variables and suitable assignment statements to record whether a prospective student has the following school-leaving qualifications: a score of 20 or more and a C or more in maths or a D or more in maths and a C or more in computer science.

3.6   The Tickets class can be used to print blank tickets. Give an object declaration and a call to varyBox that will accomplish this.

3.7   Why was the price parameter of varyBox declared as char and not int?

3.8   Give the equivalent decrement assignment statement for

```
taxrate = taxrate - 0.5;
```

3.9   Given the declaration of a mountain method, namely:

```
static void mountain (int size; char symbol);
```

decide which of the following calls are valid or not, giving reasons:

```
mountain (10,0);
mountain (8, '8');
mountain (6);
```

3.10   Suppose we wished to print just a single line of Ticket, for testing purposes. Could we call the aLine method to do this?

PROBLEMS

3.1   **Interest changes**. In Example 2.4, we looked at how the interest received would change depending on a change of rate in a given month. In order to plan ahead, we would like to know how the interest would change based on the month in which the rate change is announced. Write a program to print out a table showing how the interest would change from January to November. Use the same data as in Example 2.4.

3.2   **Another song**. Another song that can go on a bit is:

There were 10 green bottles hanging on the wall,
10 green bottles hanging on the wall
And if one green bottle should accidentally fall
There'll be 9 green bottles hanging on the wall.
9 green bottles hanging on the wall
And if one green bottle should accidentally fall
There'll be 8 green bottles hanging on the wall.

etc.

I green bottle hanging on the wall
And if one green bottle should accidentally fall
There'll be 0 green bottles hanging on the wall.

Using the technique discussed in Example 3.3, design an algorithm to print out such a song, and program it to start with 5 green bottles.

3.3   **A number triangle**. Write a program that uses for-statements and `print`/`println` statements to produce the following triangle:

```
1
2 2
3 3 3
4 4 4 4
5 5 5 5 5
```

Adapt the program to print the triangle so that the numbers are centred, as below. Adapt it again to print the triangle upside down.

```
    1
   2 2
  3 3 3
 4 4 4 4
5 5 5 5 5
```

3.4   **Shaded boxes**. Write a program to print out boxes consisting of 'darker' and 'lighter' sides, like this:

```
+--
++-
+++-
++++
```

3.5   **Conversions**. A conversion table can be viewed as a general algorithm. Establish this fact by adapting the program in Example 3.4 to print out the conversion from miles to kilometres (1 mile = 1.6km) and again to print dollars to graz (1\$ = 0.45G).

3.6   **Printing names.** Write methods to print out the letters of the alphabet that form your name, in a large format using asterisks. Each letter is formed on a 7 by 9 grid and drawn downwards, so that when the letters are printed out underneath each other, the name can be turned sideways and read. For example, for William, we need five methods, one to do each of the letters W, i, l, a and m, and the letters might look like this:

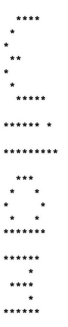

Create a class containing the methods, then write a program to call the methods in the right order to print your name. Should the methods be class methods or instance methods?

3.7   **Labels.** Adapt the program in Example 3.6 to print three labels with your name and address across the page, and do this eight times to fill the page. If you line the output up carefully, you can photocopy it on to standard-sized sticky labels.

3.8   **Clearer tables.** The conversion table of Example 3.4 is not quite right because the values increase across the page, rather than down, which is more normal. Can you work out how to change the program so as to print the values increasing in columns?

3.9   **Times tables.** In the olden days, exercise books used to have multiplication tables printed neatly on the back. These would be arranged three across and four down, with each row being of the form:

```
4 times table         5 times table         6 times table
1 x 4 = 4             1 x 5 = 5             1 x 6 = 6
2 x 4 = 8             2 x 5 = 10            2 x 6 = 12
3 x 4 = 12            3 x 5 = 15            3 x 6 = 18
4 x 4 = 16            4 x 5 = 20            4 x 6 = 24
5 x 4 = 20            5 x 5 = 25            5 x 6 = 30
6 x 4 = 24            6 x 5 = 30            6 x 6 = 36
7 x 4 = 28            7 x 5 = 35            7 x 6 = 42
8 x 4 = 32            8 x 5 = 40            8 x 6 = 48
9 x 4 = 36            9 x 5 = 45            9 x 6 = 54
```

```
10 × 4 = 40          10 × 5 = 50          10 × 6 = 60
11 × 4 = 44          11 × 5 = 55          11 × 6 = 66
12 × 4 = 48          12 × 5 = 60          12 × 6 = 72
```

Write a program that makes good use of methods and parameters to print out a complete set of all the first 12 multiplication tables.

3.10   **Timetable**. It is always useful to have a blank timetable to fill in for one's lectures. Write a program that will print out such a timetable, with Monday to Friday across the top, and the hours 8 to 15 down the left. The timetable should have suitable borders.

3.11   **Histogram**. A histogram is generally a useful graph to draw. See if you can create a class based on that in Example 3.5 which includes bar and axis methods and can be called to print histograms for a variety of data. Test it by mapping the value of sin x against values of degrees from 0 to 90. Think of other examples that could be tried. (Note: they will have to be based on calculations since we have not learnt to read in values yet, or you could come back to this problem after Chapter 4.)

3.12   **Other tables**. Take the large conversion table program and alter it to produce other tables, such as:

●   Celsius to Fahrenheit,

●   miles to kilometres,

●   litres to gallons,

●   dollars to your currency.

CHAPTER 4

Changing the state

4.1 Inputting interactively

A program will most often need to acquire values for its variables from the outside world. Such values form the **data** for the program and could consist of tables stored on disk, replies to questions or just lists of values to be typed in. The term **stream** is applied to the sequence of data items that will come from one source. Thus the keyboard is modelled by a stream, as is a file on disk. In this section we look at keyboard input, and follow it by looking at file input and output in Section 4.2.

Input files

The Java equivalent of `System.out` is `System.in`. Although `System.in` is also a predeclared field, its class is `InputStream`, which is an **abstract** class in Java terms. Abstract classes are covered fully in Chapter 9, but what we need to know here is that we cannot always create objects of abstract classes. The `System.in` item must be supplied as a constructor parameter to another class called `InputStreamReader`, thereby creating a usable object. In addition, keyboard input works best when buffered, so we then pass this object to another class, `BufferedReader`, and all is set up.

We acknowledge that this is a complex way of handling matters, but the following form shows that the actual programming involved is not excessive.

Declaring the keyboard for input

```
import java.io.*;
BufferedReader stream = new BufferedReader
            (new InputStreamReader(System.in));
```

Before the class statement, we must import the `java.io` package in which the three classes are defined. Then the declaration declares a new stream, connected to `System.in`, with all the facilities of the `BufferedReader` class. A typical such declaration is:

```
BufferedReader in = new BufferedReader
                (new InputStreamReader(System.in));
```

which will declare `in` as the stream that is connected to the keyboard. In Section 4.2 we shall see how to connect streams to files as well.

One side effect of reading is that something could go wrong, for example the data might end unexpectedly or have the wrong format. Such events are called **exceptions** and we shall see later in the chapter how to deal with them. However, Java requires that we indicate in every method those exceptions that can occur. Therefore if we are going to read, we need to add the phrase

```
throws IOException
```

after the appropriate method.

Reading strings

Similar to the `println` method, the `BufferedReader` class provides a `readLine` method which will read in a full line of text to the given string. The form is:

Reading a string

```
string = stream.readLine();
```

Notice two differences between this form and that for printing:

- The suffix is `-Line` not `-ln`;
- The method is typed, not void, so is called in an assignment, not on its own.

EXAMPLE 4.1 Greetings

Problem Suppose we would like to greet someone in French.

Solution Write a program with the greeting built in and ask the user to type the name.

Program The program is quite straightforward.

```
import java.io.*;

class Greetings {

    /*  A simple greetings program   by J M Bishop  Oct 1996
     *  -------------------------    Java 1.1  Dec 1997

    public static void main (String [] args) throws IOException {

        BufferedReader in = new BufferedReader
                (new InputStreamReader(System.in));

        System.out.println("What is your name?");
        String name = in.readLine();
        System.out.println("Bonjour " + name);
    }
}
```

Testing Here is a sample run, using plain type for the input and bold for output as before.

What is your name?
Pierre Marchand
Bonjour Pierre Marchand

readLine reads a whole line from the keyboard, until return is pressed.

Java's approach to reading numbers

Java can easily read values of the other types of data if they are already in binary form and stored in a file. However if we want to interact with a program from the keyboard, the idea is that we should read a string and do the conversion explicitly in the program. The conversion routines are supplied with object classes associated with the primitive types, as well as through special classes available in the java.text package (discussed in Chapter 7). The same classes can be used for output formatting.

Although powerful, these classes are not simple to use, which is a shame because reading a number is, after all, an operation that we may need to perform frequently. Here is what a read of a real number would look like:

```
double d = Double.valueOf(in.readLine().trim()).doubleValue();
```

Of course, such complexity can be easily hidden in a method and similar methods can be made for real numbers and the other types. To collect the methods together, we create a class that will provide the functionality required.

In fairness, it must be said that the java.text classes are well put together and make for very versatile programming in the international context, as they cover such input as percentages and currencies, as well as numbers. This aspect is covered in Chapter 7.

Java Gently's Text class

The class defined for *Java Gently* is called Text[1] and it provides the methods shown in the following form:

```
The Text Class

void      prompt      (String s)
int       readInt     (BufferedReader in)
double    readDouble  (BufferedReader in)
String    readString  (BufferedReader in)
char      readChar     (BufferedReader in)
String    writeInt    (int number, int align)
String    writeDouble (double number, int align, int frac)
BufferedReader open (InputStream in)
BufferedReader open (String filename)
printWriter create  (String filename)
```

prompt is a method that will print out a string, but then keep the cursor on the same line so that a reply can follow immediately. readInt and readDouble return numbers as required. readString is not exactly the same as the built-in method readLine because all of the Text class's methods have the property that multiple values can be typed on a single line. This feature is illustrated in the next example and exploited in the Olympic medals system (Example 4.9). readChar reads a single character. All of the four reading methods rely on the item being read being 'delimited' by something such as a space, tab, comma or end of line. Unfortunately, this means that we cannot read successive characters, only those separated by such delimiters.

The next two methods provide a means for controlling numeric output. The align parameter specifies the minimum number of characters that should be used to print the number. Thus if the number is 123 and the align parameter is 6, there will be three spaces in front of 123 when output. In this way, numbers can be neatly lined up in columns. Both writeInt and writeDouble have the property that if the number will not fit in the gap given, the gap will be expanded to the right, and the digits before the decimal point will be printed in full anyway. For real numbers, the frac para-

---

[1] There is fortunately no confusion with Java's text package because that has a small t. Moreover java.text is a package, whereas our Text is a class. Our Text class pre-dates java.text package, which came out with version 1.1.

meter is definite: there will always be that number of digits in the fractional part, and any further digits are truncated. For example, suppose we say:

```
System.out.println(Text.writeDouble(x, 10, 4));
```

then for various values of x we get:

```
-1234.5678              -1234.5678
1234.56789               1234.5678
45.67                      45.6700
4                           4.0000
4.56789                     4.5678
0                           0.0000
123456789            123456789.0000
777777.88888            777777.8888
```

Finally, there are methods for opening the System.in stream, and opening and creating files (more about which later). Using open is slightly shorter than the form shown above and has the advantage that one need not remember the second class name involved (i.e. InputStreamReader). Notice that there are two versions of open, but that these are different because their parameter lists are different.

How to compile, store and access the javagently package is covered in Section 4.5 at the end of the chapter. The Text class is not at all long, and is discussed in full in Chapter 7. Now we look at an example that uses Text to good advantage.

EXAMPLE 4.2 Summing a sequence of numbers

Problem There is a sequence of numbers that needs to be summed, and the precise length of the sequence is unknown when the program is written.

Solution It is quite straightforward to read the numbers into the computer, adding each one in turn to a total. The problem is how to know when the end of the numbers has been reached. There are four ways:

1.   **State in advance** how many items there must be and keep a running count.

2.   **Precede the data by a count** of how many items there actually are, and keep a running count.

3.   Make use of an **end-of-file exception** to mark the end of the items.

4.   Put a **special terminating value** at the end of the items, such as zero or 999.

The first two methods are applicable to counting-loops, since they rely on the number of items being known before reading starts. In method 3 the number of items is not relevant; rather, the reading stops when a certain condition is achieved, and we show

how to detect it in the next section. The last one is applicable to conditional loops, and is discussed in the next chapter.

Of the two methods for counting-loops, the second is more general, since the same program will be able to read in 10 numbers, or 55, or 1000, with just the data being changed. Let us consider it as a model for our solution.

Algorithm The algorithm is depicted in Figure 4.1.

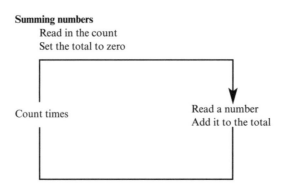

Figure 4.1 *Algorithm for summing numbers.*

Program The program reflects the algorithm. It makes use of the Text class to prompt the user, and to read the numbers.

```
import java.io.*;
import javagently.*;

public class Summation1 {

    /* The first Summation program    by J M Bishop Aug 1996
     * --------------------------      Java 1.1 Oct 1997
     *
     * Reads in numbers interactively and displays their sum.
     * Illustrates the declaration of an input stream
     * and simple use of the Text class.
     */

    public static void main(String[] args) throws IOException {

        int count;
        double total = 0;
        double number;

        BufferedReader in = Text.open(System.in);

        System.out.println("****** Summing numbers ******");

        Text.prompt("How many numbers?");
        count = Text.readInt(in);
```

```
    for (int i = 1; i <= count; i++) {
      System.out.print(i+"> ");
      number = Text.readDouble(in);
      total += number;
    }

    System.out.println("That's enough, thanks.");
    System.out.println("The total is "+total);
  }
}
```

Testing Running the program will produce the following dialogue on the screen.

```
****** Summing numbers ******
How many numbers?  5
1>   23
2>   -18
3>   45
4>   11
5>   2
That's enough, thanks.
The total is 63.0
```

Notice that we try to make the running of the program as helpful to the user as possible. In Java, there are very fancy ways of doing this, as we shall investigate in Part II.

The flexible features of *Java Gently's* Text class

The Text class has a forgiving nature: it will detect bad numbers and permit you to type them in again. It allows – and ignores – blank lines and spaces between data items. It does not allow them inside strings, so, if we write a Text version of the greeting program, only one of Pierre's names would appear:

```
import java.io.*;
import javagently.*;

class Greetings2 {
  public static void main (String [] args) throws IOException {

    BufferedReader in = Text.open(System.in);

    Text.prompt("What is your name?");
    String name = Text.readString(in);
    System.out.println("Bonjour " + name);
  }
}
```

```
What is your name? Pierre Marchand
Bonjour Pierre
```

Greeting2 detects only a single word: that is, Pierre, not Pierre Marchand.

`Text` does actually allow multiple items on a line, we just have to be aware that we want them. So a third version of the greetings program for a two word name would be:

```
import java.io.*;
import javagently.*;

class Greetings3 {
  public static void main (String [] args) throws IOException {

    BufferedReader in = Text.open(System.in);

    Text.prompt("What is your name?");
    String firstname = Text.readString(in);
    String secondname = Text.readString(in);
    System.out.println("Bonjour " + firstname+" "+secondname);
  }
}
```

What is your name? Pierre Marchand
Bonjour Pierre Marchand

Although forgiving, `Text` is very firm, and if it wants two names it will get them or die in the attempt. Thus the second call to `readString` will wait until another string is entered.

4.2 File input and output

Although it is a relief to be able to enter input to programs at last, interactive testing can rapidly become tedious. It is often better to keep the data in a file and read it from there. Certainly for large amounts of data this is essential. The extension to the stream declaration for declaring a file for normal text input is:

Declaring a file for input

```
BufferedReader stream = new BufferedReader
       (new FileReader(filename));
BufferedReader stream = Text.open (filename);
```

Instead of supplying `System.in` as the parameter to the `InputStreamReader` constructor, we create a new object of the `FileReader` class initialized with the actual file name. For example, to read data from a file called 'numbers' we would define a stream as

```
BufferedReader fin = new BufferedReader (new FileReader("numbers"));
```

`fin` is a `BufferedReader` and therefore it can be passed to any of the `Text` methods. In a program, one can have several streams open for input simultaneously.

There is also the `open` method provided by *Java Gently's* `Text` class. So the above example can also be given as:

```
BufferedReader fin = Text.open ("numbers");
```

EXAMPLE 4.3   Inputting from a file

For example, suppose we adapt the `Summation1` program so that the count is read from the keyboard, but the numbers themselves are read from a file. We could dispense with the prompts in this case. The program becomes:

```
import java.io.*;
import javagently.*;

public class Summation2 {

    /* The second Summation program    by J M Bishop Aug 1996
     * ---------------------------      Java 1.1 Oct 1997
     *
     * Reads in numbers from a file and displays their sum.
     *
     * Illustrates the declaration of input from both
     * the keyboard and a file.
     */

    public static void main(String[] args) throws IOException {

        int count;
        double total = 0;
        double number;

        BufferedReader in = Text.open(System.in);
        BufferedReader fin = Text.open("numbers");

        System.out.println("****** Summing from numbers file ******");

        Text.prompt("How many numbers?");
        count = Text.readInt(in);

        for (int i = 1; i <= count; i++) {
            number = Text.readDouble(fin);
            total += number;
        }

        System.out.println("That's enough, thanks.");
        System.out.println("The total is "+total);
    }
}
```

If the same five numbers given in Example 4.2 were on the file, then the screen output would be:

```
**** Summing from numbers file ****
How many numbers? 5
That's enough, thanks.
The total is 63.0
```

Outputting to a file

It is very useful to be able to send output to a file. Not only does it make it easy to retain the results and print them out, but very often programs produce too much output to appear sensibly on the screen. In the same way as we set up a file input stream, we can set up a file output stream. The form is:

Declaring a file for output

```
PrintWriter stream = new PrintWriter
   (new FileWriter ("filename"));
PrintWriter stream = Text.create ("filename");
```

We recall that `println` and so on are part of the `PrintStream` class. `PrintStream` has been superseded by `PrintWriter` now, and all these useful methods have moved over. In order to use them on the file, we create a `PrintWriter` object. The object supplied to initialize it is a new `FileWriter` object, created with the file name that we want. So an example would be:

```
PrintWriter fout = new PrintWriter(new FileWriter("results"));
```

Once again, we can just use the `Text` class's method, which in this case is called `create`, which would give:

```
PrintWriter fout = Text.create("results");
```

An important consideration for output files is that they must be closed before the program ends, otherwise all the writing done to them is lost. The method in `PrintWriter` is:

```
fout.close();
```

EXAMPLE 4.4 Saving a label

As a simple example, consider printing a label directly to a file. The program would be:

```
import java.io.*; import javagently.*;


class SaveaLabel {
/* Label saving program       by J M Bishop revised Dec 1996
 * --------------------        Java 1.1
   Prints a single label to a file.
   Illustrates file declarations and writing
   to a file and the screen in the same program */


public static void main (String [] args) throws IOException {

  PrintWriter fout = Text.create("label.out");

  System.out.println ("Printing the label to label.out");
  fout.println ("-------------------------");
  fout.println ("|                       |");
  fout.println ("|  Ms Mary Brown        |");
  fout.println ("|  33 Charles Street    |");
  fout.println ("|  Brooklyn             |");
  fout.println ("|                       |");
  fout.println ("-------------------------");
  fout.close();
  System.out.println ("Program finished");
  }
}
```

The output produced by this program would be:

On the screen:

```
Printing the label to label.out
Program finished
```

In the file label.out

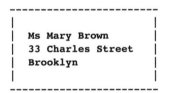

The fact that the names of the i/o classes are not symmetric can be very confusing. In order to clarify what is going on, Figure 4.2 summarizes the relationships between the different classes for default streams such as `System.in` and `System.out` and streams based on files. Part of the problem is the changes wrought between Java 1.0 and Java 1.1. All of the classes we use now are new, except that `System.in` and `System.out` are still defined on the old classes, `InputStream` and `OutputStream` respectively. Presumably this was done in order to keep the `System` class stable.

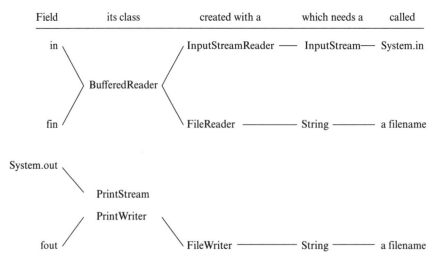

Field	its class	created with a	which needs a	called
in		InputStreamReader —— InputStream—		System.in
	BufferedReader			
fin		FileReader ————————— String ————		a filename

System.out

PrintStream

PrintWriter

fout ————— FileWriter ——————— String ———— a filename

Figure 4.2 *Summary of input and output classes.*

4.3 Selection with if-else

Two methods of changing the values of variables have been covered so far: assignment and reading in. We now consider how to check the values in variables, and choose alternative actions based on the result of the check. Java has two **selection** statements known as the **if-statement** and the **switch-statement**. We look at the if-statement here, and the switch-statement in the next chapter.

Form of the if-statement

The general form of the if-statement is:

If-statement
| ```
if (condition)
   statement;
else statement;
``` |

The condition is a boolean expression as covered in Section 3.2. Examples are:

```
speed > speedlimit
(age >= 16) & (age < 75)
isaMinor
year == 1066
day != 29
initial != 'J'
```
```

In the if-statement we refer to the statement following the brackets as the **then-part** and to the statement following the `else` as the **else-part**. The whole if-statement is executed as follows. First, the condition is evaluated. If this result is true, the then-part is executed, and the else-part is skipped. If the result is false, the then-part is skipped and the else-part is executed. A simple example would be:

```
if (number >= 0)
  System.out.println("Positive")
else System.out.println("Negative");
```

The following diagram explains the example further:

```
                        true      write out Positive
        number >=0
                        false
                                  write out Negative
```

In the form of the if-statement, the `else` is given in italics. This means that it is optional and the statement can be used in an 'if-then' version. For example,

```
if (day == 25)
  System.out.println("Christmas, Hooray");
```

In either case, the then- and else-statements can be blocks, which would be surrounded by curly brackets.

EXAMPLE 4.5   Summing three ways

Problem A sequence of numbers needs to be summed, and separate sums kept of the positive and negative numbers as well.

Solution Start with the `Summation1` program in Example 4.2. Add in two new totalling variables, and use an if-statement to cause values to be added to one or the other.

Algorithm The loop in algorithm form is shown in Figure 4.3.

Summing numbers three ways

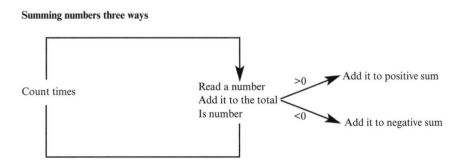

Figure 4.3 *Algorithm to add numbers three ways.*

Program The program implements the algorithm by reusing the `Summation1` program and adding the if-statements required. Notice that we start out with the most common case – greater than zero. The remaining, and less common, case comes next by default: that is, we do not even ask whether a number is negative since if it is not positive it *must* be negative.

But, what if it is zero? In this program it does not matter, since adding zero to either total has no effect! Notice, however, that adding zero takes place in the less common case, with the negative numbers.

```java
import java.io.*;
import javagently.*;

class Summation3 {

    /* The Three sums program        by J M Bishop Sept 1996
     * ---------------------          Java 1.1 October 1997
     *
     * Adds a sequence of numbers and also keeps
     * totals of the positive and negative ones separately.
     * Illustrates the if-else statement.
     */

    public static void main(String[] args) throws IOException {

        BufferedReader in = Text.open(System.in);

        int count;
        double total = 0;
        double posTotal = 0;
        double negTotal = 0;
        double number;

        System.out.println("****** Three sums ******");
        Text.prompt("How many numbers?");
        count = Text.readInt(in);          = new Integer (keyboard.readLine());

        for (int i = 1; i <= count; i++) {
            Text.prompt(i+">");
            number = Text.readDouble(in);
            total = total + number;
            if (number > 0)
                posTotal += number;
            else
                negTotal += number;
        }

        System.out.println("That's enough, thanks.");
        System.out.println("The total is "+total);
        System.out.println("The positive total is "+posTotal);
        System.out.println("The negative total is "+negTotal);
    }

}
```

Testing A complete run would look like this:

```
****** Three sums ******
How many numbers?   5
1>   20
2>   11
3>   -3
4>   0
5>   -2
That's enough, thanks.
The total is 26.0
The positive total is 31.0
The negative total is -5.0
```

Blocks in then- and else-parts

Suppose that in the threeSums program, it is also required to know how many positive and negative numbers were read. Then two more counters are needed and, to each part of the if-statement, an extra statement is added to do the counting. Thus, the if-statement would become:

```
int posCount, negCount;

if (number >= 0) {
   posTotal += number;
   posCount++;
   }
else {
   negTotal += number;
   negCount++;
   }
```

Successive else-ifs

Sometimes there are more than two possibilities that need to be considered. One way in which this is done is by **successive else-ifs**. The condition of the first if-statement eliminates one case, leaving the rest to the else-part. The else-part in its turn introduces another if-statement which selects out another condition and leaves the rest to its else-part, and so on. Else-ifs are illustrated nicely in an example that assigns a grade for various ranges of marks, thus:

```
int marks;
char grade;

if       (marks >= 80) grade='A';
else if  (marks >= 70) grade='B';
else if  (marks >= 60) grade='C';
else if  (marks >= 50) grade='D';
else                   grade='E';
```

Notice a few points about this statement:

- The conditions are carefully ordered, so that each eliminates a certain range of marks. Thus, the line that writes out a D for anything over 50 will be reached only when it has already been established that the mark is under 60.

- The last class, E, is given for all the rest of the marks, and does not need a condition.

- The layout of successive if-statements is important for readability, and should try to reflect the pattern of conditions as much as possible.

- the statements appear on the same line as the condition for clarity of reading.

A secondary consideration is that the most frequently occurring conditions should be checked first. If it is more likely that people will fail, then it will be marginally more efficient to arrange the order of the conditions thus:

```
int marks;
char grade;
if         (marks < 50)   grade='E';
else if    (marks < 60)   grade='D';
else if    (marks < 70)   grade='C';
else if    (marks < 80)   grade='B';
else                      grade='A';
```

EXAMPLE 4.6 The highest number

Problem Find the largest in a sequence of numbers.

Solution A program can read in the numbers one at a time, remembering the highest so far, and updating this if necessary. We note that negative numbers should be catered for as well.

Algorithm This is a very interesting algorithm. We start by assuming that we have found the highest of n numbers. Then the $n+1$th number is read. To find the highest of the $n+1$ numbers, all that needs to be done is to compare the new number with the highest so far, and if it is higher, to replace the highest. This process can then be repeated for as long as required.

The question is, how does the process start? Well, the highest number of a sequence that is one long must be just that number. So we start by reading in one number, make it the highest and proceed from there. The algorithm is shown in Figure 4.4.

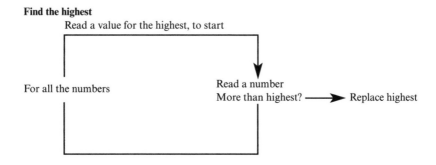

Figure 4.4 *Algorithm for finding the highest number.*

Program

```java
import java.io.*;
import javagently.*;

public class HighestValue {

  /* The Highest Value Program    by  J M Bishop  Aug 1996
   * ------------------------      Java 1.1 October 1997
   *
   * Finds the highest in a list of numbers.
   * Illustrates the if-statement
   */

  public static void main(String[] args) throws IOException {

    BufferedReader in = Text.open(System.in);

    System.out.println("*****  Finding the highest number *****");

    // Find out how many numbers will be coming
    Text.prompt("How many numbers (1 or more)?");
    int n = Text.readInt(in);

    // Start off the sequence
    System.out.println("Type them in");
    Text.prompt("1>");
    int highest = Text.readInt(in);

    // Read and check the rest of the numbers
    int number;
    for (int i = 2; i <= n; i++) {
      Text.prompt(i+">");
      number = Text.readInt(in);
      if (number > highest)
        highest = number;
    }
```

(handwritten annotation) number = new Integer (keyboard . Readline ( ) . intValue( ))

```
    System.out.println("That's enough, thanks");
    System.out.println("The highest number was "+highest);
  }


}
```

Testing It is a good idea to test such an algorithm with the first number being the highest, then with the last, and then with one in the middle. Another test would be to have all the numbers except one equal. This is left up to the reader, but here is one run:

```
*****  Finding the highest number *****
How many numbers (1 or more)?  5
Type them in
1>   56
2>   -99
3>   23
4>   70
5>   -4
That's enough, thanks
The highest number was 70
```

The next example has a more complex structure, and requires if-statements, coupled with methods. It also uses characters rather than integers for the data that is to be compared.

EXAMPLE 4.7 Counterfeit cheques

Problem Counterfeit cheques are in circulation and the banks have discovered that they all have the same distinctive properties. In the 10-digit cheque number, if there are:

- three or more zeros in succession,

- and/or four or more non-zeros in succession,

then the cheque could be counterfeit. We would like the computer to assist in warning of a possible counterfeit.

Solution When the cheques are handled by the bank's computers, the first thing that is read is the number. For the purposes of this example, we could write a program to read in cheque numbers and to analyse them for the above properties. The analysis could detect the occurrence of either of the runs described above and if either is found then the cheque can be marked as suspect.

Algorithm The algorithm for analysing a number involves reading it in, digit by digit, and counting the number of zeros and non-zeros. However, these have to occur in runs, so once a run is 'broken', the relevant count will be reset. It will therefore be necessary to remember that a critical count was reached at some stage: this is best done with a boolean variable. Figure 4.5 shows what the algorithm looks like.

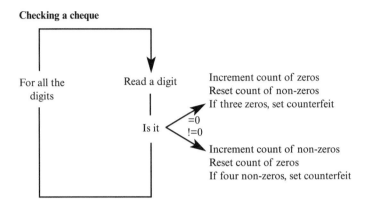

Checking a cheque

For all the digits

Read a digit

Increment count of zeros
Reset count of non-zeros
If three zeros, set counterfeit

Is it $=0$ $\neq 0$

Increment count of non-zeros
Reset count of zeros
If four non-zeros, set counterfeit

Figure 4.5 *Algorithm for checking a cheque.*

Program The program follows the algorithm closely, making use of two methods for clarity. The digits will be read as characters, but one of the features of the Text class is that any items must be delimited by what is known as 'white space' – spaces, ends-of-lines, tabs. Thus the digits of the cheque have to be entered with spaces following each one, so that they can be read using readChar. Section 7.1 explains how to fix this problem.

```java
import java.io.*;
import javagently.*;

public class Cheque {

   /* Counterfeit cheque detector    by J M Bishop Sept 1997
    *                                 Java 1.1 October 1997
    * Checks a cheque number for the occurrence
    * of >= 3 zeros
    * or >= 4 non-zeros in a row
    * The digits of the number must be separated by spaces.
    *
    * Illustrates if-then-else and static methods
    */

   static final int noOfDigits = 10;
   static boolean counterfeit = false;
   static int countOfZeros = 0;
   static int countOfNonzeros = 0;

   static void recordZero() {
      countOfZeros ++;
      countOfNonzeros = 0;
      if (countOfZeros == 3)
         counterfeit = true;
   }
```

class variables

```
    static void recordNonzero() {
      countOfNonzeros ++;
      countOfZeros = 0;
      if (countOfNonzeros == 4)
        counterfeit = true;
    }

    public static void main(String[] args) throws IOException {

      BufferedReader in = Text.open (System.in);

      System.out.println("***** Checking for counterfeits *****");
      System.out.println("Enter a cheque number of ten digits "+
          "separated by a space and ending with a return");
      char digit;
      for (int i = 0; i < noOfDigits; i++) {
        digit = Text.readChar(in);
        if (digit == '0')
          recordZero();
        else
          recordNonzero();
      }
      if (counterfeit)
        System.out.print("\tCOUNTERFEIT");
      else
        System.out.print("\tOK");
      System.out.println();
    }

}
```

Testing Cheque numbers should be chosen so as to test the special cases. For example, sample runs of the program with input and output might be:

```
****** Checking for counterfeits ******
Enter a cheque number with digits separated by a space
0 0 0 3 3 0 0 4 4 0
          COUNTERFEIT

****** Checking for counterfeits ******
Enter a cheque number with digits separated by a space
0 0 3 3 3 0 0 3 3 3
          OK

****** Checking for counterfeits ******
Enter a cheque number with digits separated by a space
4 4 4 4 0 0 5 5 0 0
          COUNTERFEIT

****** Checking for counterfeits ******
Enter a cheque number with digits separated by a space
1 2 3 4 5 6 7 8 9 0
          COUNTERFEIT
```

The restriction that the digits of a cheque number have to be separated by spaces will be removed once we discuss string handling in more detail in Chapter 7.

4.4 Introduction to exceptions

If-statements provide a means of control over the state of the current method. We can check the values of data to which we have access and react accordingly. But what happens if a condition is set in another method and we, the caller of the method, should react to it? The if-statement is not powerful enough to handle this. We need another construct.

Java's role in Web programming puts it in the position of the old adage that 'if things can go wrong they will': a user could disconnect, a file could have been deleted, incorrect input could be entered, a host server might be unavailable. In order to operate within such a volatile environment, Java has a special concept known as an **exception**.

An exception is an object that signals that some unusual condition has occurred. Java has many predefined exception objects, and we can also create our own. The point about exceptions is that they are intended to be **detected** and **handled**, so that the program can continue in a sensible way if at all possible. Should an exception occur outside our immediate environment, we shall be informed as to what has happened. We then have the opportunity to handle the situation that has arisen. If we do not react, the method we are in is terminated and the exception is sent up to the method that called us. This process may repeat until eventually an unhandled exception will pass to the Java virtual machine which will terminate the program.

Figure 4.6 illustrates the process of one method calling another and having a handler ready for a possible exception. Depending on how the rest of A is structured, it may be able to continue operating after it handles the exception, or it may exit.

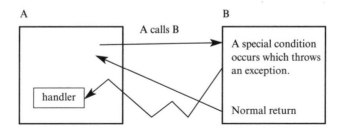

Figure 4.6 *The process of exception handling.*

Now let us consider a concrete example related to the summation program. It is unlikely that a user of a program will wish to count precisely the number of values to be entered beforehand. It would therefore be useful to be able to detect in some other way that the data is at an end. The third method mentioned in the list in Example 4.2 is to use Java's exceptions. In the reading methods supplied with Java, a check is made each time as to whether the input has been exhausted (either by the file ending or by the user indicating end-of-input in the usual way on the keyboard). If the check turns up true, then the read method causes an `EOFException` (for end-of-file exception). The summation program must then react to this.[2]

---

[2] In other languages, the end of input condition can be checked separately in advance using an if-statement and the method can decide how to proceed based on the outcome. This is not the case in Java: in order to handle variable length input, we *must* use exceptions.

The four essentials of exceptions

To use exceptions, we have to do four things:

1. **Try**: create a block around statements where the result of any method calls or other operations might cause an exception and preface them with the keyword `try`.

2. **Catch**: follow the try-statement with one or more handlers prefaced by the keyword `catch`.

3. **Throw**: if the exception is not dealt with at all, it will automatically be passed up to the calling method; if we catch it and deal with it partially, we can still pass it up with a throw statement.

4. **Declare**: mention in the method declaration which exceptions it may throw back to its caller.

In general, but not always, the event that causes the exception is triggered in a method lower down the calling path, and we do not know the precise reason why it is thrown at us. That is why exceptions have very explanatory names, which are usually enough to guide us in their handling.

Indeterminate loops

If there are indeterminate amounts of data, then the loop must similarly be an indeterminate one. The for-statement is powerful enough to handle this variation. All we do is omit any ending condition. The loop will then continue, until presumably an exception gets in the way and causes control to transfer out of the loop. In fact, all three parts of the for-statement are optional. The really basic indeterminate loop is:

```
for (; ;)
```

However, while the loop is in progress, it is often necessary to keep count of iterations, so that more probably we would have

```
for (int count; ; count++)
```

Although exceptions are one way of getting out of a loop, Java does provide another way using a break-statement. However, the `break` can only be activated by an if-statement based on conditions that are calculable in the loop itself. Thus we can say

```
if (number == 999) break;
```

but we cannot, in Java, use the if-statement and break-statement to detect the end of data.

The end-of-file exception

One of the most useful exceptions is that which signals the end of data. On the keyboard, the user types in data and when finished, presses the character that the system uses for ending the stream. This may be cntrl-D, cntrl-Z or esc, for example. The presence of this special character is detected by the `Text` class and is relayed to the caller by throwing the `EOFException`. It is therefore up to us to catch it. How this is done is shown in the next example.

EXAMPLE 4.8 Summation with exceptions

Problem There is a sequence of numbers that needs to be summed, but we do not know how many there are, even when the program starts running.

Solution The solution used in Example 4.5 is not possible here, because it relies on the user giving the number of numbers when the program starts. Instead, we must make use of the third option, that of detecting and reacting to the `EOFException`.
    For the sake of explanation, let us assume that the numbers will be read in from the keyboard. We shall make use of `Text`, `prompt` and `readDouble` to obtain the same sequence of interaction as in Example 4.5.

Algorithm Figure 4.7 shows the algorithm.

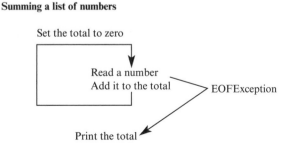

Figure 4.7 *Algorithm for summation with an exception.*

Program The loop has to be an indeterminate one: we achieve this by leaving the check-part blank in the for-loop. Since we shall now want to know how many numbers were read, the for-loop serves the purpose of keeping track of the tally.

```
import java.io.*;
import javagently.*;

public class Summation4 {
   /* The generalized Summation program   by J M Bishop Aug 1996
    * -------------------------------------   Java 1.1 October 1997
    *
```

```
 * Reads and sums numbers until the end of data is indicated.
 * Illustrates the correct use of the EOFException.
 */

public static void main (String [] args) throws IOException {

    int count = 0;
    double total = 0;
    double number;

    BufferedReader in = Text.open(System.in);

    System.out.println("****** Summing n numbers ******");
    System.out.println("Type numbers, ending with control-D (unix)"+
        "or control-Z (Windows)");

    try {
      for (count = 1; ; count++) {
        Text.prompt(count+">");
        number = Text.readDouble(in);
        total += number;
      }
    } catch (EOFException e) {
      System.out.println("That's enough, thanks.");
      System.out.println("The total of the "+(count-1)+
          " numbers is "+total);
    }
  }
}
```

Testing If this program was run then the screen might have the following on it:

```
****** Summing numbers ******
Type numbers, ending with cntrl-D
1>   23
2>   -18
3>   45
4>   11
5>   2
That's enough, thanks.
The total is 63.0
```

Notice that the control-D typed is not visible on the output, but it was there!

Recovering from an exception

The previous example showed how we could handle an exception in order to conclude a program gracefully. There may also be cases where we do not wish to end the method, but to go back and retry the operation that caused the exception. An example of such a situation is the opening of a file. If we have the file name incorrect, we may wish to give the user the chance to enter another name. The algorithm is shown in pseudo-code in Figure 4.8. This algorithm is used in the case study.

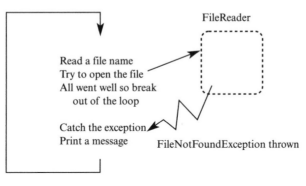

Figure 4.8 *An algorithm for opening a file securely.*

User-defined exceptions

Apart from the exceptions already defined in the Java library packages, users can also set up their own exceptions, peculiar to the situation in hand. To define such an exception, the form is:

Defining a new exception

```
class name extends Exception {
  public name () { }
  public name (String s) { }
}
```

We now have an exception class called `name` and we can throw exception objects of this class as in:

Throwing and catching a new exception

```
throw new name ("message");

catch (name e) {
  do something with e.getMessage();
}
```

The message can be used by the exception handler (the catch statement) to give information to the user by calling the `getMessage` method, or it can be empty (accounting for the two options in the declaration above). Opportunities for using user-defined exception arise later in the book.

EXAMPLE 4.9 Olympic medals

Problem The number of gold, silver and bronze medals won at the Olympic Games by each country has been stored in a file. We would like to display these results, as well as the total number of medals for each country, then we would like to investigate ways of making the file opening process more secure, by checking whether the file we want to open actually exists, and giving the user a chance to try again if not. Maybe there should be a limit on the number of tries allowed, and this possibility is investigated.

Solution We start by imagining a loop very similar to that in the summation program, using the EOFException (Example 4.8). The data is stored in a file, so we do not prompt for input, and we get four values at a time – country, gold, silver and bronze. Country will be a string, and the other three will be integers. Sample test data would be:

```
Australia  9  9  22
China  16  22  12
Cuba  9  8  8
France  15  7  15
```

In fact, this part of the program is easy. The part we want to study now is how to check whether the file name is valid. When we call Text.open there is a possibility that the FileNotFoundException will be raised. We should catch it and let the user try again. This can be done with the for-try sequence as just shown earlier in Figure 4.8.

Program We shall first give the program, then describe its constituent parts.

```
import java.io.*;
import javagently.*;

class Olympics {

    /* Olympic medals program   revised J M Bishop Dec 1996
     * --------------------- Java 1.1 October 1997
     *
     * Reads in and totals medals gained by countries in an
     * Olympic Games.
     * Illustrates recovering from an exception
     * (the for-try sequence) as well as ending with
     * an exception (the try-for sequence).
     */

    public static void main(String[] args) throws IOException {

        System.out.println("**** Olympic medals ****");
        System.out.println();

        /* Declare the keyboard stream, and initialize
         * the file stream to go there too.
         * Java requires that objects used later on definitely
         * have a value, and within a 'try' one cannot be sure
```

```
    * that a value has been assigned.
    * The same applies to giving filename an initial value.
    */

BufferedReader in = Text.open(System.in);
BufferedReader fin = Text.open(System.in);
String filename = "";

for (;;) {
  try {
    Text.prompt("What file for the medals statistics?");
    filename = Text.readString(in);
    BufferedReader fin = Text.open(filename);
    // Success, so break out of the loop
    break;
  } catch (FileNotFoundException e) {
    System.out.println(filename+" does not exist.");
    System.out.println("Try again");
  }
}

String country;
int gold, silver, bronze, total, all = 0;
System.out.println("\nCountry\t\tGold\tSilver\tBronze\tTotal");

try {
  for (;;) {
    country = Text.readString(fin);        Country = fin.readline();
    gold = Text.readInt(fin);
    silver = Text.readInt(fin);
    bronze = Text.readInt(fin);
    total = gold + silver + bronze;
    System.out.print(country);
    if (country.length() < 8)
      System.out.print("\t");
    System.out.println("\t"+gold+"\t"+silver+"\t"+bronze+
        "\t"+total);
    all += total;
  }
} catch (EOFException e) {
  System.out.println(all+" medals won.");
}
    }
  }
}
```

Algorithm The first point to discuss is why the `FileNotFoundException` requires a for-try sequence, and the `EOFException` uses a try-for sequence. What exactly is the difference? The for-try sequence is shown diagrammatically in Figure 4.8. It is used when we want to try something repeatedly. After the catch statement, control passes back up to the front of the loop. In the case of the try-for sequence, once the exception is detected, the loop ends. Hence the catch statement appears outside the loop, and the loop is terminated by replacing it with this handler.

The second point concerns the comment on initial values for objects. It is the case that any assignments made within try-statements cannot be guaranteed to have happened. The Java compiler will therefore complain if variables and objects are not given default values before we embark on a try statement.

Testing As expected, the output from the program is:

```
**** Olympic medals ****

What file for the medals statistics? medlas
medlas does not exist.
Try again
What file for the medals statistics? medals

Country          Gold   Silver   Bronze   Total
Australia          9       9       22       40
China             16      22       12       50
Cuba               9       8        8       25
France            15       7       15       37
Germany           20      18       27       65
Hungary            7       4       10       21
Italy             13       9       12       34
Poland             7       5        5       17
Russia            26      21       16       63
South.Korea        7      15        5       27
Spain              5       6        6       17
Ukraine            9       2       12       23
United.States     43      32       25      100
519 medals won.
```

Extension Now let us put a limit on the number of retries the user has for entering the file name. If we simply put a count in the for-loop, then after say five tries, the loop will end naturally. At this point, `fin` will still have its default value, being the keyboard, and the program will limp along reading data from there instead of from a file. The revised section of code would be:

```
for (int count = 0; count < 5; count++) {
  try {
    Text.prompt("What file for the medals statistics?");
    filename = Text.readString(in);
    BufferedReader fin = Text.open(filename);
    // Success, so break out of the loop
    break;
  } catch (FileNotFoundException e) {
    System.out.println(filename+" does not exist.");
    System.out.println("Try again");
  }
}
```

The problem is that we would rather stop the program if the file is not opened successfully, but we do not know at the end of the loop why the loop ended. In addition, we would like to be able to put all this code into a method so we can use it later on in other programs as well. Suppose we split it up as follows:

```
Text.prompt("What file for the medals statistics?");
String filename = "";
BufferedReader fin = open();

BufferedReader open () throws IOException {
  for (int count = 0; count < 5; count ++) {
    try {
      filename = Text.readString(in);
      return Text.open(filename);
    } catch (FileNotFoundException e) {
        System.out.println(filename+" does not exist.");
        System.out.println("Try again");
    }
  }
  return Text.open(System.in);
}
```

The method is a typed one, and returns a valid file reference. Here the `return` statement serves as assignment and a breaking out of the loop. If the `Text.open` fails five times, then `System.in` is returned as the default as before.

4.5 Creating and accessing packages

The `Text` class is stored in a package called `javagently` and in order to access it, a suitable import statement must be added to the program, i.e.

```
import javagently.*;
```

Although at present the `javagently` package only contains the one class, it could have more added, so we use the `.*` convention when importing. Therefore

```
import javagently.Text;
```

would be equally effective.

Since `javagently` is our own package, it does not come precompiled with the Java Development Kit or with the Java IDE you may be using. We therefore first have to create it before the import statement will work. Follow these easy steps:

1. At a level above that where you are working, create a directory called `javagently`.

2. Download the `Text.java` file from the website into this directory or type it in from Section 7.2.

3. In this directory, compile `Text.java`.

4.   There will now be the `Text.java` and `Text.class` files in the `javagently` directory.

5.   Using the method particular for your machine, add the directory immediately above `javagently` to your classpath (not to the path).

6.   Put

```
import javagently.*;
```

at the start of your program.

Figure 4.9 summarizes the result of these steps for a typical situation on a PC.

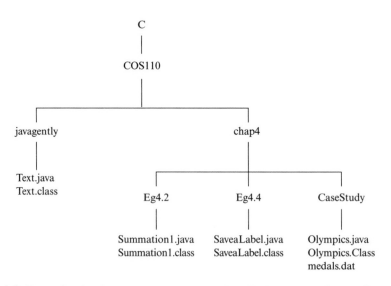

Figure 4.9 *Example of a directory structure for using the* `javagently` *package.*

An import statement in a Java class causes a look up process via the classpath. Thus we include the `C:\COS110` directory in the classpath, because that is where `javagently` resides. We do not include `C:\COS110\javagently` in the classpath, because the package is not in that directory! Any and all of the Java classes in `chap4`, or anywhere else under the COS110 directory, can make use of `javagently` in this way.

EXAMPLE 4.10   Secure file opener

Referring back to Example 4.9, since opening a file is probably going to be a facility that will be needed in various programs, we shall see how to set it up as a standard utility in its own package, just like `Text` in `javagently`. If we are writing our own package, the same steps as above apply, with the additional requirement that the class and its methods must be declared as public. Here is the new open method enclosed in a class called `FileMan` and destined for a package called `myutilities`.

```
package myutilities;

import java.io.*;
import javagently.*;

public class FileMan {

  /* The File Manager class     by J M Bishop  Dec 1997
   * ----------------------      Java 1.1
   *
   * Provides for a file to be opened, with five tries at a
   * correct file name.
   * Illustrates the use of exceptions.
   */

  public FileMan () { };

  public static BufferedReader open () throws IOException {

    BufferedReader in = Text.open(System.in);
    String filename = "";

    for (int count = 0; count < 5; count ++) {
      try {
        filename = Text.readString(in);
        return Text.open(filename);
      } catch (FileNotFoundException e) {
          System.out.println(filename+" does not exist.");
          if (count < 4) System.out.println("Try again");
      }
    }
    throw new FileNotFoundException ();
  }
}
```

The code has some interesting features, most important of which is that at the end of the loop, if no valid file name is entered, the `FileNotFoundException` is thrown again explicitly. The idea is that the exception should be picked up by the calling program and dealt with. This is shown in Olympics, version 2.

```
import java.io.*;
import javagently.*;
import myutilities.*;

public class Olympics2 {

  /* Olympic medals program  revised J M Bishop Dec 1996
   *                Java 1.1 October 1997
   *
```

```
   * Reads in and totals medals gained by countries in an
   * Olympic Games.
   * Illustrates catching an exception thrown explicitly
   * from another class, as well as ending with
   * an exception (the try-for sequence).
   */

public static void main(String[] args) throws IOException {

  System.out.println("**** Olympic medals ****");
  System.out.println();


 try {
   System.out.print("What file for the medals statistics?");
   BufferedReader fin = FileMan.open();

   String country;
   int gold, silver, bronze, total, all = 0;
   System.out.println("\nCountry\t\tGold\tSilver\tBronze\tTotal");

   try {
   for (;;) {
     country = Text.readString(fin);
     gold = Text.readInt(fin);
     silver = Text.readInt(fin);
     bronze = Text.readInt(fin);
     total = gold + silver + bronze;
     System.out.print(country);
     if (country.length() < 8)
       System.out.print("\t");
     System.out.println("\t"+gold+"\t"+silver+"\t"+bronze+
         "\t"+total);
     all += total;
   }
   } catch (EOFException e) {
   System.out.println(all+" medals won.");
   }
  } catch (FileNotFoundException e) {
   System.out.println
       ("Check the file name and run the program again.");
  }
 }
}
```

Using the packaged opener has made our program much shorter: this is the beauty of methods, classes and packages.

SUMMARY

There are two ways of changing the state of a variable: by assignment and by reading in values. In order to read in Java, we have first to connect to a stream. Thereafter we can read strings. Through the javagently class we can also read numbers and characters. In addition, files can be declared for both input and output and programs, and can receive and send data to multiple streams.

There are also two ways of changing the course of the program based on conditions that occur. The if-statement is suitable for checking the local state within a method. It can have an else-part, as well as successive else-ifs. When the condition occurs in another method, it is signalled back by means of an exception. Exceptions can be caught and handled. There are standard ways of recovering from an exception and trying again.

QUIZ

4.1   The following program extract is meant to swap the integer values in x and y if necessary, so that x lands up with the lower one. What will actually happen? Correct the extract.

```
if (x > y)
    int temp = x;
    x = y;
    y = x;
```

4.2   Give declarations to set up an input file called 'marks' which will have the name marksIn in the program.

4.3   What will the Text class do if a string is typed in where a number is required?

4.4   Given the suggestion in Example 4.6, devise another set of test data for exercising the highestValue program.

4.5   In the following try-statement, where could exceptions occur? What are their names?

```
try {
    for (int count = 0; ; count++) {
        x = Text.readDouble (in);
        y = 1/x;
        System.out.println (x, y);
    }
}
```

4.6   In Example 4.9 (Olympic medals), why was it necessary to use a dot in the country with more than one word, rather than a space, for example United.States instead of United States?

4.7   How is end-of-file signalled on your system when inputting from the keyboard?

4.8   Given the following statements and data, what will be printed out?

Statements	Data	
int i, j, k;		
Text.readInt (i);	67	56
Text.readInt (i);	98	kilos
Text.readInt (j);	11.5	33
Text.readInt (k);		
System.out.println (i, j, k);		

4.9   The following set of statements is inefficient. Why is this so? Rewrite it more efficiently.

```
if (pre == 'm') System.out.print ("milli");
if (pre == 'c') System.out.print ("centi");
if (pre == 'K') System.out.print ("kilo");
System.out.println ("metre");
```

4.10   If one wanted to read in amounts such as 65kg or 7s, how could the data be set up so that this could be done simply?

PROBLEMS

4.1 **Conversions.** Adapt the program in Example 3.4 so as to read in the limits required for the table.

4.2 **Fibonacci.** The Fibonacci series consists of a series of numbers in which the first two are 1 and each successive number is the sum of the two that precede it, that is:

1 1 2 3 5 8 13 21 34 55 . . .

Write a program to print the first 50 terms of the series.

4.3 **Average ages.** A Youth Club has 24 children grouped in four 'rings'. The children are aged 7 to 11. Write an interactive program to read in the ages for each ring and to work out the average age per ring for a group of 24 children, as well as the average overall age.

4.4 **Fuel consumption.** Adapt the program written for Problem 2.4 so as to read in all the values that may vary.

4.5 **Weighted averages.** Adapt the program in Problem 2.3 to read in the marks from a file and print each student's average as well as the overall average. Use exceptions to detect the end of the file.

4.6 **One man went to mow.** Fix Example 3.3 so that the last line is correctly printed out for one *man*.

4.7 **Better `FileMan`.** Extend the `FileMan` class to have another method, also called open, but which has a parameter specifying how many tries should be allowed. Can the existing open method be rationalized then?

4.8 **Stopping the song.** Consider Example 3.3 again. Alter the program so that it will stop after each verse of the song, and wait for some command to continue or not. Alternatively, make it react to a cntrl-Z or cntrl-D by stopping at the end of the next verse.

CHAPTER 5

Controlling the flow

5.1 Conditional loops with `while` and `do`

This book introduced loops early in order to emphasize the power of programming in handling repetitive tasks in a simple way. The two kinds of loops examined so far have been:

- counting loops based on the for-statement;

- indeterminate loops based on the for-statement, but with breaks and exceptions providing for exits from the loop when certain conditions or signals are encountered.

As was explained in the discussion on exceptions, the place where the exception is thrown is often one level lower than the place where it is caught. The implication is then that the condition for the loop to end is hidden, except in so far as it is conveyed in a meaningful exception name, such as `EOFException`.

We now consider a third and important group of loops, those that are based on conditions that are visible and detectable where the loop itself is defined.

The form of conditional loops

Conditional loops are phrased in terms of while- or do-statements. A general form of a loop using the while-statement is:

While-statement

```
Initialize the conditions
while (conditions) {
  Statements to perform the loop
    and change the conditions
}
```

After statements to initialize variables involved in the conditions, the loop itself starts by checking the conditions. If they evaluate to true, the body of the while-statement is entered and executed. When the end of the loop is reached, control goes around again to the beginning and the conditions are checked again. This process is repeated until the test of the conditions evaluates to false, at which point the looping stops, and control is passed to the statement following the body of the loop.

EXAMPLE 5.1 Highest common factor

Problem We wish to find the highest common factor (HCF) of two numbers.[1]

Solution One possible solution would be to find all the factors of each number and then compare both lists for the highest one. Fortunately, there is a quicker way!
   Suppose a and b are the numbers, a is larger than b and their HCF is f. Then $a - b$ and b will also have an HCF of f. If we use this fact, repeatedly replacing the larger of the two numbers by their difference, until the two numbers are the same, then this figure will be the HCF, even if it is 1.

Algorithm The above discussion can be expressed in the algorithm in Figure 5.1.

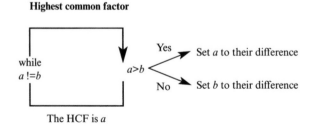

Highest common factor

Figure 5.1 *Algorithm for the highest common factor.*

---
[1] Some may know the HCF as the GCD – greatest common divisor.

Examples

a	b		|a - b|
65	39		26
26	39		13
26	13		13
13	13	HCF	

a	b		|a - b|
99	66		33
33	66		33
33	33	HCF	

Program Notice that the loop only has one statement, and therefore the curly brackets were omitted.

```java
import java.io.*;
import javagently.*;

class FindHCF {

  /* The HCF Program      by J M Bishop Aug 1996
     Calculates the highest common factor of two integers.
     Illustrates a while loop. */

  public static void main (String [] args) throws IOException {

    BufferedReader in = Text.open(System.in);

    System.out.println("***** Finding the HCF *****");
    Text.prompt("What are the two integers? ");
    int a = Text.readInt (in);
    int b = Text.readInt (in);
    System.out.print("The HCF of "+a+" and "+b+" is ");

    while (a != b)
      if (a > b) a -=b;
      else       b -=a;
    System.out.println(a);
  }
}
```

The general form of the do-statement is similar, as shown below. The do-loop starts off by going through its body at least once before checking the conditions. This can sometimes be a desirable property, but in general the while-statement is favoured by programmers. Unlike a while, the curly brackets are compulsory.

Do-statement

```
Initialize the conditions
do {
  Statements to perform the loop
    and change the conditions
} while (condition);
```

The two very important points about conditional loops are that:

- the condition must be initialized;

- the condition must change during the loop.

If the condition is not initialized, then the loop will be working on incorrect or even undefined information. If it is not altered during the loop, then there will be no chance of it changing and causing the loop to end.

Before going on to a problem, consider a small illustrative example of conditional loops, bearing in mind the importance of formulating them correctly. In order to convey the sense of the looping process, the example makes use of booleans and methods, which have the effect suggested by their names.

Developing a conditional loop

The first example simulates trying to find a pair from a drawerful of mixed coloured socks.

```
PickaSock();
PickAnotherSock();
while (!aPair()) {
  DiscardaSock ();
  PickAnotherSock ();
}
```

The loop is initialized by having two socks in hand: this is essential so that the check for a pair can be correctly performed. The loop is correctly formulated in that the condition will change each time round, as a new sock is selected. There are, however, two crucial flaws in the loop.

Suppose a pair is never found. The condition is not met so the loop continues, but the method to `PickAnotherSock` will eventually fail, and the whole operation will crash. The other problem is similar – suppose there were no socks in the drawer to start with. In this case, neither of the initializing statements can be performed, and the program as it stands will not be able to execute. These two situations can be summed up as:

- guard against not being able to begin;
- guard against never ending.

The remedy is to provide additional conditions as the guards. In this case, we need to know if sufficient socks (that is, at least two) exist to be able to test for a pair, and then we need to know when the drawer becomes empty. Both conditions are based on the number of socks in the drawer, and we assume that this figure can be provided in some way. The corrected version of the loop then becomes:

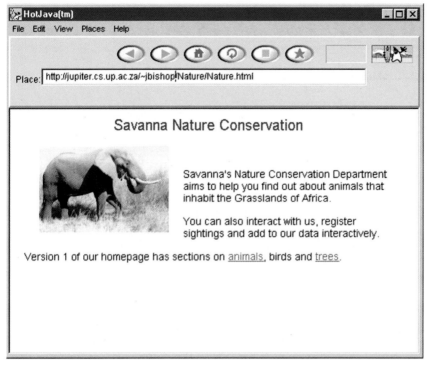

Plate 1 *The first page of the web site, showing two links to animals and trees.*

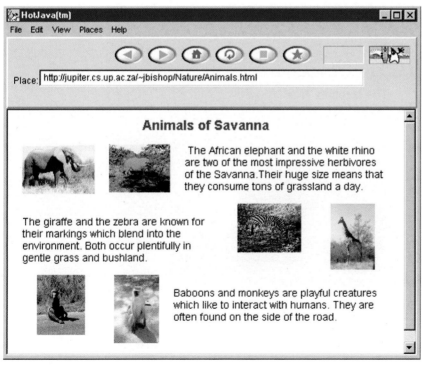

Plate 2 *The second web page, showing images and text.*

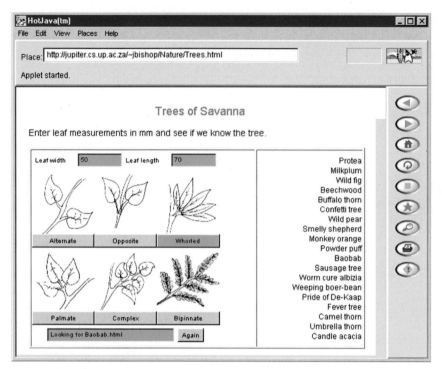

Plate 3 *The Trees web page with an applet at the bottom.*

Plate 4 *The result of the applet's deduction of your tree.*

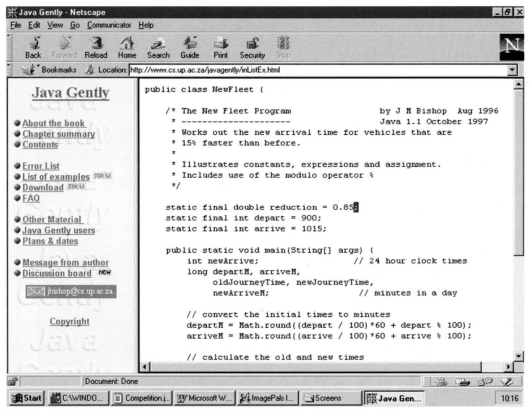

Plate 5 *An example program on the* Java Gently *web site.*

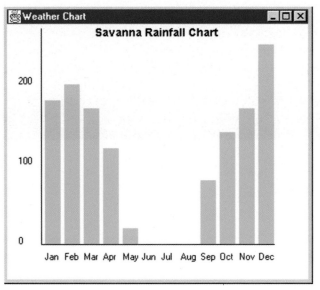

Plate 6 *Weather chart drawn with graphics.*

Plate 7 *Selecting a time zone under Windows.*

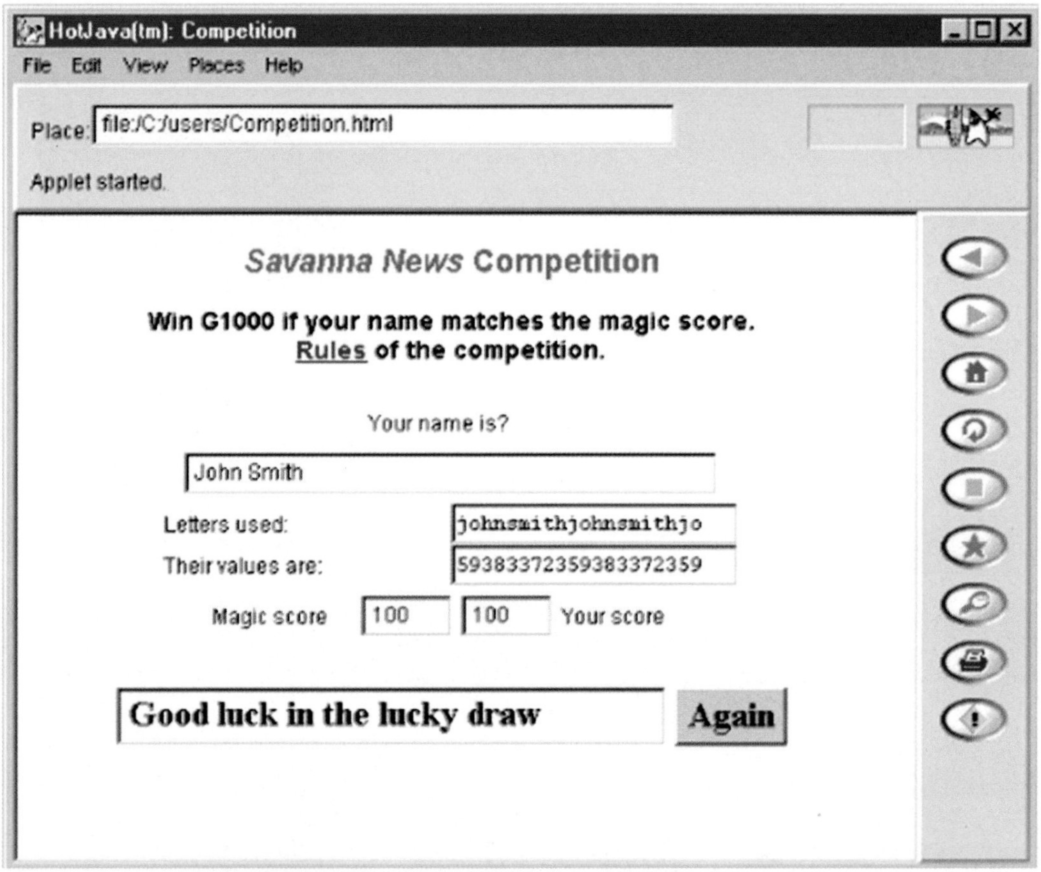

HotJava(tm): Competition
File Edit View Places Help
Place: file:/C:/users/Competition.html
Applet started.
Savanna News Competition
Win G1000 if your name matches the magic score.
Rules of the competition.
Your name is?
John Smith
Letters used:
johnsmithjohnsmithjo
Their values are:
59383372359383372359
Magic score
100
100
Your score
Good luck in the lucky draw
Again

Plate 8 *The Competition applet running in Hot Java.*

Traffic Lights Version 3
Savanna Traffic Light Simulation
1000
500
1000
500
1000
500
2000
500
4000
500
5000
1000
New Set
Walk
Duration
1000
Walk
Close

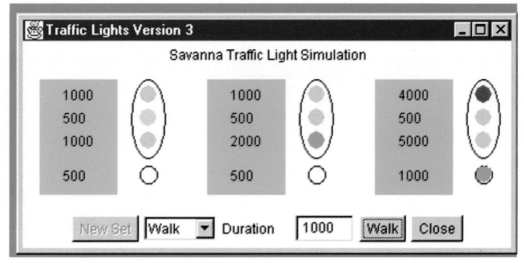

Plate 9 *The final traffic light simulation, with variable light duration.*

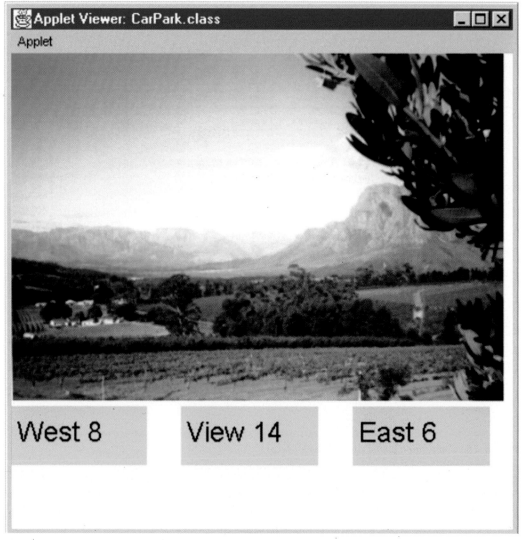

Plate 10 *The car-parks for the view site showing the counters.*

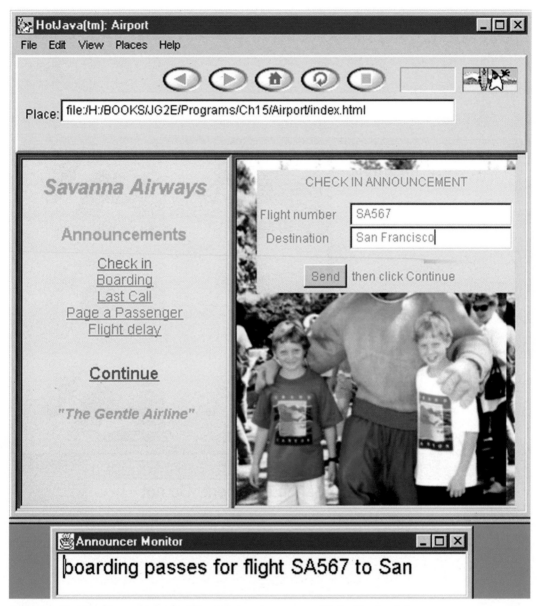

Plate 11 *The Checkin applet for the Airport Announcer system with the Monitor below.*

Plate 12 *The first screen for the Airport system, together with a security announcement.*

```
if (NumberofSocksinDrawer >= 2) {
  PickaSock ();
  PickAnotherSock ();
  while (NumberofSocksinDrawer > 0 && !aPair()) {
    DiscardaSock () ;
    PickAnotherSock () ;
  }
}
{At this point, a pair may or may not have been found}
```

There is one final consideration with any conditional loop. If there is more than one part to the condition governing the loop, it may be necessary to know at the end which part caused the loop to stop. In the example, it seems sensible to be able to decide whether the search was successful or not. This is called **a follow-up action**, and is performed by re-checking some of the conditions, as in:

```
if (aPair()) System.out.println("Got a pair of socks.");
else System.out.println("Bad luck, no pair found.");
```

Notice that when conditions are connected (as they often are), one must be careful as to which is tested. In this case, it would not have been correct to test for the drawer being empty as in:

```
if (NumberofSocksinDrawer == 0)
   System.out.println("Bad luck, no pair found.");
else System.out.println("Got a pair of socks.");
```

since the pair could have been found on the very last time round the loop. The drawer would also be empty, but that is irrelevant for this purpose.

Exercise Write the necessary if-statements to report on whether a pair was found or not, whether the drawer was empty initially, or whether it became empty during the search.

5.2 The switch-statement

The if-statement is a two-way selection statement based on conditions. However, if there are several simple tests for given values, successive else-if statements can become unwieldy. Java provides for so-called **keyed selection** with the switch-statement. The form of the switch-statement is:

Switch-statement

```
switch (switch-expression) {
    case value : statement; break;
    case value : statement; break;
    . . .
    default : statement; break;
}
```

The switch-statement considers the value of the switch-expression and, starting at the first case value, endeavours to find a match. If a match is found, then the corresponding statement is executed and the **break** causes control to pass to the end of the whole switch. The **default** keyword is a catch-all for values that have not been mentioned. The break statements and the default part are not strictly compulsory but it is considered good programming practice to have them. Without a break, control falls through to the next case. This could be useful if the statement part is empty, as shown in the examples that follow.

The switch-expression must produce a value that is an integer or character. It may not be real. The case values are expressions of the same type as the key-expression, and there may be one or more case value for a given statement. The key-values do not have to be in any order but may occur only once.

As an example, consider the little jingle which gives the number of days in a month:

> Thirty days hath September, April, June and November.
> All the rest have thirty-one, excepting February alone,
> Which has but twenty-eight days clear,
> And twenty-nine in each leap year.

If we assume that month has an integer value with January being 1, then a switch-statement can be used to look at the month and set days to the appropriate value as follows (ignoring leap years):

```
switch (month) {
    case 9:
    case 4:
    case 6:
    case 11: days = 30; break;
    case 2: days = 28; break;
    default: days = 31; break;
}
```

As always, the statement mentioned after each case can be a compound statement and include several statements. Such is the situation when establishing the correct number of days for February, taking account of leap years. Instead of doing a calculation of the year (divisible by 4 and so on), we simply ask whether the year is leap or not:

```
switch (month) {
  case 9:
  case 4:
  case 6:
  case 11:
    days = 30; break;
  case 2: {
    System.out.println("Is this a leap year?");
    char ans = Text.readChar(in);
    if (ans == 'Y') days = 29; else days = 28;
  } break;
  default: days = 31; break;
}
```

Switch-statements are the subject of the next example. The switch expressions are characters, which is quite often the case.

EXAMPLE 5.2 Exchange rates

Problem SavBank issues foreign exchange in four major currencies for customers, but the rates change daily.

Solution Set up a method which uses a switch to convert graz into one of the major currencies. These are Y (yen), $ (dollars), D (marks) and F (francs). The rates should be read in with suitable prompts each morning. (You could also include sterling if your keyboard has a pound sign.)

Algorithm The solution can be divided into two parts: the entry of the exchange rates, and the method which does the conversion and prints the foreign currency value. Clearly a switch-statement is ideal for the second part, and it will look something like this:

```
switch (currencySymbol) {
  case 'Y': factor = yenExchange; break;
  case '$': factor = dollarExchange; break;
  case 'D': factor = markExchange; break;
  case 'F': factor = francExchange; break;
  default : .....;
}
```

What should be done in the default case, which would be reached if an invalid symbol is entered? Obviously, a message must be displayed, informing the user that the symbol was invalid. But how to try again? One possibility would be to declare and raise an exception. This would be overkill, however, since we have all the information to hand, and we stipulated repeatedly in Chapter 4 that exceptions are for cross-method communication.

Instead we declare a simple boolean variable that will be set to false, and should the currency symbol be valid, it will be set to true. The switch-statement is then encased in a while-statement based on the boolean. Figure 5.2 sums this up.

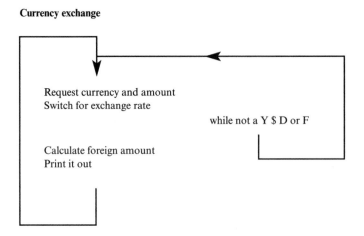

Currency exchange

Request currency and amount
Switch for exchange rate

while not a Y $ D or F

Calculate foreign amount
Print it out

Figure 5.2 *Algorithm for currency exchange.*

A further question is how to interact with the user. A question and answer session can become tedious and unclear. Instead, we use a tabular format, where the user fills in the first two columns and presses return, then the program tabs to the third column and gives the result. The output would then look like this:

```
SavBank Foreign Exchange Section
=================================
Graz into gives
1000  $
              217.391 dollars
1000  Y
              25000 yen
1000  M
              Valid currencies are Y$DF. Try again
        D
              333.333 marks
1000  F
              1098.9 francs
```

Program This version of the program sets up the exchange rates as constants, to emphasize the use of the switch-statements.

```
import java.io.*;
import javagently.*;
```

```
class ForeignExchange {

  /* The Foreign exchange program      by J M Bishop Oct 1996
   * --------------------------         Java 1.1 Dec 1997
   * Changes graz into yen, dollars, marks for francs.
   * Illustrates the use of switches. */

  static final double yenExchange = 0.04;
  static final double dollarExchange = 4.6;
  static final double markExchange = 3.0;
  static final double francExchange = 0.91;

  public static void main (String [] args) throws IOException {

    BufferedReader in = Text.open(System.in);
    double amount;
    double factor = 0;
    char c = '$'; // by default

    System.out.println("SavBank Foreign Exchange Section");
    System.out.println("=================================");
    System.out.println("Graz into gives");
    for (; ;) {
    try {
      amount = Text.readDouble (in);

      boolean found = false;
      while (! found) {
        c = Text.readChar (in);
        Text.prompt("\t\t");
        switch (c) {
          case 'Y' : factor = yenExchange; break;
          case '$' : factor = dollarExchange; break;
          case 'D' : factor = markExchange; break;
          case 'F' : factor = francExchange; break;
          default  : System.out.println
                        ("Valid currencies are Y$DF. Try again");
                     Text.prompt("\t");
        }
        found = (c=='Y' | c=='$' | c=='D' | c=='F');
      }

      System.out.print (Text.writeDouble(amount/factor, 8,3));"
      switch (c) {
        case 'Y' : System.out.println (" yen"); break;
        case '$' : System.out.println (" dollars"); break;
        case 'D' : System.out.println (" marks"); break;
        case 'F' : System.out.println (" francs"); break;
      }
    }
    catch (EOFException e) {}
    }
  }
}
```

Case ranges

In the previous example, the switch expression was a single variable, and it mapped directly on to the case values. Sometimes, there are many values for each statement, but there is a simple way of adjusting them so that there is only one per statement. For example, suppose that given an examination mark, it is required to set a symbol depending on the multiple of 10, with anything 80 and over being A, 70 and over being B, and so on down to anything under 40 being F. The switch to achieve such a mapping is:

```
switch ((int) (mark / 10)) {
    case 10:
    case 9:
    case 8:  symbol = 'A'; break;
    case 7:  symbol = 'B'; break;
    case 6:  symbol = 'C'; break;
    case 5:  symbol = 'D'; break;
    case 4:  symbol = 'E'; break;
    default: symbol = 'F'; break;
}
```

This is the clearest and most efficient way of solving this problem, but it is not the only way. The same effect could be achieved using successive if-else statements as described in Section 4.3. However, it is usually easier to see what is going on in a table as opposed to a calculation, so switch-statements should be used in preference to if-statements where possible.

When not to use switches

The clarity of the switch makes it a natural choice for many types of selections. However, it cannot be used in situations where the selection is based on conditions. For example, the following is not valid Java:

```
/* NOT VALID JAVA */
switch (number) {
    case < 0: Addtonegatives;
    case = 0: Donothing;
    case > 0: Addtopositives;
}
```

The cases must be actual values. A suitable approach here would employ successive if-else statements.

Another place where switch-statements are inappropriate is for checking strings. A string is a more complex entity than a switch can handle. Later on we shall see how to match strings as keys to values (Section 6.4).

5.3 Conditional loops and input data

Dealing with the outside world in the form of a user's input is a very important part of a program. In Chapter 4, we assumed that the input would end when the end of data was detected by an exception. There are other more subtle ways of telling the program to stop, and the next two examples explore these.

EXAMPLE 5.3   Controlling an engine

Problem An engine is controlled by numbers that may change, but must always be in descending order. As soon as the sequence is no longer descending, the engine stops. How would this aspect of its operation be programmed?

Solution We assume that the numbers will be read into a program, and that for the purposes of the investigation they can then be ignored. What is important is to get the algorithm for checking on the sequence correct.

Algorithm To check that a number is in sequence, we have to have both it and the previous number in hand. Each time round the loop, we replace the previous number with the one read in. As far as starting off goes, we cannot make an assumption as to the value of the first number, so the remembered number cannot be preset to a special value. Instead, the first number is read in separately, and then the loop starts.

Program The relevant loop would be:

```
int n = Text.readInt(in);
do {
  previous = n;
  n = Text.readInt(in);
} while (n <= previous);
```

Extension Since we have established that a program to control the engine is feasible, the maker of the engine has asked that it be written, but with the following additional conditions:

- the first number must be positive;
- the numbers must not go below 0.

For each number, he asks that we print out that many dots.

Algorithm The condition on the while-statement will need two parts now: to check the new number against 0 and to check it against `previous`. In addition, an if-statement is needed at the beginning to check that the very first number is positive. Printing the dots is best done in a separate method. Since it will depend upon n, we give the method a parameter to make this easy to do.

Program

```
import java.io.*;
import javagently.*;

  class controller {

    /* The Engine controller program      by J M Bishop Aug 1996
     * --------------------------------      Java 1.1
     * Reflects the operation of an engine until it
     * is shut down by a change in the sequence of
     * numbers expected.
     * Illustrates multiple conditions for starting
     * and ending a loop.
     */

    static void react (int dotcount) {
       for (int dot = 0; dot < dotcount; dot ++)
         System.out.print (".");
       System.out.println ();
    }

    static void instructions () {
      System.out.println("Type in the readings as they come");
      System.out.println("The engine will keep working while"+
        " readings are the same");
      System.out.println("or decreasing. It stops normally on" +
        " an increased reading and");
      System.out.println(" abnormally on a negative one.");
    }

    public static void main (String [] args) throws IOException {

      BufferedReader in = Text.open(System.in);
      System.out.println("***** Controlling an engine *****");

      Text.prompt("Type in the start-up value");
      int n = Text.readInt(in);
      if (n <= 0)
        System.out.println("The engine cannot work on that.");
      else {
        instructions ();
        int previous;

      do {
        react (n);
        previous = n;
        n = Text.readInt(in);
      } while (n>=0 & n <= previous);

      if (n<0) System.out.println("Abnormal shutdown");
      else System.out.println("Engine shut down okay");
    }
  }
}
```

Testing Sample input and output for the program would be:

```
***** Controlling an apparatus *****
Type in the start-up value 12
Type in the readings as they come
The engine will keep working while readings are the same
or decreasing. It stops normally on an increased reading and
abnormally on a negative one.
. . . . . . . . . . . .
11
. . . . . . . . . . .
9
. . . . . . . . .
5
. . . . .
2
. .
4
Engine shut down okay
```

The testing should include the cases for abnormal shutdown and where the data starts off negative. The next example looks at how to design a loop that can take care of all possible happenings in the input data.

EXAMPLE 5.4 Missing the target

Problem We would like to show how loops can handle the three cases of guarding against

• not being able to begin;

• never ending;

• reaching the end.

Solution We shall work with the following simple loop:

```
int target = Text.readInt(in);
do {
   int number = Text.readInt(in);
} while (number != target);
```

Reading is a special operation in a loop, in that it involves processing data, and it *also* changes the outcome of the value of variables. Thus, a read performs the dual function of the body of a loop and changing the conditions.

Algorithm Now consider the first two guards mentioned previously: the loop may not be able to start if no data exists, and it may never end if the target does not appear. If the target does not appear, then the data has ended, so both cases reduce to an end of data condition, both of which which will be signalled by the EOFExcep-tion. So the simple try- and catch-statements with the loop are:

```
try {
   int target = Text.readInt(in);
   do {
      int number = Text.readInt(in);
   } while (number != target);
}
catch (EOFException e) {
   System.out.println("The data has run out.");
}
```

This loop is unsatisfactory because the catch is a catch-all: we would like to be able to distinguish between the two reasons for an EOFException to be raised. One way is to add more try-statements, and then record the status in a boolean which protects the next stage:

```
boolean endofdata = false;
try {
   int target = Text.readInt(in);
}
catch (EOFException e) {
   System.out.println("No starting value.");
   endofdata = true;
}
if (!endofdata) {
try {
      do {
        int number = Text.readInt(in);
      } while (number != target);
      System.out.println("Finished correctly");
   }
   catch (EOFException e) {
      System.out.println("Target not found.");
      endofdata = true;
   }
}
```

Algorithm 2 With exceptions, it is better to keep try-statements to a minimum and handle catches together. One way of doing this is to use nested trys, and to throw an inner exception out to the outermost level. In so doing, we can change its name to a user-defined exception. Since an exception is a class declaration, it appears before the one for the class containing the main program. Thus we have:

```
import java.io.*;
import javagently.*;

class TargetNotFoundException extends Exception {} ;

class exceptions {
   public static void main (String [] args) throws IOException {

      BufferedReader in = Text.open(System.in);

      try {
         int target = Text.readInt(in);
```

```
    try {
      do {
        int number = Text.readInt(in);
      } while (number != target);
    }
    catch (EOFException e) {
      throw new TargetNotFoundException();
    }
  }
  catch (EOFException e) {
    System.out.println("No starting value.");
  }
  catch (TargetNotFoundException e) {
    System.out.println("Target not found.");
  }
 }
}
```

The next example takes the issue of reading further, by looking at reading structured values in one class, and throwing a user-defined exception to another class when things go wrong.

EXAMPLE 5.5   Testing a dates class

Problem We want to read in safely a structured value such as date, and test the method we devise.

Solution A date is a very useful item in programming. Java has built-in classes for dates, but they are fairly complex, and are covered in Chapter 7. Here we look at defining our own small date class, but take into account simple checking procedures for the fields of a date. For example, the month must lie between 1 and 12, and so on.

Algorithm The question is, what facilities should the dates class provide? A minimal set would be:

- constructing a date, and checking its elements
- converting a date to a string for later use in `println`
- comparing two dates.

Specifically, the class excludes any input or output itself: this should be done in the calling program. Thus instead of saying

```
D = readDate();
```

we call a constructor with the already read in component values.

```
D = new Dates (y, m, d);
```

Similarly, instead of having a method such as

```
writeDate(D);
```

we provide a `toString` method which gives automatic access to `println` as follows:

```
System.out.println(D);
```

In summary, Figure 5.3 shows a desirable class diagram.

Dates

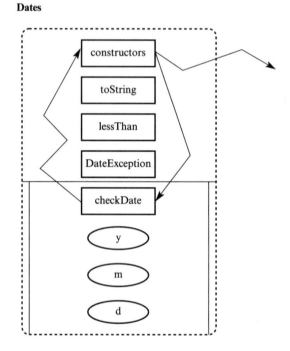

Figure 5.3 *Class diagram for a dates class, showing the progress of the* `DateException`.

Program The class makes use of a switch statement (which is why it is in this chapter!) and creates and throws a user-defined exception. Because it is such a useful class, we add it to the `myutilities` package.

```
package myutilities;

public class Dates {

    /* The Dates Class       by J M Bishop   December 1997
     *  ---------------       Java 1.1
     *
     * Provides a class for dates objects
     * with a few minimal facilities.
     */
```

```
public class DateException extends Exception {
  DateException (String s) {
    super(s);
  }
}

public Dates () {}

public Dates (int y, int m, int d) throws DateException {
  checkDate (y,m,d);
}

private int year, month, day;

private void checkDate (int y, int m, int d)
                          throws DateException {
  if ((m<1) | (m>12))
    throw new DateException("Error in month");
  else if ((d<1) | (d>31))
    throw new DateException("Error in day");
  else {
    year = y;
    month = m;
    day = d;
  }
}

public String toString () {
  String s = String.valueOf(day) + " ";
  switch (month) {
    case 1: s = s + "Jan"; break;
    case 2: s = s + "Feb"; break;
    case 3: s = s + "Mar"; break;
    case 4: s = s + "Apr"; break;
    case 5: s = s + "May"; break;
    case 6: s = s + "Jun"; break;
    case 7: s = s + "Jul"; break;
    case 8: s = s + "Aug"; break;
    case 9: s = s + "Sep"; break;
    case 10:s = s + "Oct"; break;
    case 11:s = s + "Nov"; break;
    case 12:s = s + "Dec"; break;
  }
  s = s + " " + String.valueOf(year);
  return s;
}

public boolean lessThan (Dates D) {
  boolean b = year < D.year;
  b = b || year == D.year && month < D.month;
  b = b || year == D.year && month == D.month && day < D.day;
  return b;
}

}
```

Now for a small testing program.

```
import myutilities.*;
import javagently.*;
import java.io.*;

class testdate {

  /* Testing the dates class     by J M Bishop  Dec 1997
   * ----------------------     Java 1.1
   */

  public static void main (String args [])
    throws IOException, Dates.DateException {

    BufferedReader in = Text.open(System.in);

// The date objects must first be set up before values
// are entered, because the entering is done in a try-
// catch statement.
    Dates d1 = new Dates ();
    Dates d2 = new Dates ();

    try {

// Two ways of putting values in the dates.
// The first uses constants in a constructor,
// the second reads values then calls the constructor.

      d1 = new Dates (1998,12,25);
      Text.prompt("Type a date (year first)");
      int y = Text.readInt(in);
      int m = Text.readInt(in);
      int d = Text.readInt(in);
      d2 = new Dates (y,m,d);
    } catch (Dates.DateException e) {
      System.out.println(e.getMessage());
    }
    System.out.print(d1 + " is ");
    if (d1.lessThan(d2))
     System.out.print("earlier than ");
    else
      System.out.print("later than ");
    System.out.println(d2);
  }
}
```

Testing Typical output from a few runs would be:

```
Type a date (year first) 1997 10 7
25 Dec 1998 is later than 7 Oct 1997

Type a date (year first) 2001 1 1
25 Dec 1998 is earlier than 1 Jan 2001
```

```
Type a date (year first) 1997 31 12
Error in month
25 Dec 1998 is later than 0  0
```

5.4 Case Study 2: Rock–scissors–paper game

There is a popular two-person game in which each player makes a choice of rock, scissors or paper, and who is the winner depends on the following rules:

- rock beats scissors (it can smash them);

- scissors beat paper (they can cut it);

- paper beats rock (it can wrap it).

If both players make the same choice, then it is a draw.

We would like to program the computer to play this game against a human. Each will make a choice and the computer will work out who won.

Solution

Programming any two-person game involves seven steps:

1. Give instructions (or omit them if requested to do so).
2. Initialize the game, if necessary.
3. Set up a loop to play the game repeatedly until told to stop.
4. Generate the computer's choice.
5. Get the user's choice.
6. Decide who has won.
7. Play again, or if no more, sign off.

We shall look at each step in turn.

Step 1: instructions

Computer games should always give instructions for new users. These should include not only a description of the rules, but also how to enter replies. Two issues that should always be addressed here are whether replies need to be followed by return, and whether capital letters are acceptable as well as lower-case letters. We shall require the user to type in R, S, P or a Q to end. We shall not permit lower-case letters.

Step 2: initialize

We need to ask the question here as to how the computer is to make its choice. Ideally, we want a random choice, and therefore need to use random numbers. Java provides a class in the `util` package called `Random`. The specification of `Random` is:

```
public class Random extends Object {
// constructors
  public Random ();
  public Random (long seed);
// instance methods
  public double nextDouble();
  public float  nextfloat();
  public int    nextInt();
  public long   nextLong();
  public synchronized double nextGaussian();
  public synchronized void   setSeed (long seed);
}
```

Once a `Random` object is created (with or without a starting value, called a *seed*), the next random number of any of the four types mentioned can be obtained. We want an integer, and we would like to seed it from data supplied by the user, so we could use:

```
private static Random dice = new Random(Text.readInt(in));
int next = dice.nextInt ();
```

The problem is that `next` will have any integer value, and we want one between 0 and 2. We can obtain this simply by taking the remainder after dividing by 3, thus:

```
if (next < 0) next = -next;
mychoice = next % 3;
```

Step 3: set up a loop

We are going to use an indeterminate while-loop because the place where we stop the loop (based on a Q being input) is in between getting our choice and getting the computer's choice. We exit the loop with a break. The loop is the main feature of the main class that plays the game, as follows:

```
import java.io.*;
import javagently.*;

class playGame {

  /* The Playing Game program      by J M Bishop   Aug 1996
   * -----------------------        Java 1.1
   * Calls methods in the RSP class to get
   * my choice and the computer's choice and
   * display who has won until Q is typed.
   * Illustrates conditional loops and objects
   */

  public static void main (String [] args) throws IOException {

    BufferedReader in = Text.open(System.in);

    RSPGame mygame = new RSPGame ();
    mygame.startGame (in);
```

```
      while (true) {
        mygame.makemyChoice();
        if (mygame.getyourChoice (in)=='Q') break;
        mygame.winner();
      }
      System.out.println("Thanks for playing");
  }
}
```

Step 4: generate the computer's choice

We have already seen that this will be done by random numbers. The computer will be submitting 0, 1 or 2 and the user will be submitting R, S or P. In fact, this will not cause problems.

Step 5: getting the user's choice

Here we have to program defensively. We must check that the character entered is indeed one of the permissible ones. If it is not, we should give a message and try again. A do-loop is in order because the test comes after the input has been done. The basic sequence is:

```
do {
   Text.prompt("Your choice of R S P or Q to stop ?");
   yourchoice = Text.readChar(in);
} while (yourchoice!='R' & yourchoice != 'S'
        & yourchoice != 'P' & yourchoice != 'Q');
```

This sequence will force the player to use capital letters. Notice that the initial message serves as an error message as well.

Step 6: decide who has won

This is algorithmically the most intricate part. We have three choices for the computer, and each of these has three outcomes, depending on the player's choice. This could mean a selection statement with nine arms! Fortunately, there is a better way, using a method with parameters.

Let us consider the first case of the computer having a rock. Then, depending on the player's choice, the computer judges the result as:

- scissors – win,
- paper – lose,
- rock – draw.

The same process is repeated for the computer having a scissors, except that the list of player's choices is in a different order. Clearly, a method will be appropriate here, and the result is shown in the program below.

Step 7: sign off

We can have a very simple sign off, such as thanking the user, or we can print out statistics on how many games were won either way.

Program

The program follows the strategy outlined above, and makes good use of all the control instructions introduced in this chapter. The program is arranged in two classes: the structure of the `playGame` class is more or less independent of the game being played, except that it refers to the `makemyChoice` and `getyourChoice` methods as belonging to `RSPGame`. In the `RSPGame` class, there are three private variables/objects and one private method. Figure 5.4 gives the class and method diagram for the program.

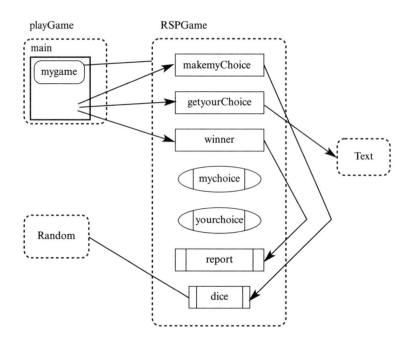

Figure 5.4 *Class and object diagram for the rock–stone–paper game.*

```
import java.io.*;
import javagently.*;
import java.util.Random;

class RSPGame {

    /* The RSP Game class          by J M Bishop Aug 1996
     * ------------------          Java 1.1  Dec 1997
```

```
 * offers four methods:
 * startGame, getmyChoice, getyourChoice and Winner.
 * getyourChoice returns a character so
 * that we can stop if it was a Q.
 * Illustrates typed methods switches, loops and Random.
 */

private static int mychoice;
private static char yourchoice; // R S P
private static Random dice;

void startGame (BufferedReader in) throws IOException {
  System.out.println("Let's play RSP");
  System.out.println("To show I'm not cheating, start me off by"+
    " giving me a number.");
  dice = new Random(Text.readInt(in));
}

void winner () {
  // In the calls to report, the first parameter is my choice.
  // The second one is the choice that I could beat.
  // The third one is the choice that would beat me.

  switch (mychoice) {
    case 0 : report ('R','S','P'); break;
    case 1 : report ('S','P','R'); break;
    case 2 : report ('P','R','S'); break;
  }
}

void makemyChoice () {
  // nextInt returns an integer in its full range.
  // We have to reduce it to 0, 1, 2

  int next = dice.nextInt();
  if (next < 0) next = -next;
  mychoice = next % 3;
}

char getyourChoice (BufferedReader in) throws IOException {
  do {
    Text.prompt("Your choice of R S P or Q to stop ?");
    yourchoice = Text.readChar(in);
  } while (yourchoice!='R' & yourchoice != 'S'
          & yourchoice != 'P' & yourchoice != 'Q');
  if (yourchoice != 'Q')
    System.out.print("You drew "+yourchoice+" and ");
  return yourchoice;
}

private static void report (char me, char Iwin, char youWin) {
  System.out.println("I drew a "+me);
  if (yourchoice == Iwin)
```

```
      System.out.println("I win");
    else if (yourchoice == youWin)
      System.out.println("You win");
    else
      System.out.println("It's a draw");
    }
  }
```

Testing

A typical run could go something like this:

```
Let's play RSP
To show I'm not cheating, start me off by giving me a number.
67
Your choice of R S P or Q to stop ? R
You drew R and I drew a S
You win
Your choice of R S P or Q to stop ? S
You drew S and I drew a R
I win
Your choice of R S P or Q to stop ? P
You drew P and I drew a R
You win
Your choice of R S P or Q to stop ? P
You drew P and I drew a P
It's a draw
Your choice of R S P or Q to stop ? S
You drew S and I drew a P
You win
Your choice of R S P or Q to stop ? R
You drew R and I drew a S
You win
Your choice of R S P or Q to stop ? Q
Thanks for playing
```

As you can see, the computer's choices are random, and it does lose sometimes!

SUMMARY

The while-loop is the basic controlling loop. It checks the condition at the start of the loop. The do-loop checks the condition at the end. In either case, we can check one or more conditions in the middle and exit the loop using a break-statement. Boolean variables are useful when programming while-loops, in order to keep the value of conditions established before the time comes to check whether to continue. The use of while-loops is intimately entwined with reading input data, and, as was explained in the previous chapters, it is necessary to handle some of the ending conditions via exceptions.

The switch-statement provides for multi-way decision making based on values. Several values can lead to the same statement. The values may only be integers or characters.

QUIZ

5.1 Each of the following three loops is meant to read characters until a $ is found. Do they all have the same effect?

```
char ch;
for (;;) {
  ch = Text.readChar(in);
  if (ch == '$') break;
}

char ch;
do {
  ch = Text.readChar(in);
} while (ch != '$');

char ch;
while (ch != '$')
  ch = Text.readChar(in);
```

5.2 Write a switch-statement that will print out the name for each of the days of the week, given a number from 0 to 6.

5.3 What would be suitable target ending values for the following sets of data:

- ages of people
- air temperatures
- years

5.4 Write out suitable instructions for the RSP game in the Case Study.

5.5 What happens when a switch statement is entered with a case value that is not one of those listed and there is no default case?

5.6 What would be the while-statement equivalent of the indeterminate for-statement

```
for (;;)
```

5.7 If we want to have the chance of trying an operation again once an exception has been thrown into a while-statement, should we use a do-try or a try-do sequence? (Hint: See Examples 4.9 and 5.4 for explanations of the difference.)

5.8 Write a while-loop which will print out all the even numbers from 0 to 20.

5.9 Draw an algorithm diagram for the last program in Example 5.4.

5.10 Suppose we decided to change the `getyourChoice` method in the Case Study into a boolean method and return

```
return yourchoice == 'Q';
```

How would the calling method change?

5.1 **Postage stamps**. Savanna Mail has decided to have machines that print out postage stamps up to a maximum value of G99.99. The stamps have a basic design as follows:

```
-----------
| SAVANNA |
| G14.30  |
| BY AIR  |
-----------
```

The three zones of postage rates per 10 grams are as follows:

A   50c

B   90c

C   G1.10

and the postage is doubled for airmail. Write a program that prompts the user for the mass of an article, the zone to which it is going and whether it should go by air or not, and then prints out the correct stamp. Use a class for the stamps, and create three objects for the different zones. Refer to the Case Study in Section 3.7 for a model.

5.2 **Rainfall figures**. The rainfall figures in mm are available for each day of the past four weeks. We want to know the total rainfall for each week, the most recent wettest day and the driest week.

Write a program that will read in several sets of 28 rainfall figures and print out the three bits of information required. Sample data and results would be

```
Sample data          Sample results
3 0 0 7 8 21 0       39 mm
0 1 1 0 0 0   4       6 mm
9 6 7 0 0 0   0      22 mm
0 0 0 0 0 0   1       1 mm
The wettest day was day 6.
The driest week was week 4.
```

5.3 **Golf scores**. The Savanna Golf Course has nine holes. At each hole, a player is expected to be able to sink the ball in the hole in one to five shots. This gives a course average or par of 30. A player's score for the course is the sum of the numbers of shots for each hole. Depending on past performance, a player is granted a handicap which is subtracted from his or her score to give his or her actual result for a game. Players are also interested in knowing whether they have scored under par or not. When players play together, the winner is the one with the lowest score. If the scoring of a golf game were computerized, sample input and output might be:

Player	Handicap	Shots per hole	Total	Result	Under Par?
1	6	1 3 6 2 1 4 3 2 4	26	20	yes
2	3	2 2 2 2 4 4 4 2 2	24	21	yes
3	2	4 5 4 3 4 1 3 5 4	33	31	no

The winner is player 1 with a handicapped result of 20

Write a program that

- reads in the shots per hole for several players;
- calculates each total score, handicapped score and par decision;
- determines the winning player and the winning score.

5.4 **Sensitive drugs**. A sensitive drug cannot sustain a change in temperature of more that 30 °C in a 24 hour period. The temperatures are monitored and recorded every two hours. Write a program the laboratory technician can run once a day to determine whether or not to throw the drug away.

5.5 **Parking meters**. The Savanna Traffic Department wants to decide whether or not to mount a campaign against illegal parking. A number of traffic inspectors are sent to different zones in the city where parking time is restricted. The different zones have different time restrictions. Each of the traffic officers has to monitor any 10 cars in their zone and record the actual time the vehicle was parked in the time restricted zone. If 50% or more of the cars were parked for a longer period than allowed, the traffic department will decide to launch a massive campaign. Write a program that

- reads in the number of zones;
- reads the time limit and actual parking time for ten vehicles for each of the zones;
- determines the number of cars exceeding the time limit in each of the zones;
- decides whether a campaign should be mounted or not;
- identifies the zone where the situation is the worst.

Sample input and output might be:

```
Please enter the number of zones: 3
Area  Limit  Parking times                              Over limit
1      60     20 40 70 35 45 78   34 56 73   5           3
2      45     62 47 68 40 53 62 120   8 15 72            7
3      30     66 32 41 89   7 25   29 33 54 17           6
A campaign must be mounted.
Concentrate on area 2
```

5.6 **Engineering apparatus**. A certain engineering apparatus is controlled by the input of successive numbers. If there is a run of the same number, the apparatus can optimize its performance. Hence we would like to arrange the data so as to indicate that a run is coming. Write a program that reads a sequence of numbers and prints out each run of numbers in the form (n*m) where m is the number to be repeated n times. These instructions are printed in brackets on a new line, to indicate that they are going to the apparatus. Note that a run could just consist of a single number. The numbers are terminated by a zero, which halts the apparatus. Sample input and output would be:

```
Sample input and output
20 20 20 20 20 20 20 20 20 20 50
(10*20)
50 50 50 50 60
(5*50)
60 60 60 60 20
(5*60)
30
(1*20)
```

```
30 30 30 90
(4*30)
0
(1*90)
(0)
```

5.7   **Rabbits!** A scientist needs to determine when she will run out of space to house her rabbits. She starts with two rabbits and it is known that a pair of adult rabbits (those more than three months old) produce on average two rabbits every three months. The scientist has space to house 500 rabbits. Write a program that will determine how many months it will be before she runs out of space. Adapt the program to print out a table of the rabbit populations (adult, non-adult and total) every three months for five years. Assume no rabbits die.

5.8   **Fibonacci again.** Problem 4.2 involved printing out the Fibonacci sequence. Alter the program so that only every third value is printed out. What do you notice about these values?

5.9   **Setting exchange rates.** Improve the Exchange rates program (Example 5.2) so that the rates can be read in before trade begins each day.

5.10   **Better date checker.** The checkDate method in the dates class (Example 5.5) is rather crude. Improve it so that it takes account of the precise number of days allowed for a particular month. (Hint: see Section 5.2.)

5.11   **Times class.** Develop a class similar to dates to store and compare times (hours, minutes and seconds).

CHAPTER 6

Arrays and tables

6.1 Simple arrays

We are beginning to realize that there is a need to be able to store and manipulate multiple values in a program. If there are relatively few values, simple variables can possibly be used, but consider the following example.

Suppose we have several hundred scores between 0 and 19 which have to be analysed for frequency of occurrence of each score. We could set up 20 counters, one for each score. As the scores are read in, the counter corresponding to the score could be incremented. It would be very unwieldy if we had to invent 20 different names for the counters, and then use a big switch-statement every time one of them needed updating. What we need is the concept of the *i*th **variable** so that we can read a value, say *i*, and then update $counter_i$. Programming languages provide for this facility with the **array**.

Form of an array

An array is a bounded collection of elements of the same type, each of which can be selected by indexing with an integer from 0 upwards to a limit specified when the array is created. The relevant form is:

Array declaration

```
type arrayname [ ] = new type [limit];
type arrayname [ ] = {values};
```

Arrays can be declared to contain any type or class, but the index and hence the limit must always be an integer. The limit gives the number of elements in the array, with each element being indexed by a number in the range from 0 to *limit* – 1. Examples of array declarations of the first form shown above are:

```
int frequencies [] = new int [20];
Dates holidays [] = new Dates [16];
String countries [] = new String [175];
```

The `frequencies` array will have 20 integers, numbered 0 to 19. There will be 16 dates[1] in the `holidays` array, numbered 0 to 15, and 175 strings stored in the `countries` array numbered 0 to 174. Notice that array names are frequently given as plurals.

The second form creates an array with initial values. The size of the array is then deduced from the number of values given, for example:

```
char vowels [ ] = {'a','e','i','o','u'};
```

The `vowels` array has five characters, numbered from 0 to 4.

To access an array element, we give the name of the array variable and an index expression enclosed in square brackets. The index is sometimes known as the **subscript**. For example, we could have:

```
for (int i=0; i<20; i++) frequencies[i] = 0;
holidays [0] = new Dates (1997,1,1);
countries[44] = "Great Britain";
System.out.println(vowels[3]);
```

Remember that arrays are always indexed starting at 0, so that the last example here will print the fourth element, which is 'o', not 'i'.

EXAMPLE 6.1   Frequency count

Problem The frequencies of several hundred scores between 0 and 19 have to be calculated.

Solution The solution has already been outlined at the beginning of the section. We set up an array and as each score is calculated or read, the appropriate element of the array is incremented. The algorithm is so simple that we go straight on to the program.

---

[1] The `Dates` class as used here is the one defined in Section 5.3. Java has a `Date` class, which is considered in Chapter 7.

Program The program uses the random number generator to create 100 numbers between 0 and 19 for testing purposes. The important line is

```
scoreFreqs [score]++;
```

which is where the relevant element of the array is incremented.

```java
import java.util.Random;

class Frequencies {
    /* The Frequencies Program       by J M Bishop Dec 1996
     * ----------------------        Java 1.1
     * Counts the frequencies of scores from 0 to 19.
     * Tested by generating random numbers.
     * Illustrates simple array handling
     */

    static final int maxscore = 20;
    static final int n = 100;

    public static void main (String [] args) {

        int scoreFreqs [] = new int [maxscore];
        int score;
        Random TestScore = new Random ();

        for (int i=0; i<n; i++) {
            score = Math.abs(TestScore.nextInt() % 20);
            scoreFreqs [score]++;
        }

        System.out.println("Table of Score Frequencies\n"+
                           "==========================\n");
        for (int i = 0; i<maxscore; i++) {
            Text.writeInt(i,6);
            Text.writeInt(scoreFreqs[i],6);
            System.out.println();
        }
    }
}
```

Testing Sample output would be

```
Table of Score Frequencies
==========================
       0      4
       1      3
       2      5
       3      4
       4      8
       5      3
       6      4
       7      4
```

8	3
9	9
10	4
11	4
12	4
13	6
14	4
15	4
16	9
17	6
18	6
19	6

This program has been written without methods or classes. Clearly, it could have been formally broken up and parameter interfaces created. However, in this case, we deemed it simpler to present the program as one unit, so that the idea of arrays can be understood on its own. In later examples, we shall see how arrays interface with classes in different ways. We now consider the properties of arrays in a formal way.

Properties of arrays

1. **Element type.** Arrays can be formed of any type or class, from integers to dates to arrays themselves. The last leads to multi-dimensional arrays, discussed in detail in Section 6.2.

2. **Size.** The size of an array is limited only by the computer's memory, which is usually adequate for most applications. The size is **fixed** at the time that the array is created, and cannot be changed thereafter.

3. **References.** When an array is declared, a **reference** is set up for it. This reference will point to the place where the array's elements are stored. The declaration

```
int A [] = new int [4];
```

therefore has the effect shown in Figure 6.1. The declaration can be done in two stages: one to declare the array name and create the reference, and then later another to set up the storage. The equivalent Java statements would be:

```
int A [];
A = new int [4];
```

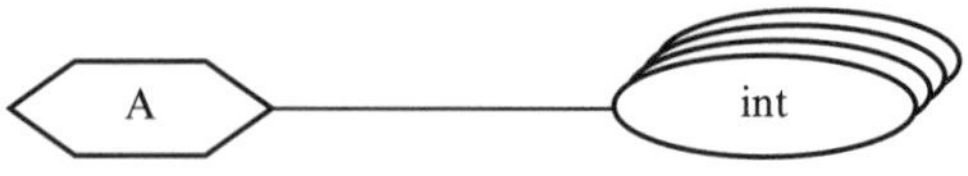

Figure 6.1 *An array stored as a reference and values.*

4. **Operator.** The only operator that applies to a whole array is assignment. Assigning one array to another, though, does not create a copy of the whole array. Instead, it copies the references, so that both arrays will refer to the same storage, and changes made to one will affect the other. Copies of the actual values of arrays can be made in the same way as copies of objects can, by a method called **cloning**, and this topic is taken up in Section 8.3. Should we wish to copy an array at this point, we could do it simply by creating a new array and copying each element over using a loop.

5. **Element access.** Java is quite firm about allowing access only to array elements that actually exist. Every time an array is accessed, the index supplied is checked against the bounds given in the array declaration. If the index is out of bounds, an `ArrayIndexOutOfBoundsException` is raised. The exception can be caught and handled, and if it is not, the program halts. For example, with the above declarations, both `frequencies[100]` and `vowels[5]` would cause errors.

6. **Length.** The length of an array can be established by means of a special property associated with every array, called `length`. Thus

    ```
    frequency.length
    ```

    will yield 20. In other words, `length` returns the limit used in the declaration. Notice that `length` is not a method, but a property, and therefore does not have brackets after it.

7. **Parameters.** Arrays can be passed as parameters to methods. A very convenient feature of Java is that the formal parameter in the method does not have to specify the length of the array it expects. The method can accept arrays of the correct type of any length, and processes them by using the `length` property described in point 6. A prime example is the main method which declares

    ```
    main (String [] args)
    ```

    If there are any arguments, `main` could print them out using a for-loop as follows:

    ```
    for (int i=0; i<args.length; i++)
      System.out.println(args[i]);
    ```

Array and class interaction

There are at least three different ways in which arrays and classes can interact.

1. An array of a class of objects (Figure 6.2).

    ```
    Dates holidays [] = new Dates [4];
    ```

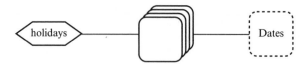

Figure 6.2 *An array of objects.*

2. A class containing an array and methods that operate on it (Figure 6.3).

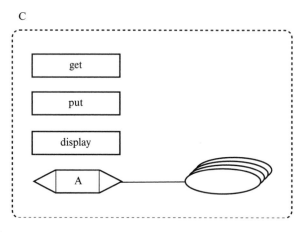

Figure 6.3 *A class containing an array.*

```
class C {

    int get (int i) {
        return A[i];
    }
    void put (int i, int x) {
        A[i] = x;
    }
    void display () {
        for (int i=0; i<A.length, i++)
            System.out.println(A[i]);
    }

    private int A [] = new int [4];
}
```

A is marked as private because in this class, the only access to the array is via the methods. Notice that A is not static: objects of class C can be declared, and each one will get its own instance of the A array.

3. A class containing methods that operate on array parameters (Figure 6.4).

C

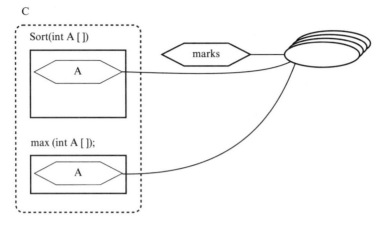

Figure 6.4 *Methods that have array parameters.*

```
int marks [] = new int [n];
Sort (marks);
System.out.println(max(marks));
```

Figure 6.4 shows that there exists only one array, `marks`. The methods in `C` have formal parameters which are array references. When the call is made, the reference is directed to `marks`, and the method operates on that array.

The first technique was used in Example 6.1. The others are illustrated in examples that follow.

Arrays as an abstraction

In this book, we delayed introducing arrays in order to emphasize the control operations in processing data. Very often, one will find a solution to a problem that makes use of an array, where in fact it is not strictly necessary. Is this wrong? No, it is not wrong; it merely represents a different abstraction of a solution.

Consider the following problem: we need to read in 20 values and find the smallest and the largest. There are two approaches to the solution:

- Read in the 20 values, keeping track of the smallest and largest 'on the fly'.

- Read the 20 values into an array, then scan the array through twice to find the smallest and then the largest values.

Instinctively, the first approach seems more efficient, and on the face of it, it is no more complicated than the second. But the balance changes if we take into account methods that we already have in stock.

Suppose we already have methods to calculate the minimum and maximum values from a given array. Then, the comparative algorithms would be as shown in Figure 6.5.

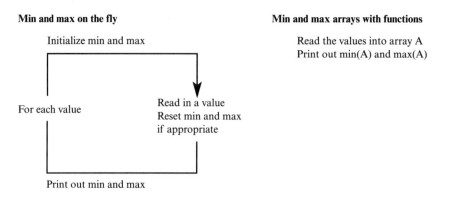

Min and max on the fly

Initialize min and max

For each value

Read in a value
Reset min and max
if appropriate

Print out min and max

Min and max arrays with functions

Read the values into array A
Print out min(A) and max(A)

Figure 6.5 *Two algorithms for finding the minimum and maximum in an array.*

The concept we are highlighting here is called **separation of concerns**. In the first algorithm, all the operations are mixed up in one process. In the second, we identify three concerns which can be handled separately in both time and space. These are the reading, finding the minimum and finding the maximum. The development of each process can proceed independently in time, and they are also identified separately in space as three different methods. In the long run, the second approach can enable us to reap the benefits of readability and be more easier to manage.

These ideas are illustrated in Example 6.2 which, strictly speaking, does not *need* an array, but which uses one to good effect to make an easily understandable program. On the other hand, later examples do need an arrays, as did Example 6.1.

EXAMPLE 6.2   Diving competitions

Problem The judging of diving competitions relies on judges from several countries. In order to avoid bias, such as judges rewarding competitors from their home country with higher scores, the result for a single dive is calculated as the average of all the scores, less the highest and lowest score. We would like to computerize these calculations.

Algorithm As outlined just above, there are two possible approaches to this problem. The three values required – that is, the sum, the lowest and the highest scores – can all be calculated on the fly while the scores are read in. Alternatively, we can read the values in and then assess them. Assuming we choose the second approach, then there are once again two options. These are to compute the three values simultaneously in a single loop, or to have three different loops, perhaps in three different methods, to calculate them. Since the calculations are really so simple, we shall adopt the first approach this time, and do them all together.

Class design The program breaks naturally into two parts. There is a class for reading in the scores, eliminating the outer ones, and so on. Then the main program is concerned with computing the final result for each dive.

The relationship between a class for judges and the array of scores falls into the second category of array and class interaction described above. The scores are kept in a class and we have two methods, `getScores` and `assessScores`, to read them in and total them. The broad outline of the class relationship is shown in Figure 6.6.

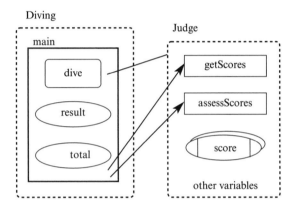

Figure 6.6 *Class diagram for the diving program.*

The array declaration is:

```
private int score [];
```

The number of judges is set up by the constructor, so that we also have the case here where the array is introduced, and then its size created later:

```
Judge (int n) {
  noofJudges = n;
  score = new int [noofJudges];
}
```

In addition, associated with the array are four other variables, notably:

```
int minJudge, maxJudge, minScore, maxScore;
```

While `score` is private and accessible only through the methods, these other variables can be accessed directly. It would be too tedious to create additional methods just to send them across as values: moderation in everything!

Program Here follows the class:

```
import java.io.*;
import javagently.*;

class Judge {
   /* The Judge Class by       J M Bishop Dec 1996
    * ---------------          Java 1.1
    * Stores and assesses diving scores.
    * All the variables are visible, except the
    * array of scores itself.
    * Illustrates arrays
    */

   int noofJudges;
   int minJudge, maxJudge, minScore, maxScore;

   Judge (int n) {
     noofJudges = n;
     score = new int [noofJudges]
   }

   void getScores (BufferedReader in) throws IOException {
     System.out.println("Type in the "+noofJudges
                        +" scores in order");
     for (int i=0; i < noofJudges; i++)
        score [i] = Text.readInt(in);
   }

  int assessScores () {
     minScore = 10;
     maxScore = 0;
     int sum = 0;
     for (int i=0; i < noofJudges; i++) {
       sum += score[i];
       if (score[i] <= minScore) {
         minScore = score[i]; minJudge = i;
       }
       if (score[i] > maxScore) {
         maxScore = score[i]; maxJudge = i;
       }
     }
     minJudge++; maxJudge++;
     return sum;
   }

   private int score [];

}
```

And here is the program. Notice that we use the `writeDouble` method of the `Text` class to ensure that we get only a reasonable number of fractional digits when the calculations are done. Three seems to be standard.

```
import javagently.*;

class Diving {
  /* The Diving program       by J M Bishop Dec 1996
   * ------------------       Java 1.1
   * Uses the Judge class to record the
   * correct scores for dives.
   * Illustrates class methods, arrays
   * and typed functions.
   */

  static final int noofDives = 3;

  public static void main (String [] args) throws IOException {

    System.out.println ("Diving Score Calculator\n" +
                        "=======================\n");

    BufferedReader in = Text.open(System.in);

    double result, total = 0;
    Judge dive = new Judge (8);

    for (int i=0; i < noofDives; i++) {
      System.out.println("Dive no: "+(i+1));
      dive.getScores (in);
      result = (double) (dive.assessScores ()
              - dive.minScore - dive.maxScore)
              / (double) (dive.noofJudges - 2);
      total += result;
      System.out.println("Scores " + dive.minScore
            + " from judge "
            + dive.minJudge + " and " + dive.maxScore
            + " from judge "
          + dive.maxJudge + " excluded.");
      System.out.println("Result is: " + Text.writeDouble(result,5,3));
    }
      System.out.println("Diving average is : "+
          Text.writeDouble(total/noofDives,5,3));
  }
}
```

Testing A test run of the program would produce:

```
Diving Score Calculator
=======================
Dive no: 1
Type in the 8 scores in order
7 8 7 4 8 6 9 7
Scores 4 from judge 4 and 9 from judge 7 excluded.
Result is: 7.166
Dive no: 2
Type in the 8 scores in order
8 8 8 8 4 8 10 8
Scores 4 from judge 5 and 10 from judge 6 excluded.
```

```
Result is: 8.000
Dive no: 3
Type in the 8 scores in order
7 7 7 7 7 7 7 7
Scores 7 from judge 8 and 7 from judge 1 excluded.
Result is: 7.000
Diving average is : 7.388
```

6.2 Tables

Tables appear commonly in computer applications. The data is arranged in rows and columns. Since Java permits array elements to be of any type, including arrays themselves, arrays of multiple dimensions can be built up, known as a multi-dimensional arrays. Most of the time, through there will not be more than two dimensions, and the resulting structure is known as a matrix. For a typical matrix such as that shown in Figure 6.7, the declaration would be:

```
double matrix [][] = new double [4][5];
```

Rows are always mentioned first in the declaration. This enables a single row of the matrix to be represented. For example,

```
matrix [3]
```

would give the shaded row in Figure 6.7. Each element of the row can be selected by indexing twice, as in:

```
matrix [3] [1]
```

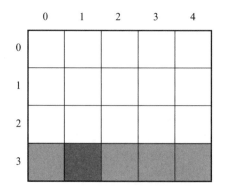

Figure 6.7 *A typical matrix.*

which would give the darker element. To swap two rows, *i* and *j*, of the matrix, we could say:

```
int row [] = new int [5];
row = matrix[i];
matrix[i] = matrix[j];
matrix[j] = row;
```

EXAMPLE 6.3 Gold exploration

Problem Savanna Exploration Inc. has obtained data of infrared readings of a portion of desert where gold is believed to be present. The data should show up the boundaries of a gold reef, based on readings that are greater than the average of those around them. Can you help find the gold?

Solution The map of the readings can be considered, a point at a time, and a corresponding map printed out showing those with higher than average infrared levels. For example, given the following data on a sample 8×8 grid:

```
21 21 22 30 40 21 34 45
21 22 23 30 45 21 37 40
22 23 24 45 46 47 38 39
22 23 24 35 46 47 38 38
23 24 25 36 46 49 37 36
23 24 25 37 39 48 36 35
23 24 25 25 26 25 26 25
23 25 26 27 28 29 30 31
```

we could deduce the corresponding map:

```
******* Savanna Exploration Inc. *****
Where is your gold map? maly.dat
maly.dat does not exist.
Try again.
mali.dat
We shall find gold!
Map of possible boundaries of the gold reef
===========================================
   0  1  2  3  4  5  6  7
0
1               *     *
2      *     *  *  *
3               *  *
4      *     *  *  *
5            *     *
6
7
Good luck prospecting!
```

Algorithm The high-level algorithm is:

> **Gold exploration**
> Read in the data
> Assess each point, creating the corresponding map of blanks and asterisks
> Print the map

Each of these steps can be refined into double loops scanning the whole matrix. For example, assessing a point consists of adding up the values to its north, south, east and west and dividing by 4. If the point itself has a higher reading than its neighbours, we mark it as part of the reef on the map. Thus there are two matrices: data and map.

```
point = data[i][j];
average = (data[i-1][j]+data[i+1][j]
              +data[i][j-1]+data[i][j+1])/4;
if (point > average) map[i][j] = cover;
```

We must also consider how to deal with data points on the edge of the grid. We shall assume that there is sufficient redundancy in the data to allow us to ignore the points on the boundary. Thus we run the assessing loops from 1 to rowmax-1 and 1 to colmax-1 respectively.

Class design The design consists of two classes: one concerned with the gold maps, and one concerned with activating them. The design of the Gold class is once again category two: there is a class containing arrays with methods that can be called to act upon them. The arrays and all their supporting variables and constants are private as there is no need for them to be known outside the class. The class diagram is very similar to that of Example 6.2. This time you are encouraged to draw it yourself.

Program The Gold class is:

```
import java.io.*;
import javagently.*;

class Gold {

    /* The Gold class       by J M Bishop    Jan 1997
     * --------------             Java 1.1
     * Transforms raw geological
     * readings into a character map of a possible
     * gold reef.
     * Illustrates two different multi-dimensional
     * arrays in a class.
     */

    Gold (int r, int c) {
        rowmax = r;
        colmax = c;
```

```
      data = new double [rowmax] [colmax];
      map = new char [rowmax] [colmax];
    }
    void readIn (DataInputStream in) throws IOException {
      for (int i=0; i<rowmax; i++)
        for (int j=0; j<colmax; j++)
          data[i][j] = Text.readDouble(in);
    }

    void assess () {
      double point, average;
      for (int i=0; i<rowmax; i++)
        for (int j=0; j<colmax; j++)
          map[i][j] = blank;
      for (int i=1; i<rowmax-1; i++)
        for (int j=1; j<colmax-1; j++) {
          point = data[i][j];
          average = (data[i-1][j]+data[i+1][j]
                    +data[i][j+-1]+data[i][j+1])/4;
          if (point > average) map[i][j]=cover;
      }
    }

    void print () {
      System.out.println("Map of possible boundaries " +
                    "of the gold reef");
      System.out.println("===============================" +
            "=============\n");
      for (int j=0; j<colmax; j++) System.out.print(j+" ");
      System.out.println();
      for (int i=0; i<rowmax; i++) {
        System.out.print(i+" ");
        for (int j=0; j<colmax; j++)
          System.out.print(map[i][j]+" ");
        System.out.println();
      }
      System.out.println("Good luck prospecting!");
    }

    private int rowmax, colmax;
    private double data [][];
    private char map [][];
    private static final char blank = ' ';
    private static final char cover = '*';
}
```

Then calling it we have the short Explore class, which makes use of the file opening class we developed in Case Study 2. If a file is not found, we open up a default map which we know is around, called gold.dat.

```
import java.io.*;
import myutilities.*;
import javagently.*;
```

```
class Explore {

  public static void main (String [] args) throws IOException {

    System.out.println("******* Savanna Exploration Inc. *****");
    System.out.print("Where is your gold map? ");
    try {
      BufferedReader fin = FileMan.open();
    } catch (FileNotFoundException e) {
      BufferedReader fin = Text.open("gold.dat");
      System.out.println("Using my own map in gold.dat.");
    }
    System.out.println("We shall find gold!");

    Gold mine = new Gold (8,8);
    mine.readIn(fin);
    mine.assess();
    mine.print();
  }
}
```

Only one instance of the Gold class is created, but of course we could have several, and thus process several sets of data and make several maps.

Testing The expected output to the file has already been given.

The next example illustrates the use of the third technique for the array–class interaction that we mentioned. It is typical of statistical type programs, where a bank of functions is programmed separately for arrays and matrices which are passed as parameters. Fortunately, the reference facility that Java uses for arrays enables the methods to be written independently of the size of the arrays, thus achieving considerable generality. In Chapter 9 we shall see how this generality can be extended to the types of the elements as well.

EXAMPLE 6.4   Rainfall statistics

Problem The Savanna Weather Department has kept statistics on monthly rainfall figures for the past 20 years. Now it would like to calculate:

- the average rainfall for each month, and
- the standard deviation for each month.

Solution The table of rainfall figures that is provided by a clerk will look something like this:

Year	Jan	Feb	Mar	Apr	May	Jun	Jul	Aug	Sep	Oct	Nov	Dec
1987	20	22	17	14	5	0	0	0	7	12	30	20
1988	22	24	19	12	0	0	3	0	8	15	20	25
1989	17	17	17	15	0	0	0	0	6	17	8	20
1990	10	10	10	5	0	0	0	0	0	12	10	15
1991	10	10	10	5	0	0	0	0	0	12	10	15
1992	20	22	17	14	5	0	0	0	7	12	30	20
1993	22	24	19	12	0	0	3	0	8	15	20	25
1994	17	17	17	15	0	0	0	0	6	17	8	20
1995	25	30	25	15	7	0	0	0	20	15	20	30
1996	25	30	25	15	7	0	0	0	20	15	20	30

The data can be read in by drawing such a table on the screen and letting the user type in each value in turn, or by reading the values from a file. As the values are read in, they are stored in a matrix which is indexed by both the months and the years. Since the rainfall for a month seems to be the crucial figure, the matrix should be structured so that a whole column can be moved around at once. In other words, we would like to represent the matrix as in Figure 6.8.

To do this, we make months the first subscript, and the range of years the second, that is:

```
static final int maxyear = 7;
double rainTable [] [] = new double [12][maxyear];
```

`rainTable[5]` then gives all rainfall for all the available years for June (remember arrays start at 0, so June is 5). This is the shaded area in Figure 6.8.

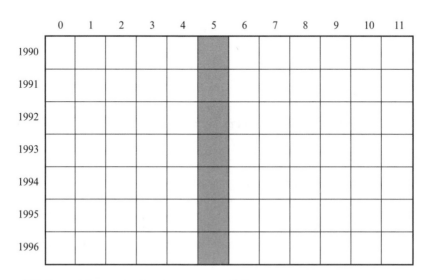

Figure 6.8 *Part of the matrix for storing rainfall data.*

Once the rainfall figures are safely in the matrix, methods can be designed to perform the required calculations. Each will make use of the matrix and be passed a column of one month's rainfall figures.

Solution Some elementary statistics is in order at this point. If we have a set of measurements x_i we can analyse them to find the mean $\bar{x}$ which gives the average measurement, and the standard deviation s, which shows the amount by which measurements are likely to differ from the mean. In other words, the standard deviation indicates the spread of the measurements.

The mean of a set of measurements x_i $(i = 1, n)$ is defined to be:

$$\bar{x} = \frac{\sum\limits_{i=1}^{n} x_i}{n}$$

and the formula for the standard deviation is:

$$s = \sqrt{\frac{\sum\limits_{i=1}^{n} (x_i - \bar{x})^2}{n-1}}$$

We can allow for expected errors and intrinsic randomness by saying that the result of a set of measurements will be within a certain standard deviation. In many cases we can say that the true result is in the range $x \pm 2s$: that is, the mean plus or minus twice the standard deviation.

Class design Calculating the mean – or average – could be done fairly simply as we read in each new value. However, because the formula for the standard deviation uses the mean, we have to calculate it after the mean has been arrived at. Thus, we store the values in an array, and process them from there in a second stage. If we adopt technique three for class–array interaction and have the matrix in the main class, with columns of it being repeatedly passed as parameters to methods in another class, then the method to calculate the monthly average could be declared as:

```
static double monthlyAverage (double monthlyRain [], int n)
```

Alternatively, the declaration could be:

```
double monthlyAverage (int m, int n) ;
```

where the first parameter indicates an index into the rain table, and the rain table is stored in the class itself (technique two). If the whole column is sent, accessing the elements is by single indexing. If the index alone is sent as a parameter, then the method has to perform double indexing to get to each element. On balance, technique three is a better choice.

If the value calculated by monthlyAverage is assigned to a variable a, it can be passed to the next method which uses it to calculate the standard deviation. The declaration for this function is therefore:

```
double monthlyStdDev
    (double monthlyRain [], int n, double mean);
```

Program This version of the program assumes input from a file called rain.dat with output to rain.out. First of all, here is the Rain class with the two statistical methods.

```
class Rain {

  /* The Rain class      by J M Bishop    Jan 1997
   * --------------       Java 1.1
   * Has methods for calculating the mean and standard
   * deviation.
   * Illustrates passing arrays as parameters.
   */

  static double monthlyAverage (double monthlyRain [], int n) {
    double total = 0;
    for (int y=0; y<n; y++)
      total += monthlyRain[y];
    return total / n;
  }

  static double monthlyStdDev (double monthlyRain [],
                               int n, double mean) {
    double total = 0;
    for (int y=0; y<n; y++)
      total += (mean-monthlyRain[y])*(mean-monthlyRain[y]);
    return Math.sqrt(total/(n-1));
  }
}
```

And here is the main class that declares the matrix, reads in the data, and then makes use of the Rain class.

```
import java.io.*;
import javagently.*;

class Weather {

  /* The Weather program      by J M Bishop Jan 1997
   * Calculates mean and standard deviation of rainfall
   * for each month over the number of years provided.
   * Illustrates handling of a matrix and passing columns
   * as parameters.
   * The data must be in the form:
   * year followed by the 12 rainfall figures for
   * the months of that year.
   */
```

```
static int startYear, endYear = 0;
static double rainTable [] [] = new double [12] [70];

static void readIn () throws IOException {

  BufferedReader fin = Text.open("rain.dat");

  int actualYear = 0; // e.g. 1985
  int yearIndex = 0;

  // The actual years are read in and might not be sorted
  // or contiguous. The yearIndex starts at 0 and is used
  // to store the data in an orderly manner.

  try {
    while (true) {
      actualYear = Text.readInt(fin);
      System.out.print(actualYear +" ");
      if (yearIndex == 0) startYear = actualYear;
      for (int m = 0; m<12; m++) {
        rainTable[m][yearIndex] = Text.readDouble(fin);
        System.out.print(
            Text.writeDouble(rainTable[m][yearIndex],5,0));
      }
      System.out.println();
      yearIndex++;
    }
  }
  catch (EOFException e) {

    // Pick up the last year of data read in.
    endYear = actualYear;
    System.out.println("Data read for "+startyear+" to "+
        endyear+"\n\n");
  }
}

static void showResults () {
  System.out.println("Rainfall statistics for " +
    startYear + " to " + endYear);
  System.out.println("=========================" +
      "============\n");
  System.out.println("Month\tMean\tStd Deviation");
  int nyears = endYear-startYear+1;
  double a, s;
  for (int m=0; m<12; m++) {
    a = Rain.monthlyAverage (rainTable[m], nyears);
    s = Rain.monthlyStdDev (rainTable[m], nyears, a);
    System.out.println(Text.writeInt(m+1,2)
              +Text.writeDouble(a,11,2)
              +Text.writeDouble(s,10,4));
  }
}
```

```
public static void main (String [] args) throws IOException {
  readIn ();
  showResults ();
}
}
```

Testing For the data shown above, the output to the file would be:

1987	20	22	17	14	5	0	0	0	7	12	30	20
1988	22	24	19	12	0	0	3	0	8	15	20	25
1989	17	17	17	15	0	0	0	0	6	17	8	20
1990	10	10	10	5	0	0	0	0	0	12	10	15
1991	20	22	17	14	5	0	0	0	7	12	30	20
1992	22	24	19	12	0	0	3	0	8	15	20	25
1993	17	17	17	15	0	0	0	0	6	17	8	20
1994	25	30	25	15	7	0	0	0	20	15	20	30
1995	25	30	25	15	7	0	0	0	20	15	20	30
1996	10	10	10	5	0	0	0	0	0	12	10	45

```
Data read for 1985 to 1994

Rainfall statistics for 1987 to 1996
====================================
Month   Mean    Std Deviation
  1     18.80   5.3913
  2     20.60   7.1055
  3     17.60   5.0596
  4     12.20   3.9665
  5      2.40   3.1692
  6      0.00   0.0000
  7      0.60   1.2649
  8      0.00   0.0000
  9      8.19   6.8766
 10     14.20   2.0439
 11     17.60   8.3692
 12     25.00   8.4983
```

The use of `writeInt` and `writeDouble` enabled us to output a nice table again.
Example 10.2 and Plate 6 show this output graphically.

6.3 Sorting and searching

Sorting and searching are very common operations in computing, and many systems
provide high-level commands that enable data to be sorted or searched in any specified
way. These commands rely on one of a number of algorithms, and every programmer
should know at least one sorting algorithm and one searching algorithm by heart. We
start by introducing simple ones: selection sort, which performs in time proportional
to the square of the number of items being sorted, and linear search which is propor-
tinal to the number of items, as its name suggests. Other algorithms (for example,

Quicksort and binary search) perform faster, but are perhaps more difficult to understand and remember. They are covered in Chapter 15.

Selection sort

Sorting items means moving them around in a methodical way until they are all in order. A method used by some card players is to sort cards by holding them in the right hand, finding the lowest one and taking it out into the left hand, then finding the next lowest and taking it out, until all the cards have been selected, and the left hand holds the cards in order. The following sequence illustrates how this method works.

Left hand	**Right hand**
	7 3 9 0 2 5
0	7 3 9 – 2 5
0 2	7 3 9 – – 5
0 2 3	7 – 9 – – 5
0 2 3 5	7 – 9 – – –
0 2 3 5 7	– – 9 – – –
0 2 3 5 7 9	– – – – – –

We could implement this by having two arrays and picking the numbers out of one, adding them to the other. However, there is a way of keeping both lists in the same array, the one growing as the other shrinks. Each time an element is picked out, the gap it leaves is moved to one end, thus creating a contiguous area, which is used to hold the new list. The move is done by a simple swap with the leftmost element of the right hand. So, the example would proceed as follows:

Left hand	**Right hand**
	7 3 9 0 2 5
0	3 9 7 2 5
0 2	9 7 3 5
0 2 3	7 9 5
0 2 3 5	9 7
0 2 3 5 7	9
0 2 3 5 7 9	

The underlined digits are those that moved at each phase. Each time, a reduced list is considered, until only one element is left. The algorithm can be phrased more precisely as shown in Figure 6.9.

Because sorting is clearly going to be useful in many contexts, it makes sense to put it in a method from the beginning. The parameters would be the array to be sorted, and the number of items that are active in it. Of course, we shall have to say in the formal parameter what type of items are being sorted. In Section 9.2 we explain how we can relax this requirement.

Selection sort

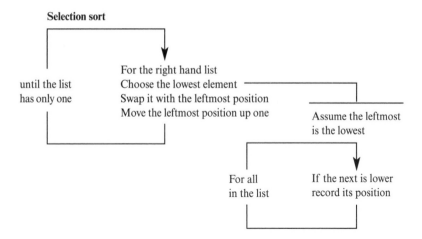

Figure 6.9 *Algorithm for selection sort.*

```
static void selectionSort (double [ ] a, int n) {
  double temp;
  int chosen;

  for (int leftmost = 0; leftmost < n-1; leftmost++) {
    chosen = leftmost;
    for (int j = leftmost+1; j < n; j++)
      if (a[j] < a[chosen]) chosen = j;
    temp = a[chosen];
    a[chosen] = a[leftmost];
    a[leftmost] = temp;
  }
}
```

Sorting is a frequent requirement in computing, and it is useful to have a sorting algorithm handy. The above algorithm can be applied to arrays of any size, and containing any elements, and can be used to sort in descending order just by changing the comparison from < to >. Notice, however, that if we wish to sort from highest to lowest, then the value that moves to the left each time will be the largest, not the smallest. The example sort given here sorts an array of doubles, and uses the < operator for the comparison. If the items being sorted are objects, then < will not work and will need to be replaced by a method, typically called lessThan or compareTo.

Searching

A simple linear search involves proceeding through an array until an item is found or until the end of the array is reached. If we only want to return whether or not the item is there, then a boolean method does the trick, as in:

```
boolean search (double[] a, int n, double x) {
  for (int i = 0; i < n; i++)
```

```
        if (x == a[i]) return true;
      return false;
   }
```

However, if we also want to return where in the array the item was found (so that we can update it, perhaps) then a more complex method is needed. We leave this to Section 15.2, as the above is sufficient as a companion to the sort for now.

EXAMPLE 6.5   Sorting words in a file

Problem   The mandate is : 'illustrate sorting and searching'.

Solution   In this example, we do not have a particular problem to solve, but need to create the problem to fit a technique we have learnt. A suitable scenario would be to read in every word of a file, construct an array containing only the unique words, sort the array and print it.

Algorithm   In diagrammatic terms, Figure 6.10 illustrates the part of the program that creates the array of unique words.

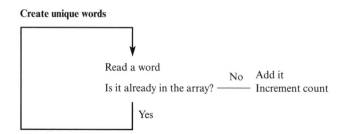

Figure 6.10 *Algorithm for creating an array of unique words.*

After this, we print the array, call the sort, and print again.

Program   In using `selectionSort`, we shall be sorting strings. As will be fully discussed in the next chapter, < cannot be used on `String`. Instead we need the `compareTo` method, which has the following results:

```
a.compareTo(b)    a less than b       result will be negative
                  a same as b         result will be 0
                  a greater than b    result will be positive
```

The same method will be used in the search. The program follows.

```
import java.io.*;
import javagently.*;
import myutilities.*;


public class SortWords {

    /* The Sort Words program    by J M Bishop  Feb 1997
     *                           Java 1.1 October 1997
     *
     * Reads in and then sorts up to 100
     * different words.
     * Illustrates sorting and searching an array.
     */

    static void selectionSort(String[] a, int n) {
        String temp;
        int chosen;

        for (int leftmost = 0; leftmost < n-1; leftmost++) {
            chosen = leftmost;
            for (int j = leftmost+1; j < n; j++)
                if (a[j].compareTo(a[chosen])<0)
                    chosen = j;
            temp = a[chosen];
            a[chosen] = a[leftmost];
            a[leftmost] = temp;
        }
    }

    static boolean search (String[] a, int n, String x) {
        for (int i = 0; i < n; i++)
            if (x.compareTo(a[i])==0) return true;
        return false;
    }

    static void display(String[] a, int n) {
        for (int i = 0; i < n; i++) {
            System.out.print(a[i]+"\t");
            if (i>0 && i % 7 == 0) System.out.println();
        }
    }

    public static void main(String[] args) throws IOException {

        String [] group = new String[100];
        System.out.print("Where are the words? ");
        BufferedReader fin = FileMan.open();

        int count=0;
        try {
            while (count < 100) {
                String word = Text.readString(fin);
```

(handwritten annotations): array fill ← ; ← no of elems in array.

(handwritten annotation): ← 7 elems per line

(handwritten annotation): FileReader f = new FR (filename) Buffered Reader fin = new BR (f).

(handwritten annotation): word = fin. Readline ()

(handwritten annotations: "array", "0", "static", "method returns boolean.", "while group loop")

```
      if (! search(group,count,word)) {
         group[count] = word;
         count ++;
      }
   }
} catch (EOFException e) {
   System.out.println(count + " words read.\n\n");
}

System.out.print("Original\n");
System.out.print("========\n");
display(group,count);

selectionSort(group, count);

System.out.print("\n\nSorted\n");
System.out.print("======\n");
display(group,count);
   }
}
```

Testing We have set up the program to use `FileMan.open` to open the file, so we can supply any data we like. Just for interest's sake, the test run below uses the selection sort in a file. In order to maximize the common words, we reorganized the file so that there were spaces between words and symbols. The results are quite interesting.

```
Where are the words? sort.java
30 words read.
Original
========
static   void  selectionSort  (           String     [ ]        a
,        int   n              )           {          temp        ;
chosen   for   leftmost       =           0          <           -
1        ++    j              +           if         .           compareTo
}


Sorted
======
(        )     +              ++          ,          -           .           0
1        ;     <              =           String     [           ]
a        chosen  compareTo    for         if         int         j
leftmost n     selectionSort              static     temp        void        {
}
```

The output gives some idea of Java's 'collating sequence', in other words how it sorts operators and letters and numbers.

6.4 Dictionaries

In this section we look at a very useful extension of the table concept, that of the dictionary. A dictionary, as the name suggests, has the following properties:

- keys are mapped to values,
- keys and values can be anything,
- there is a fast way of finding a key.

In a real dictionary, words are mapped to explanations, and the speed of searching is obtained because the keys are sorted alphabetically. Knowing this, we can arrive very rapidly at the right place for a word (see Section 15.2 for more on searching).

The problem is that arrays as we have studied them up to now are inadequate to represent the dictionary concept. There are several drawbacks to arrays:

- they are of a fixed size, set inside the program, and cannot grow;
- the index is always an integer;
- the index always starts at zero.

The fixed size restriction can be sidestepped by making the array very large, and working within it. We did this in the previous example (Example 6.5). Although the array was defined as being 100 long, we kept an internal tally of the number of used elements in it, which hovered around 30.

For the second restriction, consider the following, fairly common, requirement: we would like to store values for each of the letters of the alphabet. An array would be the ideal choice, but we cannot index one with char, nor can we easily convert chars to integers and back.

Finally, Example 6.4 (Rainfall statistics) has already shown that even if the index is an integer, there are cases where the data does not start from zero. Adjustments are necessary to fit it into a zero-starting array.

Fortunately, Java provides more sophisticated array handling facilities in the form of standard classes in the `java.util` package. The first class, `Vector`, mirrors the array idea, but removes the fixed size restriction. The second class, `Hashtable` (based on class `Dictionary`), provides a full mapping service in what is also known as an **associative array**.

The `Vector` class

The `Vector` class defines sequences of objects where the sequence can grow in size as required. In fact, it grows automatically, without even being explicitly asked to! Objects are put in and taken out of the vector using methods. A method is also used to access elements. We shall not look further at vectors in this chapter for two reasons: firstly, the next class is more general and interesting, and, secondly, the terminology used for defining vectors is quite different from Java's other classes, and is generally considered to be most confusing.

Hash tables

What we really want is a dynamically sized structure, which also has the property that the indices can be, well, anything. Java's hash tables fit this bill completely. A hash table is an collection of pairs of items (key,value). The key is the index (in array terms) and the value is what is associated with the key. We can therefore see that an array is a special case of a hash table, with the key being of type int. With hash tables, though, the key can be of any type or class, including double, String, Students, Dates or whatever. Figure 6.11 illustrates a hash table.

Key	Value
plums	soft, red, deciduous fruit
oranges	orange, sweet, citrus fruit
lemons	yellow, tart, citrus fruit
apples	red, green or yellow hard deciduous fruit
kiwis	green, interesting fruit

Figure 6.11 *An example of a dictionary or hash table.*

If we compare Figure 6.11 with the example shown in Figure 6.8, we notice that the essential difference is that with an array (or matrix) the indices are external to the table, whereas here they are part of it – the key part. Also, values are not inserted contiguously from the beginning: there may be gaps. This does not affect the access of the data, as we shall see. In fact, it makes it faster!

A word about the term 'hash' table. Hash refers to the fact that the items are not stored sequentially in the table, but in a manner that makes them efficient to retrieve. In fact, in a fairly empty table, the efficiency can approach that of an array. As a result, hash tables are not ordered by key, and if we print out what is in one, the items will appear in some seemingly random order. It is a pity that we cannot continue to use the word dictionary, as this better describes what we are after, but it is better to be specific.

Some of the ways of declaring and manipulating a hash table are summarized in the form:

Hash table declaration and access

```
Hashtable name = new Hashtable ( );
void      put (Object key, Object value);
Object    get (Object key);
boolean   containsKey (Object key);
boolean   contains (Object value);
void      remove (Object key);
```

The class `Object` is defined by Java as the superclass of all classes. There will be more about it in the next three chapters. In the meantime all we need to know is that `Hash-table` is defined based on `Object` so that it can be used with any class.

For example, suppose we wish to associate names with dates. We could do the following:

```
Hashtable holidays = new Hashtable ();
Dates d;

holidays.put ("Christmas", new Date (1998,12,25));
holidays.put ("New Year", new Date (1998,1,1));
d = (Dates) holidays.get ("Christmas");
```

The last statement will successfully get the date 25 Dec 1997 out of the table. But why does the cast to `(Dates)` appear in the assignment? The reason is that hash tables are potentially available for any kinds of objects. The result type of a `get` is `Object`. In order to ensure that we have obtained an object of type `Dates`, Java requires that we **cast** the `Object`. The format for doing this is the same as for casting primitive types, which we discussed in Section 3.2. There is more on casting in Section 8.3.

Envelopes

One of the strict rules in Java is that variables and objects cannot be mixed. For most of the time, this causes little inconvenience, but there are times when a standard package, such as `HashTable`, requires an object, and we wish to send it, say, a variable of type `int`. In order to do so, we first place it in what is known as an **envelope** class, thus making it into an object. The envelope class provides access to the value and also has various conversion methods available.

The Java `lang` package has envelope classes associated with each of the primitive types, which classes are called `Boolean`, `Character`, `Double`, `Float`, `Integer` and `Long` (notice the capital letters). As their names suggest, they provide class-level versions of their respective primitive data types.

As an example, the important methods of the `Integer` class are given in the following form:

```
Integer and int conversions

// constructor
   Integer (int value);
// class methods
   static  Integer valueOf (String s);
   static  String  toString (int i);
   static  int     parseInt (String s);
// instance method
   int     intValue ();
```

The constructor and the instance method provide for moving back and forth between types and classes. Thus if i is an `int`,

```
Integer Iobj = new Integer (i);
```

makes an object out of it. To get the `int` back in order, say, to print it, we use:

```
System.out.println(Iobj.intValue());
```

The other selected methods convert from strings and back. The other envelope classes have corresponding methods.

Enumerations

Another class that is closely associated with hash tables is `Enumeration`. In fact, `Enumeration` is not a class: it is a special kind of class called an interface.[2] Interfaces are discussed in Section 9.2, but for now we can just make use of the facilities offered for the purposes of enhancing the power of hash tables.

Enumerations provide a means for iterating over a collection of objects. There are only two methods:

Enumerations

```
Object   nextElement ();
boolean hasMoreElements ();
```

Once we declare an enumeration, `nextElement` will repeatedly provide the next element, and we can do this until `hasMoreElements` becomes false. For example, if `table` is a `Hashtable` and has been filled with keys that are `Strings` (the type of the values does not matter at this point), then the loop for printing out the keys will be

```
System.out.println("In the table");
for (Enumeration e = table.keys(); e.hasMoreElements();) {
   String s = (String) e.nextElement();
   System.out.println(s);
}
```

Notice that because of the casting required (as explained just above), the update part of the loop is done as a separate assignment in the body, rather than with the initialize and check parts, as is usual. Putting this all together, we can tackle Example 6.6.

EXAMPLE 6.6   Student marker

Problem We would like to store student marks and query them, based on names.

---

[2] A term commonly used in other languages for an enumeration is an **interator**.

Solution Here we have a classic case for a hash table. The names and marks can be read in and each pair can be put in the hash table. Then querying is a simple `get` operation, perhaps preceded by a `containsKey`, just to check that the name was spelt correctly. We shall assume that there are six marks per student and that the program must in addition calculate a final mark based on a weighted average. This gives us more scope to practise arrays as well.

Class design There should obviously be a student class, with the three items, name, marks and final mark. The technique for array–class interaction is the first one: the table is declared as being a collection of objects of the class `Student`. The class diagram would be as shown in Figure 6.12.

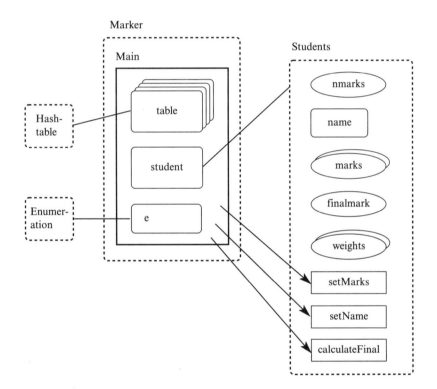

Figure 6.12 *Class diagram for the student marks program.*

Program Here is the `Student` class:

```
import java.io.*;
import javagently.*;

public class Students {

        /* The Students class    by J M Bishop  Dec 1996
        *                        Java 1.1 October 1997
```

```
    * Stores names and 7 marks.
    * Everything is directly accessible
    * by users of the class.
    */

   static final int nMarks = 6;
   String name;
   int[] marks = new int[nMarks];
   int finalMark;
   int[] weights = { 5, 10, 5, 15, 15, 50 };
   public Students() {
   }

   void setMarks(BufferedReader in) throws IOException {
       for (int i = 0; i < nMarks; i++)
           marks[i] = Text.readInt(in);
   }

   void setName(BufferedReader in) throws IOException {
       name = Text.readString(in)+" "+Text.readString(in);
   }

   void calculateFinal () {
       finalMark = 0;
       for (int i = 0; i < nMarks; i++)
           finalMark += marks[i]*weights[i];
       finalMark = finalMark/100;
   }

}
```

The Marker program follows the lines set out above. Of interest are the lines where objects from the hash table are retrieved, and a type cast must be done.

```
import java.io.*;
import java.util.*;
import javagently.*;

public class Marker {

    /* The Marker Program      by J M Bishop  Dec 1996
     *                          Java 1.1 October 1997
     * Registers the marks of students and enables them to be queried.
     * Illustrates the use of a hash table
     */

    public static void main(String[] args) throws IOException {

        BufferedReader fin = Text.open("marks.dat");
        BufferedReader in = Text.open(System.in);

        Hashtable table = new Hashtable(20);

        for (int i = 0; i < 10; i++) {
            Students student = new Students();
```

```
        student.setName(fin);
        student.setMarks(fin);
        student.calculateFinal();
        table.put(student.name, new Integer(student.finalMark));
    }

    System.out.println("In the table are");
    for (Enumeration e = table.keys(); e.hasMoreElements();) {
        String name = (String)e.nextElement();
        System.out.println(name);
    }

    while (true) {
        try {
            System.out.print("Whose mark would you like to know?");
            String s = Text.readString(in)+" "+Text.readString(in);
            if (table.containsKey(s)) {
                Integer result = (Integer) table.get(s)
                System.out.println((result.intValue()));
            } else {
                System.out.println("Sorry, try again.");
            }
        } catch (EOFException e) {
            break;
        }
    }
  }
}
```

Testing The following test was run on a set of test data:

```
In the table
Derrick Kourie
Mary Brown
John Botha
Carol Steele
Peter Beukes
Francois Jacot
Elizabeth Rogers
Louis Botha
Jean Barkhuizen
William Bishop
Whose mark would you like to know? Mary Brown
85
Whose mark would you like to know? William Bishop
80
Whose mark would you like to know? Carol Steele
81
Whose mark would you like to know? Francios Jacot
Sorry, try again.
Whose mark would you like to know? Francois Jacot
73
Whose mark would you like to know?
```

The program could detect that Francios Jacot – a misspelling – was not in the table, through the `containsKey` call, and reacted appropriately.

SUMMARY

Arrays provide for multiple values referred to by the same name. Arrays in Java are of fixed size, but they can have multiple dimensions. There are several ways in which arrays and classes interact, and the correct technique must be chosen for each problem's solution. A useful feature in Java is the ability to declare a method with an array parameter whose length is not specified. Sorting also makes use of arrays, and the selection sort is explained and presented in as general a way as possible.

Finally, we consider how the restrictions of fixed size arrays as well as indexing only with integers can be relaxed. The best answer is to use Java's hash tables which can store values of any class, indexed by any other class, and enable the table to be interrogated and values or keys retrieved. To iterate through the hash tables, we use the enumeration interface supplied along with hash.

QUIZ

6.1   Draw diagrams to show the references and storage created by the following declarations:

```
int counters [] = new int [5];
String names [] = {"Adam", "Eve", "Joseph", "Sarah"};
```

6.2   Define each of the following terms: array, table, matrix, vector, dictionary.

6.3   In Example 6.2 (Diving competitions), the array of scores is declared as:

```
private int score [];
```

Where is it given a length and by which class?

6.4   What is wrong with the following statements?

```
int A [] = new int A[10];
System.out.println (A[A.length()]);
```

6.5   We have declared an array:

```
double B [] = new double [100];
```

Would it be possible to send it to the `monthlyAverage` method defined in Example 6.4 to calculate the mean and, if so, what would the call look like?

6.6   If `"yen"` and 167.9 form a pair of a double number, with a string key, what would be the statement required to put the pair into a hash table called `exchangeRates`? What would be the statement required to get the 167.9 out again and print it, given the key `"yen"`?

6.7   In the multi-dimensional array shown in Figure 6.8, which will be the first index, the rows or the columns?

6.8   In which package can the `Hashtable` class be found?

6.9   The following statements will not compile. What is wrong? Can you fix them?

```
Hashtable holidays = new Hashtable ();
holidays.put ("Foundation Day", new Dates (97,6,6));
Dates d = holidays.get ("Foundation Day");
```

6.10   What error message is printed by Java if you try to access an array with an invalid index?

PROBLEMS

6.1 **Mains voltage.** The mains voltage supplied by a substation is measured at hourly intervals over a 72 hour period, and a report made. Write a program to read in the 72 readings and determine:

- the mean voltage measured;
- the hours at which the recorded voltage varies from the mean by more than 10%;
- any adjacent hours when the change from one reading to the next is greater than 15% of the mean value.

Include in your program an option to display a histogram of the voltage over the 72 hours, using the method developed in Example 3.5.

6.2 **Useful methods.** Write a class with methods which take an array of integers as one of their parameters and do the following:

- find the maximum of all the elements;
- determine whether all the quantities in the array are equal;
- determine the number of times a value greater than a given level occurs.

We would also like to add the following facilities:

- find the maximum of all the elements, plus all the positions where it occurs;
- determine the range of values spanned by the array.

Discuss why this may be more difficult and propose a class–array design that might be able to provide for the methods.

6.3 **Sum of squares.** Write a typed method which is given two integers as parameters, and returns as its value the sum of the squares of the numbers between and inclusive of the two parameters. Show how to call the method to print the value of $\sum i^2$ where i runs from 1 to 10. How would the program change if the data was to be read in and stored initially in an array?

6.4 **Standard passes.** The Senate at Savanna University has decreed that at least 75% of students in each course must pass. This means that the pass mark for each course will differ. Write a program that will read in a file of marks and determine the highest pass such that the Senate's rule applies.

6.5 **Judges' countries.** In Example 6.2, instead of printing out the judges' numbers, we would like to print out the country from which they come. Use an array to set up a list of country names for the judges on duty, and adapt the program to make the output more explanatory. Consider carefully whether to have an array of countries in `Judge` alongside the scores, or whether to create another class consisting of a name and a score.

6.6 **Population increase.** Since 1980, the Savanna population statistics have been stored on a computer file, with each line containing the year followed by the total people counted for that year. Write a program that will read this file and find the two consecutive years in which there was the greatest percentage increase in population. The data is not guaranteed to be in strict year order and may need to be sorted first.

6.7 **Bilingual calendars**. Design a program to print out a calendar, one month underneath each other. Then using hash tables, set up versions for the months and days of the week in another language (say, French, Spanish or German), and let the user select which language the calendar should be printed in.

6.8 **Bureau de change** Every day Savanna Bank posts exhange rates on the web on www.res-bank.co.za. The data is on a web page and can be selected as a table in any currency. For example, if we chose ZAR (South African Rands), the start of the table would look like this:

```
Currency unit                          ZAR/Unit           Units/ZAR
==============================     ==================     ================
DZD Algerian Dinars                    0.777              12.9
USD American Dollar                     4.556              0.2195
ARP Argentinian Pesos                   4.556              0.2195
AUD Australian Dollars                  3.356              0.2980
ATS Austrian Schillings                 0.3614             2.767
BSD Bahamian Dollars                    4.556              0.2195
BBD Barbados Dollars                    2.265              0.4415
DEF Belgian Francs                      0.1231             8.121
```

The Bank would like to provide a simple program to interact with users, reading in a currency and amount, and outputting how much foreign exchange is due. For example, a session might go like this:

```
Welcome to Savanna Bank.
What currency?  Austrian
What amount?    2500
Amount before commission: 6917.5 Austrian Schillings
```

Using the Student Marker program as a model, and making use of hash tables, write a system to accomplish the above.

Note: if the above URL fails, there is a copy of a data file on the Java Gently web site called curtable. Look under the section on Other Material

CHAPTER 7

Formatting

In this chapter we consider the various ways that Java provides for formatting text, both internally and externally. Initially, Java 1.0 did not have much in this regard, but Java 1.1 has extensive facilities for handling data in a manner that is locale dependent. This means that programs can present themselves in the most appropriate style for the country in which they run. In many ways, such presentation details could be regarded as not essential in a first course, but we give them here to show how different Java is from languages that preceded it. In this chapter, Section 7.1 is essential reading for what follows, and Section 7.2 contains very useful information. Sections 7.3 and 7.4 can be covered later if necessary.

7.1 Strings and string handling

Strings were the first data items that we introduced in *Java Gently* and they have been used extensively since. It is now time to take a formal look at what they really are and what facilities are available for them. Strings are special in Java for several reasons:

1. `String` is a class so that strings are objects and not variables.

2. There is a special notation for string constants which is a shorthand for creating string objects with known contents.

3. Strings, unlike other objects, have an operator defined for them, i.e. the + for concatenation.

4. Once created, the contents of a `String` object cannot be changed.

5. Another class, `StringBuffer`, enables changes to the contents of a string.

6. There is a difference between an empty (but initialized) string and a null (i.e. not initialized) string.

So, for example, if we make the declaration:

```
String bigOne = "hippopotamus";
```

an object will automatically be created and initialized (without us using new) and will contain a reference called `bigOne`, as in Figure 7.1.

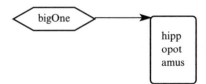

Figure 7.1 *Example of how a string is stored.*

Compare this declaration with a similar one for `Dates` (as defined in Example 5.5):

```
Dates graduation = new Dates (1998,5,4);
```

Here the constant is given in brackets and the new operator is used.

Regarding empty and null strings, consider the following two statements:

```
String s1;
String s2 = "";
```

`s1` will have a special value called null until it is given some other string value. Such a string is not valid for string manipulation methods, and if an attempt is made to access it, a `NullPointerException` will be thrown by the system. `s2`, on the other hand, can be used in string manipulation: it just has no contents. The difference between the two is brought out in Example 7.1.

The strings created in quotes or read into objects of the `String` class cannot be altered. There is another Java class, `StringBuffer`, which allows for this sort of thing. The `String` class has several constructors, some of which are shown in the next form:

Creating a string

```
String ();
String(String value);
String(char[] value);
String(char[] value, int offset, int count)
String(StringBuffer buffer)
```

Thus we can create a string from another string, or from a character array or from a `StringBuffer`.

There are many methods available in the `String` class, and the form shows a selection of them:

Manipulating strings

```
// class methods
  String    valueOf (int i)
  String    valueOf (double d)
  ... and 9 others
// instance methods
  char      charAt (int index)
  int       compareTo (String s)
  boolean   equals (Object obj)
  int       indexOf (String s)
  int       indexOf (String s, int fromindex)
  int       length ()
  String    substring (int begin, int end)
  boolean   startsWith (String prefix)
  char []   toCharArray ()
  String    toLowerCase ();
  String    trim ();
  ... and 33 others
```

`length` will give the length of string. Notice that unlike for an array, this is a method call, so the brackets are required. Although a string cannot be indexed directly, it is made up of characters and the character at any index position can be obtained via `charAt`. The whole string can also be transformed into a character array if required. For example,

```
String bigOne = "hippopotamus";
char study [];
study = bigOne.toCharArray();
```

produces an array of length 12 with each character from the original string. `indexOf` operates as a searching mechanism, enabling one to find a substring in a string. So, for example,

```
String bigOne = "hippopotamus";
int bang = bigOne.indexOf("pop");
int fizz = bigOne.indexOf("up");
```

will produce 3 in `bang` but –1 in `fizz`. Similarly, a substring can be extracted, as in

```
String bigOne = "hippopotamus";
String small = bigOne.substring(3,5);
```

which would give `"pop"` in `small`.

`compareTo` and `equals` enable whole strings to be compared. The comparison operators <, > and == should not be used for this purpose. The reason is connected with the fact that strings are objects; the full implications are carefully discussed in Section 8.3. The difference between assigning string values and their references is also covered in Section 8.3. Meanwhile, we note how the comparison methods would be used. `equals` returns a boolean as expected, for example:

```
String bigOne = "hippopotamus";
String small = bigOne.substring(3,5);
System.out.println (bigOne.equals(small));
```

will give false. The comparison works as follows:

```
a.compareTo(b)a less than b      result will be negative
              a same as b        result will be 0
              a greater than b result will be positive
```

The comparison is a straight alphabetical one. So, for example,

```
String bigOne = "hippopotamus";
String small = bigOne.substring(3,5);
System.out.println (bigOne.compareTo(small));
```

will produce –1. In other words, 'hippopotamus' does come alphabetically before 'pop'.

One of the common operations in programming is to convert strings to numbers and back again. The `valueOf` methods can take any of the primitive types and produce a string from it. We would only want to use `valueOf` if we want to keep the string in the program for a while, rather than print it out immediately.

EXAMPLE 7.1   Removing double spaces

Problem Standards have been set up which indicate that in typed paragraphs, there should only ever be single spaces. We would like to process existing text and replace any double spaces by single ones.

Solution We can read a file a line at a time, looking for double spaces using the string method `indexOf` and proceed accordingly.

Algorithm String manipulation algorithms can be very tricky. This one is best taken in stages. Let us start by reading one line of text and printing out the line together with the position of the first occurrence of a double space. The Java would be:

```
s = fin.readLine();
System.out.println(s.indexOf(" ",s) + " " + s);
```

If we enclosed this in a program to process a whole file, we could get output such as

```
0    Algorithm String manipulation algorithms can be very tricky.
33   This one is best taken in stages.  Let us start by reading one
-1   line of text and printing out the line together with the
52   position of the first occurrence of a double space.  The Java
10   would be:
```

which indicates that the first line has a double space at the beginning; the second and fourth lines have doubles somewhere in the middle; the third line has no double space, so indexOf returns –1; and the last line has a double space at the end, that is, after the colon.

To find more than one occurrence of double space in a string we shall have to loop round, checking from where we left off each time. The basic loop looks like this:

```
startingFrom = 0;
while (true) {
  spaceAt = s.indexOf("  ",startingFrom);
  if (spaceAt==-1) break;
  s = s.substring(0,spaceAt)+" "
    + s.substring(spaceAt+2,s.length());
  startingFrom = spaceAt+2;
}
System.out.println(s);
```

In other words, we recreate s each time from the part from 0 to the double space, plus a single space, plus the remainder of the string. We know we have finished processing the string when the indexOf method returns –1.

Program The full program incorporates these sections, and also checks for the end of file. It does so by looking for a null string. For testing purposes, the program is set up to read from the keyboard, but the fin stream could just as easily be directed to a file of the user's choice using FileMan.open.

```
import java.io.*;
import javagently.*;

class Spaces {

  /* Removing spaces program    by J M Bishop  Dec 1997
   * ----------------------     Java 1.1
   *
   * Replaces double spaces by single.
   * Illustrates use of string handling methods.
   */

  public static void main (String args []) throws IOException {
```

```
      System.out.println("Program to convert double spaces");
      System.out.println("to single ones.");
      BufferedReader fin = Text.open(System.in);

      String s = "";
      int spaceAt, startingFrom;
      try {
        while (true) {
          s = fin.readLine();
          if (s==null) throw new EOFException();

          startingFrom = 0;
          while (true) {
          spaceAt = s.indexOf("  ",startingFrom);
            if (spaceAt==-1) break;
            else if (spaceAt==0)
                s = s.substring(1,s.length());
            else s = s.substring(0,spaceAt)+" "
                  + s.substring(spaceAt+2,s.length());
            startingFrom = spaceAt+2;
          }
          System.out.println(s);

        }
      }
      catch (EOFException e) {}
   }
}
```

Testing The following shows some simple test data entered interactively.

```
Program to convert double spaces
to single ones.
Line one  with one double.
Line one with one double.
Line one  with  two.
Line two with two.
Line three ends with one.
Line three ends with one.
  Line four starts with one.
 Line four starts with one.
Line five has a   triple.
Line five has a  triple.
```

Obviously, there are many improvements that could be made to this program, and they are picked up in the problems at the end of the chapter.

The `StringBuffer` class

As we have mentioned, strings themselves are immutable. If we want to change the length or contents of a string, we basically have to break it up into bits and rejoin them, making a new string, as explained in Example 7.1. `StringBuffer` is an alternative class which provides methods such as `append`, `insert` and `setcharAt`, all of which enable efficient alterations to existing strings.

Strings and character arrays

Unlike other languages, strings in Java are definitely different from character arrays. However, conversion between them is possible, as mentioned above. An example of where such conversion would be very useful is in the counterfeit cheque example (4.7). In order to read in individual characters of the cheque number, we had to separate them by spaces, which was quite artificial. Instead, we can read in a string, convert it to an array, and peel off each character in turn.

The main loop of that example then changes from:

```
char digit;

for (int i = 0; i < noOfDigits; i++) {
  digit = Text.readChar (in);
  if (digit == '0')
    recordZero();
  else
    recordNonZero();
}
```

with data such as 1 0 0 6 7 0 2 2 1 5 to

```
String s = Text.readString(in);
char digits [ ] = s.toCharArray();

for (int i = 0; i < digits.length; i++) {
  if (digits[i] == '0')
    recordZero();
  else
    recordNonZero();
}
```

with the much more conventional data of 1006702215.

7.2 Tokenizers and the Text class

We mentioned in Chapter 4 that reading numbers was somewhat awkward in Java, and introduced the Text class as a means for providing these simple facilities. In this section we now look at the inside of that class, to see how it actually performs its task. But first we have to examine an important Java feature: the tokenizer.

Tokenizers

We have already mentioned that Java is slightly deficient in the input arena, and that the `Text` class was created to make up for the problem. Java's approach is to read strings, and to provide a very efficient means of breaking a string up into tokens and then to convert the token to the required type. Tokens are substrings separated by characters such as a comma, a space or a tab. In this way we can pick off substrings from the input and pass them to the string versions of the envelope class routines for conversion in order to get the values we want.

The methods provided by the `StringTokenizer` class, which is in `java.util`, are:

```
StringTokenizer declaration and access

StringTokenizer (String s);
StringTokenizer (String s, String delimiters);
StringTokenizer (String s, String delimiters,
                 boolean returnasTokens);

String  nextToken ();
String  nextToken (String delimiter);
boolean hasMoreTokens ();
int     countTokens ();
```

Having read in a string, we delare a tokenizer on it, as in:

```
StringTokenizer T = new StringTokenizer (S);
```

We then look through the tokens, checking for the end, as follows:

```
while (T.hasMoreTokens()) {
   System.out.println(T.nextToken());
}
```

Changing the delimiter set

We can also change the default delimiters from the usual space, tab and end-of-line, to something else. For example, if we were analysing a program, we would want semicolon, brackets and so on to also be delimiters. Otherwise they will be part of the tokens. Suppose we have the line

```
spaceAt = s.indexOf("  ",startingFrom);
```

With default delimiters, the tokens would be:

```
spaceAt
=
s.indexOf("  ",startingFrom);
```

which probably is not what we wanted. We could get a better effect by declaring:

```
StringTokenizer T = new StringTokenizer (S," .(,); =:",false);
```

which increases the delimiter set and excludes delimiters from the tokens. This gives:

```
spaceAt
s
indexOf
"   "
startingFrom
```

which is more like it. We now consider how envelopes and tokenizers are used in the Text class.

EXAMPLE 7.2   The Text class

Problem What really goes on behind the scenes in the Text class?

Solution We now have covered enough of the language to explain this useful addition to our programming repertoire. The class is not long, but it does make use of tokenizers and envelopes. The methods provided by the class were given in Chapter 4, and are repeated here:

The Text class methods	
``` void ```	``` prompt (String s) ```
``` int ```	``` readInt (BufferedReader in) ```
``` double ```	``` readDouble (BufferedReader in) ```
``` String ```	``` readString (BufferedReader in) ```
``` char ```	``` readChar (BufferedReader in) ```
``` String ```	``` writeInt (int number, int align) ```
``` String ```	``` writeDouble (double number, int align, int frac) ```
``` BufferedReader ```	``` open (InputStream in) ```
``` BufferedReader ```	``` open (String filename) ```
``` PrintWriter ```	``` create (String filename) ```

The Text class is composed of a set of methods which can be called in any order. There is no initializing to be done, so the methods must be sure to initialize themselves. The methods are static, and the class is not intended to be instantiated. It operates as a service provider in the same way as the Math class.

Algorithm The general algorithm for each of the reading methods is illustrated by that for reading an integer (Figure 7.2). The routine can initialize itself by detecting a null token. If this is the case, it reads a line and generates the tokenizer. It then calls nextToken, to get a token, and tries to convert the token to a number. Both statements can go wrong:

- The call to nextToken can fail if there are no more tokens. The appropriate action is therefore to read another line.

- The conversion can fail if the substring forming the token does not represent a number of the proper kind. Again an exception is raised. Here we just print a message and try again.

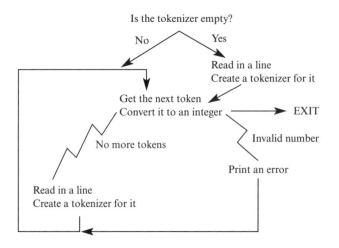

Figure 7.2 *Reading an integer using the tokenizer.*

If both statements complete successfully, the method exits.

The class also has a prompt method for writing out a short message and staying on the same line, as well as write and open methods (discussed in Chapter 4).

The class contains interesting statements in each of the numeric conversion methods. The integer one uses the parse method from the Integer envelope class:

```
return Integer.parseInt(item);
```

However, the Double class does not have a corresponding parse method, and the conversion is a bit more complex:

```
return Double.valueOf(item.trim()).doubleValue();
```

Let us consider what this does. item is a string returned from the tokenizer. Working from the inside outwards, we first trim it of spaces, using a method from the String class. Then we call the Double.valueOf method to convert the string to an object of type Double. Finally, we take the object out of its envelope and turn it into a double type. This statement is certainly worth putting into a typed method!

Program

```
package javagently;

import java.io.*;
import java.util.*;
import java.text.*;

public class Text {

  public Text () {};

  /* The All New Famous Text class     by J M Bishop  Aug 1996
   *              revised for Java 1.1 by Alwyn Moolman Aug 1997
   *
   * Provides simple input from the keyboard and files.
   * Now also has simple output formatting methods
   * and file opening facilities.
   *
   * public static void   prompt (String s)
   * public static int    readInt (BufferedReader in)
   * public static double readDouble (BufferedReader in)
   * public static String readString (BufferedReader in)
   * public static char   readChar (BufferedReader in)
   * public static String writeInt (int number, int align)
   * public static String writeDouble
   *              (double number, int align, int frac)
   * public static BufferedReader open (InputStream in)
   * public static BufferedReader open (String filename)
   * public static PrintWriter create (String filename)
   */

  private static StringTokenizer T;
  private static String S;

  public static BufferedReader open (InputStream in)  {
    return new BufferedReader(new InputStreamReader(in));
  }

  public static BufferedReader open (String filename)
   throws FileNotFoundException {
    return new BufferedReader (new FileReader (filename));
  }

  public static PrintWriter create
    (String filename) throws IOException {
    return new PrintWriter (new FileWriter (filename));
  }

  public static void prompt (String s) {
    System.out.print(s + " ");
    System.out.flush();
  }
```

```java
public static int readInt (BufferedReader in) throws IOException {
    if (T==null) refresh(in);
    while (true) {
      try {
        return Integer.parseInt(T.nextToken());
      }
      catch (NoSuchElementException e1) {
        refresh (in);
      }
      catch (NumberFormatException e2) {
        System.out.println("Error in number, try again.");
      }
    }
  }

public static char readChar (BufferedReader in) throws IOException {
    if (T==null) refresh(in);
    while (true) {
      try {
        return T.nextToken().trim().charAt(0);
      }
      catch (NoSuchElementException e1) {
        refresh (in);
      }
    }
  }

public static double readDouble (BufferedReader in) throws IOException {
    if (T==null) refresh(in);
    while (true) {
      try {
        String item = T.nextToken();
        return Double.valueOf(item.trim()).doubleValue();
      }
      catch (NoSuchElementException e1) {
        refresh (in);
      }
      catch (NumberFormatException e2) {
        System.out.println("Error in number, try again.");
      }
    }
  }

public static String readString (BufferedReader in) throws IOException {
    if (T==null) refresh (in);
    while (true) {
      try {
        return T.nextToken();
      }
      catch (NoSuchElementException e1) {
        refresh (in);
      }
    }
  }
}
```

```
private static void refresh (BufferedReader in) throws IOException {
  S = in.readLine ();
  if (S==null) throw new EOFException();
  T = new StringTokenizer (S);
}

//  Write methods
//  ------------

private static DecimalFormat N = new DecimalFormat();
private static final String spaces = "                    ";

public static String writeDouble (double number, int align, int frac) {
  N.setGroupingUsed(false);
  N.setMaximumFractionDigits(frac);
  N.setMinimumFractionDigits(frac);
  String num = N.format(number);
  if (num.length() < align)
    num = spaces.substring(0,align-num.length()) + num;
  return num;
}

public static String writeInt (int number, int align) {
  N.setGroupingUsed(false);
  N.setMaximumFractionDigits(0);
  String num = N.format(number);
  if (num.length() < align)
    num = spaces.substring(0,align-num.length()) + num;
  return num;
}

}
}
```

The writing methods make use of Java's text package, which is the subject of the next section.

7.3 Formatting numbers with the `java.text` package

In the write methods of our own Text class, we made use of features of the `java.text` package, which is new in Java 1.1. In this section we describe and assess this approach to writing numbers.

The concept of a formatter

Java differs from other languages in that the formatting for numbers is not given in the print statements, but in a separate object altogether. Then in the print statement, the relevant format object is joined up with the item to be printed. Several format objects can exist in a program together at any one time, and they can be used and reused at will.

The formatters that are available in `java.text` are `DateFormat`, `Simple-DateFormat`, `NumberFormat`, `DecimalFormat` and a somewhat different one called `MessageFormat`. We discuss the date formatters in the next section and concentrate on number formatters here.

`NumberFormat` and its subclass `DecimalFormat` provide facilities for formatting all kinds of numbers, including percentages and currencies, in various forms. First we create a format, then we can customize it in two ways:

- for particular formatting requirements, such as the number of fractional digits to be printed for a real number;

- for different locales around the world, which have different conventions for decimals, currency symbols, thousand groups and so on.

The latter is a very powerful aspect of Java and puts the language in a class of its own for world-wide computing.

Since `NumberFormat` is an abstract class, creating a format is done by class methods, as given in the form:

Creating number formatters

```
NumberFormat getInstance ()
NumberFormat getCurrencyInstance ()
NumberFormat getNumberInstance ()
NumberFormat getPercentInstance ()
```

Each of the four creation methods has a corresponding version that mentions a new locale, other than the default one, that should be used. Perhaps a better way of handling locales is to switch between them, as shown in Example 2.6. We will discuss this further later on in the section.

To use a formatter, the following instance methods apply. Since all the other numeric types can operate within long and double, only two methods are needed.

Using number formatters

```
String format (double number);
String format (long number);
```

So, for example, to compare the default writing of numbers with the default settings of the formatter, consider:

```
NumberFormat N = NumberFormat.getInstance ();

system.out.println(Math.PI + "   " + 10000);
system.out.println(N.format (Math.PI) + "   " + N.format (10000));
```

which would print out

```
3.141592653589793  10000
3.141  10,000
```

The printing out of numbers with commas is not very common, except in financial matters, so we would want to customize the format in most cases. To do so, we make use of the following instance methods:

Customizing a number formatter

```
void setMaximumIntegerDigits (int newvalue);
void setMinimumIntegerDigits (int newvalue);
void setMaximumFractionDigits (int newvalue);
void setMinimumFractionDigits (int newvalue);
void setGroupingUsed (boolean newvalue);
```

For each of the set methods, there is a corresponding get method which can, if needed, provide the current settings.

Note that it is a good idea to use short identifiers for formatters since, with `format`, they tend to clutter up print statements.

Formatting real numbers

To see the effect of changing the various settings for real numbers, the best example is to dissect the `Text.writeDouble` method. It is:

```
public static String writeDouble
              (double number, int align, int frac) {
  N.setGroupingUsed(false);
  N.setMaximumFractionDigits(frac);
  N.setMinimumFractionDigits(frac);
  String num = N.format(number);
  if (num.length() < align)
    num = spaces.substring(0,align-num.length()) + num;
  return num;
}
```

The three set calls establish that there must be no grouping of thousands and that the number of fractional digits is fixed. If we set the minimum but not the maximum then we would get spaces as padding, whereas usually we want zeroes. The number is then formatted and put into a local string, because there is one adjustment to be made. The number formatter has a default setting of 1 for the minimum integer digits, so we will always get a number such as 0.567 rather than .567. If we set the maximum to (align-frac) then we will get numbers of fixed width, but there will be leading zeroes, not spaces. Therefore we add the extra spaces by means of string manipulation instead.

Setting the maximum integer digits has another danger: Java will truncate anything else. Thus with a maximum digits of 3, 1000 will be printed as 0. In general therefore, the old `Text` class is still a useful tool.

In the `DecimalFormat` class there is a facility to set up a pattern to be used in formatting. However, creating a pattern such as ###0.### requires string handling as well if the number of hashes is a variable. We shall consider patterns again when customizing dates.

Currencies

As part of the number formatting facilities, we can get any currency printed out nicely.[1] To print a number as a currency, we use:

```
NumberFormat C = NumberFormat.getCurrencyInstance();
System.out.println (C.format(10000));
```

which could give in return:

```
$10,000.00
```

Currencies are fun because Java will pick up the correct currency formatting and currency symbol from the computer and use it. Example 7.3 illustrates what happens.

EXAMPLE 7.3   Currency conversion table

Problem   We would like to investigate the effect of locale changes on the printing of currencies.

Solution   We set up a small test program that gets five exchange rates and then prints out a table with the amount converted from graz.

Program   The program is very simple. A currency format is created for each of the locales that are involved. The rates are read in and then the converted amounts printed.

```
import java.text.*;
import javagently.*;
import java.util.*;
import java.io.*;
import myutilities.*;

class Currency {

    public static void main (String args []) throws IOException {
```

---

[1] Percentages seem to be somewhat problematic at present, so we shall not consider them here.

```
BufferedReader in = Text.open("rates.dat");

System.out.println("Currency conversion table");
System.out.println("==========================");
System.out.println();
System.out.println("The exchange rates are:");
System.out.println("graz\tdollars\tpounds\tyen\tmarks\tfrancs");
double d = Text.readDouble(in);
double p = Text.readDouble(in);
double y = Text.readDouble(in);
double m = Text.readDouble(in);
double f = Text.readDouble(in);
System.out.println("1\t"d+"\t"+p+"\t"+ y+"\t"+ m+"\t"+ f);
System.out.println();

NumberFormat Nd =
      NumberFormat.getCurrencyInstance(Locale.US);
NumberFormat Np =
      NumberFormat.getCurrencyInstance(Locale.UK);
NumberFormat Ny =
      NumberFormat.getCurrencyInstance(Locale.JAPAN);
NumberFormat Nm =
      NumberFormat.getCurrencyInstance(Locale.GERMANY);
NumberFormat Nf =
      NumberFormat.getCurrencyInstance(Locale.FRANCE);

for (int graz = 1000; graz < 10000; graz+=1000)
  System.out.println('G'+Text.writeInt(graz,3) + '\t' +
    Nd.format(graz/d) + '\t' +
    Np.format(graz/p) + '\t' +
    Ny.format(graz/y) + '\t' +
    Nm.format(graz/m) + '\t' +
    Nf.format(graz/f));
  }
}
```

Testing The output from the program will be:

```
Currency conversion table
==========================

The exchange rates are:
graz         dollars      pounds      yen         marks         francs
1            4.8845       8.047       0.0378      2.7361        0.8174

G1000        $204.72      £124.26     ¥26,455     365,48 DM     1 223,39 F
G2000        $409.45      £248.53     ¥52,910     730,96 DM     2 446,78 F
G3000        $614.18      £372.80     ¥79,365     1.096,45 DM 3 670,17 F
G4000        $818.91      £497.07     ¥105,820    1.461,93 DM 4 893,56 F
G5000        $1,023.64    £621.34     ¥132,275    1.827,41 DM 6 116,95 F
G6000        $1,228.37    £745.61     ¥158,730    2.192,90 DM 7 340,34 F
G7000        $1,433.10    £869.88     ¥185,185    2.558,38 DM 8 563,73 F
G8000        $1,637.83    £994.15     ¥211,640    2.923,86 DM 9 787,12 F
G9000        $1,842.56    £1,118.42   ¥238,095    3.289,35 DM 11 010,52 F
```

The output is very interesting, considering that we did no work ourselves!

Inputting formatted data

We have concentrated up to now on outputting data. The java.text package also provides for inputting formatted data in each of its classes. Formatted data is distinguished from unformatted data in that the items need not be delimited by spaces and so on, but must appear in particular columns in the input line. They may even abut each other as in the following:

```
76 89123 45 10  6100
```

If this data is interpreted with a format of maximum and minimum digits as 3, then the resulting numbers are 76, 89, 123, 45, 10, 6 and 100.

  The general term for getting input data in Java is **parsing**, which is analogous to formatting for output. However, data these days is very seldom presented without delimiters of some sort, and in general tokenizers, as discussed in Section 7.2, are adequate for most needs. A distinct disadvantage of parsing via the formatters is that the results are presented as objects, so one still has to do the conversion to primitive types.

7.4 Dates, calendars and time

The Date class, which is part of the util package, represents dates and times in a system-independent way. Its complete specification is given in the form:

The Date class specification

```
public class Date extends Object {

// Constructors
    public Date ();
    public Date (long time);

// Instance methods
    public boolean after (Date when);
    public boolean before (Date when);
    public boolean equals (Object obj);
    public long    getTime ();
    public int     hashCode ();
    public long    setTime (long time);
    public String  toString ();
}
```

Date gives an example of what a standard class in Java looks like. As you can see, it starts off with two constructors. The first one, which has no parameters, will put the computer's current date and time in the new object. Thus if we say

```
Date today = new Date ();
```

we create an object containing today's date and time, as taken from the computer's clock. The second constructor creates a date from the number of milliseconds from some arbitary date. In `Date` itself, there is no easier way to create a specific date, and we need another class, `Calendar`, for this purpose.

After the constructors come the methods, and the interesting ones to us at this stage are `getTime` and `toString`. Given our `date` object, we can print it straight through `println` as follows:

```
System.out.println(today);
```

`today` will first be converted to a string and then printed. The conversion is carried out by the `toString` method, which should be present in all classes that want their objects to be printed. The format for the conversion means that the date will always be printed in the following form, shown with an example:

```
Day Month Date Hours:Mins:Secs Zone Year
Sat Dec 06 17:11:54 EST 1997
```

If the zone of the computer is not one of Java's recognizable time zones, then an offset from GMT is given, as in

```
Thu Dec 25 00:00:00 GMT+00:00 1997
```

Other formats are possible via `java.text`, as discussed below.

Originally in Java 1.0, the `Date` class was much bigger and included methods for getting and setting parts of the date, among others. These functions have now been taken over by another much more complex class, `Calendar`. Rather than itemize `Calendar`, we just list here the parts we shall need for the next example:

- constants indicating the various fields, e.g. `YEAR` or `MINUTE`
- constants for the days and months, e.g. `MONDAY` or `DECEMBER`
- a class method that creates an object, i.e. `getInstance`
- instance methods for getting and setting parts of the date, i.e. `get` and `set`

`get` and `set` require field parts to be specified, for example

```
int y = get(Calendar.YEAR);
set (Calendar.YEAR, 2001);
```

In addition, set can be given three values, year, month and day, but note that it is best to use the constant names provided for the months, e.g. `Calendar.MAY` not 4.

EXAMPLE 7.4 Shopping Days

Problem We would like to calculate the number of shopping days to Christmas, assuming that we are already in the month of December.

Algorithm Given the assumption that we are already in December, the algorithm is very simple, as we only have to subtract the dates of the two Dates.[2] Working from November or October would require more calculating skills than we want to use at present.

Program It starts by importing the util package, then introduces itself and starts its main method.

```
import java.util.*;

public class Shopping {

    /* Shopping Program          by J M Bishop Dec 96
     * ----------------          Java 1.1 by J M Bishop Dec 97
     * Calculates the number of shopping days to Christmas,
     * and is only meant to be run in December.
     *
     */

    public static void main(String[] args) {

      Calendar today = Calendar.getInstance();
      Calendar christmas = Calendar.getInstance();

      christmas.set(
          today.get(Calendar.YEAR), Calendar.DECEMBER, 25);

      System.out.println("Only run this program in December!");
      System.out.println("Christmas is on "+ christmas.getTime());
      System.out.println("Today is "+ today.getTime());

      System.out.println("There are "
              +(christmas.get(Calendar.DATE)-
                  today.get(Calendar.DATE))
              +" shopping days to Christmas.");
    }
  }
```

Counting lines within the main method, the two dates are declared on lines 1 and 2 as Calendar objects using the getInstance class method to set them up. Lines 3 and 4 make the program independent of which year we are in, by getting the year from today to set the year for Christmas. This program will not even have trouble running after the year 2000!

---

[2] Java's terminology here is potentially confusing: Date is the class, but the number of the day in the month, e.g. the 8th, is also referred to as the date, thus we have getDate and setDate. The reason for the use of date in this second context is clearly to avoid a conflict with Day, which is one of the seven Sun, Mon, Tues and so on. This is perhaps the type of confusion you should not introduce into your classes once you start defining them.

Lines 5 and 6 print out the two dates and then on line 8 we subtract their day numbers for the final message. Notice here that we have to put the subtraction expression in brackets so that the result of it, which is an integer, is the expression which is converted to a string for printing. The compiler will complain if we do not do this. (Try it and see.)

Testing The results of a test run of the program would be:

```
Only run this program in December!
Christmas is on Thu Dec 25 00:00:00 EST 1997
Today is Sun Dec 07 12:00:11 EST 1997
There are 18 shopping days to Christmas.
```

Date formatting

In the same way as we can format numbers and currencies, we can also format dates. From the DateFormat class of java.text we create a formatter with a specific style, being one of DEFAULT, FULL, LONG, MEDIUM or SHORT. Thus instead of the simple

```
System.out.println("Today is "+ today.getTime());
```

in the above program, we can be more specific and say:

```
DateFormat D = DateFormat.getDateInstance(DateFormat.FULL);
System.out.println("Today is "+ D.format(today));
```

which would print out the more user-friendly version of:

```
Sunday, December 7, 1997
```

The various options are explored in the next example.

Similarly, we can select a time formatter and print the time in a variety of ways. The method here is getTimeInstance.

Date parsing

A useful feature of the DateFormat class is the method to parse a date from a string. It enables us to read dates. For example, if we declare an ordinary date formatter as:

```
DateFormat DF = DateFormat.getDateInstance();
```

and have data such as

```
1997-Aug-15
```

we can read it with:

```
Date D = DF.parse(Text.readString(in));
```

Parse can raise an exception, so it is necessary to catch it here or mention it in all the methods associated with the call. Catching it could look like this:

```
DateFormat DF = DateFormat.getDateInstance();
Date D = new Date();
String s = Text.readString(in);
try {
 D = DF.parse(s);
} catch (ParseException e) {
  System.out.println("Error in date " + s);
}
```

The default date format is the simple one shown above. Of course, other date formats can be insisted upon by changing the style of the formatter, as shown in the next example.

EXAMPLE 7.5   Formatting and parsing dates

Problem Illustrate the various options for input and output of dates in Java.

Solution The solution, as always, is to set up a test program. The one that follows is carefully crafted not only to give the necessary illustrative output, but also to exercise some of the other interesting aspects of date formatting in Java. Specifically:

●   date formats can be sent as parameters

●   the parse method throws a `ParseException` which indicates a date in the wrong form.

Program Notice that we have set the program up for the UK locale which will put the day before the month. It is easy to change this statement. The default is US, which would put the month before the day. See Example 7.7 for more on dates and locales.

```
import java.text.*;
import java.util.*;
import javagently.*;
import java.io.*;

class CustomDates {

   /* Testing date formatting    by J M Bishop Dec 1997
    * ---------------------    Java 1.1
    *
    * Writes dates in multiple formats and
    * prompts for dates back in the same form.
    */
```

```
CustomDates () {
}

static BufferedReader in = Text.open(System.in);
static Date d = new Date ();
static Date my = new Date();

static void echoDate(String style, DateFormat Din,DateFormat Dout)
                       throws IOException {
  System.out.println(style+"\t"+Din.format(d));
  String s = in.readLine();
  System.out.println("\t\t\t"+s);
  try {
    my = Din.parse(s);
  }
  catch (ParseException e) {
    System.out.println("Invalid date "+s);
  }
  System.out.println("\t\t\t"+Dout.format(my));
}


public static void main (String args []) throws IOException {

  Locale.setDefault(Locale.UK);
  DateFormat DS = DateFormat.getDateInstance(DateFormat.SHORT);
  DateFormat DM = DateFormat.getDateInstance(DateFormat.MEDIUM);
  DateFormat DL = DateFormat.getDateInstance(DateFormat.LONG);
  DateFormat DF = DateFormat.getDateInstance(DateFormat.FULL);
  DateFormat DD = DateFormat.getDateInstance(DateFormat.DEFAULT);

  echoDate("SHORT",DS,DF);
  echoDate("MEDIUM",DM,DF);
  echoDate("LONG",DL,DF);
  echoDate("FULL",DF,DF);
  echoDate("DEFAULT",DD,DF);
}
}
```

Testing

```
SHORT   13/12/97
20/10/04
        20/10/04
        Thursday, 20 October 1904
MEDIUM  13-Dec-97
20-Oct-04
      20-Oct-04
      Thursday, 20 October 1904
LONG 13 December, 1997
20 October, 2004
      20 October, 2004
      Wednesday, 20 October 2004
```

```
FULL Saturday, 13 December 1997
Saturday, 20 October 2004
        Saturday, 20 October 2004
        Wednesday, 20 October 2004
DEFAULT13-Dec-97
20-Okt-04
        20-Okt-04
Invalid date 20-Okt-04
        Wednesday, 20 October 2004
```

We notice two points from this output:

1. Java seems to have a Year 2000 problem! It is not until the date style is given as LONG that a four digit year is allowed.

2. In FULL style, if an invalid day is entered, the formatter ignores it and presents the correct one.

Time zones

In its mission to be a truly world-wide and web-oriented language, Java provides for detecting the time zone of the computer running the program. From the time zone, the zone code, the offset from Universal Time[3] and information about daylight saving can be established.

EXAMPLE 7.6   Testing time zones

What follows is a small test program to show the information that can be deduced about the computer's time zone.

```java
import java.util.*;

class WorldTime {

    /* Time Zone program    by J M Bishop December 1997
     *                          Java 1.1
     * Uses the Java libraries to display
     * time anywhere in the world.
     */

    public static void main (String [ ] args) {
        TimeZone here = TimeZone.getDefault();
        Date today = new Date();
        System.out.println(today);
        System.out.println("We are in " + here.getID() + " time zone");
        System.out.println("with " + here.getRawOffset()/3600000 +
                            " offset from UTC");
```

---

[3] Universal Time is taken from 0° longitude and used to be known as GMT (Greenwich Mean Time).

```
        System.out.println("Daylight Savings Time used here is " +
                        here.useDaylightTime());
        System.out.println("and being now in Daylight Savings Time is "
                        + here.inDaylightTime(today));

    }
}
```

Sat Dec 06 17:11:54 EST 1997
We are in EST time zone
with -5 offset from UTC
Daylight Savings Time used here is true
and being now in Daylight Savings Time is false

Once you have run the WorldTime program, it is quite fun to change your time zone and run it again. On a Windows system, you do this by going into Help, selecting time zones and clicking the arrow. You are given a map of the world and can select any vertical time zone slice, as well as a specific region for that zone. Figure 7.3 shows this screen.

Localized date formatting

In Chapter 2 we discussed locales and showed how the locale of a program can be changed, thus indicating a different display language. By using locales, we can obtain dates printed in different languages and different formats. We can even create our own, if the language is not one known to the Java Locale class (the full list was given in Section 2.5).

EXAMPLE 7.7 Multilingual dates

Problem We would like to demonstrate Java's ability to print dates in various languages.

Solution Use the DateFormat and Locale classes.

Algorithm Printing the dates can be done by a method

```
    static void printDates (Locale L) {

        System.out.println("We are in " + L.getCountry() +
            " speaking " + L.getLanguage());

        DateFormat D = DateFormat.getDateInstance();
        System.out.println(D.format(today));

        D = DateFormat.getDateInstance(DateFormat.FULL);
        System.out.println(D.format(today));
        System.out.println();
    }
```

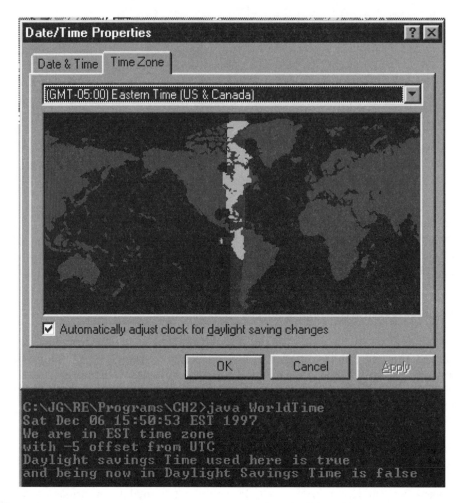

Figure 7.3 *Selecting a time zone under Windows. (See also Plate 7.)*

This will give the country and language, then print the date in default form (quite short) and full form (but without the time). To call it, we use:

```
Locale.setDefault(Locale.GERMANY);
printDates(Locale.getDefault());
```

In other words, we overwrite the default locale of the computer, and pass this to `print-Dates`. The result should be:

```
We are in DE speaking de
11.12.1997
Donnerstag, 11. Dezember 1997
```

Java is really providing quite an impressive facility here.

Program The program put together with several such changes of locale is:

```java
import java.util.*;
import java.io.*;
import javagently.*;
import java.text.*;

class VaryDates {

  /* Vary Dates program    by J M Bishop December 1997
   * ------------------    Java 1.1
   * Uses the Java libraries to display
   * dates for different locales.
   */

   static Date today = new Date();

  static void printDates (Locale L) {

    System.out.println("We are in " + L.getCountry() +
        " speaking " + L.getLanguage());

    DateFormat D = DateFormat.getDateInstance();
    System.out.println(D.format(today));

    D = DateFormat.getDateInstance(DateFormat.FULL);
    System.out.println(D.format(today));
    System.out.println();
  }

  public static void main (String [ ] args) throws IOException{

    System.out.println(today);

    Locale genuine = Locale.getDefault();
    printDates(genuine);

    Locale.setDefault(Locale.GERMANY);
    printDates(Locale.getDefault());

    Locale.setDefault(Locale.UK);
    printDates(Locale.getDefault());

    Locale.setDefault(Locale.FRANCE);
    printDates(Locale.getDefault());

    Locale.setDefault(Locale.US);
    printDates(Locale.getDefault());

    Locale.setDefault(Locale.JAPAN);
    printDates(Locale.getDefault());

  }
}
```

Testing Running the program gives:

```
Thu Dec 11 20:24:36 GMT+00:00 1997

We are in SOUTH AFRICA speaking en
11-Dec-97
Thursday, December 11, 1997

We are in DE speaking de
11.12.1997
Donnerstag, 11. Dezember 1997

We are in GB speaking en
11-Dec-97
Thursday, 11 December 1997

We are in FR speaking fr
11 dÈc 97
jeudi, 11 dÈcembre 1997

We are in US speaking en
11-Dec-97
Thursday, December 11, 1997

We are in JP speaking ja
97/12/12
1997? 12? 12? ???
```

The displaying is not always perfect, but there certainly are a variety of formats and the words do come out in different languages. It is interesting to note if we switch locales to Japan, it is already tomorrow, and the date has changed to 12 December. Java also cannot print the Japanese characters so does its best with numbers.

Extension As promised, we can also teach the computer about new locales. To do this, we declare a new locale as in

```
Locale Afr = new Locale("Afrikaans","Suid-Afrika");
```

Then we have to pull in another class called DateFormatSymbols in which we can set the names of the days and months in the new language. For example, the months go like this:

```
String AfrMonths [] = {"Januarie", "Februarie", "Maart", "April",
      "Mei", "Junie", "Julie", "Augustus", "September",
      "Oktober", "November", "Desember"};

DateFormatSymbols DAfr = new DateFormatSymbols(Afr);
DAfr.setMonths (AfrMonths);
```

Then we set up the format patterns for the country, using a string pattern. The pattern facility is provided in a subclass of DateFormat called SimpleDateFormat, and typical format declarations would be:

```
SimpleDateFormat Dshort = new SimpleDateFormat("yyyy/MM/dd");

SimpleDateFormat Dfull = new SimpleDateFormat
                    ("EEEE dd MMMM yyyy", DAfr);
```

Dshort specifies a pattern; Dfull specifies a pattern and a set of DateFormat-Symbols which will include all the names of months, etc. Putting this all together, we get the following statements which can be put at the end of VaryDates.

```
String AfrMonths [] = {"Januarie", "Februarie", "Maart",
    "April", "Mei", "Junie", "Julie", "Augustus", "September",
    "Oktober", "November", "Desember"};

String AfrDays []= {"Saterdag", "Sondag","Maandag", "Dinsdag",
    "Woensdag", "Donderdag","Vrydag"};

Locale Afr = new Locale("Afrikaans","Suid-Afrika");
Locale.setDefault(genuine);

DateFormatSymbols DAfr = new DateFormatSymbols(Afr);
DAfr.setMonths (AfrMonths);
DAfr.setWeekdays (AfrDays);

System.out.println("We are in " + Afr.getCountry() +
    " speaking " + Afr.getLanguage());

SimpleDateFormat Dshort = new SimpleDateFormat("yyyy/MM/dd");
System.out.println(Dshort.format(today));

Dfull = new SimpleDateFormat("EEEE dd MMMM yyyy", DAfr);
System.out.println(Dfull.format(today));
```

The output would be:

```
We are in SUID-AFRIKA speaking afrikaans
1997/12/11
Donderdag 11 Desember 1997
```

There are more facilities available in all these classes, and you can look them up in the Java API help.

SUMMARY

Strings are not arrays in the Java context, but are objects instantiated from a special String class. They have their own properties and characteristics. Conversion methods between strings and character arrays and between strings and numbers do exist. However, the conversions sometimes need the help of envelope classes, which turn variables into objects. Strings can be processed by means of tokenizers. Together these facilities combine to provide the power needed by the Text class, which is used for all the simple input in this book.

Output formatting is provided for extensively in Java. Numbers, currencies, percentages and dates can all be customized for specific formats, as well as for locales. Choosing a locale causes the language and format of output to be adapted the conventions of that country. Time zones can also be specified and interrogated.

7.1   Write a loop to go through an array of 3 names and print out the first position of the letter 'e' in each name, if it exists.

7.2   What would be printed from the following statements:

```
String a = "abcdefg";
System.out.println(a.compareTo("aabcde"));
```

7.3   Write statements to convert a word to small letters, then capitalize the first letter.

7.4   If s is a string holding an integer number, give statements and (a) to store the integer as a variable and (b) to print the integer without first storing it.

7.5   Give two reasons why the NumberFormat class of java.text is not as useful as it could be for outputting numbers reasonably simply.

7.6   Write statements to print a salary in currency units not that of your machine (choose the units.)

7.7   If tragic is a Calendar object, use a set method to give it the date 31 August 1997.

7.8   How would Java print your birthday this year in FULL style?

7.9   In Example 7.7, was it necessary to declare and set the DateFormat D in the printDates method or could these statements be moved to the main metod and executed once?

7.10   Looking at the extension to Example 7.7, is setMonths a class method or an instance method?

7.1   **Birthdays.** The after and before methods of the Calendar class in the util package will return true or false depending on the relationship between the instance object and the parameter. For example,

```
new Calendar (1996,Calendar.DECEMBER,25).before
            (new Calendar (1996,Calendar.DECEMBER,1))
```

will be false. Write a program that sets up your birthday and the day of Easter this year and displays the result of each of the three relations – before, equals and after – between the two dates.

7.2   **Typing improvements.** There are different schools of thought for typing spaces after full-stops. It used to be that one entered two spaces, now the fashion seems to be one. Adapt Example 7.1 so that the user can choose one of these styles, and the program will standardize an input file accordingly.

7.3   **Validating codes.** Course codes at Savanna University have a precise form: four capital letters followed immediately by three digits. Write a class for such codes, and include methods to create, convert to a string and check a code for validity. Refer to Example 5.5 for ideas on how to set up such a class. Test the class with a small test program.

7.4   **Palindromes.** A palindrome is a word or sentence that reads the same forwards as backwards, disregarding punctuation. Famous palindromes are:

Madam, I'm Adam

Able was I ere I saw Elba.

Write a Boolean method that will check whether a given string is a palindrome or not. Call the method from a test program.

7.5   **Concordance**. A concordance is a list of words similar to an index, where the position of each word – its page number and line number – in a piece of text is indicated. The difference between a concordance and an index is that a concordance considers all words except common ones such as 'and', 'the' and 'is'. Write a Java system to create a concordance from a piece of text at your disposal. Use hash tables. (Hint: the hash table will have the words as keys and the page/line numbers as values. Since the words could occur more than once, the value will have to be an array of numbers, and will have to have an upper limit, say 10 occurrences recorded.)

7.6   **Multiple word names**. A problem we detected earlier (for example in the Olympic medals program in Example 4.9) is that we cannot have names with spaces in them. The reason is that a space delimits the whole name, so it cannot be *in* the name. We solved the problem by changing the data so that names such as United.States were written with a full stop in the middle.

Now that we know more about formatting, what would be the best approach to employ for a method that could read such names? Assume that the names are lined up in columns of a fixed size and that no other data items will be in that column.

Write a suitable method to read multi-word names, include it as part of a class called `Formatters` in your `myutilities` package and use it to remove the data restriction from the Olympics program.

7.7   **Your own dates**. Choose another country not supported by the standard locales and customize Java to reflect the language and conventions of that country, as we did in Example 7.5. Investigate the APIs via Java's help and try to customize the currency formatting as well. The approach is very similar to that for dates.

7.8   **Egalitarian minutes**. The Council of Savanna University has decreed that in future all minutes of meetings will omit titles of those speaking. Instead of Prof Brown, committees may choose between John Brown, Brown, JB or John, depending on circumstances. However, in any one document, ony one convention should be used. Your task is to process a document, looking for titles, i.e. Prof Dr Mr Ms Miss Rev, remove them, and replace the name that follows with the selected form.

To solve this problem, the program will need information regarding the names of the people. For example, if the John Brown format is chosen, and the program encounters Prof Brown, then it must be able to find John from somewhere. There are two options:

(a)   Interact with the secretary or whoever is running the program and get the information that way. This is simple to set up but could be tedious and error prone when running.

(b)   From the attendance and apologies lists at the beginning of the document, construct a hash table with the necessary information. Assume that these lists give everyone's details in full, e.g. Prof John Brown (JB). Make use of the `String` method `startWith` to find the lists.

You will have to decide how the hash table is to be arranged, i.e. what the key is, but remember that we can search the keys and the values, and various customized searching can also be added.

PART II

Power

CHAPTER 8

Objects at work

Java is an object-oriented language and, in Part I, we introduced and used both objects and classes in many examples. Now that we have covered the basic constructs of Java, it is time to look at the real power of objects, and how they are used in larger programs. In this chapter we discuss objects using a case study of a typical inventory program. In the next chapter we go on to look at further capabilities of objects, such as inheritance, interfaces and abstract classes, and explore some more examples. Before we look at the Case Study, let us consider once again some basic object principles.

8.1 Object protection

The general form of an object declaration is:

Object declaration

```
modifier classname objectname = new classname ( );
modifier classname objectname = new classname (parameters);
modifier classname objectname;
```

The first form introduces a new object and creates space for it according to that required by the class. The second form does the same, but also supplies parameters to the construction process. Usually these values are stored in local fields of the new object. The final version does not create space: it merely introduces the name of the object, so that it can be referred to later in the program. However, when the program runs, the object must have been created before it is used.

Designing an object really means designing a class and its members. One of the cardinal principles in such design is **separation of concerns**. What this means is that a class should endeavour to be as self-contained as possible, and to reveal to other classes only that which is necessary. Going further, it is even considered good practice to protect a field by not allowing direct access to it, but by providing get and set methods which give controlled access. Protection of this sort is indicated by **modifiers**, and a short study of Java's available modifiers is now in order.

Java modifiers

Classes, objects and members of objects can be given a modifier which indicates how they be used. Not all modifiers apply to classes: some are for objects and other members of classes (methods, variables) only. Table 8.1 gives a summary of the meaning of some of Java's main modifiers, together with the section of this book where the topic is fully discussed.

Table 8.1 *The meaning of some of the modifiers applicable to classes and members, together with the sections where they are discussed*

Modifier	Class	In	Member	In
No modifier	Accessible only within its package	8.1	Accessible only within its package	8.1
`public`	Accessible anywhere its package is	8.1	Accessible anywhere its class is	8.1
`private`	n/a		Accessible only within its own class	8.1
`protected`	n/a		Accessible within its package and its subclasses	8.1
`abstract`	May not be instantiated	9.4	A method is not implemented here but in a subclass	9.4
`final`	May not be subclassed	9.3	A field may not be changed. A method may not be overridden	2.4 9.3
`static`	A top-level class, not an inner one	8.5	Class member accessed through its class name	2.2

So far, we have considered final fields (which we referred to as constants) and have used the concept of static members extensively. We did mention abstract classes in the last chapter, but their finer nuances are covered once we delve into inheritance in Chapter 9. The meaning of inner-classes, referred to under static, is discussed in the next section. Meanwhile, let us clear up the meaning of the protection modifiers – public, protected and private – now.

Protection in objects

Like many object-oriented languages, Java recognizes that objects are an encapsulation mechanism that provides both a public and a private face. In Java, there is a choice of four levels of protection: private, protected, package (the default) and public. The meaning of these levels is defined in Table 8.1, and illustrated using Figure 8.1.

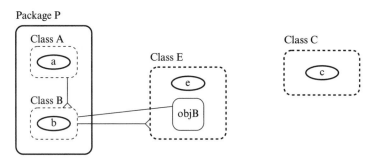

Figure 8.1 *Class diagram for illustrating protection.*

The diagram shows four classes A, B, C and E, each having one variable field, and E having an object as well, instantiated from B. A and B are in the same package, but C and E are not specifically in any package. They are therefore in what is known as the default package, which is where most of our test programs to date have been created. Java does not require that classes be in named packages. In fact the only time we have used packages so far in this book is to put Text into the `javagently` package and `FileMan` into `myutilities`. The classes also have inheritance relationships, which can stay within packages or cross package boundaries. So E inherits from B which inherits from A, although E is in a different package. (Inheritance is fully discussed in Section 9.3.)

Now we can explain the accessibility modifiers as follows, working from the least to the most accessible.

- **private** Applies only to members (not classes) and restricts access to the class that defines it. Therefore if all the variables were declared as private in the example they could only be seen in their own classes, e.g. a in A, b in B and so on.

- **package** In the absence of any other modifier, classes and members have package-wide visibility. Thus a would be seen from B and b from A. Of course, they will need to be suitably qualified in their naming, in the sense that B cannot just ask for a: it must refer to A.a (if a is static) or AObj.a if AObj is an object of class A. By the same token, A and B can see each other, but they cannot be seen outside P.

According to this definition, B could not in fact have package accessibility, because the diagram shows that it is used in an inheritance relationship by E outside the package. What package accessibility says is that the import statement has no effect on classes such as B: it still cannot be seen outside its package.

What about C and E that are not in a named package? In order to be visible to each other, they would have to be stored in the same physical directory, and therefore constitute a virtual package. Then c would be accessible from E and e from C. Once classes are in packages, though, to cross the boundaries requires an import statement.

- **protected** If we want members to be visible only to subclasses in a package (those that inherit) then we change the modifier to protected. In this way we could tighten up on a in A so that only B could see it. Protected members are therefore just like default ones, and the accessibility does not extend ouside a package, even in the case of inheritance.

- **public** The most expansive level says visibility is everywhere, provided the correct connections have been set up. What this means is that if B is public, objects of class B can be created in E or in C provided they import the package P. If C and E are in the same directory, then E can also create objects of class C (without importing). With public, an interesting point arises: making a class public does not automatically make all its members public. Everything keeps its package accessibility unless specifically changed to something else.

Where does this all lead us? Let us explore the modifiers in use in Figure 8.1 in the example that follows.

EXAMPLE 8.1 Exploring protection

Problem Does all this accessibility protection really matter, and does Java check it?

Solution The most convincing way to answer the question is to write a few small classes and experiment with various levels of accessibility. Before we do, we note the minimum levels of protection that could be allowed for the relationships in Figure 8.1 to be valid:

- A will have package accessibility because it is only used in its package.

- a also has package accessibility because it is called by B, which is within its package.

- b has public accessibility because it is could be used outside its package by E.

- B is public, so that E, which is not associated with it via inheritance, can create objects of B.

- c and e are private.

None of the items uses the protected level. In fact, protected has a very limited usage, its sole purpose being to control accessibility within a family hierarchy. More often, we want to make members private to a class, or accessible within a package (the default).

Program Now let's set up a small program to reflect Figure 8.1. Notice that we can keep adding classes to package P. Any public class should be in its own file with the same name as its class. The directory structure is also important, as the files associated with P must be in a directory called P.

```
IN DIRECTORY P, FILE A.java

package P;

class A {
  int a;
  public A () { a=1; }
}
```

```
IN DIRECTORY P, FILE B.java

package P;

public class B extends A {
    public int b;
    public B() {
      b = 1;
      a = 1;
    }
}
```

Some points need clarification here. Firstly, why is A's constructor declared as public, when A itself is not? The answer is a bit complicated. B inherits from A. When B's constructor is called, its first action is to call its superconstructor, if any, which in this case is A. Java requires that such implicit calls of constructors can only be made if they are public. For the same reason, B's constructor is public, so that E can use it.

The second point is to notice that reference is made directly to a, since A is in the same package as B, and visibility has been established through inheritance. To summarize, the three ways of obtaining visibility to a member in the same package are:

- inheritance and use a member reference

- create an object and use an object.member reference

- for a static member, use a class.member reference.

Now we look at E, in a simple version first, together with C, which can be in the same file. Since neither is used by anything else, nor has a main method, the file name is immaterial, but by convention we call it E.

```
IN any other directory, FILE E.java with CLASSPATH including P
```

```
import P.*;

class E extends B {
  private e;

  B objB = new B();

  E () {
    objB.b = 2;
  }
}

class C {
  private c;
  C {c = 1;}
}
```

This system will compile correctly, indicating that we have created a compatible set of modifiers.

To test the modifiers further, let us add the full range of four members to B and see what happens. The new B becomes:

```
package P;

public class B extends A {
    public     int bPublic;
               int bPackage;
    protected int bProtected;
    private    int bPrivate;
    public B() {
      b = 1;
      a = 1;
    }
}
```

and we reference the new fields in E, as well as make use of A, as follows:

```
import P.*;

class E extends B {
  private int e;

  A objA = new A();
  B objB = new B();

  E () {
    objB.bPublic = 2;
    obj.bPackage = 2;
    objB.bProtected = 2;
    objB.bPrivate = 2;
  }
}
```

While the new B compiles, E causes five errors. They are:

```
E.java:6 Can't access class P.A. Only public classes and interfaces in
other packages can be accessed.
```

That is clear enough. Just in case it is not, it is repeated again for line 6 when the constructor is discovered. The next error is:

```
E.java:11 Variable bPackage in class P.B not accessible from class E.
```

Notice that the compiler accepted line 10, where access to the bPublic was made. However, the last two accesses are also thrown out:

```
E.java:12 Can't access protected field bProtected in class P.B.  P.B is not
           a subclass of the currect class.
E.java:13 Variable bPrivate in class P.B not accessible from class E.
```

In general therefore, Java gives quite explanatory messages, and there is no doubt that all the errors are caught.

8.2 Designing an object-oriented program

We now consider the design and development of an example that will make considerable use of classes and have many objects instantiated from them.

EXAMPLE 8.2   Nelson's Coffee Shop

Problem Nelson's Coffee Shop is looking to computerize its inventory. It would like to investigate what information it needs about coffee stocks and what operations it should incorporate to handle them.

Solution At this stage we are not going to write the whole inventory program! We are just looking at the definition of the objects. In so doing, though, we shall bear in mind that while coffee may be the main selling item at the shop, it may in the future also sell pastries, ice-creams and so on.

Definition The shop does not sell just one kind of coffee, but many kinds, such as Java, Columbian, VIP and Kenyan. Coffee is going to be a class, and we shall create different coffee objects. In looking at stocks of coffee, we can list the data items that need to be taken into account when recording information about a particular blend. Such a list is the starting point for an object definition. At the same time, we take a guess at the general type of each data item. The first such list is shown in Table 8.2. String, real, integer and date all have existing equivalents in Java.

Table 8.2 *Data items for the coffee class*

Item	Type
Name	String
Price	Double (graz)
Amount in stock	Integer (kilograms)
Reorder level	Integer (kilograms)
Barcode	String
Sell-by date	Date

Looking at this list, we notice that it is too simple. Whereas the first five properties refer to coffee in general, the sell-by date is going to differ for each *batch* of coffee as it comes into the shop. What this means is that a batch is another object. Not only must it record the date, but it also keeps a count of the number of kilograms of coffee for that date. The main coffee object will keep a cumulative total. This relationship is illustrated in Figure 8.2.

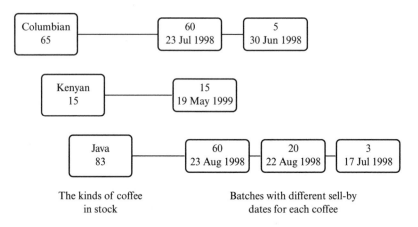

The kinds of coffee   Batches with different sell-by
in stock   dates for each coffee

Figure 8.2 *Multiple classes and objects for the coffee shop.*

The next part of the definition concerns the operations. We treat these in two groups: those for a blend of coffee (Table 8.3) and those for particular batches (Table 8.4). Starting with the coffee, there is a list of operations that seem likely. Some of these have implications for batches.We can see that there is a hierarchy between the two types of objects: coffee objects call batch operations, but not vice versa. The method to remove old stock will consider each batch in turn and nullify a batch if it finds it is too old. Similarly, selling coffee could bring a batch down to zero.

Table 8.3 *Operations on coffee blends*

Operations on coffee	Implications for batches
Prepare to enter stock	
Display coffee blend's data	
Check reorder level	
Change price	
Add stock	Add a new batch
Sell coffee	Subtract stock from relevant batches
Remove old stock	Check sell-by date

Table 8.4 *Operations on coffee batches*

Operations on batches	Implications for coffee
Add a new batch	
Display data about a batch	
Check how much is available	
Check sell-by date	
Sell	

How can an object be removed? It will all depend on how the batch objects are arranged. The only grouping structure we know of so far is an array, and we can immediately see that it is a singularly inappropriate structure if we want to delete items: all those following will have to move up, or we have to handle gaps.

Of course there is a better way, but in order not to extend this part of the example for too long, we shall tackle that in Section 8.3, and return to the coffee shop in Section 8.4. Consequently, we will not implement the methods to sell coffee or remove old stock at this point, and will be content to keep batches in an array.

Classes Now we can try to express the design in Java. Starting with the specification of the `Batch` class:

```
class Batch  {

  /* The Batch class                  by J M Bishop Oct 1996
   * --------------                    Java 1.1 October 1997
   * for products with sell-by-dates.
   * Can be tested with the Coffee class main program. */
  private double inStock;
  private Date sellByDate;

  Batch (double k, Date d)
```

```
double   available ( );
boolean sell (double k);
void     display ();
boolean pastSellByDate();
private double inStock
private Date sellByDate

}
```

The details of the methods have not yet been filled in. Let us first look at how they are used. To create a new batch, the Coffee class will include a statement of the form:

```
freshBatch = new Batch (kilos, roastDay);
```

The new batch will have to be linked to the other batches in some way, but we shall leave that issue for the time being. When coffee is sold, the method responsible must first check the availability in the oldest batch and sell as much as it can there. If the order is not complete, the next batch is offered. Let us assume that in an array of batches, batch B[i] contains the oldest coffee. The statement to call it to sell k1 kilograms will be:

```
B[i].sell(k1);
```

If we needed to reduce stock from another batch, identified by B[j], then

```
B[j].sell(k2);
```

would refer to a different stock and date. The two would not be confused, because they are in different objects.

With respect to accessibility, Batch is always going to be used with coffee, so there is no need to make it public at this stage. The four methods it provides to the coffee class can therefore also have default accessibility. However, the fields a batch uses should not be accessed from outside, and therefore are declared as private.

The definition of the Coffee object proceeds in a similar way. Its outline is:

```
class Coffee {

    /*  The Coffee class        by J M Bishop Oct 1996
     *  ---------------         Java 1.1 October 1997
     *  keeps an inventory of batches of coffee of a
     *  particular kind or blend
     */

    Coffee ( );

    Coffee (String s)

    void prepareToStock (BufferedReader in);
    boolean newBatchIn (BufferedReader in);
```

```
    void display ();
    double sell (double k);
    boolean stocksLow ();
    void changePrice (double p);
    void checkSellByDate ();

    private String name;
    private double price;    // per kg
    private double stock;    // kgs
    private double reorder; // kgs;

    private Batch B [ ] = new Batch [10];
    private int batches = 0;
}
```

As with a batch, the variables are all declared as private, which means that they cannot be altered from outside, only from methods within the class itself. The constructor has no parameters, and in fact does nothing either: all the setting of values is done inside prepareToStock. Why did we do it this way? The reason is that the details of the coffee will be read from a file; they are not available in the program itself. In the next version of the program, we will add a second constructor.

Both the prepareToStock method and newBatchIn will be reading data, and they both get passed the data stream concerned from the main program, which creates coffee objects. The class diagram so far is shown in Figure 8.3. Notice that Coffee uses some of the methods of Batch, and there is therefore a solid arrowed line to it. Also, the array of batches kept in Coffee is declared as of the class Batch, and this instantiation is shown by a plain line. The private variables are shown grouped with private lines down the side of the class. (See Figures 3.4 and 3.5 for the class notation.)

Data An important consideration for the operation of the reading in of coffee is how the data should be arranged. We choose to keep it on file at this stage, but as soon as we get to Chapter 11 (not very far away now) we shall be able to input data with a graphical user interface. The alternative, that of prompting the user on the screen, line by line, is really very tedious and not part of modern programming any more.

The data can be arranged on file as follows:

```
name
price reorder-level
stock sell-by-date       (repeated for each batch)
0
```

with an example being

```
Columbian
59.95 10
10 15-Apr-97
25.5 31-May-97
0
```

```
Java
63.50 30
20 23-May-97
100 12-Jul-97
12.25 1-Aug-97
0
Kenyan
60.75 10
15.75 20-May-97
0
```

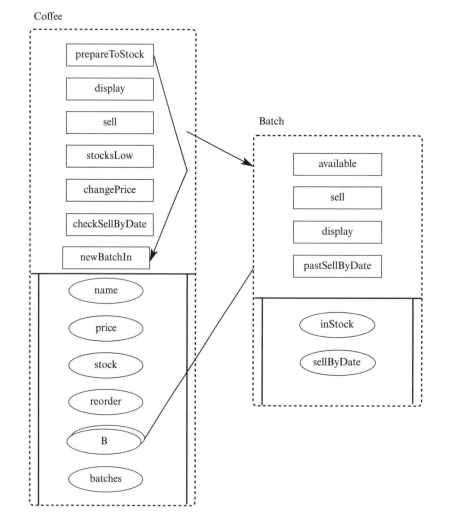

Figure 8.3 *Class diagram for the* Coffee *and* Batch *classes.*

The zero after each set of batches is necessary to enable the loop to end. (See Section 5.3 for a discussion on this issue.) The date is going to be read in as a string and converted to a `Date` object. How this is done was discussed in Section 7.4.

Program And finally we have the program. It consists of three classes, `Batch`, `Coffee` and main program, `CoffeeShop`. The latter contains a little test main program that causes the data to be read in and printed out. Nothing else happens at this stage, but of course we have achieved a lot: we have written a large-ish object-oriented program, and it contains two kinds of user-defined objects. Just as a matter of interest, can you count how many other kinds of objects it contains as well?

```
import java.io.*;
import java.util.*;
import java.text.*;

class Batch  {

  /* The Batch class                    by J M Bishop Oct 1996
   * ---------------                     Java 1.1 October 1997
   * for products with sell-by-dates.
   * Can be tested with the Coffee class main program. */

  private double inStock;
  private Date sellByDate;

  Batch (double k, Date d) {
    inStock = k;
    sellByDate = d;
  }

  double available ( ) {
    return inStock;
  }

  DateFormat DF = DateFormat.getDateInstance();

  boolean sell (double k) {
    inStock -= k;
    System.out.println("Sold "+k+" from batch "
              + DF.format(sellByDate));
    return instock <=0;//sold out
  }

  void display () {
    System.out.println("\t\t"+DF.format(sellByDate) +
        " : " + inStock + "kg");
  }

}


//=======================================================
```

```java
import java.io.*;
import java.util.*;
import javagently.*;
import java.text.*;

class Coffee {

  /*  The Coffee class        by J M Bishop Oct 1996
   *  ----------------        Java 1.1 October 1997
   *  keeps an inventory of batches of coffee of a
   *  particular kind or blend
   */

  Coffee ( ) {}

  Coffee (String s) {name = new String (s);};

  void prepareToStock (BufferedReader in)
             throws IOException {
    name = Text.readString(in);
    price = Text.readDouble(in);
    reorder = Text.readInt(in);
    batches = 0;
    stock = 0;
  }

  DateFormat DF = DateFormat.getDateInstance();

  boolean newBatchIn (BufferedReader in)
          throws IOException {
    double a = Text.readDouble(in);
    if (a == 0)
      return false;
    else {
      stock += a;
      Date d = new Date ();
      String s = Text.readString(in);
      try {
        d = DF.parse(s);
      } catch (ParseException e) {
        System.out.println("Error in date " + s);
      }
      B[batches] = new Batch (a,d);
      batches ++;
      return true;
    }
  }

  void display () {
    System.out.println(name+" @ G"+
          Text.writeDouble(price,1,2)+" per kg");
    for (int i = 0; i < batches; i++)
      B[i].display ();
    System.out.println("\t" + stock + "kg in stock. Reorder level is "
                +reorder+"kg\n");
  }
```

```
   private String name;
   private double price;    // per kg
   private double stock; // kgs
   private double reorder; // kgs;
   private Batch B [ ] = new Batch [10];
   private int batches=0;
}

// =======================================================

import java.io.*;
import java.util.*;
import java.text.*;
import javagently.*;

class CoffeeShop {

   /* A test Coffee Shop program    by J M Bishop Oct 1996
    * -------------------------    Java 1.1 October 1997
    * checks that data can be read into the
    * Coffee and Batch classes, and printed out again.
    * Uses an array to store several objects of each.
    */

  public static void main (String [] args) throws IOException {

     BufferedReader in = Text.open("coffee.dat");

     // Introductory messages
     Coffee C [ ] = new Coffee [10];
     int blend;
     System.out.println("Nelson's Coffee Shop");
     System.out.println("Inventory control");
     System.out.println("Stocking from coffee.data");

     // Read in the data for the coffees or blends
     for (blend=0; blend<10; blend++) {
       try {
         C[blend] = new Coffee ();
         C[blend].prepareToStock (in);
         boolean morebatches = true;
         while (morebatches)
           morebatches = C[blend].newBatchIn (in);
       }
       catch (EOFException e) {
         System.out.println("That's the shop stocked for today\n");
         break;
       }
     }

     // Display all the details
     DateFormat DF = DateFormat.getDateInstance(DateFormat.FULL);
     System.out.println("The contents on " + DF.format(new Date()));
     for (int i = 0; i<blend; i++)
       C[i].display();
  }
}
```

Testing For the data above, the output would be:

```
Nelson's Coffee Shop
Inventory control
Stocking from coffee.data
That's the shop stocked for today
The contents on Saturday, December 13, 1997
Columbian @ G59.95 per kg
        15-Apr-97 : 10.0kg
        31-May-97 : 25.5kg
     35.5kg in stock. Reorder level is 10.0kg
Java @ G63.50 per kg
        23-May-97 : 20.0kg
        12-Jul-97 : 100.0kg
        01-Aug-97 : 12.25kg
    132.25kg in stock. Reorder level is 30.0kg
Kenyan @ G60.75 per kg
        20-May-97 : 15.75kg
     15.75kg in stock. Reorder level is 10.0kg
```

8.3 Properties of objects

We now look at more of the properties of objects, and how they can be manipulated in a program.

Null objects

Objects that have not been through a construction process are given the special value null by the Java virtual machine. We can test if an object is null, for example

```
if (s == null)
```

If we try to access members of a null object, then Java will raise an exception, called a nullPointerException.[1]

The this identifier

Every object can access all of its members by name. The full name for a member is this.member, where this is an identifier signifying the current object. While there is no ambiguity over member names, the use of this is unnecessary. We would employ it in a case where a method has a local field or parameter with the same name as that defined in the class: then we can refer to the class field by its full name, prefixing it with this. An example of the need for such qualification is found in the equals method in the Batch class in the next example.

---

[1] It should of course be a NullObjectException, but Java shows its C++ influences here.

Objects versus variables

How do objects differ from variables? The obvious distinction is based on storage.

- A **variable** has storage for a single value and has available a predefined set of operations, based on its type.

- An **object** has storage for a group of several values, together with a coherent set of user-defined methods that operate on them, all encapsulated in the class from which the object is instantiated.

Apart from the number of items stored, there is another very important distinction. Variables are stored as actual **values**, whereas objects are given **references** to the group of values they represent. A reference is an indirect way of getting to where the actual value is stored. Arrays are, like objects, stored via references.

Consider the declarations from the `Coffee` class, namely

```
private String name;
private double price;   // per kg
private double stock;   // kgs
private double reorder;// kgs;
private Batch B [ ] = new Batch [10];
private int batches;
```

For our first coffee, Columbian, the object's storage would be represented as in Figure 8.4. `name` is an object. It therefore has a reference to where the characters of the string are actually stored. `price`, `stock`, `reorder` and `batches` are all variables and are stored as values. `B` is an array, and therefore has a reference to its first element, `B[0]`. Each element of the array is a `Batch`, so each is a reference to an object. The first two are created with values, the others are null. The object containing all this information is named `C[0]`, within the `C` array.

The `Object` superclass

We have already been introduced to the superclass `Object` in Section 6.4. `Object` is central to the theory of classes in Java. Java achieves generality by using objects of different classes in the same parts of the program, while just calling them all `Object`s. This principle is important in cloning, which is the next topic for discussion.

Object equality and cloning

There are two implications of storing objects as references. The first concerns **equality**. A straight comparison such as

```
B[i].sellByDate == B[j].sellByDate
```

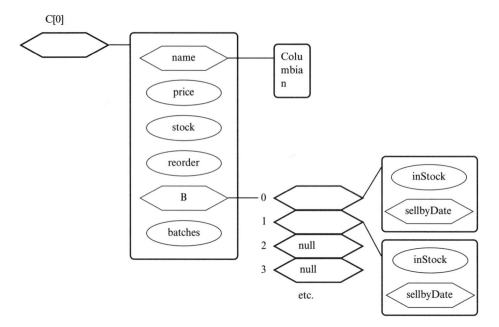

Figure 8.4 *The relationship between variables and objects.*

will compare the *references* of the two dates: that is, do they refer to the same storage? It will not compare the values, which is probably what we intended. To compare the values themselves (all together as a group) we use an `equals` method which we must define for each new class of objects. For example, in the `Batch` class we could define:

```
boolean equals (Batch b) {
   return (this.sellByDate.equals(b.sellByDate));
}
```

Because `equals` is user-defined, the user (us) must decide on what basis to establish equality. Here we have said that two batches are equal if they have the same sell-by date: it does not matter how many kilograms is in each of them. Because dates are also objects, we had to use the `Date`'s class `equals` method to perform the comparison.

The second implication is for **assignment**. Assigning two objects, for example

```
tempBatch = B[i];
```

will copy the *references*. To copy the values, we need to **clone**[2] the object using a method that once again must be defined for each new class as shown in the following forms. Using Figure 8.4 as a starting point, Figure 8.5 illustrates the difference between the assignment and cloning of objects.

---

[2] For clone, read copy if you like.

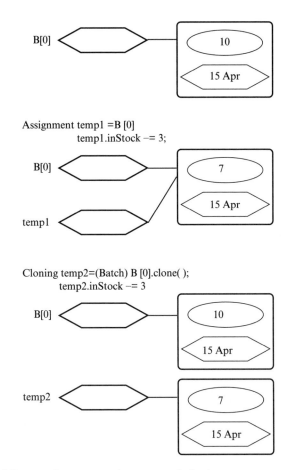

Figure 8.5 *The difference between assignment and cloning.*

For assignment, temp1's reference becomes the same as B[0]'s. Any changes made to B[0] are reflected in temp1. With cloning, a copy of the object is made, and temp2 refers to the copy. Now temp2 and B[0] can change independently.

As mentioned, the class is responsible for defining what is meant by equals and clone. For our example, a clone for Batch could be:

```
public Object clone () {
  Batch x = new Batch (inStock,null);
  x.sellByDate = new Date(sellByDate.getTime());
  return x;
}
```

Cloning a batch involves copying both data items, the stock and the date. `inStock` is a variable so it can be assigned or supplied in the constructor to the new object, as is done here. Copying the date means making a new date object and supplying the existing one to its constructor. An additional point is that cloning is a special operation in Java, and therefore any class that wants to clone must implement the `Clonable` interface. Interfaces are discussed in Chapter 10. Meanwhile, we can give the general form for a clone declaration:

Clone declaration

```
modifier class classname implements Clonable {

  public Object clone ( ) {
    classname obj = new classname (parameters);
    statements to copy the fields to obj
    return obj;
  }
}
```

Put altogether, Table 8.5 sums up the differences between variables and objects.

Table 8.5 *Variables and objects compared*

	Created from a	Stored as	Copied with	Compared with
Variable	type	value	assignment =	equality ==
Object	class	reference	`clone` method	`equals` method

Class conversions

We saw that variables of different types can be converted into each other if this is meaningful. The same applies to objects. In particular, there are methods defined for the Java superclass, `Object`, which can be used by other objects. However, before the results are assigned, an explicit type cast must be made. `clone` is one of these methods. Thus to clone a `Batch` and print it out would require:

```
Batch tempBatch = (Batch) B[0].clone();
System.out.println(tempBatch);
```

Calling the `clone` method on `B[0]` will return an `Object`. It must return an `Object` because that is what the `Clonable` interface requires. But we can convert it to a `Batch` by mentioning the class name. You can insert the clone method into `Batch` and the above statement into `Coffee` and check that it all works.

8.4 Lists of objects

One of the problems with arrays is that they are rigid, both in size and arrangement. One cannot remove an element without pushing all the later elements up, and this takes time and effort. Hashtables, discussed in Chapter 6, get away from both of these restrictions, but they store the data in a somewhat unconventional way ('hashed'). The classical alternative to an array is the **linked list**, and we shall spend this section looking at how one can be defined in Java, and how it integrates with the example in Section 8.1.

In an array, items are stored sequentially, and we know that item $i+1$ follows item i. In a linked list, the items are regarded as self-standing, but connected together by **links**. These links can be made and broken, and thus we can have a structure that, unlike an array, can grow and shrink at will while the program is executing.

Suppose we have some string objects already created in a linked list as in Figure 8.6.

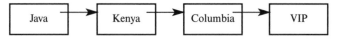

Figure 8.6 *A simple linked list of coffees.*

If the object with 'Columbia' in it needs to be removed, then we can just arrange to redirect the links as in Figure 8.7. Java will then **garbage collect** the space that the unwanted object occupied and it will be no more.

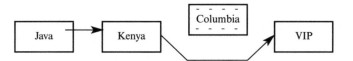

Figure 8.7 *A linked list after deleting a node.*

The question is: what are the links? They are nothing more complicated than the references that we introduced in the previous section. So in order to establish a chain of objects like this, we just need to declare an object inside itself and space for a reference – the link – will reserved. We shall call the objects forming a linked list **nodes**.

Creating a list

The Java for a general sort of node is:

```
class Node {
  /* The Node class for storing objects that are linked
     together. */
```

```
// The constructor copies in the data
// and the link to the given node
// (which may be null).
Node (Object d, Node n)   {
  data = d;
  link = n;
}

Object data;
Node link;
}
```

To create such a node, we must supply a value for its data and the node it is going to be linked to. Initially, the list will have nowhere to link to, so the following will work:

```
Node list = new Node ("VIP",null);
```

which gives us Figure 8.8.

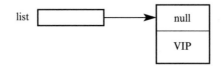

Figure 8.8 *A list with one node.*

To link the next node to the list, the statement is:

```
list = new Node ("Columbia", list);
```

Consider this statement a step at a time. new Node creates the space for a node. The data item is filled with "Columbia". The link item is filled with a reference to where list is currently referring. Then the list object is made to refer to this new one, shown in Figure 8.9.

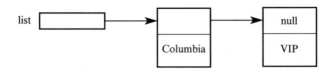

Figure 8.9 *A list after a second node has been added.*

And so the creation of the list can continue. To add the next two nodes, we could use:

```
list = new Node ("Kenya", list);
list = new Node ("Java", list);
```

Notice that we have taken the short cut of drawing the strings inside the nodes themselves. As objects in their own rights, they should of course be represented with references, so that the Columbia node, for instance, would actually look as shown in Figure 8.10.

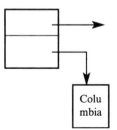

Figure 8.10 *A node with a string item.*

Removing from a list

Having created a list which has nice dynamic properties, we must consider the Java for removing an item from it. Let us start with the list shown in Figure 8.11. Assume that x, referring to Columbia, has been identified as the object to be removed. What we want to do is take the link that is referring to Columbia – that is, Kenya – and make it refer to what Columbia is presently referring to – VIP.

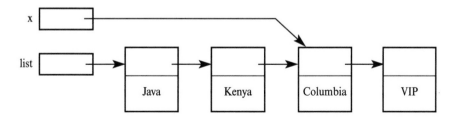

Figure 8.11 *A list before removing a node.*

The assignment should be:

```
Kenya's link = x.link;
```

However, there is a problem with the left-hand side of this assignment. We do not have a name or reference for the Kenyan node. Objects in a linked list are essentially anonymous, except for the first one, unless we travel through the list and establish temporary names for nodes. That is of course exactly what we did in order to find Columbia and have x refer to it. The answer to the problem is to keep track of *two* objects as we look for something, one running behind the other. Let us assume that this has been done, and that xPrevious refers to Kenya. The assignment then can be:

```
xPrevious.link = x.link;
```

and the resulting diagram is shown in Figure 8.12. It does not matter that Columbia is still referring to VIP as it is no longer linked into the list. However, since another object, x, is still referring to Columbia, it is not garbage collected[3] yet.

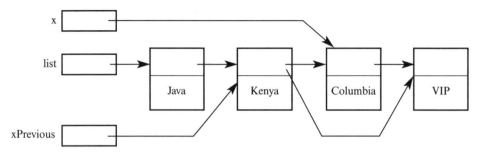

Figure 8.12 *A list after node x has been removed.*

However, there is a problem: if x refers to the first node, Java, then what is the meaning of xPrevious? It will start at null. If xPrevious is null, it will not be possible to use the assignment above. This possibility must therefore be taken care of in the remove method as follows:

```
if (xPrevious == null)
   list = x.link;
else
   xPrevious.link = x.link;
```

Searching a list

Finally, we consider how x was found in the first place. Now that we know we have to keep track of the previous node as well as the current one, we can devise the general loop for finding a sought-after value in a list as follows:

```
Node x = list;
Node xprev = null;
do {
   if (x.data.equals(soughtAfter)) break;
   xprev = x;
   x = x.link
} while (x != null);
```

We assume that data is an object, rather than a variable, and will therefore need to be compared using its equals method.

---

[3] Garbage collection is the process of reclaiming storage. Java does it automatically when objects are no longer in use.

EXAMPLE 8.3   A class for lists

Problem Given that lists are going to be useful in many circumstances, it makes sense to define them as a class and put the class in a package.

Solution A classic list class is somewhat more sophisticated in implementation than the one we have developed here, and we shall investigate it in Chapter 15. However the differences are in performance rather than functionality. In keeping with our 'Gently' approach, we shall complete the simple list class here.

Class design What are the members of such a class? The data will be three objects referring to the `start` of the list and the items we are at now and previously, `prev`. We shall declare them private to prevent untoward access, and provide all legitimate access to the list through methods.

What methods should the class include? We have already explored `add` and `remove`. In addition to these, a list must be able to return its `current` element – that is, where the user is currently in the list – and also to indicate whether the list is `empty` or not.

In order to scan through the list for various reasons, such as searching or displaying the items, we provide a trio of methods which mirror the parts of a for-loop. These are `reset`, `succ` (for successor) and `eol` (for end-of-list).

Program The proposed `List` class makes use of the `Node` class, as discussed above. It is:

```
package myutilities;

public class List  {

    /* The List class      by J M Bishop October 1997
     *                      no change for Java 1.1
     * Maintains a list of objects
     * in LIFO order and provides simple
     * iterator methods.
     */

    private Node start, now, prev;

    public List() {
        now = null;
        start = null;
        prev = null;
    }

    public void add(Object x) {
        if (start == null) {
            start = new Node(x, null);
            now = start;
        } else {
```

```
                Node T = new Node(x, now.link);
                now.link = T; prev = now;
                now = T;
            }
        }

    public void remove() {
        if (isempty() || eol()) {
            return;
        } else {
            if (prev == null) {
                start = now.link; now = start;
            } else {
                prev.link = now.link;
                now = now.link;
            }
        }
    }

    public boolean isempty() {
        return start == null;
    }

    public Object current() {
        return now.data;
    }

    public void reset() {
        now = start;
        prev = null;
    }

    public boolean eol() {
        return now == null;
    }

    public void succ() {
        now = now.link;
        if (prev == null)
            prev = start;
        else
            prev = prev.link;
    }

class Node {

    /* The Node class for storing objects that
     * are linked together.
     */

    Object data;
    Node link;
    /* The constructor copies in the data
     * and the link to the given node
```

```
     * (which may be null).
     */
    Node(Object d, Node n) {
        data = d;
        link = n;
    }

  }

}
```

Armed with `List`, we can proceed to rewrite the Coffee Shop program to avoid using arrays, as in Case Study 3. First, though, we need to pick up on one more aspect of Java classes which affects object handling options in the rest of the book.

8.5 Inner classes

In Java 1.1, classes achieved 'first class' status in that they can now be declared any-where, used as parameters, and as local members to other classes, methods and blocks. Table 8.6 summarizes the four kinds of inner classes that can be used:

Table 8.6 *Types of inner classes*

Inner class type	Defined as	Used for	Comment
Nested top-level	Static member of another class	Grouping classes	Name includes enclosing class name
Member	Ordinary member of another class	Helper class, sharing members among classes	• Access to enclosing instance of other class; • Special syntax for `this`, `new` and `super`; • Cannot have static members.
Local	Member of a method of block	Adapter class to be passed as a call-back, e.g. in event-handling	Same as for member
Anonymous	Unnamed member of a method or block	One off class defined where needed	Same as for member; no name or constructor; is only be instantiated once; defined in an expression

Nested classes

A nested class is just like any other class, but it is grouped inside another class for ease of development and handling. Often it is not convenient to have every class in a different file, and with nested classes, we can keep them together. By declaring the class as static, we indicate that it is to have the same top-level status as the enclosing class. Nested classes can be imported from within their enclosing class. In a way, they are similar in effect to Java's package concept.

Member classes

Member classes are typically helper classes for the enclosing class. They are not visible outside it, but can make use of all its members, private or not. While an inner class may not have the same name as its enclosing class, it can have the same name as other member classes of other enclosing classes, thus cutting down on the number of names one has to invent in a big system. Member classes are regarded as elegant and worth using. In fact, we have already done so in Example 8.3. Node is used exclusively by List, so we declared it as a member class of List. It does not use any of List's members, but it could.

Because of the ability to use one's own members and those of an enclosing class, member classes can distinguish two versions of this. An unqualified this refers to the member class, whereas to refer to the enclosing class we preface this with its name. Similar extensions are made for new and super.

A notable restriction of member classes is that they may not have static members. Any static members required must be grouped in the top-level class.

Anonymous classes

Anonymous classes perform the same function as local classes with the restriction that they do not have a name and therefore can only be instantiated once, at the point where they are defined. They are very useful with Java's event handlers, which we shall study in Chapters 10 and 11. To give the flavour of such a class, here is a typical usage:

```
f.addWindowListener(new WindowAdapter () {
  public void windowClosing(WindowEvent e) {
    System.exit(0);
  }
});
```

WindowAdapter is an interface (see Section 9.2) which needs to have a window-Closing method defined, so that it can be called at the appropriate moment for the window called f here. So we create a new anonymous class as a parameter to the addWindowListener method. The whole class is passed as a parameter and at the appropriate moment, windowClosing, as here defined, will be called. Anonymous classes are used often in Chapter 10.

Local classes

Local classes are much the same as anonymous ones, except that we give them names and can have more than one instantiation. The choice as to which to use is 90% a matter of taste.

8.6 Case Study 3: Nelson's Coffee Shop

Opportunity

Nelson's Coffee Shop wants to take advantage of the List class to make the stock of coffee types and batches dynamic: that is, the number does not have to be set at the start, and batches (and coffees) can be removed when sold out. The solution, of course, is to use the List class just defined.

Algorithms

The algorithmic part of the system relates to handling sales. These will be entered from an orders file with the name of the coffee followed by the number of kg. First of all, the main program must find the relevant coffee in its list, then call the sell method in that Coffee class. Two things can go wrong:

- the type of coffee is not found;
- there is not enough in stock.

In both cases, the program prints out a suitable message.

Moving now to selling, this algorithm is more complex than one would first imagine. It has to check each batch in turn, using it up and then moving to the next one if there are still kilograms outstanding on the order. The algorithm reduces to that shown in Figure 8.13. The rest of the program follows in similar vein or is fairly simple.

Converting the program

It turns out that the Batch class is independent of how it is put together in a structure. In other words, whether we have arrays of batches, or lists of batches, does not matter to Batch. The Coffee class, however, will have to change slightly. We shall call the new class Coffee2. In the Coffee class where there is an array, replace it with

```
private List BatchStock = new List ();
```

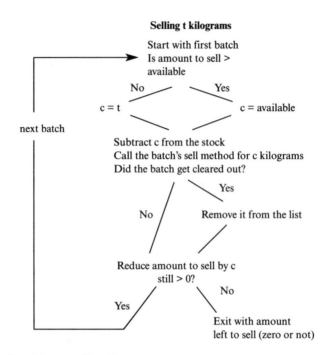

Figure 8.13 *Algorithm to sell coffee.*

This has the effect of creating an object with three node references (to start, now and prev nodes), all initialized to null. The counter, batches, can go as well. Adding a new batch becomes a call to add:

```
BatchStock.add(new Batch (a,d));
```

The loop at the end to print all the batches will use the iteration methods we defined for lists, that is,

```
for (BatchStock.reset(); !BatchStock.eol(); BatchStock.succ()) {
  Batch b = (Batch) BatchStock.current();
  b.display ();
}
```

The reason why the extra local object, b, is necessary is as follows. BatchStock is a List, and it has access to all the List methods. But they are all defined in terms of the superclass Object. There is nothing that ties the List in Coffee2 to the Batch class. We do put batches in it, but to get batches out, we must convert objects to batches. Then the assignment can take place. We now have a local reference to the current object, and can call Batch's display method on it.

Another place where care must be taken over precisely which objects we are dealing with is in the section of the main program which finds a coffee:

```
String s = Text.readString (orders);
Coffee2 blend = new Coffee2 (s);

while (!CoffeeStock.eol()) {
  Coffee2 b = (Coffee2) CoffeeStock.current ();
  if (b.equals(blend)) {found = true; break;}
  else CoffeeStock.succ();
}
```

We cannot of course use == to compare the name of the required coffee with each of the coffees in stock. In the first place, the name is a string, and the coffees are of class Coffee2. That is why we must create a temporary coffee object. Secondly, we must make sure as before that the item that comes off the list is designated as a Coffee2 object, so that the equals method defined for Coffee2 is called. This method looks only at the names. Notice that we have caused a new Coffee2 constructor to be implemented because we have to get a name into the temporary coffee object but do not need to bother about all the other fields, which are set in prepareToStock.

The list of Coffee2 objects is created in exactly the same way, using List. The only other change to the program as we had it before is that we remove the final 0 from the data in order to trigger the EOFException at the right point.

A diagram showing the main classes in the system is given in Figure 8.14.

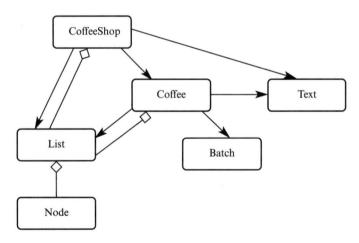

Figure 8.14 *Classes in the dynamic coffee shop.*

The arrowed lines indicate 'uses' in the sense of method calls. The diamond lines indicate composition. Thus CoffeeShop2 has a List (of coffees), as does Coffee2 (of batches). List has several nodes. Notice that CoffeeShop2 is not indicated as having any instances of the Coffee class nor does Coffee2 have any batches. This is not strictly true as they each have a temporary variable respectively. But they do not form a direct composition: the composition is done through the List class.

From the diagram we can deduce that only List knows about nodes and that Batch does not do any input. The other named class in the system is Date (not shown), and it is used by the three main classes.

Program

Given the options for inner classes explained in Section 8.5, how should our five classes be arranged? Well, Node is already a member class of List, and List is compiled into the myutilities package over in the myutilities directory. CoffeeShop2 is a top-level, main program type class. Should Coffee2 and Batch be declared in or with CoffeeShop2 or each other? In fact, the answer is no. Batch is the likeliest candidate for inclusion, but remember that it is also used by the previous version of the system, so it should then remain separate. (It does not have to, as it could be a nested class and therefore accessible to other classes.) For ease of changes and compilation, we leave Coffee2 on its own as well. The program is therefore in three compiled files as follows:

```
/**** The Batch class ****/

/*  as in Example 8.2  */

/**** The Coffee2 class ****/

import java.io.*;
import java.util.*;
import javagently.*;
import java.text.*;


class Coffee2 {

    /* The Improved Coffee class        by J M Bishop Oct 1996
     *                            Java 1.1 October 1997
     * Keeps an inventory of batches of coffee of a
     * particular kind or blend using
     * a Linked List
     */

    private String name;
    private double price;   // per kg
    private double stock; // kgs
    private double reorder; // kgs;
    private List BatchStock = new List ();

    public Coffee2() {
        /* empty construction, because all values
         * are read in via prepareToStock
         */
    }
```

```java
public Coffee2(String s) {
    name = new String(s);
}

void prepareToStock(BufferedReader in) throws IOException {
    name = Text.readString(in);
    price = Text.readDouble(in);
    reorder = Text.readInt(in);
    stock = 0;
}

DateFormat DF = DateFormat.getDateInstance();

boolean newBatchIn(BufferedReader in) throws IOException {
  double a = Text.readDouble(in);
  if (a == 0)
    return false;
  else {
    stock += a;
    Date d = new Date ();
    String s = Text.readString(in);
    try {
      d = DF.parse(s);
    } catch (ParseException e) {
      System.out.println("Error in date " + s);
    }
    BatchStock.add(new Batch(a, d));
    return true;
  }
}

double sell(double toSell) {
    double fromBatch;
    Batch b;

    for (BatchStock.reset(); !BatchStock.eol(); BatchStock.succ()) {
        b = (Batch)BatchStock.current();
        if (toSell > b.available())
            fromBatch = b.available();
        else
            fromBatch = toSell;
        stock -= fromBatch;
        boolean soldOut = b.sell(fromBatch);
        if (soldOut) {
            System.out.println("Batch now empty");
            BatchStock.remove();
        }
        toSell -= fromBatch;
        if (toSell <= 0)
            break;
    }
    System.out.println("Stock report:");
    display();
    return toSell;
}
```

```
      boolean equals(Coffee2 c) {
          return name.equals(c.name);
      }

      void display () {
      System.out.println(name+" @ G"+
            Text.writeDouble(price,1,2)+" per kg");
          for (BatchStock.reset(); !BatchStock.eol(); BatchStock.succ()) {
              Batch b = (Batch)BatchStock.current();
              b.display();
          }
          System.out.println(stock+"kg in stock. Reorder level is "+
                  reorder+"kg\n");
      }

}
```

/* The Coffee Shop 2 class and program ****/

```
import java.io.*;
import java.util.*;
import java.text.*;
import javagently.*;

class CoffeeShop2 {

    /* An Improved Coffee Shop program      by J M Bishop Oct 1996
     * ----------------------------      Java 1.1 October 1997
     * Includes the ability to sell batches of a blend,
     * starting at the oldest.
     */

    public static void stockUp(BufferedReader in, List CoffeeStock)
        throws IOException {
        while (true) {
          try {
            Coffee2 c = new Coffee2();
            c.prepareToStock(in);
            CoffeeStock.add(c);
            boolean morebatches = true;
            while (morebatches)
              morebatches = c.newBatchIn(in);
          } catch (EOFException e) {
            System.out.println("That's the shop stocked for today");
            System.out.println();
            break;
          }
        }
    }

    public static void inventoryReport(List CoffeeStock) {
      System.out.println("Nelson's Coffee Shop");
      System.out.println("Inventory control");
      System.out.println("The coffee stock on "+
          DateFormat.getDateInstance().format(new Date()));
```

```
    for (CoffeeStock.reset(); !CoffeeStock.eol();  CoffeeStock.succ()) {
      Coffee2 c = (Coffee2)CoffeeStock.current();
      c.display();
    }
    System.out.println();
}

public static void makeSales(BufferedReader orders, List CoffeeStock)
      throws IOException {
    while (true) {
      try {
        String s = Text.readString(orders);
        Coffee2 blend = new Coffee2(s);
        double amount = Text.readDouble(orders);
        System.out.println("Order for "+s+"  "+amount);
        System.out.println("=====");

        boolean found = false;
        CoffeeStock.reset();
        while (!CoffeeStock.eol()) {
          Coffee2 b = (Coffee2)CoffeeStock.current();
          if (b.equals(blend)) {
            found = true;
            break;
          } else {
            CoffeeStock.succ();
          }
        }
        if (found) {
          Coffee2 b = (Coffee2)CoffeeStock.current();
          double remainder = b.sell(amount);
          if (remainder > 0)
            System.out.println("Could not match "+remainder+"kg");
        } else {
          System.out.println("Sorry, we're out of that blend.");
        }
        System.out.println();

      } catch (EOFException e) {
        System.out.println();
        System.out.println("Shop closed");
        break;
      }
    }
}

public static void main (String [] args) throws IOException {

    BufferedReader in = Text.open("coffee.dat");
    BufferedReader orders = Text.open("orders.dat");

    List CoffeeStock = new List ();

    System.out.println("Stocking from coffee.data");
    stockUp(in, CoffeeStock);
    inventoryReport(CoffeeStock);
```

```
    System.out.println("Coffee sales");
    makeSales(orders, CoffeeStock);
  }
}
```

Testing

The original data file was:

```
Columbian
59.95 10
10 15-Apr-97
25.5 31-May-97
0
Java
63.50 30
20 23-May-97
100 12-Jul-97
12.25 1-Aug-97
0
Kenyan
60.75 10
15.75 20-May-97
0
```

Let us now add the following orders file:

```
VIP 2
Kenyan 15
Kenyan 2
Java 30
Columbian 25
Columbian 5.5
```

The intention is that the first order's name will not be found. Then all the Kenyan will go in the second order and the third order will not be able to be processed. The Java order will need to take coffee from two batches, as will the first Columbian. The last order is a straightforward one. The detailed output is as follows:

```
Stocking from coffee.data
That's the shop stocked for today

Nelson's Coffee Shop
Inventory control
The coffee stock on 13-Dec-97
Columbian @ G59.95 per kg
     15-Apr-97 : 10.0kg
     31-May-97 : 25.5kg
35.5kg in stock. Reorder level is 10.0kg
```

```
Java @ G63.50 per kg
    23-May-97 : 20.0kg
    12-Jul-97 : 100.0kg
    01-Aug-97 : 12.25kg
132.25kg in stock. Reorder level is 30.0kg
Kenyan @ G60.75 per kg
    20-May-97 : 15.75kg
15.75kg in stock. Reorder level is 10.0kg

Coffee sales
Order for VIP  2.0
=====
Sorry, we're out of that blend.

Order for Kenyan  15.0
=====
Sold 15.0 from batch 20-May-97
Stock report:
Kenyan @ G60.75 per kg
    20-May-97 : 0.75kg
0.75kg in stock. Reorder level is 10.0kg

Order for Kenyan  2.0
=====
Sold 0.75 from batch 20-May-97
Batch now empty
Stock report:
Kenyan @ G60.75 per kg
0.0kg in stock. Reorder level is 10.0kg
Could not match 1.25kg

Order for Java  30.0
=====
Sold 20.0 from batch 23-May-97
Batch now empty
Sold 10.0 from batch 12-Jul-97
Stock report:
Java @ G63.50 per kg
    12-Jul-97 : 90.0kg
    01-Aug-97 : 12.25kg
102.25kg in stock. Reorder level is 30.0kg

Order for Columbian  25.0
=====
Sold 10.0 from batch 15-Apr-97
Batch now empty
Sold 15.0 from batch 31-May-97
Stock report:
Columbian @ G59.95 per kg
    31-May-97 : 10.5kg
10.5kg in stock. Reorder level is 10.0kg

Order for Columbian  5.5
=====
Sold 5.5 from batch 31-May-97
```

```
Stock report:
Columbian @ G59.95 per kg
      31-May-97 : 5.0kg
5.0kg in stock. Reorder level is 10.0kg


Shop closed
```

Other List classes

We have explained in detail how to create a simple List class. In Chapter 15 we look at the some similar classes Java provides, as well as a more powerful list class. The mission of this book is to teach you more than just the syntax. It aims to teach you the fundamental principles of programming as well. Knowing how to program a list class is one of those principles. You may not use it hereafter, but at least you will have understood how one works, and will be able to apply this knowledge in other circumstances later on in your programming career.

SUMMARY

This has been a crucial chapter in the development of programming skills. It has included specific details about objects, how to use them in a grand plan, and the model of a linked list as the alternative data structure to an array. Full details of the meaning of protection modifiers have been spelt out, clarifying the relationship between packages, classes and methods.

Developing a class involves looking at the data items and methods required. Interaction with other classes must be considered at the start, as must the constructors. Empty constructors are possible, especially for classes dealing with input data. The declarations of objects results in a reference to storage, whereas the values of variables are stored directly. The implications of this model are that equality and copying of objects have to be done via the equals and clone methods. Clone relies on the superclass, Object, and therefore class conversions become necessary.

Lists are a prime alternative to arrays for storing sequences of data. They have the advantage that they can grow and shrink dynamically as items are added and removed. All programmers should know how to set one up.

QUIZ

8.1   In Example 8.2, if c is a Coffee object, why would the compiler reject the following statement in the main CoffeeShop program:

```
System.out.println (c.name);
```

8.2   In example 8.2, would it have been possible to have defined the prepareToStock method, which reads in values for the particular coffee's batches, so that it could be called thus:

```
prepareToStock (in, C[blend]);
```

8.3   In the Coffee class there is a reference in sell to

```
display ();
```

and in `display` to

```
b.display ();
```

What is the difference between the two calls?

8.4 Define a `clone` method for `Coffee`.

8.5 In Figure 8.1 and the accompanying program in Example 8.1, how would we have to declare e if we wanted it to be visible from C?

8.6 Draw a diagram showing how the list in Figure 8.6 would look if another coffee, say `Kona`, was added. Use the `add` method of the `List` class.

8.7 Consider the output at the end of Case Study 3 (Section 8.6). What would happen if an order for 100kg of Java came in?

8.8 Why will the following statement not give the result expected?

```
System.out.println("s is an empty string is " + s==null);
```

How should the statement be written?

8.9 What is the essential difference between a nested class and a member class?

8.10 Draw a class diagram showing all the items and associations in the `Coffee2` class. Use Figures 8.2, 8.3 and 8.13 as guides.

PROBLEMS

8.1 **Batches in order**. The `List` class used by Nelson's Coffee Shop always adds new nodes to the start of the list. The data in the `orders.dat` file was carefully arranged so that for the batches, the oldest batches were listed last and therefore would get sold first. If batches are arriving at different times of day, one could not always ensure that this happened. In the `Batch` class, add a new method that can find the correct position for a new batch, based on its sell-by date (use the `reset`, `eol` and `succ` methods). Then write another adding method in `List` – say, `insert` – that will add the new batch in the correct position.

8.2 **Coffees in order**. Using the same philosophy as in Problem 8.1, we would like to keep the coffee types in alphabetical order. Write a method for the `Coffee2` class which will find the correct position for a new coffee, and then use the same `insert` method to insert it.

8.3 **Club database.** Choose an activity with which you are familiar and design a class and object structure to store information about the people, equipment or events associated with the activity. Add methods to access the information.

CHAPTER 9

Abstraction and inheritance

9.1 Class power

Object-oriented programming has several ways in which the use of classes is made more powerful. We have already been using classes extensively for what is known as **composition**, in other words, creating an object in a class based on another class. An example of this would be the array of batches kept in the coffee class. Two other techniques that we shall now study are **abstraction** and **inheritance**.

Abstraction

Abstraction enables a class or method to concentrate on the essentials of what it is doing – its behaviour and interface to the world – and to rely on the details being filled in at a later stage. In a way, we can think of it as a more elaborate form of parameter passing, but this time at the class level. Java has two ways of providing abstraction – interfaces and abstract classes – and we will discuss both of them below.

For example, so far, all our classes have related to concrete descriptions of natural items, such as tickets, marks, coffee and so on. If we wanted to perform an operation on all these classes, such as sorting arrays of tickets, arrays of marks or arrays of coffee, then up until now we would need to have three different sort methods. Abstraction aims to cut down on repetition and aid reuse – two of our goals right from the start.

Inheritance

With **inheritance**, we concentrate on defining a class that we know about, and leave open an option to define additional versions of it later. These versions will inherit the properties and characteristics of the original class, and therefore can be smaller in themselves, and neater. In this way we build up hierarchies of classes and can focus changes and additions at the right level. Because all the classes in the hierarchy belong to the family, they have the same type in Java's typing mechanism, and one can be used where the other might be required.

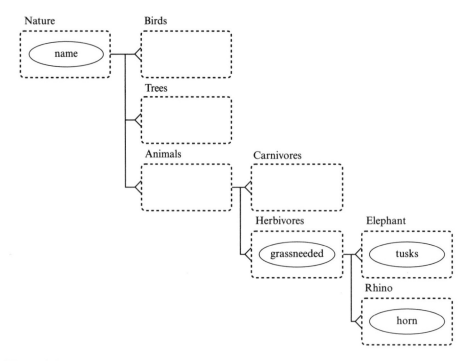

Figure 9.1 *A hierarchy in Nature.*

Consider the diagram in Figure 9.1. In Chapter 1, we saw that the Nature class consisted of animals, trees and birds. Animals could be herbivores or carnivores. Possible herbivores are elephants and rhinos. Now the field holding the name of the animal could be right in the top class, in Nature itself, since all animals, trees and birds will need a name. Similarly a method to write the name would also be placed here. If we had an elephant object and wanted to write the name, the method that would be called would be the one in Nature. However, peculiar to an elephant would be its tusk length. This field and a method to display it would be kept in `Elephant` itself. Along the way in the hierarchy, there could be a tally of how much grass a herbivore eats a day. Since this applies to all herbivores, we store the information in the `Herbivore` class. All of these design decisions are illustrated in Figure 9.1.

Figure 9.2 shows the effect of two object declarations on the classes at the lowest level of the hierarchy, `Elephant` and `Rhino`. `jumbo` and `mafuta` each have three variables, but the last one is different in each case. The other two were inherited from classes higher up. Inheritance is covered in detail in Section 9.3.

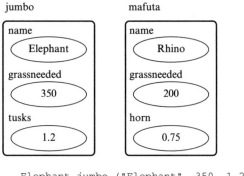

```
Elephant jumbo ("Elephant", 350, 1.2);
Rhino mafuta ("Rhino", 200, 0.75);
```

Figure 9.2 *Object declarations in the Nature hierarchy.*

9.2 Abstraction through interfaces

We have suggested that abstraction will cut down on repetition and aid the generality and reuse of the classes we write. Java provides two ways of obtaining abstraction: **interfaces** and **abstract classes**. Let us start with interfaces and then move on to abstract classes in Section 9.4.

An **interface** is a special kind of class which defines the specification of a set of methods, and that is all. The methods together encapsulate a guarantee: any class that implements this interface is guaranteed to provide these methods. We can think of an interface as defining a set of standards, and a class that implements them gets a 'stamp of approval' as having conformed to those standards. Objects of the class can therefore gain access to any methods that need an object with those standards.

The forms for an interface and for a class that implements it are:

Interface declaration

`interface` *interfacename* {
  method specifications
}

Interface implementation

```
class classname implements interfacename {
  bodies for the interface methods
  own data and methods
}
```

As an example, consider typical operations used on machines that move:

```
interface    Movable {
  boolean    start ();
  void       stop ();
  boolean    turn (int degrees);
  double     fuelRemaining ();
  boolean    changeSpeed (double kmperhour);
}
```

`Movable` defines what all movable machines must be able to do. They may do more, but this is a minimum. Now one way to implement the interface for a plane as a movable machine would be to declare a class as follows:

```
class Planes implements Movable {
  boolean start () {
    // do whatever is necessary to start
    // a plane and return true if it worked.
  }

  void    stop () {
    // do whatever is necessary to stop
    // the plane. It had better work!
  }

  boolean turn (int degrees) {
    // do whatever is necessary to turn a plane
  }

  double  fuelRemaining () {
    // return the amount of plane fuel remaining
  }

  boolean changeSpeed (double kmperhour) {
    // accelerate or decelerate if kmperhour is negative
  }
}
```

A car is also a movable machine, as is a train and a ship. In fact, a lowly lawnmower is also a movable machine and could implement the interface.

How does having the interface help us? Well, it helps when we want to use the abstract concept of movable machines. Suppose we are setting up a handheld remote control device for scale models. It will have buttons and a display corresponding to the operations we have set up in the `Movable` interface. If we do all our development of the remote control based solely on `Movable`, then we can use it at any later date with any of the actual machines mentioned. The remote control will use composition to include the `Movable` interface as follows:

```
class RemoteControl {

  private Movable machine;

  RemoteControl (Movable m) {
    machine = m;
  }
  ...
  // when the start knob is pressed on the device
  Boolean okay = machine.start();
  if (!okay) display ("No response on start");
  ...
}
```

The remote control's constructor is given an object which is of class `Movable`. It could be a plane, a car, a ship, a lawnmower or any other valid implementation of `Movable`: they are all guaranteed to have the properties of `Movable`. This object is then stored as part of the controller's private data, and whenever it calls any of `Movable`'s methods, it will be sent to the particular implementation for that class. So, for example, we could set up:

```
Planes plane = new Plane();
Ships ship = new Ship ();

RemoteControl planeRemote = new RemoteControl (plane);
RemoteControl shipRemote = new RemoteControl (ship);
```

and each will operate correctly for its own implementation of the `Movable` interface.

EXAMPLE 9.1 Sorting anything

Problem The sort we developed in Chapter 6 is obviously extremely useful and we would like to adapt it so that it is independent of what we are sorting.

Solution We consider what makes a class of objects sortable, and encapsulate this operation (or operations) in an interface called `Sortable`. Then we change the `selectionSort` method so that it works with sortable objects only. Thereafter any class that needs sorting must just implement the `Sortable` interface, and it can call the methods of the `Sort` class.

Assuming that we would like to sort countries and students, Figure 9.3 sums up the relationship between the various classes and the interface (represented by a parallelogram).

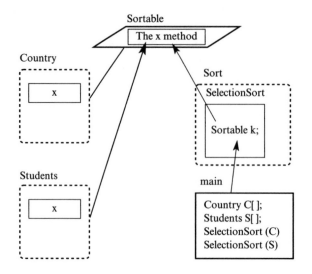

Figure 9.3 *The classes involved in abstract sorting.*

Now what is this x method referred to in the diagram? What makes sorting one class different from another? It is not the assignment of the objects, since this is defined for all types and classes. The answer is that it is the comparison between two items. The comparison triggers the interchange of items, which is how all sorts work. How this comparison is done will differ from class to class.

Algorithm Sorting is obviously a common utility so we shall put it in the myutilities package. First we set up the sortable interface as follows:

```
package myutilities;

interface Sortable {
  boolean lessThan (Sortable a);
}
```

The Sort class defined in Section 6.3 must also be changed slightly as follows:

```
package myutilities;

public class Sort {

     /* The Sort class    by J M Bishop  Feb 1997
      *                   revised October 1997
      * Provides one sorting method
      * for arrays of objects of any length.
      * where the objects' class implements the
      * Sortable interface.
      */
```

```
    public static void selectionSort(Sortable a [], int n) {
      Sortable temp;
      int chosen;

      for (int leftmost = 0; leftmost < n-1; leftmost++) {
        chosen = leftmost;
        for (int j = leftmost+1; j < n; j++)
          if (a[j].lessThan(a[chosen])) chosen = j;
        temp = a[chosen];
        a[chosen] = a[leftmost];
        a[leftmost] = temp;
      }
    }
  }
}
```

The array parameter and the temporary variable are both now declared as Sortable. Also the comparison that used to use the boolean relation < now calls the lessThan method on one of the objects, giving the other as a parameter.

Next we include in the class of objects to be sorted an implementation of the lessThan method. For example, a simple Country class would be:

```
import myutilities.*;

class Country implements Sortable {
    /* The Country class    by J M Bishop Dec 1996
     * ----------------    Java 1.1
     * stores a country name and is sortable
     */

    private String name;

    Country(String s) {
        name = s;
    }

    public boolean lessThan(Sortable a) {
        Country b = (Country) a;
        return (name.compareTo(b.name) < 0);
    }

    public String toString() {
        return name;
    }

}
```

In the implementation of lessThan we must first type cast the Sortable object passed as a parameter to a Country. The compareTo method (part of the String class) then operates on the current object's name and the name of the parameter. compareTo returns negative if the result is less, positive if it is more and 0 if it is equal.

Program Now Country, Sortable and Sort can be used in a test program as follows:

```
import java.io.*;
import javagently.*;
import myutilities.*;

class Table {

    /* The Table program     by J M Bishop Dec 1996
     * -----------------      Java 1.1 October 1997
     * for sorting a table, of countries in this case.
     * Illustrates linking up to an independent sorter.
     */

    public static void main(String[] args) throws IOException {
        Country t [] = new Country[10];
        String s;

        BufferedReader in = Text.open("Countries");
        for (int i = 0; i < t.length; i++) {
            s = Text.readString(in);
            t[i] = new Country(s);
        }

        System.out.println("Original");
        System.out.println("========");
        for (int i = 0; i < t.length; i++)
            System.out.println(t[i]);

        Sort.selectionSort(t, t.length);

        System.out.println();
        System.out.println("Sorted");
        System.out.println("======");
        for (int i = 0; i < t.length; i++)
            System.out.println(t[i]);
    }
}
```

Notice that there is actually no mention of Sortable in the program. In other words, this program could have run with the old sort. The change was effected between the object and sort. What we have gained is the flexibility to sort other classes.

Testing Just to be sure of the sort process, we give the data and output for the program:

```
Japan
Russia
Argentina
Finland
Ukraine
Zimbabwe
Algeria
France
Iceland
Israel
```

```
Original
========
Japan
Russia
Argentina
Finland
Ukraine
Zimbabwe
Algeria
France
Iceland
Israel

Sorted
======
Algeria
Argentina
Finland
France
Iceland
Israel
Japan
Russia
Ukraine
Zimbabwe
```

Extension What we really want to test is whether we have achieved the objective of independence. A quick way of doing this is to change `Table` to sort integers. However, remember that `Sortable` is dealing with objects, so we must put the integer in a class. This class can be in an inner one.

```java
import java.io.*;
import javagently.*;
import myutilities.*;

class TableInt {

    /* The TableInt program    by J M Bishop Dec 1996
     *                         Java 1.1 October 1997
     * for sorting a table, of integers in this case.
     * Illustrates linking up to an independent sorter.
     */

    public static void main(String[] args) throws IOException {
        OurInteger[] t = new OurInteger[10];
        BufferedReader in = Text.open(System.in);

        for (int i = 0; i < 10; i++)
            t[i] = new OurInteger(Text.readInt(in));

        System.out.println("Original");
        System.out.println("========");
```

```
            for (int i = 0; i < t.length; i++)
                System.out.print(t[i].val+"  ");
            System.out.println();

            Sort.selectionSort(t,t.length);

            System.out.println();
            System.out.println("Sorted");
            System.out.println("======");
            for (int i = 0; i < t.length; i++)
                System.out.print(t[i] +"  ");
            System.out.println();
        }

    class OurInteger implements Sortable {

        /* This member class encapsulates an integer
         * as an object and implements Sortable
         * for integers.
         */

        int val;

        public OurInteger(int i) {
            val = i;
        }

        public boolean lessThan(Sortable a) {
            OurInteger i = (OurInteger)a;
            return val < i.val;
        }

        public String toString () {
            return String.valueOf(val);
        }
    }

}
```

A run of the program would produce (using data typed in):

```
Original
========
5 8 1 2 0 4 3 7 9 6

Sorted
======
0 1 2 3 4 5 6 7 8 9
```

Before we leave interfaces, we stress that they can only have method specifications in them – no completed methods or variables. However, they can include constants if necessary.

9.3 Inheritance

Following the informal description of inheritance in Section 9.1, let us look at inheritance in practice in Java. Each new level of class is said to **extend** the class above it. The term conveys the impression that the new class can have more fields and methods than the original. The terms for the different class are **superclass** or **parent** (the original) and **subclass** or **child** class.

Inheritance is also transitive: that means that if a is a class and b extends it, with c extending b, then c is also related by inheritance to a. The same would be true in a family, in this case a being the grandparent, b the parent and c the child. Figure 9.1 shows this kind of hierarchy of inheritance clearly.

The process of inheriting is also sometimes referred to as deriving, but in fact Java's term – **extending** – is the most evocative of what is actually happening.

The example in Figure 9.1 can now be expressed in Java. In outline the important classes are:

```
class Nature {
  private String name;
  // much more here
}

class Animals extends Nature {
  // All sorts of things here
}

class Herbivores extends Animals {
  private protected int grassneeded;
  // plus more about herbivores
}

class Elephant extends Herbivores {
  Elephant (String n, int w, double l) {
    name = n;
    grassneeded = w;
    tusks = l;
  }
  private double tusks; // their length
  // and more on elephants
}

class Rhino extends Herbivores {
  Rhino (String n, int w, double l) {
    name = n;
    grassneeded = w;
    horn = l;
  }
  private double horn; // its length
  // and more on rhinos
}
```

The grassneeded variable in the Herbivores class has an extra modifier – protected. Protected widens the visibility of a private item to include subclasses. Thus Elephant can access grassneeded, but users of Herbivore objects cannot.

As we can see already from the constructors for Elephant and Rhino, subclasses inherit all the fields of their superclasses and can access them directly. The same applies to methods. Suppose a method is included to play the sound of an animal. We would put this in the Animals class thus:

```
class Animals extends Nature {
   // All sorts of things here
   void makeNoise (String audioclip) {
     // see Section 12.3 on how to do this
   }
}
```

Then the declaration:

```
Elephant jumbo ("Elephant", 350, 1.2);
```

would enable us to make the call

```
jumbo.makeNoise ("elephant.au");
```

Working within a hierarchy

The purpose of setting up a hierarchy of classes is to enable us to deal at different levels. At the top level, we just need to know about names of natural beings. At each level below that, we have more information and can perform in appropriate ways. The key to this multi-level operation is being able to assign objects freely within a hierarchy. Put formally:

- any object of a subclass can be assigned to an object of its superclass;

- any object of a superclass can be assigned to a subclass with an appropriate **cast**.

When these assignments are done, the object does not change at all: only the compiler's view of it, for typing purposes, is changed. As an example, if we have:

```
Animals a;

a = jumbo;          // okay
mafuta = a;         // not okay: compiler error
mafuta = jumbo;     // not okay: compiler error
mafuta = (Rhino) a; // okay
```

The example shows that we cannot assign variables across levels. jumbo and mafuta are of quite different classes and it would never make sense to assign them. But of course, we can work with them together under the Herbivore's banner, or one of the higher ones. The following example shows this:

```
Herbivores greedier;

if (jumbo.grassneeded > mafuta.grassneeded)
  greedier = jumbo;
else
  greedier = mafuta;
```

Notice that a restriction in Java is that a class may only extend one other class: there is no provision for multiple inheritance. However, classes can implement several interfaces, thereby getting much the same effect.

Superconstructing

A useful technique in a hierarchy of classes is **superconstructing**. A subclass can call the constructor of a parent to perform initialization on those variables for which the parent is responsible. This divides the work up in a cleaner way. Let us rewrite the classes as follows:

```
class Nature {
  private String name;
  Nature (String n) {
    name = n;
  }
  // much more here
}

class Animals extends Nature {
  Animals (String n) {
    super (n);
  }
  // All sorts of things here
}

class Herbivores extends Animals {
  private protected int grassneeded;

  Herbivores (String n, int g) {
    super (n);
    grassneeded = g;
  }
  // plus more about herbivores
}

class Elephant extends Herbivores {
  Elephant (String n, int w, double len) {
    super (n, w);
    tusks = len;
  }
  private double tusks; // their length
  // and more on elephants
}
```

```
class Rhino extends Herbivores {
  Rhino (String n, int w, double len) {
    super (n, w);
    horn = len;
  }
  private double horn; // its length
  // and more on rhinos
}
```

Both Elephant and Rhino are sent all three initial parameters as before, but they defer to their parent classes as to what should be done with the ones they do not themselves define. The process bubbles up: Herbivore takes care of w. It passes n up to Animals. Animals at present does nothing other than pass its parameter up to Nature.

Note that the call to the superconstructor must be the first statement in a constructor.

Shadowing variables

In addition to adding to any inherited data, a subclass can decide to replace data with its own version. It does this by declaring a variable with the same name as one higher up. Mostly we do this to change the type to something more suitable. When the object is created, all the variables still exist, but the higher one is masked out. This is called **shadowing**. For example, supposing the zoologists working with elephants want to be more precise about what they eat, they could decide to record the grass as a real number. Therefore we would add to Elephant:

```
double grassneeded;
```

When dealing with elephants, we shall get this version of the variable. Other classes will get the original integer version from the Herbivore class.

It is also possible to get at a masked variable by using the **super** prefix. Thus from Elephant,

```
super.grassneeded;
```

would refer to the original variable in Herbivores.

Overriding methods

Similar to shadowing (but not exactly the same) is **overriding**. A subclass can decide to supply its own version of a method already supplied by a superclass. We would use this facility when we start off defining a general or default method in a superclass, and as we get down the hierarchy we can provide more specialized versions.

For example, all animals sleep, so in the Animals class we could add a sleep method:

```
class Animals extends Nature {
  // All sorts of things here

  void sleep () {
    // describes the sleeping habits of animals in general
  }

  void makeNoise (String audioclip) {
    // see Section 12.3 on how to do this
  }
}
```

Then once we have researched how elephants sleep, we would add in the specialized method as follows:

```
class Elephant extends Herbivores {

  Elephant (String n, int w, double l) {
    name = n;
    grassneeded = w;
    tusks = l;
  }

  void sleep () {
    // how elephants sleep
  }

  private double tusks; // their length
  // and more on elephants
}
```

Overridden methods are more powerful than shadowed variables in the following way. When there are several instances of a method in a hierarchy, the one in the closest subclass is always used. This is true even if an object of the subclass is assigned to an object of the superclass and called from there. Consider the following, using jumbo as an example:

```
Animals a;

a.sleep();      // calls Animals version of sleep
jumbo.sleep(); // calls Elephant version of sleep
a = jumbo;
a.sleep();      // still calls Elephant version of sleep
```

Dynamic binding

Overriding uses **dynamic binding** to find the correct method. Each object has a table of its methods and Java searches for the correct versions of any overridden methods at run time. The default is that methods will need dynamic binding, and this can incur a performance overhead. If we know that a method will not be overidden, we can declare it with the modifier `final`, and save on speed. Dynamic binding is illustrated very well in the Case Study that follows.

Notice that overriding is not the same as **overloading**. Overloading involves providing several methods with the same name, but with different parameter lists, so that Java sees them as distinct entities. In overriding, the parameter lists are the same. In the Case Study we look at an example of inheritance in a small system. There will be many more examples in the next chapter as inheritance is used extensively in Java's own packages.

9.4 Abstract methods and classes

The final member of the class power trio is abstract methods and abstract classes. When used together with interfaces and inheritance, they provide for a clear and understandable way of putting together large systems.

Abstract methods

Abstract methods provide 'place holders' for methods that can sensibly be mentioned at one level, but which are going to be implemented in a variety of ways lower down. Take for example the sleep method in the Nature example. It probably does not make sense to have a general method to describe sleep patterns of all animals. But we do know that all kinds of animals have sleep patterns, and when we are dealing with objects at the `Animals` class level, it would be useful to be able to call the different methods supplied for the different classes at the bottom. What we are looking for is the concept of an abstract method. Thus we declare:

```
abstract void sleep ();
```

in `Animals`. The effect of such an inclusion in `Animals` is to turn it into an abstract class.

Abstract classes

An abstract class is any class with at least one abstract method. An abstract class cannot be used to declare objects any more: the presence of the abstract method means that it is incomplete. It must first be subclassed and the abstract method(s) filled in. In the above example, `Animals` becomes:

```
abstract class Animals extends Nature {
  // All sorts of things here

  abstract void sleep ();
  void makeNoise (String audioclip) {
    // see Section 12.3 on how to do this
  }
}
```

Now each of the bottom level of classes, such as `Elephant` and `Rhino`, can complete the definition of sleep. If `Herbivore` mentions nothing about sleeping, then by implication it must also be declared as abstract.

How would we use the hierarchy now? Well, all declarations will take place at the bottom, concrete level, for example:

```
Elephant E [] = new Elephants [10];
Rhino R [] = new Rhino [5];
```

But now we cannot declare any `Herbivores` or `Animals` as such (they are abstract). What we have gained is abstraction: we have defined what should be done, and have left it up to other classes to be responsible for doing it.

There are several examples of abstract classes in the Java packages, some of which which have already been discussed in earlier chapters (e.g. `Date`, `TimeZone`, `NumberFormat` and so on). These classes provide class methods which can be used to create an instance of the class, as we have been doing all along.

9.5 Case Study 4: Veterinary tags

The Savanna Veterinary Association several years ago developed a system of tagging pets so that if they were found straying, they could be tracked back to their owners. The tags were small and simple and had the animal's name and owner's phone number on them. If a pet was found by a member of the public, he or she could try to phone the owner in order to return it. However, the S.V.A. found that when owners moved, they did not always update their tags, and so tracking owners was more difficult.

It then started to keep a central register of all tags, so that people could phone in and check whether a pet was recorded missing or not. In addition, it wants to introduce an improved XTag which has the vet's name on it as well. Obviously, the old system must continue to run, and the new system along with it. The register is being built up over several months, and will consist of old and new tags together.

Solution I

The solution is to use inheritance. The old program already exists and runs with the old tags. What we do is define a new tags class, called XTags, which extends the old tag and has the new data item in it. But both can be stored as `Tags` – the 'family' name – in the register.

Class design

The diagram of the original system (Figure 9.4) uses technique one in class–array interaction. `main` calls the three other methods in `Vet`, and they do the processing as

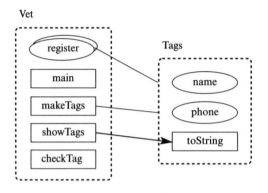

Figure 9.4 *Class diagram of the original vet program.*

required. `makeTags` will be the method that actually creates the `Tags` objects and puts them in the array, declared as:

```
static Tags register [] = new Tags [100];
```

The `Tags` class and the register

The original `Tags` class looks like this:

```
class Tags {

    /* The Tags class          by J M Bishop January 1997
     * for keeping data on a pet.
     */

    String name, phone;

    public Tags(String n, String p) {
        name = n;
        phone = p;
    }

    public String toString() {
        return name+" tel: "+phone;
    }

}
```

It has a constructor and one method – the standard `toString` method – which enables tags to be concatenated with other strings and used in `println` and other statements where strings are required. The part of `makeTags` which adds a tag to the register is:

```
Tags tag = new Tags (petsName, ownersPhone);
register[index] = tag;
```

In showTags it is printed out with:

```
System.out.println(i+"\t"+ register[i]);
```

Data for the program is in the form of pets' names and phone numbers, and it can be stored on a file or entered from the keyboard. We achieve this flexibility by using FileMan.open. If we type in invalid file names five times, the input will default to the keyboard.

The full original vet program is on the web site, but here we press on immediately to the extension to illustrate inheritance.

Extending for XTags

Now we want to add the XTags to the system. Its class is given by:

```
public class XTags extends Tags {

    /* The XTags class      by J M Bishop  January 1997
     * for extended vet tags with vet numbers.
     * Uses inheritance */

    String vet;

    public XTags(String n, String p, String v) {
        super(n, p);
        vet = v;
    }

    public String toString() {
        return name+" tel: "+phone+" Vet's tel: "+vet;
    }

}
```

Notice several points here. XTags has access to the name and phone variables in Tags. It overrides the toString method in Tags. It declares its own new field, vet. Now, armed with this new class, we can extend the class diagram shown earlier giving Figure 9.5. Notice the inheritance symbol: a line with an open 'scoop' at the child class. XTags extends Tags, so the scoop indicates that it draws in all that Tags has.

Program

Before we consider the full Vet2 program, let us look at the important section related to inheritance.

```
        char kind = Text.readChar(in);
        petsName = Text.readString(in);
        ownersPhone = Text.readString(in);
        Tags tag;
```

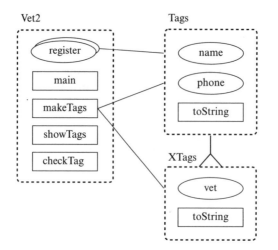

Figure 9.5 *The extended vet tag system.*

```
switch (kind) {
   case 'p':
   case 'P':
     tag = new Tags(petsName, ownersPhone);
     break;
    default:
    case 'x':
    case 'X':
       String vetsPhone = Text.readString(in);
       tag = new XTags(petsName, ownersPhone, vetsPhone);
  }

  register[index] = tag;
```

The very first line obtains information about whether the pet is to have a tag or Xtag: this is indicated by means of a 'P' (for plain) or 'X' for Xtag. Lines 2–3 are concerned with getting in the common information of pet's name and owner's phone number. Now we use a switch statement to deal with creating the two types of tags. The XTag option is also the default because we would like to move the public towards the new version. By using a multiple case labels, we can easily accommodate both capital and lower-case letters.

The statement under case 'P' comes from the old program and creates a new Tags object. However, if one of the new tags is requested, then we read in more information and create an XTag object, **but in the same tag field**. Whichever tag is created gets assigned into the register, which is still declared of the superclass, Tag. Because XTag inherits from Tag, in other words comes from the same family, it is accepted wherever a Tag would be welcome. In this way inheritance aids significantly in keeping programs reusable and maintainable.

Now here is the full updated program.

```java
import java.io.*;
import javagently.*;
import myutilities.*;
import java.text.*;
import java.util.*;

class Vet2 {

    /* The updated Vet tagging program    by J M Bishop Jan 1997
     * -----------------------------    Java 1.1 Oct 1997
     * Keeps a register of pets' tags and enables it to be
     * checked if a stray pet is found.
     * Uses two types of tags.
     * Illustrates inheritance.
     */

    static int index;
    static Tags[] register = new Tags[100];

    public static void main(String[] args) throws IOException {
      BufferedReader in = Text.open(System.in);
      BufferedReader fin = Text.open(System.in);
      // fin defaults to the keyboard in case there is no file

      System.out.println("Savanna Pet Tag System");
      Text.prompt("Where is the data?");
      try {
        fin = FileMan.open();
      } catch (FileNotFoundException e) {
        System.out.println("Enter P or X for tag type ");
        System.out.println(" then pet's name and phone " +
              "and vet's if applicable");
      }

      makeTags(fin);
      showTags();
      try {
        while (true)
          checkTag(in);
      } catch (EOFException e) {
      }
    }

    static void makeTags(BufferedReader in) throws IOException {
      String petsName, ownersPhone;

      while (true) {
        try {
          char kind = Text.readChar(in);
          petsName = Text.readString(in);
          ownersPhone = Text.readString(in);
          Tags tag;
          switch (kind) {
                case 'p':
                case 'P':
                    tag = new Tags(petsName, ownersPhone);
                    break;
```

```
                default:
                case 'x':
                case 'X':
                    String vetsPhone = Text.readString(in);
                    tag = new XTags(petsName, ownersPhone, vetsPhone);
        }
        register[index] = tag;
        index++;
      }
      catch (EOFException e) {
        break;
      }
    }
  }
  System.out.println("All "+index+" pets read in.");
  System.out.println();
}

static DateFormat DF = DateFormat.getDateInstance
                        (DateFormat.MEDIUM);

static void showTags() {

  System.out.println("The Pet Register on " +
    DF.format(new Date ()));
  System.out.println();
  System.out.println("Pet No.\tName and phone no.");
  for (int i = 0; i < index; i++)
    System.out.println(i+"\t"+register[i]);
}

static void checkTag(BufferedReader in) throws IOException {

    System.out.println();
    Text.prompt("Found pet's name as on tag:");
    String info = Text.readString(in);
    boolean found = false;
    for (int i = 0; i < index; i++)
        if (register[i].name.equals(info)) {
            System.out.println("The pet called "+
                    info+" is registered no. "+i);
            System.out.println("Full info should be "+register[i]);
            found = true;
            break;
        }
    if (!found)
        System.out.println("The pet called "+
                info+" is not registered.");
    /* After the last check has been made, an EOF is
     * entered, which can be thrown straight back at the
     * main program so that it can stop its loop.
     */
  }
}
```

Testing

The following is a sample run of the program.

```
Savanna Pet Tag System
Where is the data? vet2.dat
All 6 pets read in.

The Pet Register on 13-Dec-97

Pet No.    Name and phone no.
0          Fluffy tel: 466683
1          Seza tel: 466683
2          Puma tel: 466683 Vet's tel: 3017894
3          Buster tel: 5674563 Vet's tel: 3017894
4          Karla tel: 222546 Vet's tel: 4014999
5          Titch tel: 222546

Found pet's name as on tag: Seza
The pet called Seza is registered no. 1
Full info should be Seza tel: 466683

Found pet's name as on tag: Karla
The pet called Karla is registered no. 4
Full info should be Karla tel: 222546 Vet's tel: 4014999

Found pet's name as on tag: Corkie
The pet called Corkie is not registered.

Found pet's name as on tag: Fluffy
The pet called Fluffy is registered no. 0
Full info should be Fluffy tel: 466683

Found pet's name as on tag:
```

What we see here is that whenever toString is called from a printing of register[i], the correct version (from Tags or Xtags) is picked up from the actual object. Such **dynamic binding** is one of Java's most powerful features.

SUMMARY

Object-oriented programming is much enhanced in power by the use of abstraction and inheritance. Abstraction enables us to concentrate on the essentials of a method or class: what it must guarantee to the user. The details can then be filled in later, and perhaps by more than one implementation of the abstraction. Java provides interfaces and abstract classes and methods as means of achieving abstraction.

Inheritance serves at least two purposes. We can prolong the life of a system by creating new versions of classes which include new features, but which inherit the old. The two classes are regarded as being of the same family and therefore the child can be used wherever the parent was expected. We can also divide up information into what is essential at any level, creating a hierarchy of classes, all of which can be used together or separately.

QUIZ

9.1   A giraffe is also a herbivore. Give the class definition for a giraffe which records the length of its neck.

9.2   If car is going to implement the Movable interface, what is the minimum set of methods that it must declare?

9.3   If we want to sort giraffes based on the length of their necks, what interface must we implement?

9.4   The following is an attempt to implement a lessThan method for comparing giraffes' neck lengths. It will not compile. What is wrong with it? (Hint: look at the OurInteger class in the extension to Example 9.1.)

```
public boolean lessThan (Sortable a) {
  return (neck < a.neck);
}
```

9.5   Would the following be a valid declaration for a companion elephant to jumbo?

```
Elephant dumbo = new Elephant (1);
```

9.6   There is a temporary Elephant object called patient. Draw class diagrams for the results of the following statements.

```
Elephant patient;
patient = jumbo;
```

9.7   In Case Study 4 (veterinary tags) give an example of a method declaration which illustrates overriding.

9.8   In Case Study 4 the statement

```
System.out.println("Full info should be "+register[i]);
```

sometimes prints out two values (name and phone) and sometimes three (name, phone and vet's phone). Explain carefully how this happens.

9.9   In Case Study 4's main method there is a try-while sequence as follows:

```
try {
  while (true)
    checkTag(in);
} catch (EOFException e) {
}
```

How and where does the exception actually get detected and passed on to this handler?

9.10   Based on Figure 9.1 (the hierarchy of Nature) which of the following statements are incorrect, and why?

```
Nature n;
Animals a;
Herbivores h;
Elephant e;
Rhino r;

a = n;
e = r;
h = e;
a = h;
```

PROBLEMS

9.1 **Sorting pets**. Using the `Sortable` interface, include a facility in the veterinary system (Case Study 4) to sort pets based on their names and print out a sorted register. Questions to answer are: (a) Where is `lessThan` defined; and (b) which of the tag classes should implement `Sortable`?

9.2 **Adapting the marker**. Adapt the student marker system (Example 6.6) to include a facility to sort the students based on their final mark, and print a list in this order.

9.3 **Extending the marker**. Savanna University is introducing continuous assessment from 1998 and wants to extend the marker system so that new students will have two sorts of marks: *seen* marks, which relate to assignments and projects, and *unseen* marks which relate to tests and examinations. Decide on how to extend the `Students` class to include this facility and examine carefully what, if anything, of the `Marker` class itself needs to be changed as a result. Get the new system working.

9.4 **Model Club**. The Savanna Models Club is interested in a simulation of its remote control models (planes, trains, cars, boats). Implement the system discussed in Section 9.2, using input from the keyboard to drive a selection of models at the same time. For example, commands might be:

```
P S           // plane start
P C 10        // plane change speed to 10 k/h
P T 15        // plane turn 15 degrees
P Q           // plane stop
```

9.5 **Nelson sells ice-creams**. Nelson is contemplating selling ice-creams at his Coffee Shop during a heatwave. Obviously he has to keep track of stock and watch expiry dates and so on, so that much of the programming associated with keeping ice-cream is already part of keeping coffee. Study the Coffee Shop program and its associated classes and investigate how it could be adapted to include ice-cream. Should one use interfaces, inheritance or abstract classes, or a mixture? Is a major rewrite of the `Coffee` class necessary first?

CHAPTER 10

Graphical user interfaces

10.1 Introduction to the awt

The real world has been converted to wysiwyg[1] and GUI[2] interfaces, and Java is fully equipped to provide these soft options. The GUI part is provided inside a package called awt – abstract windowing toolkit. From now on we shall call it the awt (pronounced 'ought') package, and know that it is Java's platform-independent approach to user interfacing.

The awt is also completely driven from within the Java language. That means that any graphical layout tools that allow pointing and selecting of the visual appearance of an application, and generate the code for it, are separate from Java itself. These tools do exist, but running them will need a larger computer and more resources than one at first bargained for.

A complete tour of all the facilities available through awt is beyond the scope of this book. What we aim to do is to reveal the overall structure of the package and then to introduce several of the most used features through examples.

---

[1] What you see is what you get, prounounced 'wizzywig'.
[2] Graphical user interfaces, pronounced 'gooey'.

Overall structure of awt

The classes in the awt package can be classified as:

- graphics;
- components, including windows and menus;
- layout managers;
- event handlers;
- image manipulation.

Graphics permits the drawing of shapes, lines and images; the selecting of fonts, colours and so on. **Components** are items such as buttons, text fields, menus and scroll bars. We can put them in **containers** and then choose one of a selection of **layout managers** to arrange them suitably on the screen. The subpackage `java.awt.event` handles external **events**, such as pushing buttons and moving the mouse, through a suite of event **handlers**, **listeners** and **adapters**. Finally, `java.awt.image` is another subpackage which is used by awt to incorporate **images** in a variety of formats. Figure 10.1 gives an overall picture of the main awt.

There are four main abstract classes – `Component`, `Container`, `MenuComponent` and `Graphics`. Other abstract classes are `FontMetrics`, `Image`, `PrintJob` and `Toolkit`. `LayoutManager` is an interface (along with five other specialized ones not shown), and all the rest are classes, inheriting from the classes drawn above them. Thus `Frame` is a `Window`, which is a `Container`, which is a `Component`.

With all of these different parts to the graphical user interfacing, it is actually hard to know where to start. We shall use a very simple example – the one in Chapter 2 for drawing a virus warning box on the screen – and introduce the various parts of awt as they are needed. In particular, we shall see that there are several ways of achieving very similar effects, and that awt has a rich selection of features from which to choose.

10.2 Putting graphics in a window

Graphical interfaces are presented to the user in **windows**. Java has a `Window` class, but in practice we usually use one of its subclasses, `Frame`.

`Frame` – the basic window

We start off with `Frame` as the basic presenter of GUI items. Each application can have several windows and, for each, we declare a class that inherits `Frame` and includes the methods necessary to display information in the window and perform other actions.

In the main program a frame object is declared, created as a new instance of our class that is to occupy the frame. Then we perform three essential functions: setting the title of the window and its size, and activating the drawing of the frame itself. The methods are delared in `Frame` and `Component` (which `Frame` inherits). The form is:

Creating a frame

```
Frame f = new classname ();
f.setTitle ("title");
f.setSize (width, height);
f.setVisible (true);
```

At this point, the awt will look for a `paint` method to add any further graphics to the contents of the window. The form for a `paint` method, which overrides that defined in `Component` is:

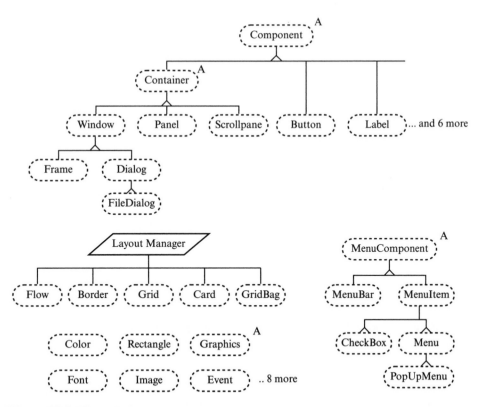

Figure 10.1 *The awt class structure.*

Redefining the `paint` method

```
public void paint (Graphics g) {
    Calls to methods in Graphics, prefixed
    by g.
}
```

The `paint` method is supplied with a `Graphics` object customized for the particular platform the program is running on. In this way, Java can take advantage of the good points of any particular platform, and make the awt present a familiar look and feel to the users of different platforms.

The `Graphics` class is quite extensive, but a summary of it is given in the form:

`Graphics` class specification

```
clearRect    (int x, int y, int width, int height);
clipRect     (int x, int y, int width, int height);
copyArea     (int x, int y, int height, int width, int dx, int dy);
draw3DRect   (int x, int y, int width, int height, boolean raised);
drawChars    (char [ ] data, int offset, int length,int x, int y);
drawLine     (int x1, int y1, int x2, int y2);
drawOval     (int x, int y, int width, int height);
drawRect     (int x, int y, int width, int height);
drawString   (String str, int x, int y);
fill3DRect   (int x, int y, int width, int height, boolean raised);
fillOval     (int x, int y, int width, int height);
fillRect     (int x, int y, int width, int height);
Color        getColor ();
setColor     (Color c);
// plus 33 others
```

Graphics includes methods for drawing rectangles, arcs, polygons and so on. For example, to draw a rectangle (as the only output), we would say:

```
public void paint (Graphics g) {
   g.drawRect (10, 10, 200, 100);
}
```

which starts at a point 10 pixels in from the top left corner of the screen, and draws a rectangle 200 wide by 100 deep (Figure 10.2).

Writing in an awt window with **drawString**

Working with the `Graphics` package, the equivalent of `println` in awt is *draw-String*. For example, we could say:

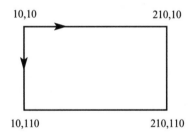

Figure 10.2 *Drawing a rectangle in the* Graphics *package.*

```
g.drawString ("Hello Pierre",30,15);
```

which would write the string 'Hello Pierre' 30 pixels in from the left and 15 pixels down from the top of the screen. The size and number of pixels varies from screen to screen, but typically a screen will have 600×400.

The difference between println and drawString is that drawString gives a choice of fonts, font styles and font sizes, and these affect the dimension of each letter. Consequently the positioning of the start of a string can be difficult. Most books on Java and programs on the Web use actual numbers to fix the *x*, *y* coordinates of the start of a piece of text (as we did above). When trying to get a program to work to one's satisfaction, these numbers can change many times, so it is better to base everything on the relative size of letters. FontMetrics is an awt abstract class which has methods for finding out the size of letters, but for the time being we shall just assume that a letter is five pixels wide and a pleasing line spacing is 15. In other words, if we declare the following constants at the start of a program:

```
static private final int letter = 5;
static private final int line = 15;
```

an equivalent call to drawString to the one above would be:

```
g.drawString ("Hello Pierre", 6*letter, line);
```

meaning six letters in from the left and one line down.

We are now ready for our first example, a very simple one indeed.

EXAMPLE 10.1 Virus warning using graphics

Problem The virus warning of Exercise 2.3 should appear in its own window and be more striking.

Solution Use an awt window and the drawString and rectangle facilities as described above. To make the rectangle striking, we need colour. Colour is provided by the setForeground and setBackground methods in the Component class, using the colour constants defined in the Color[3] class. We will use a cyan background, Color. cyan.

Program We set up letter and line constants and base the text writing on multiples of these. To enhance readability, the parameters are lined up in the paint method. The drawRect and resize methods also use suitable multiples of letter and line.

```
import java.awt.*;
import java.awt.event.*;

public class GraphicWarning extends Frame {

    /* The Graphic warning Program     by J M Bishop Oct 1996
     *                           Java 1.1 by T Abbott Oct 1997
     * produces a warning message on the screen in cyan
     * and black.
     * Illustrates setting up a window, painting in it
     * and enabling the close box.
     */

    static private final int line = 15;
    static private final int letter = 5;

    public GraphicWarning( ) {
      setBackground(Color.cyan);
      setForeground(Color.black);
    }

    public void paint(Graphics g) {
      g.drawRect(2*letter, 2*line, 33*letter, 6*line);
      g.drawString("W A R N I N G", 9*letter, 4*line);
      g.drawString("Possible virus detected", 4*letter, 5*line);
      g.drawString("Reboot and run virus", 5*letter, 6*line);
      g.drawString("remover software", 7*letter, 7*line);
    }

    public static void main(String[] args) {
      Frame f = new GraphicWarning(");
      f.setTitle("Draw Warning");
      f.setSize(50*letter,10*line);
      f.setVisible(true);
      f.addWindowListener(new WindowAdapter () {
        public void windowClosing(WindowEvent e) {
          System.exit(0);
        }
      });
    }

}
```

---

[3] Notice that it is color without a 'u', American style.

Testing Figure 10.3 shows the output of the program (reduced to black and white, unfortunately). To stop the program, we click on the close button on the right.[4] The window closes, and the final statement is a call to `System.exit(0)`. How the program is enabled to close in this way is discussed next.

Figure 10.3 *Graphic output for the virus warning program.*

Closing a window

A program that runs in a window needs some way of stopping. One of the accepted methods is for the user to click on the window close box in a top corner. Clicking is an **event** and can be detected by one of the **listeners** in the Event package in the awt. In the main method, we establish a link to such a window listener from the frame being built, by calling the method `addWindowListener` and instantiating a new version of a window adapter. In the implementation of the adapter that follows we override the `WindowAdapter` method called `windowClosing` and perform the appropriate action, which is to call `System.exit(0)`.

The sequence of definitions and actions for closing a window is summarized in the following form:

Closing a window

```
f.addWindowListener(new WindowAdapter () {
   public void windowClosing(WindowEvent e) {
      System.exit(0);
   }
});
```

Everything in this form is a keyword (in bold) or an identifier already defined in the awt package (in plain) – except for the event parameter e which is not used, so it can always remain as e anyway. The form becomes a mantra that can be put in the main method of all GUI programs. It uses an **anonymous class**, as introduced in Section 8.5. The syntax is novel, so let us go through it carefully again.

---

[4] This picture shows Windows output which is similar to Unix; on a Macintosh the close box will be on the left.

WindowAdapter is a simple abstract class that implements the WindowListener interface and provides dummy bodies for various methods contained therein. We can decide which to override, and in this case the only interesting method is windowClosing (there are six others). The instantiation of a new WindowAdapter object and the overriding of windowClosing are done inline, as part of the parameter to addWindowListener.

The alternative to an anonymous class would have been to supply (new x()) as the parameter and then define x as a local class, with a heading that extends WindowAdapter and a body just the same as that shown here, i.e. an implementation of windowClosing. All in all, the anonymous class is neater.

EXAMPLE 10.2 A weather chart

Problem Draw a histogram of rainfall figures for Savanna, based on the data of Example 6.4.

Solution By using Example 6.4, we can get in the data for several years, calculate the mean for each month (as before) and then use this figure to draw a histogram bar in graphics.

Algorithm The program will follow the pattern described above. The class will inherit Frame. Its main program will contain exactly the same instructions as in our previous example to set up the window properly.

The constructor is rather novel. We shall use it to read in all the data, a task previously performed by a readIn method. The contents, however, does not change. The most important part of the program is how to draw a satisfactory graph. We would like output such as Figure 10.4 and Plate 6.

Let us take each of the parts of the chart in turn.

1. **The axes.** Firstly, drawing the lines for the axes establishes a basis for the other parts. 'Zero' on the graph will be at about $x=50$, $y=300$, where the values are pixels, and the orientation is given as in Figure 10.2.
2. **The bars.** Next, to draw the bars, we use fillRect and must supply parameters as shown in the graphics form given at the start of this section. In other words, we need a bottom point, a width and a height. The width is some constant, such as 20. The height is the actual value of the month's mean rainfall, which we shall multiply by 10 so that it is decently represented on the screen (that is, a rainfall of 10 mm will use 100 pixels). The y starting point of the rectangle is then y-height where y is our zero point (300, as defined above). Lastly, the x starting point is a bit complicated, because it will vary for each month. The formula is based on the width and on a gap between bars as follows:

```
g.fillRect(month*(width+gap)+gap+x, y-a, width, a);
```

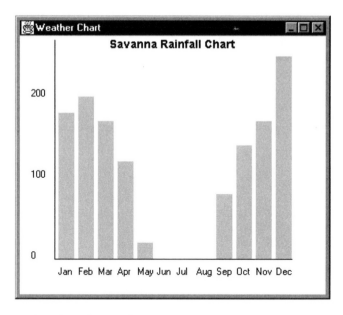

Figure 10.4 *Weather chart drawn with graphics. (See also Plate 6)*

3. **The labels.** Labelling the axes involves two loops which are fairly easy to un-
    derstand, though admittedly take some time to develop correctly from scratch!
    The x-axis makes use of an array of string names for the months.
4. **The title.** Finally, writing out the title shows how we can change fonts in Java.
    There is a `Font` class which can be instantiated with three parameters: font
    name, style and size. The available font names are: `Serif`, `SansSerif`, `Mon-`
    `ospaced`, `Dialog` and `DialogInput`. The styles are `PLAIN`, `BOLD` and
    `ITALIC` and the sizes the usual point measurements, for example 12 is normal,
    24 is large, and you should not go below 8. Changing the font is done for the
    last `drawString`, so we do not need to change it back again.

Program For what it does, the program is short, compared with Example 10.1 which did
very little. This shows that graphics, like all programming, can be very powerful when
repetition is involved. But if every little thing has to be custom-made and mentioned individually, then the programming can get long and tedious, as we shall see in later examples.

```
import java.io.*;
import javagently.*;
import java.awt.*;
import java.awt.event.*;

class WeatherChart extends Frame {

    /* The Weather Charting program    by J M Bishop Dec 1997
     *                                       Java 1.1
     * Draws a histogram of monthly rainfall
     * from data taken over a few years.
```

```
      * The data must be in the form:
      * year followed by the 12 rainfall figures for
      * the months of that year.
      * Illustrates simple graphics.
      */
   static final int base = 1950;
   static int startYear, endYear, nYears = 0;
   static double[][] rainTable = new double[12][70];

   public void paint (Graphics g) {
      int x = 50;
      int y = 300;
      int width = 20;
      int gap = 5;
// the axes
      g.drawLine (x,y,x+12*(width+gap),y);
      g.drawLine (x,y,x,30);
// labelling the axes
      for (int m = 0; m < 12; m++)
        g.drawString(Months[m],m*(width+gap)+gap+x,y+20);
      for (int i = 0; i <y; i+=100)
        g.drawString(String.valueOf(i),20,y-i);
// the title
      Font heading = new Font("SansSerif",Font.BOLD,14);
      g.setFont(heading);
      g.drawString("Savanna Rainfall Chart",120,40);
      g.setColor(Color.cyan);
// the bars
      for (int month = 0; month < 12; month++) {
        int a = (int) Rain.monthlyAverage
                (rainTable[month], nYears)*10;
        g.fillRect(month*(width+gap)+gap+x, y-a,width,a);
      }
    }

   public WeatherChart () throws IOException {
       BufferedReader fin = Text.open("rain.dat");

       int actualYear = 0;        /* e.g. 1987 */
       int yearIndex = 0;         /* e.g. 0 */
       try {
         while (true) {
           actualYear = Text.readInt(fin);
           if (yearIndex == 0)
              startYear = actualYear;
           for (int m = 0; m < 12; m++)
              rainTable[m][yearIndex] = Text.readDouble(fin);
           yearIndex++;
         }
       } catch (EOFException e) {
         /* Pick up the last year of data read in. */
           endYear = actualYear;
           nYears = endYear-startYear+1;
       }
    }
```

```
public static void main(String[] args) throws IOException {
    Frame f = new WeatherChart ();
    f.setTitle("Weather Chart");
    f.setSize(400,350);
    f.setVisible(true);
    f.addWindowListener(new WindowAdapter() {
      public void windowClosing(WindowEvent e) {
        System.exit(0);
      }
    });

}

private static String Months [] = {"Jan","Feb","Mar","Apr",
    "May","Jun","Jul","Aug","Sep","Oct","Nov","Dec"};

}
```

Awt class and method summary

Before leaving this section, we just tie up a few loose ends related to where the main classes of the awt fit in, and what are the methods they provide that we find are the most useful. Based on the short introduction in Section 10.1 backed up by Figure 10.1, we see that we could well have been using `Frame`, `Window`, `Container` and `Component`, as well as `Graphics`. In fact, we have mostly been using `Component` (awt's master class) and `Graphics`. One method, `setTitle`, comes from `Frame`, and `Container` is only used once we start looking at grouping components, as shown in the next section. To summarize, Figure 10.5 shows a complete class diagram for Example 10.2, with all its connections to the classes in the Java awt package.

10.3 Laying out buttons and other components

Although versatile, the `Graphics` class is not all that convenient for handling text. Java's awt provides a different range of classes for this purpose. These are the components shown under `Component` in Figure 10.1. The two simplest are `Label` and `Button` which provide for limited text. There are more such components, some of which are studied in later sections. There is a summary of all of them at the end of this section.

The `Label` class provides for the output of simple text via a parameter to its constructor, as in:

Creating a Label

```
add(new Label ("Text"));
```

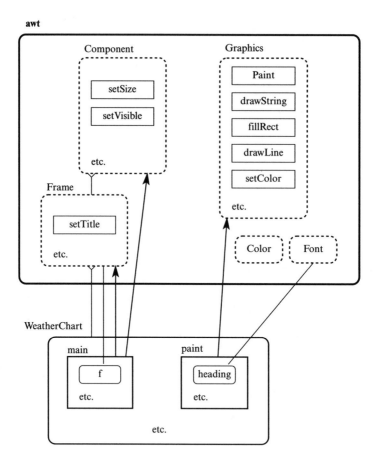

Figure 10.5 *Class diagram for* WeatherChart *showing awt connections.*

Thus we could say:

```
add(new Label ("School:"));
```

to get the label School: displayed on the screen. Button is similar, but has the additional facility of being reactive; that is, we can press the labelled button on the screen and the program can make something happen.

Creating a Button

```
// as a name
private Button buttonname;

// as a component
buttonname = new Button ("Text");
  add(buttonname);
```

The add method is defined in the Container class, so what we are doing here is adding the button to the default container of the frame we are working in. We shall see soon how to declare other containers.

For the difference between declaring labels and buttons is that labels are passive: you cannot react to them, so it is seldom necessary to give names to their objects. Buttons on the other hand will certainly be referred to later in the program, so they need permanent names. It is also the case that the name will be used outside the constructor, which is why we declared it before creating the button.

For example, to set up a Submit button and put it in the window, we could say:

```
// as a name
private Button submitButton;

// as a component
submitButton = new Button ("Submit");
  add(submitButton)
```

Why are there no parameters indicating *x,y* positions on the screen when we add the components to the frame? The reason is that these components (unlike graphics drawings) work with **layout managers**.

Layout managers

Layout managers take over control of the positioning of components that are added to a window, and arrange them sensibly. If the window is resized by the user, the layout manager endeavours to adjust the components in the new area so that they are all still visible.

Java has five such managers, but we shall look at only the first three: flow, border and grid. They all implement the interface LayoutManager, as shown in Figure 10.1. The form for incorporating a layout manager is:

Incorporating a layout manager
setLayout (NEW *Manager*(*parameters*));

where setLayout is a call to a method in Container, the abstract class from which Window and hence Frame inherit. The default layout manager is BorderLayout, but FlowLayout is actually more useful for our purposes. It also has the desirable property that it is the default manager for applets. An example layout set up is:

```
setLayout (new FlowLayout(FlowLayout.CENTER,horigap,vertigap));
```

The first parameter indicates that the items added to the frame should be centred: they could also have been left or right justified. The horigap and vertigap parameters are constants that indicate the minimum distance (in pixels once again) between items in the frame. All three parameters are optional. Examples of flow layout are given in the sample programs later on.

Reacting to buttons

In addition to closing the window, we now also need to react to buttons being pressed. Like the `windowListener`, there is an `actionListener` defined in `awt.event`. This listener interface has only one method to be implemented: `actionPerformed`. So the strategy for buttons is to link them to the `actionListener`, and to provide a version of `actionPerformed`. The linking is done in the constructor immediately after the button is declared and added to the container. The three statements for a submit button would be:

```
submitButton = new Button ("Submit");
   add (submitButton)
   submitButton.addActionListener (this);
```

The reference to `this` indicates that the current frame will be responsible for defining the `actionPerformed` method. When we set up such a link in the class diagram, it would be useful to distinguish GUI components and listeners from other classes. Referring to Figure 3.4, the symbol for a component is a double edged box and for a listener a sideways cone. The handler is a normal rectangular method symbol. So the above statement would be represented as in Figure 10.6.

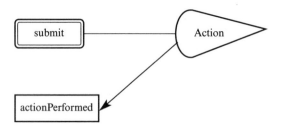

Figure 10.6 *A class diagram of a button, listener and handler.*

`ActionPerformed` has one parameter, which is an `ActionEvent`, and it can be successively interrogated to see whether it matches any of the buttons that could be pressed. The following form spells this sequence out:

Reacting to a button

```
public void actionPerformed (ActionEvent e) {
  if (e.getSource () == buttonname1) {
    statements
  } else
  if (e.getSource () == buttonname2) {
    statements
  }  // etc
}
```

If there are several buttons, all with different string labels, then the only way to distinguish between them is to have a sequence of if-else statements, checking for each possibility. In an algorithm form, we would draw a diagram as in Figure 10.7. A button press is just one kind of event so a diagram such as this will become very useful when the logic of handling events is more complicated. How to handle others will be discussed in Section 11.2.

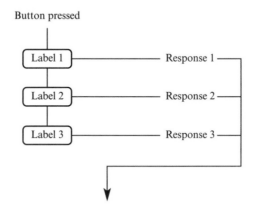

Figure 10.7 *Algorithm for responding to a button press.*

Extended indentation guidelines

Up until now, indentation in our programs has followed the traditional approach inherited from older languages such as Pascal and C, that is that we indent whenever there is a new method or statement block. Statements within the same block remain at the same level of indentation.

With GUI programming, one finds that there are often very long sequences of statements involved with setting up a number of components on the screen. Each component can have three or more statements associated with it. There is no prescribed order in which the statements have to be executed, but normally we deal with each component in turn and follow a create–link–add pattern. For Java programs, therefore, I have decided to introduce a new indenting scheme which regards the creation of a component as introducing a new level. Then all statements referring to that component can easily be seen. This effect has already been used in the `submitButton` example above, and is evident in the next example and the ones that follow.

EXAMPLE 10.3 Warning with two responses

Problem Improve the warning notice by including two buttons. One should enable the user to acknowledge the message, but wait. In this case, the whole window should turn red. The other button should pretend to force a reboot.

Algorithm Use the flow layout manager, labels and buttons to achieve the necessary effect. Select background and foreground colours from the Color class. For the actions, the Reboot button being pressed causes a simulated reboot in a similar way to closing the window. Pressing the Wait button changes colours as specified. Figure 10.8 shows the algorithm in diagrammatic form. The class diagram is show in Figure 10.9.

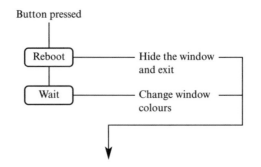

Figure 10.8 *Algorithm for responding to Reboot and Wait buttons.*

Notice that the class diagram shows associations not actions: wait and reboot are linked to the action listener that we will call actionPerformed. Although the linking is done inside the constructor, this fact is not shown as such in the diagram. Also, the window listener is shown as being linked to the whole frame, which it is in a way, although the instantiation in the main method refers more specifically to a local component, f, i.e.

```
Frame f = new ButtonTest("Button Test", message, 4);
```

Program The program is quite simple, and illustrates the essential sequential nature of GUI programming. The message to be displayed is passed to the new extension of the Frame as an array of strings. Each line is displayed through adding it as a label.

```
import java.awt.*;
import java.awt.event.*;

public class ButtonTest extends Frame implements ActionListener {

    /* The Button test Program by J M Bishop Sept 1996
     *  Java 1.1 version by T Abbott and J M Bishop Oct 1997
     * Prints a warning message, but when a Wait
     * button is pressed, it turns the window red.
     * Illustrates Buttons. Listeners and the
     * handling of events.
     * Under some browsers the change of colour does not work.
     */
```

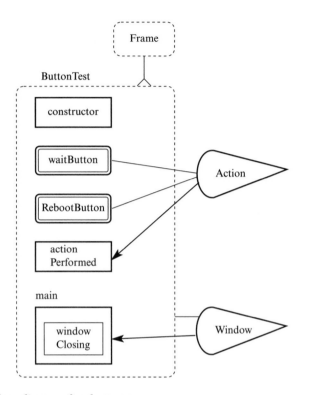

Figure 10.9 *Class diagram for the* ButtonTest *program.*

```
private static final int horigap = 15;
private static final int vertigap = 10;
private Button waitButton;
private Button rebootButton;

public ButtonTest(String title, String[] message, int n) {
/* The constructor is responsible for setting
 * up the initial buttons and colour background.
 */
  setBackground(Color.cyan);
  setForeground(Color.black);
  setLayout(new FlowLayout(FlowLayout.CENTER, horigap, vertigap));
  for (int i = 0; i < n; i++)
    add(new Label(message[i]));
  waitButton = new Button("Wait");
    add(waitButton);
    waitButton.addActionListener(this);
  rebootButton = new Button("Reboot");
    add(rebootButton);
    rebootButton.addActionListener(this);
}
```

```
public void actionPerformed(ActionEvent e) {
  if (e.getSource() == rebootButton) {
    setVisible(false);
    dispose();
    System.exit (0);
  } else if (e.getSource() == waitButton) {
    setForeground(Color.white);
    setBackground(Color.red);
  }
}

public static void main(String[] args) {
  String[] message = {
       "W A R N I N G",
       "Possible virus detected.",
       "Reboot and run virus",
       "remover software" };

  Frame f = new ButtonTest(message, 4);
  f.setTitle("Button Test");
  f.setSize(180,200);
  f.setVisible(true);
  f.addWindowListener(new WindowAdapter () {
    public void windowClosing(WindowEvent e) {
      System.exit(0);
    }
  });
}

}
```

Testing The first display from this program will be as shown in Figure 10.10.

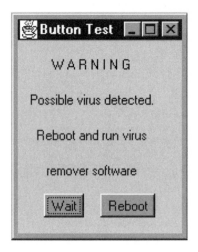

Figure 10.10 *Output from the* ButtonTest *program.*

Other layout managers

In addition to flow, the other four layout managers and their features are:

- **Border.** Allows positioning of items (scroll bars, menus, buttons, etc.) in fixed size borders indicated by a parameter which can nominate the `North`, `South`, `East` or `West` of the window, with the remainder of the space being the `Center`.[5]

- **Card.** Overlapping panels of information can be selected by clicking on tabs on the top of each panel.

- **Grid.** The frame is divided into a specified number of rows and columns which can be selected by number.

- **Grid bag.** Fine-grained layout where each component is given exact pixel constraints. Although complex to use, it is the most versatile and portable.

Since `LayoutManager` is an interface, it is possible to define your own layout manager, with customized (and sometimes very pleasing) results.

Other component options

Labels and buttons are components, and we indicated that there were other similar classes. To round things off, we name them and indicate their main functions here.

1. **`TextComponent`**, together with its two subclasses `TextArea` and `TextField`, handles multiple lined text, text selecting and editing.
2. **`Scrollbar`** is useful with text and enables the contents of the container to move in the window.
3. **`ScrollPane`** is a container that enables a component with a larger area to be moved underneath it with scroll bars so that a portion is visible at any one time.
4. **`Canvas`** is an additional window area that can be used for drawing in, so as not to interfere with buttons.
5. **`Checkbox`** provides for yes/no or on/off selection. An example would be selecting bold on a tool bar in a text processor.
6. **`Choice`** provides dropdown lists from which choices can be made. One choice can be made.
7. **`List`** is similar to choice except that the items are always on screen, and multiple selections can be made.
8. **`Menus`** can be created on the menu bar of the window, with pull down items. One can be selected at a time. Some options can be made unselectable when necessary.
9. **`Popup menus`** can be created anywhere in a window, and can have side submenus. Items can also be unselected.
10. **`Print`** is a command which can cause all or some of a window to be printed, in hardcopy, to a printer – a most useful feature, as it saves having to go through a screen dump process outside of Java.

Some of these options are used in other examples in this and later chapters.

---

[5] Note the American spelling once again for `center`.

10.4 Panels and canvases for grouping

Java provides higher-level groupings of components, which can then be moved around together in a window and are protected from overwriting each other. The first is a panel, which is used to keep groups of like components such as buttons. The panel is then passed to the layout manager as an entity. For example, submit and clear buttons could be grouped as follows:

```
Panel p = new Panel ( );
  p.add (new Button ("Submit"));
  p.add (new Button ("Clear"));
```

(Notice the use of indentation for the panel once again.) The panel can then be added to the frame in its constructor. In order to get the buttons always at the bottom of the screen, we can use BorderLayout and position the panel in the South area. BorderLayout is already the default manager for frames, while FlowLayout is the default for panels. Thus we can leave out calls to set them up, unless we wish to alter the gaps and so on. When adding to the BorderLayout, the first parameter selects one of five areas, as shown in Figure 10.11.

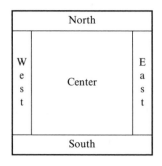

Figure 10.11 *Areas recognized by* BorderLayout.

The borders are narrow, being deep enough for one component only. Thus a couple of buttons will fit, or a heading, or a scroll bar but no more. An equivalent to the constructor in Example 10.3 is:

```
public ButtonTest(String title, String[] message, int n) {
    // using BorderLayout as the default

    super(title);
    setBackground(Color.cyan);
    setForeground(Color.black);

    Panel m = new Panel ();
      for (int i = 0; i < n; i++)
```

```
        m.add(new Label(message[i]));
      add ("Center", m);
   Panel p = new Panel p ();
      // use Flow layout as the default
      waitButton = new Button("Wait");
        waitButton.addActionListener(this);
        p.add(waitButton);
      rebootButton = new Button("Reboot");
        rebootButton.addActionListener(this);
        p.add(rebootButton);
   add ("South", p);
}
```

Canvases

The function of a canvas is to provide an area where drawing can take place. The drawing could be controlled and initiated by the program (for example, designs, logos, ticking clocks) or user-supplied drawing with a mouse. The next example explores both panels and canvases.

EXAMPLE 10.4 Traffic lights

Problem The Savanna Traffic Department would like to simulate traffic light times, and watch how pedestrian button requests affect the changing of the lights.

Solution Design a screen along the lines of Figure 10.12. Then handle the interaction of the lights and buttons as required. Such interaction needs event-based programming, so we shall take it up in Section 11.3 and complete the example there. Meanwhile we shall work on setting up the window ready for action.

Class design Put the traffic light in a canvas, with the circles, and so on, drawn using methods from Graphics. Put the buttons in one panel and the title in another. The class diagram for the program is shown in Figure 10.13. To keep the diagrams simpler, we shall leave out the listener for the window closing event from now on. Notice that the diagram shows that the walk button is not connected to anything yet.

Traffic extends Frame, as it must in order to display graphics. The buttons and title objects are both instances of the Panel class. Lights is a private object which is an instance of a small member class called LightsCanvas. LightsCanvas inherits from Canvas and has a single method, paint, which calls methods in Graphics.

In this program, we link the Close button up to the appropriate listener, but we do not yet supply any action for Walk: that comes later.

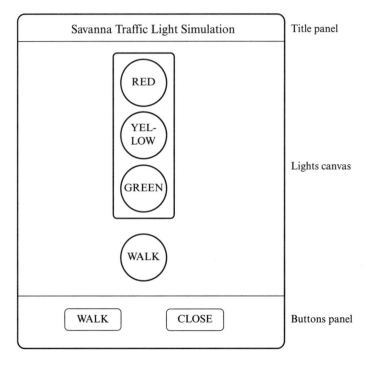

Figure 10.12 *Mock up of the screen for the traffic light simulation.*

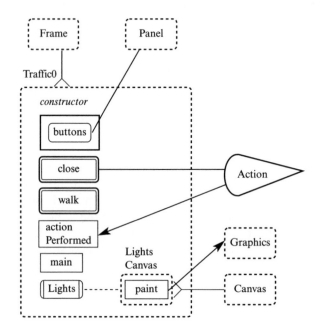

Figure 10.13 *Class diagram for the initial traffic light simulation.*

Program

```java
import java.awt.*;
import java.awt.event.*;

public class Traffic0 extends Frame implements ActionListener {

    /* The first Traffic light program
     *                                by J M Bishop Oct 1996
     *                       Java 1.1 by T Abbott October 1997
     * Displays a representation of traffic lights,
     * in preparation for a simulation.
     * NOTE: The walk button is not activated yet.
     * Illustrates panels and canvases and the
     * BorderLayout manager.
     */

    private LightsCanvas lights;
    private Button close;
    private Button walk;

    public Traffic0() {
        setTitle("Traffic Lights version 0");
        Panel title =
            new panel ();
        add(title.new Label("Savanna Traffic Light Simulation"));
        add("North", title);
        lights = new LightsCanvas();
            add("Center", lights);

        Panel buttons = new Panel();
            walk = new Button("WALK");
                buttons.add(walk);
            close = new Button("CLOSE");
                close.addActionListener(this);
                buttons.add(close);
        add("South", buttons);
    }

    public void actionPerformed(ActionEvent e) {
        setVisible(false);
        dispose();
        System.exit(0);
    }

    public static void main(String[] args) {
        Frame f = new Traffic0();
        f.setTitle("Traffic Lights Version 0");
        f.setSize(300,210);
        f.setVisible(true);
        f.addWindowListener(new WindowAdapter () {
            public void windowClosing(WindowEvent e) {
                System.exit(0);
            }
        });
    }
```

```
class LightsCanvas extends Canvas {
  public void paint(Graphics g) {
      g.drawOval(97, 10, 30, 68);
      g.setColor(Color.red);
      g.fillOval(105, 15, 15, 15);
      g.setColor(Color.yellow);
      g.fillOval(105, 35, 15, 15);
      g.setColor(Color.green);
      g.fillOval(105, 55, 15, 15);
      g.fillOval(105, 85, 15, 15);
      g.setColor(Color.black);
      g.drawString("RED", 15, 28);
      g.drawString("YELLOW", 15, 48);
      g.drawString("GREEN", 15, 68);
      g.drawString("WALK", 15, 98);
  }
 }
}
```

Testing See Figure 10.14. In colour, the three lights show up well (see Plate 9); in black and white the colours are not easily identifiable! To ensure at least an outline for each light, we should add drawOval with the same centre to the corresponding fillOval, using one pixel more in each direction, and drawn in black. For example:

```
g.setColor (Color.red);
g.fillOval (105, 15, 15, 15);
setColor (Color.black);
g.drawOval (105, 15, 16, 16);
```

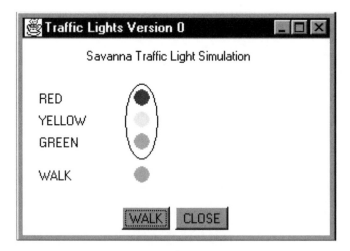

Figure 10.14 *The output of the initial traffic light simulation.*

SUMMARY

Graphics programming is fun but time-consuming. The graphics methods of Java are contained in the Graphics class and accessed by defining versions of the paint and repaint methods. All drawing takes place in a Frame, which is a subclass of the abstract class Component. Other components are Buttons, Labels, Textfields and so on, all of which can be used to construct interactive user interfaces. The layout of containers on the screen can be left up to default flow managers, or can be controlled in a number of ways, such as grids and borders. Java provides the full range of check buttons, menus, choices, scrollbars and so on that one needs.

QUIZ

10.1 The following declaration is not valid. Why not?

```
Component area = new Component ();
```

10.2 How does the paint method in a program such as Example 10.3 actually get called?

10.3 What is the default layout manager for a Frame?

10.4 Write awt calls to set up a choice list for the days of the week.

10.5 Why are the lights in Figure 10.14 not in the centre of the screen?

10.6 Give a Font declaration to enable drawString to write your name in the centre of the screen in large italics in the font that looks like Times Roman. (Study Example 10.2 for the names of Java 1.1's fonts.)

10.7 In Example 10.3, rewrite the relevant statements in the constructor so that it uses Border-Layout, with the WARNING in the north, the buttons in the south, and the rest in the centre. The effect should be the same as Figure 10.10.

10.8 In Example 10.4, why does Traffic0 have to declare that it implements ActionListener?

10.9 What statements would be used to add a close button to the Weather Chart program (Example 10.2)?

10.10 In the alternative ButtonTest constructor (Section 10.4) the last two statements are:

```
    p.add (new Button ("Reboot"));
add ("South", p);
```

Why does the last statement not have an object before the add? Explain what the statements do, and why they are indented in this specific way.

PROBLEMS

10.1 **Two traffic lights.** Improve the lights system to display two identical traffic lights on the screen.

10.2 **Digital watch.** Design the display and knobs of a digital watch to appear in a window. (Later on in Chapter 14 we shall see how to make it work.)

10.3 **Remote control.** Implement a user interface for the remote control device described in Section 9.2.

10.4 **Mobile phone.** Design and program a screen version of a mobile phone.

CHAPTER 11

Event-driven programming

Clearly, responding to events is an important part of GUI programming. Java's `awt.event` package provides the means for listenening for events, recording information about events as they occur, and linking up to user-defined event handlers. In this chapter we consider:

● how are events classified and corresponding listeners and handlers set up?

● how can sequences of events be managed?

In preparation, we start off by completing our look at components, with special attention to text fields, an essential part of user interaction

11.1 Interaction with text fields

To get text into a GUI program, Java provides a component `TextComponent` with two subclasses, `TextField` and `TextArea`. `TextArea` is for multi-line text and works in conjunction with scroll bars. We shall just consider the single-line text fields. To declare a component as a `TextField`, we use the form:

Creating a text field

```
private TextField t;

t = new TextField("initial value",n);
 add(t);
```

---

n is the number of characters one expects in the field, but will not fully define its width, since the width is also influenced by the font chosen and the layout manager used. However, the field will scroll if the user enters more than *n* characters, so there is no problem in guessing *n* incorrectly. Some of the methods available on a Text-Field are:

Text field methods

```
String      getText ();
void        setText ("value");
void        setEditable (booleanvalue);
boolean     isEditable ();
void        selectText (start, end);
```

---

getText and setText are the read and write equivalents for a TextField. Each field can also be open for input – that is, editable (the default) – or it can be locked. In the first state, it will be white, and the user must move the mouse there, click and start typing, ending with a return. If it is not editable, the field might be grey and data cannot be entered – this option depends on the computer being used. The need for these two states is illustrated in the next section. Finally, selectText allows a given part of the field to be highlighted, usually in blue.

Text fields usually have labels associated with them. To set up text fields to collect a person's name and age together in a Panel we would use:

```
Panel p = new Panel ();
  TextField name = new TextField("",40);
    p.add (new Label ("Name"));
    p.add (name);
  TextField age = new TextField("",5);
    p.add (new Label ("Age"));
    p.add (age);
```

which would give:

Notice that the flow layout manager would have taken care of setting the boxes out neatly in a frame of the right size. If the frame is bigger, the 'Age' label might land on the top row, whereupon some adjustment might be necessary to achieve the desired effect.

Inputting numbers

You may have noticed that there is only one get method for `TextField`, and it returns a `String`. Thus we are faced once again with translating the contents of the string to a number, if that is what we want. We discussed this process in Section 7.2, where the following key statement was used for integers:

Translating a string to an integer
`i = Integer.parseInt(s);`

Exactly the same technique can be used in GUI programming. However, a simple statement such as this assumes that nothing will go wrong in the conversion, such as a non-numeric character in the string. The `Text` class took care of these problems, and one could envisage a similar class being written, called say `GUIText`, which would perform exactly the same function, but with input from a `TextField` instead of a `BufferedReader`. For now we shall live dangerously, and leave the development of `GUIText` as a worthwhile exercise for the reader.

Avoiding input

We mentioned at the end of Section 10.3 that there were several other components in the awt, some of which provide for selections from lists or choices. Essentially, these save the user from typing in a lot of data, and also create a more secure environment because there is no opportunity for unexpected input. Take a simple example. If we want the user to give us a day of the week, we do not ask for text to be typed into a text field, with all its accompanying checking. Instead we provide a `Choice` list, which gives the seven choices, and the user simply selects one with the mouse. `CheckBox`, `List`, `Menu` and `Popup` have similar uses. An example of the use of a `Choice` is given in the next development of the traffic light program.

EXAMPLE 11.1 New traffic lights display

Problem Looking at the traffic light example, the simulation is intended to consider the effectiveness of different timings for the lights. For example, should red be on for longer than green, and so on.

Solution For an easy-to-use simulation, we must have the ability to change the time each light is on. In other words, we must read in new values. Doing so requires

● the selection of one of the four lights;

● the entering of the new duration.

The necessary components can be added to the buttons panel and appear at the bottom of the screen. They are a choice list for the four lights and a duration text field for entering a number of seconds.

Program We have not learnt enough yet to know how to make the lights flash: this will be covered in Chapter 13. However, we can still react to the choosing of the light and setting of the duration by outputting a suitable message alongside the light. An appropriate revised constructor for such a frame is:

```java
public Traffic1() {
  setTitle("Traffic Lights Version 1");

  Panel title = new Panel();
    title.add(new Label("Savanna Traffic Light Simulation"));
    add("North", title);

  lights = new LightsCanvas();
  add("Center", lights);

  Panel buttons = new Panel();
    colours = new Choice ();
      colours.addItem("Red");
      colours.addItem("Yellow");
      colours.addItem("Green");
      colours.addItem("Walk");
      buttons.add(colours);

    duration = new TextField("", 3);
      buttons.add(new Label("Duration"));
      duration.setEditable(true);
      buttons.add(duration);

    walkButton = new Button("Walk");
      buttons.add(walkButton);

    closeButton = new Button("Close");
      closeButton.addActionListener(this);
      buttons.add(closeButton);
    add("South", buttons);
}

private TextField duration;
private Choice colours;
private Button walkButton;
private Button closeButton;
```

Testing The output of the constructor is shown in the next example in Figure 11.4.

Although this constructor sets up components for choosing colour and duration, it does not indicate how events relating to such choices will be handled. A link to a handler is set for the Close button, as usual, but we now need to consider how to widen event handling for more kinds of components, and to look at more complicated event sequences.

11.2 Events, listeners and handlers

The classification of events is tied to the types of components that generate the events, but there is not one event type for each component type. Rather there are 11 **event** types and they are shared by the many **component** types. Each event type has a **listener** associated with it (though `MouseEvent` has two), and each listener requires that a corresponding **handler** must implement one or more of its methods.

For example, we have already seen that a button component is associated with an `ActionEvent` and an `ActionListener` and that the `actionPerformed` method must be implemented. Table 11.1 gives the full list of Java events, listeners and methods with the components they handle. All the listeners are interfaces, so those that are referred to in a program must be listed in the class header.

To understand Table 11.1, let us take an example from the previous program. In it, we defined a choice box, and we obviously will need to react to that. `Choice` is a component which is related to an `ItemEvent`, and needs an `ItemListener`. The method `itemStateChanged` must be implemented. What does such an implementation look like? Well, let us consider a handler we have seen already. When we implemented the `actionPerformed` method in Example 10.3, it looked like this:

```
public void actionPerformed(ActionEvent e) {
   if (e.getSource() == rebootButton) {
      setVisible(false);
      dispose();
      System.exit (0);
   } else if (e.getSource() == waitButton) {
      setForeground(Color.white);
      setBackground(Color.red);
   }
}
```

Thus `ActionEvent` uses the `getSource` method to return the object that caused the event. This object reference can be successively interrogated to establish which event occurred, and then the appropriate action can be taken. `getSource` is a method defined in a class called `EventObject` which is actually so high up in the hierarchy, it is in `java.util`, not `java.awt`! In every one of the event classes, there is a corresponding and more specific method which can be used instead of

Table 11.1 *Classification of events, listeners, methods and components*

Event	Listener	Methods	Components
ActionEvent	ActionListener	actionPerformed	Button List MenuItem TextField
AdjustmentEvent	AdjustmentListener	adjustmentValueChanged	ScrollBar
ComponentEvent	ComponentListener	componentHidden componentMoved componentResized componentShown	Component
ContainerEvent	ContainerListener	componentAdded componentRemoved	Container
FocusEvent	FocusListener	focusGained focusLost	Component
ItemEvent	ItemListener	itemStateChanged	CheckBox Choice List
KeyEvent	KeyListener	keyPressed keyReleased keyTyped	Component
MouseEvent	MouseListener	mouseClicked mouseEntered mouseExited mousePressed mouseReleased	Component
	MouseMotionListener	mouseDragged mouseMoved	
TextEvent	TextListener	textValueChanged	TextComponent
WindowEvent	WindowListener	windowActivated windowClosed windowClosing	Window

getSource. The problem is one of remembering all the names and return values, as they do not follow a pattern in the same way as the listeners and other methods do, as shown in Table 11.1. For example, for an ActionEvent, the alternative method to getSource is getActionCommand and it returns a string. Thus

```
    if (e.getSource() == rebootButton) {
```

would become

```
    if (e.getActionCommand() == "Reboot") {
```

However, for an ItemEvent (as generated by a Choice) the method is getItem-Selectable and it returns a value based on an interface called ItemSelectable. To keep things simple, we shall stick to getSource as a means of identifying events.

11.3 Managing sequences of events

In terms of the awt's interaction with the user, events are single happenings, but together they can form a chain of events. In other words, a certain event need not always elicit the same response. There may be two or three responses, depending on the events that have gone before.

How do we record what has gone before? In most cases, we use suitably named boolean variables which indicate whether or not a previous event happened. For example, in the panel in Example 10.4 which enabled the selection of a light, and then the entering of a new duration, we could force these two to happen in this order. We may also like to disable both of these components until a Change button has been pressed. We indicate the flow of this logic in Figure 11.1.

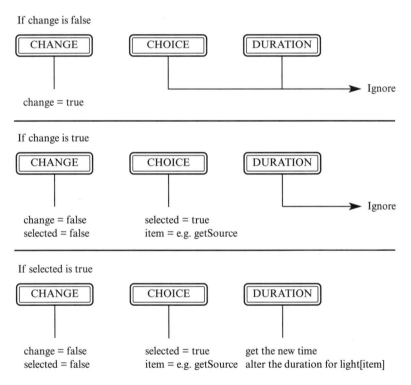

Figure 11.1 *Example of handling a sequence of events.*

Notice some interesting consequences of this logic. The change button acts as an on–off button, so that no matter what progress had been made with selecting a choice, if change is then pressed, the choice will be cancelled. Also, choice can be called over and over, with new selections being made until the user is satisfied. Finally, once a duration is selected, both choice and change go back to their original states so that the process must begin again. The logic did not have to be so: one could have said that having selected a duration, we can leave change on and leave the choice where it is, thus enabling a new duration to be entered immediately for the same item.

The point is that whatever logic we choose, we must be clear about it and it must contain no dead ends. It is not customary to provide a guide to the user about what to do, since just clicking the buttons will soon make the sequence clear.

EXAMPLE 11.2 Traffic light calibration

Problem We continue with Example 10.4, getting the user interface ready for changing the length of time that a light will shine.

Solution The display has been set up in the revised constructor we developed in the previous example. We need to connect the various components up to listeners and establish appropriate event handlers for their activation. The three components are the colours choice box, the duration text field and the walk button. At present we cannot do anything about the walk button, so we leave it unactivated.

To simulate changing the duration of the lights in response to a value typed in, we just write the value next to the light. This means that every time a duration is entered, the central graphic must be redrawn with the new values. The `actionPerformed` event therefore is responsible for calling `repaint`.

Algorithm A suitable algorithm for the event handling of the new program is given in Figure 11.2.

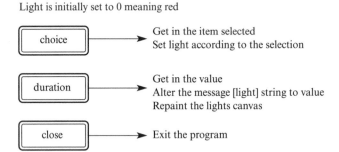

Figure 11.2 *Event handlers for version 1 of the traffic light calibration program.*

The enhanced class diagram for the new program is given in Figure 11.3.

Program

```
import java.awt.*;
import java.awt.event.*;
```

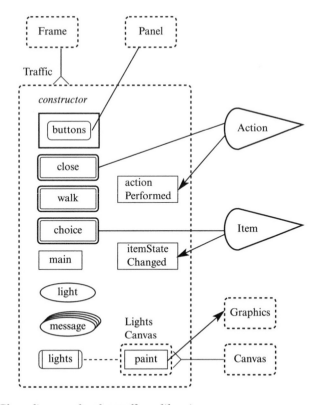

Figure 11.3 *Class diagram for the traffic calibration program.*

```
public class Traffic1 extends Frame
                   implements ActionListener, ItemListener {

   /*  The second Traffic Light program
    *                          by J M Bishop Oct 1996
    *           Java 1.1 version by T Abbott Oct 1997
    *        enhanced and revised by J M Bishop Oct 1997
    *  Adds options to set the duration for a light to
    *  be on, but choice is merely recorded, not
    *  acted upon at this stage.
    */

   private LightsCanvas lights;
   private TextField duration;
   private Choice colours;
   private Button walkButton;
   private Button closeButton;

   public Traffic1() {
      setTitle("Traffic Lights Version 1");

      add("North",new Label("Savanna Traffic Light Simulation"));
```

```
      lights = new LightsCanvas();
      add("Center", lights);

      Panel buttons = new Panel();
        colours = new Choice ();
          colours.addItem("Red");
          colours.addItem("Yellow");
          colours.addItem("Green");
          colours.addItem("Walk");
          buttons.add(colours);
          colours.addItemListener(this);

        buttons.add(new Label("Duration"));

        duration = new TextField("", 3);
          duration.setEditable(true);
          duration.addActionListener(this);
          buttons.add(duration);

        walkButton = new Button("Walk");
          // no action yet
          buttons.add(walkButton);

        closeButton = new Button("Close");
          closeButton.addActionListener(this);
          buttons.add(closeButton);
      add("South", buttons);
  }

  public void actionPerformed(ActionEvent e) {
    if (e.getSource() == closeButton) {
     setVisible(false);
     dispose();
      System.exit (0);
    } else if (e.getSource() == duration) {
      message[light] = duration.getText();
      lights.repaint();
    }
  }

  public void itemStateChanged(ItemEvent e) {
    if (e.getItemSelectable()==colours) {
      String s = (String) e.getItem();
      if (s=="Red")    {light = 0;} else
      if (s=="Yellow") {light = 1;} else
      if (s=="Green")  {light = 2;} else
      if (s=="Walk")   {light = 3;}
    }
  }

  public static void main(String[] args) {
    Frame f = new Traffic1();
    f.setSize(350, 210);
    f.setVisible(true);
```

```
    f.addWindowListener(new WindowAdapter () {
      public void windowClosing(WindowEvent e) {
        System.exit(0);
      }
    });
  }

  private int light = 0;
  String [ ] message = {"default","default","default","default"};

  class LightsCanvas extends Canvas {
    public void paint(Graphics g) {
    g.drawOval(87, 10, 30, 68);
    g.setColor(Color.red);
    g.fillOval(95, 15, 15, 15);
    g.setColor(Color.yellow);
    g.fillOval(95, 35, 15, 15);
    g.setColor(Color.green);
    g.fillOval(95, 55, 15, 15);
      // walk light is also green
    g.fillOval(95, 85, 15, 15);
    g.setColor(Color.black);
    g.drawString("RED", 15 ,28);
    g.drawString("YELLOW", 15, 48);
    g.drawString("GREEN", 15, 68);
    g.drawString("WALK", 15, 98);
    g.drawString(message[0], 135 ,28);
    g.drawString(message[1], 135, 48);
    g.drawString(message[2], 135, 68);
    g.setColor(Color.black);
    g.drawString(message[3], 135, 98);
    }
  }

}
```

Testing The expected output is shown in Figure 11.4.

The formulation of the traffic light simulation has been deliberately vague on the question of how the lights actually count down and change. In order to make this kind of animation work, we shall need some of the threaded facilities available in the java.net package. Networks are covered in Chapter 13, when the example is picked up again. The Case Study, however, puts into practice the ideas regarding event handling which we have developed in this section.

11.4 Case Study 5: Supermarket till

The solution to the following problem exploits different components of a GUI interface as well as event handling.

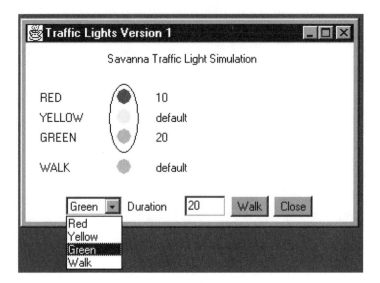

Figure 11.4 *Output from traffic light calibration program.*

Problem

Savanna Grocers wishes to computerize the weighing of fruit and vegetables at its tills. It envisages a display with buttons for the different produce and a space to enter the mass. At present the scales are not directly linked to the till, and there is not a special unit to print a price sticker, but the price of each item should be entered on the usual till slip.

Solution

The sequence of events required is shown in Figure 11.5. Thus if the strawberries weigh 3 kg, we enter 3 in the mass field. The cost per unit is given in graz, let us say G12 per kilogram. The mass times unit cost, which is G36, will appear in the cost field, and a line is printed for the complete transaction.

The solution devolves nicely into two parts: the design of the screen, and the organization of the event handling.

The design of the screen

Apart from the mass and cost text fields with their accompanying labels, there must be a button for each type of produce. These can be laid out in rows and columns like calculator buttons. In this case, the best layout manager is not flow, but grid. With `GridLayout` we specify the expected number of rows and columns, and Java will line

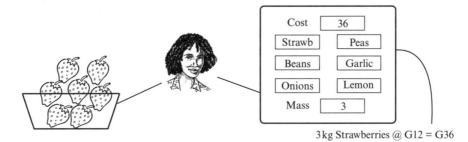

3 kg Strawberries @ G12 = G36

Figure 11.5 *A model for the grocery till.*

the components up in these boxes as they are added. The result is more symmetric and fixed than with `FlowLayout`.

All in all, we have three panels on the screen, which fit into a `BorderLayout` as follows:

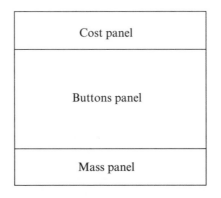

The buttons panel contains a button for each item of produce, plus three others for controlling the till, WEIGH, PRINT and CLOSE. CLOSE is not really needed since the system stops when we close the window, but it could be used to cause the printing of a running total or something like that.

Event handling

We start by listing the possible events:

WEIGH pressed
produce button pressed (e.g. peas)
mass entered
PRINT pressed
CLOSE pressed
window close

Not all of these are always valid. We want to force an ordering of events for weighing produce so that everything is entered before PRINT is pressed, that is:

these three in any order   press **WEIGH**
press a produce button
click on mass field, enter mass, press **RETURN**

press **PRINT**

Now we tabulate the events and indicate their effect:

WEIGH   opens up mass field
a produce button   sets unit cost and sets chosen
text in weigh field   sets mass and sets weighed
PRINT   prints the cost and resets everything

However, these effects cannot be achieved if the sequence of events is not correct. So we need to build that in too with the help of a couple of boolean variables (Figure 11.6).

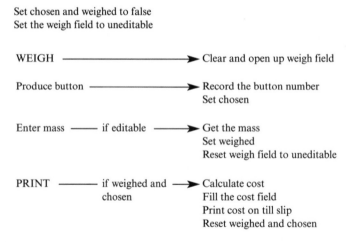

Figure 11.6 *Handling events in the grocery till.*

Data entry

There remains the question as to how to get the basic data into the program: that is, the produce names and their unit costs. Since the items could vary from day to day, and their prices certainly will, it would make sense to have this information stored in a file. For ease of getting the program up, though, we shall embed a few items in the program for now, and leave the extension to a file as an exercise.

Program

The program is as follows. Notice that in the constructor, we declare one panel, p, but instantiate it three times for each of the three different panels we need.

```
import java.awt.*;
import java.awt.event.*;

public class Till extends Frame implements ActionListener {

  /*  The Grocery Till program          by J M Bishop Oct 1996
   *      Java 1.1 version by T Abbott and J M Bishop Oct 1997
   *  Simulates the operation of a grocery till for
   *  up to 12 products, together with the costs per
   *  kilogram.
   *  Illustrates Panels, different layout managers,
   *  (including grid), user event handlers and the
   *  handling of events that should occur in a
   *  specified order.
   */

  private TextField weighField, totalField;
  private Button[] itemButtons;
  private Button weighButton, printButton, closeButton;

  public Till() {
    setLayout(new BorderLayout());

    Panel p = new Panel();
      p.setLayout(new FlowLayout());
      totalField = new TextField(6);
      totalField.setEditable(false);
      p.add(new Label("COST"));
      p.add(totalField);
    add("North", p);

    p = new Panel();
      p.setLayout(new GridLayout(5, 3));
      itemButtons = new Button[items.length];
      for (int i = 0; i < items.length; i++) {
        itemButtons[i] = new Button(items[i]);
        itemButtons[i].addActionListener(this);
        p.add(itemButtons[i]);
      }
      weighButton = new Button("WEIGH");
        weighButton.addActionListener(this);
        p.add(weighButton);
      printButton = new Button("PRINT");
        printButton.addActionListener(this);
        p.add(printButton);
```

```
      closeButton = new Button("CLOSE");
        closeButton.addActionListener(this);
        p.add(closeButton);
    add("Center", p);

  p = new Panel();
    p.setLayout(new FlowLayout());
    weighField = new TextField(4);
      weighField.setEditable(false);
      weighField.addActionListener(this);
      p.add(weighField);
    p.add(new Label("MASS"));
    p.add(new Label("Type return after the amount"));
    add("South", p);

  pack();
}

public void actionPerformed(ActionEvent e) {
  Object source = e.getSource();
  if (source == closeButton) {
    System.exit(0);
  } else
  if (source == printButton) {
    printItems();
  } else
  if (source == weighButton) {
    resetWeighField();
  } else
  if (source == weighField) {
    readWeighField();
  } else
    selectItem(e.getActionCommand());
}

/* Here follows the main control of the program.
 * The event and action handlers above call these
 * methods, which ensure that there is only a reaction
 * if certain conditions (e.g. other previous events)
 * have already been met.
 */

public void resetWeighField() {
  weighField.setText("");
  weighField.setEditable(true);
}

public void readWeighField() {
  if (weighField.isEditable()) {
    weighField.setEditable(false);
    weighField.selectAll();
    kg = (double)Integer.parseInt(weighField.getText());
    weighed = true;
  }
}
```

```
public void printItems() {
  if (weighed && chosen) {
    total = kg*unitCosts[select];
    totalField.setText("G "+total);
    System.out.println(kg+"kg "+items[select]+" @ G"+
            unitCosts[select]+" = G"+total);
    kg = 0;
    weighed = false;
    chosen = false;
    total = 0;
    weighField.select(0,0);
  }
}


public void selectItem(String item) {
  select = 0;
  while (!item.equals(items[select]))
    select++;
  chosen = true;
}

public static void main(String[] args) {
  Frame f = new Till( );
  f.setTitle("Savanna Grocers");
  f.setVisible(true);
  f.addWindowListener(new WindowAdapter() {
    public void windowClosing(WindowEvent e) {
      System.exit(0);
    }
  });
}

private String[] items = { "Apples", "Pears", "Oranges",
                           "Potatoes", "Lemons", "Squash",
                           "Onions", "Garlic", "Avocados",
                           "", "", "" };
private double[] unitCosts = { 6.00, 5.00, 7.00,
                              3.00, 10.00, 4.00,
                              4.00, 12.00, 15.00,
                              0, 0, 0 };

private double total;
private double kg;
private boolean chosen = false;
private boolean weighed = false;
private int select = 1;
}
```

Examining the `actionPerformed` method, we see that there are five if-statements. These correspond to the five events, excluding closing a window which is handled separately in the `main` method. Three of the events are unconditional: CLOSE, WEIGH and pressing a produce button. They always cause the action as given. The other two rely on previous events, so that the `weighField` can get input only if it is editable, and the PRINT button causes a reaction only if weighed and chosen have already been set.

Testing

The screen looks like Figure 11.7 after a few items have been entered.

Figure 11.7 *The Till program screen after a few selections.*

SUMMARY

User input is handled through text fields, as well as menus, choice boxes and so on. The latter restrict the user's options, but can make interaction more accurate and fast.

Once a screen has been laid out and displayed, interaction with the user begins. Moving the mouse, clicking a button or entering text constitutes an event. Events are linked to listeners and the listeners call back handlers which perform the correct actions. Event-driven programming requires careful algorithm development, especially for events that have to be forced into a certain order, for example weighing before printing.

QUIZ

11.1   Give the statement needed to read in an integer value i from a text field t.

11.2   Given a panel p, write awt calls to create a textfield called name with 'NAME' to its left and add it to p.

11.3   What special facilities do `TextArea` and `ScrollPane` offer? (Consult the Java help for information.)

11.4   What event is caused by typing into a text field? Is this the same event as pressing a button?

11.5   What is the method call used in `ActionPerformed` to decide what kind of event has occurred?

11.6   Create a typed method for reading in a double value from a `TextField` and show how it could be called from the `readweighField` method of the `Till` class.

11.7 Is there space in the `Till` class to add another three products? What would happen if we added another six?

11.8 What is the effect of `SetEditable` on a text field?

11.9 If you wanted to force the user to choose a product before pressing weigh, what would you have to do?

11.10 Why is message not private in the Till program?

PROBLEMS

11.1 **Shape selector**. A teacher wishes to let toddlers draw shapes (circle, square, triangle) in three colours (red, blue, yellow). The children cannot read. Provide a suitable GUI interface for selecting a shape and colour and drawing the object at a position given by a mouse click.

11.2 **GUI Text**. Implement a companion class to `Text` (Sections 4.2 and 7.3) for input from `TextFields`.

11.3 **Improving the grocery range**. Alter the Till program so as to have the items and costs stored on a file and read in at the start of the main program before the window is activated. Will the `GridLayout` size be affected or will it automatically accommodate more buttons?

11.4 **Till slip**. Create a proper till slip for a weighed item in a separate window, using a pleasing design similar to that of your local supermarket.

11.5 **Several tills**. Experiment with the Till program to bring up several Till windows at once by creating several `Frames` objects. Can you work with them alternately?

11.6 **GUI Coffee Shop**. Create a design for a full screen version of Nelson's inventory control program. Rewrite the classes so as to access the screen effectively. Find out what events may occur, and set up a suitable event handler.

CHAPTER 12

Applets in action

12.1 From applications to applets

A great deal of the excitement surrounding Java has had to do with its integration into the World Wide Web. As we shall see, once the mechanics of accessing Java through the web have been sorted out, and we have looked at the facilities available in the standard Java packages, it will be very easy for you to branch off on your own and create applets bounded only by your imagination.

So what is an applet? An applet is a Java program that operates within a browser, and hence can appear in a web page. The applet runs on the user's computer, even though it may have been fetched from far away.

The combination of factors that make this particular (and unique to Java) operation possible are **interpretation**, rather than full compilation of programs, and the **enabling** of the Java Virtual Machine in all web browsers. Interpretation means that Java applications (which we have studied so far) can move around the web and be executed on a variety of machines. Java browser enabling extends this facility to create the concept of applets. As the name suggests, applets are normally small programs, each devoted to a single task on a single browser page. At this point, the reader might like to refer to the diagrams and screen shots in Figures 1.1 to 1.6 (Plates 1–4), when applets were first introduced in the book.

The advantages of having applets in a web page are that:

1. The work is done on the machine where the results are needed, rather than sent there, so there is **less traffic** on the network.
2. The user's machine can be **dedicated** to the applet and can run it much faster than could a share of a server machine where the web page resides.
3. The **full facilities** of the Java programming language are available,[1] unlike some specially designed web languages which have restricted calculation and structuring powers. In particular, the standard awt is used for user interface communication.

To get an idea of how an applet differs from an application, let us go back to the first awt example in Chapter 9 and convert it to an applet.

Converting an application to an applet

The steps to achieve the conversion are as follows:

1. Check that all **input/output** relevant to the user goes through the awt interface. For example, replace

   ```
   System.out.println("This is a warning");
   ```

   with

   ```
   g.drawString("This is a warning", 0,0);
   ```

2. Remove any means for **stopping** the program (e.g. close buttons). Applets end when their viewer or surrounding browser pages end. They are not allowed to call `System.exit()`.
3. `Applet`'s **default layout** is flow, so if the frame was relying on border layout by default, add a call to make it specific, thereby overriding flow layout: for example, add

   ```
   setLayout (new BorderLayout ());
   ```

4. Import the `applet` package and in the main **window**, extend `Applet`[2] instead of `Frame`. For example, replace

   ```
   class graphicWarning extends Frame {
   ```

   with

   ```
   class appletWarning extends Applet {
   ```

5. Replace the class's **constructor** by a redefinition of the `init` method, which will be called by `Applet` to make any one-off initializations. For example,

   ```
   graphicWarning {
   ```

---

[1] Barring some security restrictions discussed below.

[2] `applet` with a small a is the name of the package that is imported; `Applet` with a capital A is the name of the class that is extended.

becomes

```
void init {
```

6. Remove the **main** method from the program, as the applet package will take over its functions such as creating a window and setting its size and visibility.
7. Create an **HTML** file that refers to the applet's class file or include HTML instructions (called **tags**) in a existing web page (see form below).
8. **Run** the HTML file through an applet viewer or through a web browser such as HotJava, Netscape, Mosaic or Explorer.

There are some consequences of no longer importing `Frame` (point 4 above). A call to `setTitle` must be removed (applets use the file name as a default title) and any other `Frame`-specific method calls must be replaced by `Applet` ones: for example, `dispose` becomes `destroy`.

Simple HTML

HTML stands for Hypertext Markup Language. We need to know only the bare basics of it to run applets. In fact, the form for activating an applet consists of one tag as follows:

HTML tags for an applet

```
<APPLET code="name" width=n height=m>
</APPLET>
```

An HTML page created via the editor of a browser may generate additional tags indicating the start and end of the HTML and the Body, but the above is sufficient.

Point 8 above indicates that there are two ways of running an applet. Let us first consider how to do this through the applet viewer supplied with Java. In the next sections we shall consider how to integrate applets with a browser.

EXAMPLE 12.1 Virus warning applet

Opportunity The warning program has become popular, and others would like to use it.

Response If the program is changed into an applet, it can be downloaded onto any other machine and run there. (Of course, this is a very simple program which would not draw much on the resources on either side, but we are using it for illustrative purposes.)

Design Following the steps above, we can convert the application of Example 10.1 into an applet. The HTML file that must be created contains the following:

```
<APPLET code="warningApplet.class" width=200 height=200>
</APPLET>
```

Program The program was pretty simple to start with, so it does not require much conversion. Points 2, 3 and 5 above do not apply in this case. Notice that as an applet, it is shorter than the original because the main program has gone: its function has been taken over by the Java runtime system in the browser or viewer.

```java
import java.awt.*;
import java.applet.*;

public class warningApplet extends Applet {

  /* A Warning box in an applet    by J M Bishop  Oct 1996
   * ==========================    Java 1.1
   * Must be run via its corresponding html file
   * in a browser or the appletviewer
   */

  static private final int line = 15;
  static private final int letter = 5;

  public void paint(Graphics g) {
    g.drawRect(2*letter, 2*line, 33*letter, 6*line);
    g.drawString("W A R N I N G", 9*letter, 4*line);
    g.drawString("Possible virus detected", 4*letter, 5*line);
    g.drawString("Reboot and run virus", 5*letter, 6*line);
    g.drawString("remover software", 7*letter, 7*line);
  }
}
```

Testing The output from the applet (Figure 12.1) looks exactly the same as that from an application, except that the title bar of the window is set up by the applet viewer as the file's name and there is a clear indication that the window is created by an applet. Figure 12.1 shows the window along with a listing of the HTML file.

How applets work

If an applet does not have a main program, how does it get started, and how does it stop? An applet is started up by the Java runtime system, which then looks to call one of the following four methods – which the applet has provided – at the appropriate time:

Applet methods
init()
destroy()
start()
stop()

Figure 12.2 shows the relationship between an applet and the Applet class running in a Web browser. The init method is called in place of a constructor, to provide

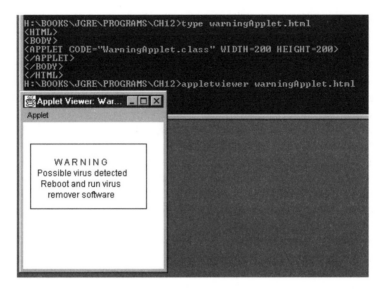

```
H:\BOOKS\JGRE\PROGRAMS\CH12>type warningApplet.html
<HTML>
<BODY>
<APPLET CODE="WarningApplet.class" WIDTH=200 HEIGHT=200>
</APPLET>
</BODY>
</HTML>
H:\BOOKS\JGRE\PROGRAMS\CH12>appletviewer warningApplet.html
```

Applet Viewer: War...
Applet

WARNING
Possible virus detected
Reboot and run virus
remover software

Figure 12.1 *Applet output for the Warning program.*

the initial setting up of the applet. Here the programmer would put the drawing of the user interface, its buttons and menus, and any other passive initialization. The `start` method on the other hand, is called if there are dynamics to set up in an applet, such as animation and extra threads of control. (Threads are discussed in the next chapter.)

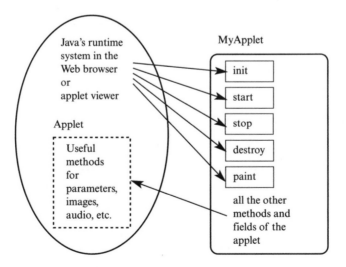

Java's runtime system in the Web browser or applet viewer

MyApplet

Applet

Useful methods for parameters, images, audio, etc.

init
start
stop
destroy
paint

all the other methods and fields of the applet

Figure 12.2 *The relationship between an applet and the* `Applet` *class.*

At this point, the system calls any other methods which the program (in either its application or applet form) has overridden, such as `paint`. In Example 12.1, only the `paint` method is present, as the applet had no reason to define any of the others. The applet then returns to a passive state and waits for something to happen. There are two possibilities: the applet can become invisible, by means of the user scrolling it off the page in the browser, or there can be a normal GUI event such as a mouse down or a button press. If an applet becomes invisible, its `stop` method is called, which has the responsibility of halting any animation and so on. When it becomes visible again, `start` is called. Any of the other events are handled in the normal way via the awt methods redefined in the original program (such as `actionPerformed`).

Finally, a `destroy` method can be provided so that the applet can release any resources it may have before the viewer ends or the browser moves to a different page. If we return to the page with our applet on it, the applet will start from scratch again, going through its `init` sequence.

The above four methods are defined by the `Applet` class, but are overridden by the user, who provides the functionality. There is also a group of methods defined in the `Applet` class which we can use directly. These include methods to load images, audio and HTML parameters, and to establish where the applet is and where it came from. These methods are introduced in later sections and chapters.

12.2 Applets in browsers

Before Java, web browsers were mainly static, presenting information to the viewer exactly as it was stored at the original site. There were facilities for returning data to the host via form collecting and mailing, but Java's idea of having calculations at the host site is novel. With applets being able to be included in web pages, what comes down the link can now present a dynamic interface to the user (refer back to Figure 1.1).

Work can be done and results can be returned to the host machine. Without Java, the same sequence of events as in Figure 1.1 occurs when web browsing, except that the display includes only text and images.

Where are the applets?

If an applet is stored on a host machine, then it is accessible to any other machine on the internet via its World Wide Web protocol and name or URL.[3] The `warningApplet`'s URL would be something like:

```
http://www.cs.up.ac.za/javagently/warningApplet.html
```

where the HTML file is stored on a web-accessible directory. The class file it refers to must be in the same directory, if it has the simple name as given in the tag:

---

[3] URL stands for universal resource locator.

```
<APPLET code="warningApplet.class" width=200 height=200>
```

If the applet is in another directory, then the tag must specify its full URL.

We consider now an example of an applet that actually interacts with the user, and compare its operation locally through the applet viewer and remotely via a browser.

EXAMPLE 12.2 Supermarket till applet

Opportunity The directors of Savanna Grocers see the opportunity of keeping the master version of the supermarket till program in one place, and letting the various tills download it as required. There could well be advantages for updating, for franchising and for changing computers.

Response Convert the program into an applet as per the instructions. Create an HTML file and access it via a browser loaded on each till.

Program The changes are absolutely minimal. The constructor changes its name to `init` and the `main` method is removed. Since applets cannot close themselves, we also remove the close button and the corresponding handler for it in `actionPerformed`.

```
import java.awt.*;
import java.awt.event.*;
import java.applet.*;

public class TillApplet extends Applet implements ActionListener {

    /*  The Grocery Till applet    by J M Bishop Oct 1996
     *  =======================    Java 1.1 version
     *                             by T Abbott and J M Bishop Oct 1997
     *  Simulates the operation of a grocery till for
     *  up to 12 products, together with the costs per
     *  kilogram.
     *  Illustrates Panels, different layout managers,
     *  (including grid), user event handlers and the
     *  handling of events that should occur in a
     *  specified order.
     *  Runs as an applet via its corresponding html file.
     */

    private TextField weighField, totalField;
    private Button[] itemButtons;
    private Button weighButton, printButton, closeButton;

    public void init () {
        ... as for the constructor but with the close button removed
    }
```

```
public void actionPerformed(ActionEvent e) {
    ... as before but with reference to System.exit() for the
    ... close button removed.
}

/* Here follows the main control of the program.
 * The event and action handlers above call these
 * methods, which ensure that there is only a reaction
 * if certain conditions (e.g. other previous events)
 * have already been met.
 */

    ... exactly as before

private String[] items = { "Apples", "Pears", "Oranges",
                           "Potatoes", "Lemons", "Squash",
                           "Onions", "Garlic", "Avocados",
                           "", "", "" };
private double[] unitCosts = { 6.00, 5.00, 7.00,
                               3.00, 10.00, 4.00,
                               4.00, 12.00, 15.00,
                               0, 0, 0 };

private double total;
private double kg;
private boolean chosen = false;
private boolean weighed = false;
private int select = 1;
}
```

Testing If we run the applet via the applet viewer, then the till applet's output is the same as that of the original application, except for the absence of the close button. Figure 12.3 gives a picture of the screen, together with output that is still being printed for the till slip, that comes out on the command line window. The applet responds to the application in the same way but is closed by closing the applet viewer itself: there is no close button.

Now if we store the HTML file in a location that is accessible on the web, we can start up a browser (such as HotJava in this case) and request the location specified. The result is shown in Figure 12.4. There are two differences between what the user sees of the applet in the viewer and browser environments:

- The applet viewer still gives access to the screen for printing. Under the browser, open up the Java Console window to see the output (usually available on the File menu).

- The applet viewer can be stopped by closing the viewer's window, whereas under a browser, the applet ends only when the page it is running in is closed.

In all other respects applets behave the same under either environment.

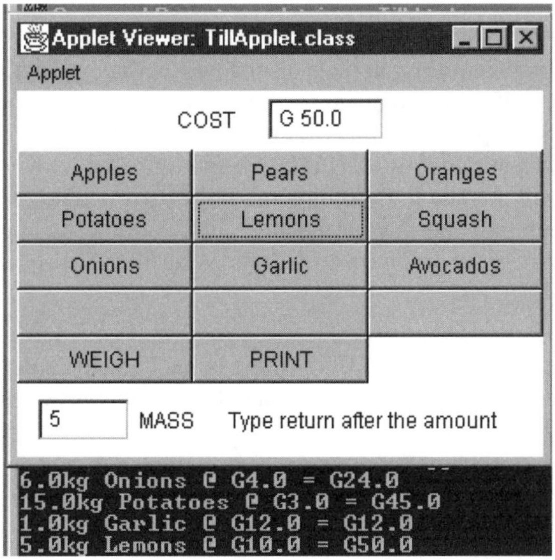

Figure 12.3 *Applet output from the Till program via a viewer.*

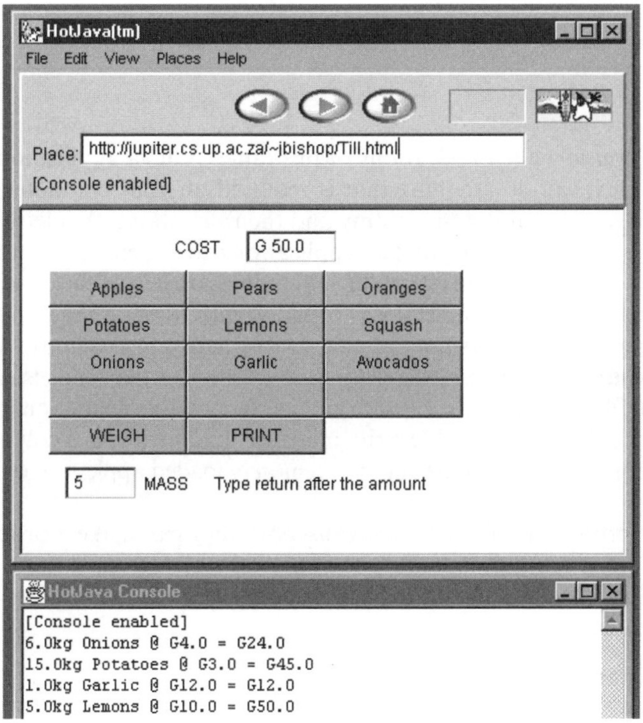

Figure 12.4 *The Till applet running under the HotJava browser.*

Applet security

A potential concern when using applets on the web is that a program you download could be corrupt, and cause damage to your system. In every possible way, Java guards against this happening. In the first place, there is a validity check on the byte-code that arrives at your computer. If it had been tampered with *en route*, your Java Virtual Machine will not run it. Secondly, the JVM itself will not perform any operation that could potentially harm your machine. For example, an applet from far away cannot find out your password, nor can it delete your files. The full set of rules is summarized in Table 12.1.

Operation	Java application	Applet in an applet viewer	Local applet in a browser	Remote applet in a browser
Access local files	✓	✓		
Delete a local file	✓			
Run another program	✓	✓		
Find out your name	✓	✓	✓	
Connect back to the host	✓	✓	✓	✓
Connect to another host	✓	✓	✓	
Load the Java library	✓	✓	✓	
Call exit	✓	✓		
Create a pop-up window	✓	✓	✓	✓

Table 12.1 *Applet security*

Let us consider the implications of this table. A Java application is a full program and as such can do anything that is required on your computer. An applet is quite different, and is subject to scrutiny and the rules above. Applets running in the applet viewer can do everything that an application can, except for deleting files. However, once they run within a browser, their activities are curtailed somewhat.

Within a browser, an applet does not end: it ends when the page it is in is replaced by another page. Thus it does not call exit, nor is there any close box. Applets in web pages are **seamless**, as shown in the Case Study. The fact that applets cannot read or write the local file system can be a disadvantage. In fact, this restriction can be lifted by the applet user defining a special security manager. Finally, the last column in the table shows that additional restrictions apply to remotely loaded applets, and these are all to the good.

These restrictions are in a good cause, but they can make a programmer's life difficult. The work-arounds that must be employed when an applet cannot read a local file are described next and illustrated in Example 12.3.

The PARAM facility

We are already aware that getting data into an applet cannot always be done by just reading a file. If the applet is running in a browser, then there is a facility to set up data in the web page, and for the applet to fetch it from there. The mechanism is fairly cumbersome, so is best used for one-off set-up type data.

Interaction between applets and web pages is achieved through the PARAM facility. PARAM operates by having named parameters listed in the HTML document that the applet can read using an Applet class method called getParameter. Parameters are listed between the <APPLET> and </APPLET> tag brackets and each parameter must be of the form:

HTML parameter

```
<PARAM NAME = "formal" VALUE = "actual">
```

NAME indicates that the string that follows is the name of the parameter that is being sought. Within the same set of angle brackets, forming a pair, there is the VALUE to be assigned to that parameter. The value is also a string, but obviously it can be parsed as a number or whatever other type is required. A possible application of PARAM in the till example would be to move the prices of the products from the applet to the web page, specifying them as:

```
<PARAM NAME="garlic" VALUE="12">
```

To access the parameters we use the string method getParameter as follows:

```
unitCosts[i] = Integer.parseInt(getParameter(items[i]));
```

Here, items[i] is a string, such as "garlic", and getParameter will find the parameter with that name and return the corresponding value, which would be the string "12". The PARAM facility is used in Example 12.3 and the Case Study, and is required in some of the problems that follow.

Signed applets

All the above restrictions apply to untrusted code. Some of them could get in the way within a single company, where applets are written at head office and fetched to branches. There may well be the need to read local files at the branches, for example. The JDK provides for applets to be created with digital signatures, via a special utility called the javakey tool. The company must maintain a small database of trusted applets, which can be entered in the base, with their public and private keys. Then the applet is saved as an archive or JAR[4] and the JAR file is passed through the javakey tool. The HTML file that is going to run the applet then includes an additional tag to fetch the signed archive file, before the code file it contains is executed.

The above applies to the JDK: other IDEs and browsers may have other ways of declaring and handling trusted applets.

---

[4]JAR stands for Java archive.

EXAMPLE 12.3   The newspaper competition

Problem The *Savanna News* runs a weekly competition based on readers' names. A value is assigned to each letter of the alphabet and there is a winning score. If you are one of the readers whose name adds up to the winning score, then you can enter for a prize. To even things out, every name is expanded or contracted to 20 letters, without spaces or punctuation. The competition is repeated every week with different letter values and a different winning score each week. All those who enter have a chance of winning the weekly 1000 graz prize.

Example

```
Alphabet          a b c d e f g h i j k l m n o p q r s t u v w x y z
Values            5 1 3 6 7 9 2 3 7 5 4 1 3 8 9 7 5 4 3 2 1 3 2 4 5 4
Winning score     100
```

Names	Letters used	Score
Judy Bishop	JudyBishopJudyBishop	94
John Smith	JohnSmithJohnSmithJo	100
Roelf van den Heever	RoelfvandenHeeverRoe	118
Timothy Fox-Fox-Robinson	TimothyFoxFoxRobinso	116

So John Smith can enter the competition this week. The others can try again when the letter values change next week.

Now the editor would like the competition to be available on the Web so that people can try out their names and get an up-to-date immediate response.

Solution Write a Java applet, of course! This competition is ideal for an applet because it contains information that is maintained centrally (the letter values) and that must be protected, but we want everyone to be able to do the calculation. Moreover, doing it by hand is actually quite tedious, so the calculation facility offered by applets is valuable.

Screen design It is useful to start off with a screen design for the applet, indicating what fields we need to reserve for input and output while iterating with the user. In addition, we can decide what information can be kept in the Web page, and what has to go in the applet. Plain text is cheaper to display via HTML than via an applet. Figure 12.5 gives an indication of what the screen could look like.

Algorithm The competition applet splits into two parts. The first one handles the setting up of the screen and the data; the second one handles the input of names and the calculation of the result through a GUI interface. Figure 12.5 gives an idea of the layout. Setting up the data requires more thought.

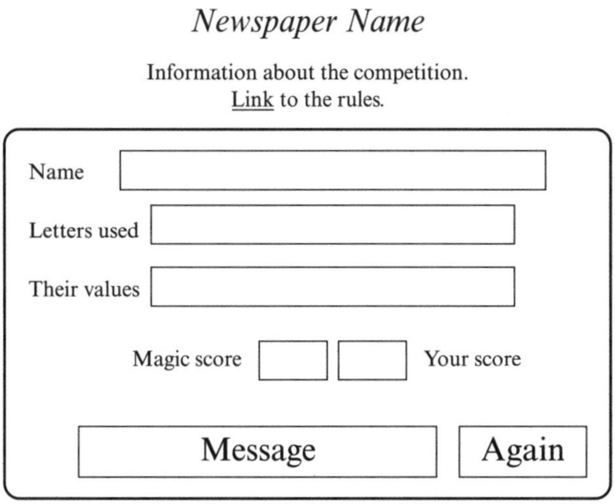

Newspaper Name

Information about the competition.
Link to the rules.

Figure 12.5 *Screen design for the newspaper competition.*

We want to associate values with characters. In other words, we want a table relating characters to integers. Unfortunately, as we discovered in Section 6.4, Java does not allow arrays to have any index type except integer. Instead, we have to use a hash table, where the characters and corresponding integers are both stored using put, and extracted using get.

The question then is: how do we get the values into the applet? What we want is for the values to be easily alterable by newspaper staff who may not be programmers. If we create them as fixed constants, then each week we shall have to recompile the program when the values change, which is not convenient. Two other options are:

1. Have the values stored in the web page as parameters and get them from there.
2. Connect to a file on the main newspaper computer and read the values remotely.

Either of these suggestions is feasible. How to connect to a remote resource is covered in Chapter 14, so we shall use the parameter facility here. The parameter names will be Score and a, b, c, d and so on for each letter of the alphabet.

The interface has two input fields – the name and an Again button – and five display fields – the letters used, their values, the magic score, your score and a message. Setting up the strings to be displayed is best described in Java itself in the applet below.

For the input, the actionPerformed method must handle events on the field and the button. Clicking the Again button will set the fields to their original state, which is easy. Handling the name is more complex. The algorithm required is:

Checking a name for a win

Get the text
Trim it of trailing blanks
Convert it to lower case
Remove all spaces and punctuation
Cut the name to 20 chars max or repeat the name to 20 chars
Consult the hash table for the values for each letter and compute the Total
Total is winning score?

yes   no

Good luck message   Bad luck message

To work on the name, we use several of the methods supplied with the `String` class, such as `trim`, `toLowerCase` and `toCharArray`. The last converts a string into an equivalent array of characters, which is more convenient for our purposes. The extracted name is also an array of characters, as is its equivalent array of letter values. These are both displayed in the output.

Web page The web page has the headings and the parameters. Here it is, as produced through a browser editor.

```
<HTML>
<HEAD>
   <META HTTP-EQUIV="Content-Type" CONTENT="text/html; charset=iso-8859-1">
   <META NAME="GENERATOR" CONTENT="Mozilla/4.03 [en] (Win95; I) [Netscape]">
   <TITLE>Competition</TITLE>
</HEAD>
<BODY>

<CENTER>
<H3>
<B><FONT COLOR="#3366FF"><FONT SIZE=+2>Savanna News
Competition</FONT></FONT></B></H3></CENTER>

<CENTER><B>Win G1000 if your name matches the magic score.</B></CENTER>

<CENTER><B><A HREF="Rules.html">Rules</A> of the competition.</B></CENTER>

<CENTER><B></B> </CENTER>

<CENTER><APPLET CODE="Competition.class" WIDTH=350 HEIGHT=240>

<PARAM NAME="Score" VALUE="100">
<PARAM NAME="a"     VALUE="5">
<PARAM NAME="b"     VALUE="1"> <PARAM NAME="c"     VALUE="3">
<PARAM NAME="d"     VALUE="6"> <PARAM NAME="e"     VALUE="7">
<PARAM NAME="f"     VALUE="9"> <PARAM NAME="g"     VALUE="2">
<PARAM NAME="h"     VALUE="3"> <PARAM NAME="i"     VALUE="7">
<PARAM NAME="j"     VALUE="5"> <PARAM NAME="k"     VALUE="4">
```

```
<PARAM NAME="l"    VALUE="1"> <PARAM NAME="m"    VALUE="3">
<PARAM NAME="n"    VALUE="8"> <PARAM NAME="o"    VALUE="9">
<PARAM NAME="p"    VALUE="7"> <PARAM NAME="q"    VALUE="5">
<PARAM NAME="r"    VALUE="4"> <PARAM NAME="s"    VALUE="3">
<PARAM NAME="t"    VALUE="2"> <PARAM NAME="u"    VALUE="1">
<PARAM NAME="v"    VALUE="3"> <PARAM NAME="w"    VALUE="2">
<PARAM NAME="x"    VALUE="4"> <PARAM NAME="y"    VALUE="5">
<PARAM NAME="z"    VALUE="4">
</APPLET></CENTER>

</BODY>
</HTML>
```

Applet Some of the interesting code in the applet includes the extraction of the name from the textfield and its conversion into a character array, done by:

```
c = nameField.getText().trim().toLowerCase().toCharArray();
```

getText returns a string. trim and toLowerCase are both string methods which return strings. Finally, toCharArray takes a string and converts it into a character array.

The next section of code takes each element of this array and looks up its letter value in the hash table. The hash table stores strings, so the result of

```
String s = (String) values.get(String.valueOf(d[i]));
```

is a string. To build up another character array of the letter values (which are all under 10 and therefore single digits) we can just extract the first character of the string using charAt. However, to create the score, we do finally have to convert the string to an int. These two lines perform this task:

```
e[i] = s.charAt(0);
total += Integer.parseInt(s);
```

A further point of interest is that we use a variety of fonts in the applet. The ordinary font is:

```
Font g = new Font("SanSerif",Font.PLAIN,12);
```

but for the letters and their values we use a fixed spaced font, set up by:

```
Font h = new Font("Monospaced",Font.PLAIN,12);
```

and then message uses a larger font:

```
Font f = new Font("Serif",Font.BOLD,20);
```

The Java applet follows. It is not all that long, but is effective.

```
import java.awt.*;
import java.applet.*;
import java.awt.event.*;
```

```java
public class Competition extends Applet implements ActionListener {

  /*  The Competition applet       by J M Bishop Oct 1996
   *  =====================        Java 1.1 Jan 1998
   * Runs a competition screening mechanism.
   * Illustrates interaction between an applet
   * and a web page.
   */

  private static int winningScore;
  private TextField targetField, nameField,
          lettersField, valuesField, scoreField, resultField;
  private Button againButton;
  private Hashtable values = new Hashtable ();
  private String openingMessage = "See if your name is a winner!";
  private static final int lettersCounted = 20;
  String  letters [] = {"a","b","c","d","e","f","g","h","i","j",
          "k","l","m","n","o","p","q","r","s","t","u","v","w",
          "x","y","z"};

  public void init () {

    // First, generate the letter values and
    // Create the hash table by using values in the
    // PARAM tags of the web page.
    // Both the key and value are strings.

    winningScore = Integer.parseInt(getParameter("Score"));
    for (int i = 0; i<26; i++)
      values.put(letters[i], getParameter(letters[i]));

    // draw the user interface
    setLayout (new BorderLayout ());

    Panel p = new Panel ();
      Font g = new Font("SanSerif",Font.PLAIN,12);
      p.setFont(g);
      nameField = new TextField ("",40);
        p.add (new Label ("Your name is?"));
        p.add (nameField);
        nameField.addActionListener(this);
      Panel r = new Panel();
        Font h = new Font("Monospaced",Font.PLAIN,12);
        r.setLayout(new GridLayout(2,2));
        lettersField = new TextField("",20);
          lettersField.setEditable(false);
          r.add(new Label("Letters used:"));
          r.add (lettersField);
          lettersField.setFont(h);
        valuesField = new TextField("",20);
          valuesField.setEditable(false);
          r.add(new Label("Their values are:"));
          r.add (valuesField);
          valuesField.setFont(h);
      p.add(r);
```

```
      targetField = new TextField
                    (Integer.toString(winningScore),4);
        targetField.setEditable(false);
        p.add (new Label ("Magic score"));
        p.add (targetField);
      scoreField = new TextField ("",4);
        p.add (scoreField);
        p.add (new Label ("Your score"));
        scoreField.setEditable(false);
    add ("Center", p);

    Panel q = new Panel ();
      resultField = new TextField (openingMessage);
        resultField.setEditable(false);
        Font f = new Font("Serif",Font.BOLD,20);
        resultField.setFont(f);
        q.add (resultField);
      againButton = new Button("Again");
        q.add (againButton);
        againButton.addActionListener(this);
    add ("South", q);
  }

  public void actionPerformed (ActionEvent evt) {
    Object source = evt.getSource();

    // Again resets everything. It is always available
    if (source == againButton) {
      nameField.setText("");
      scoreField.setText("");
      resultField.setText(openingMessage);
    }

    // A name was entered
    else
      handleName();
  }

  void handleName() {
    char c [];
    char d [] = new char[lettersCounted];
    char e [] = new char[lettersCounted];

    // Convert name to lower case and strip blanks
    c = nameField.getText().trim().toLowerCase().toCharArray();
    int n=0;
    for (int i=0; i<c.length & n<lettersCounted; i++) {
      if (Character.isLetter(c[i])) {
        d[n] = c[i];
        n++;
      }
      if (i==c.length-1) i=-1;
    }

    // The stripped down array is now in d[0] to d[n]
    // and we put the corresponding values in e[].
    int total = 0;
```

```
for (int i=0; i<n; i++) {
    String s = (String) values.get(String.valueOf(d[i]));
    e[i] = s.charAt(0);
    total += Integer.parseInt(s);
}

// Calculate and compare the score. Display a message.
scoreField.setText(Integer.toString(total));
lettersField.setText(String.valueOf(d));
valuesField.setText(String.valueOf(e));
if (total == winningScore)
    resultField.setText("Good luck in the lucky draw");
else
    resultField.setText("Bad luck! Try again next week");
    }

}
```

Testing The applet can be tested with the names above, or with a variety of other names. The run shown in Figure 12.6 has hit on a name with the lucky score.

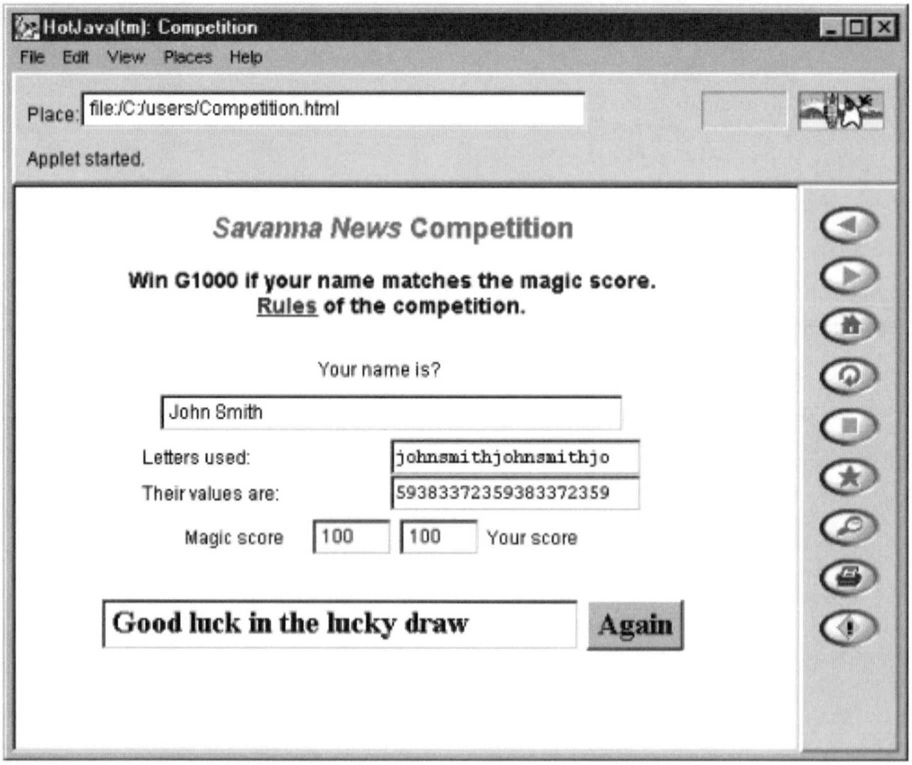

Figure 12.6 *The Competition applet running in HotJava.*

12.3 Sound and images

One of the joys of Java is being able pull in sound and images easily and effectively into a program.

Sound

The `Applet` package has an interface called `AudioClip` which has three methods: `play`, `stop` and `loop`. The `Applet` method `getAudioClip` will return an object which implements this interface, and then we can play that object. The form is:

`AudioClip` declaration and play

```
AudioClip name;
name = getAudioClip (getCodeBase (), filename);
name.play();
```

The `getCodeBase` method in `Applet` finds out where the applet is running, so that the sound can be played there. The file, at the moment, must be an .au file, not a .wav file, but see below for future developments.

Suppose we have a file called 'ouch.au' and want to play it. The following statements will set this up:

```
AudioClip ouch;
ouch = getAudioClip (getCodeBase (), "ouch.au");
ouch.play();
```

There is also a shorthand version of the above which uses anonymous clips as follows:

```
play(getCodeBase (), "ouch.au");
```

The first form is preferable if you are going to use the clip more than once in a program. Sound is used in Example 12.4.

Images

Images are pixel data that is stored in a file, brought over the network, or created in realtime by a graphics engine or video camera. Java has extensive facilities for handling all these, and in particular for addressing the problems of working in a distributed, networked environment. You will have already experienced the varying speeds at which images are downloaded within a browser. One of the more useful options in a browser is to set autoloading of images, meaning that the text will continue to come in while the image is also being displayed. Thus we are not held up just for a picture we may have already seen and do not particularly want.

Java can perform the same kind of control through objects called `Observers`. We can also animate images, control flickering and filtering and run through videos at varying speeds. All of this is a topic on its own. In this chapter, we shall look at a simple fetch of a single image, and the usual way of moving it around on the screen.

Like audio clips, Java has a class for images, and the form for getting one is exactly the same as above, with `AudioClip` replaced by `Image`. Thus an example of fetching an image would be:

```
Image me;
me = getImage (getCodeBase (), "bishop.gif");
```

To display the image, we access the `drawImage` method within the `Graphics` class of the awt. The form for displaying an image is:

Display an image
`g.drawImage (name, x, y, observer);`

The *x* and *y* coordinates specify the top left corner of the spot where the image should be drawn on the screen. In most cases our applet is the observer and therefore we use `this` as the fourth parameter. For example:

```
g.drawImage (me, 0, 0, this);
```

Media tracking

While observers let us carry on with what we are doing while images are being loaded, we may wish to do the opposite: ensure that an image is loaded before continuing. It is important to do so when an applet is loading images in its `init` method. If an image is set to load, and the applet asks how big it is, it may get a spurious answer. So we set a media tracker on it. The form is:

Media tracker

`MediaTracker tracker = new MediaTracker(applet);`
`tracker.addImage(image, 0);`
`try {tracker.waitForID(0);}`
`catch (InterruptedException e) {}`

The tracker will watch the image and when a signal such as the zero (selected by us) is returned, we catch it and deduce that the image has been loaded. The Case Study uses this method successfully.

Moving images

The technique for moving an image around on the screen is a well-known one. Java just makes it easier. In many other systems, when you take an image and draw it where else, you also have to take care to wipe out the old one. In Java, the use of the `paint` method means that the screen is written correctly as we want it each time. What we have to do is make sure that we specify the coordinates for moving objects in a relative way: that is, using variables rather than constants for their coordinates. Example 12.4 shows how this is done.

Reacting to mouse events

In Sections 10.3 and 11.2 we described the different events, listeners and handlers that Java provides. Thereafter, we used mainly the `ActionEvent`, with its associated `ActionListener` and `ActionPerformed` handler method. `ActionListener` is actually special, because it has only one handler method. If you refer to Table 11.1, you will see that most other events have several methods.

The point is that the listeners are abstract interfaces, and when one uses an interface, you have to provide real versions of **all** its abstract methods, even if you do not use them. Thus to detect a mouse press, we would have to define a `mousePressed` method (which is fine) and also dummy versions of all the other four mouse-related methods in the `MouseListener` class. To save on such wasted coding, the `java.awt.event` package includes for each of the abstract listener interfaces an implementation of it called an **adapter**. The abstract adapter class supplies dummy versions of all the methods in the listener. Then instead of implementing the listener, we inherit the adapter, and override only those methods that we really need. Figure 12.7 shows how this sequence applies to the two mouse listeners available for mouse events.

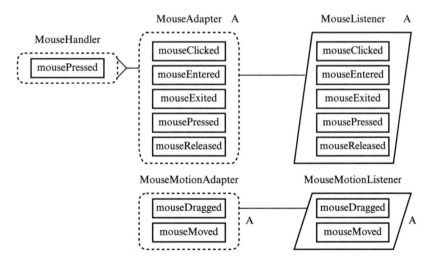

Figure 12.7 *Class diagram of mouse listeners and adapters.*

So if an applet wants to listen to the mouse, it includes the following in its `init` method:

```
this.addMouseListener(new MouseHandler());
```

and an inner class called `MouseHandler` where the code for the `mousePressed` event is given. The next example illustrates the use of both the mouse listener and the mouse motion listener.

EXAMPLE 12.4 Catching the duke

Problem We would like to have a little game where an image moves around the screen, and we move the mouse to try to catch it. The game should have sound as well.

Solution First we need to get hold of a gif file and two au files – one for a hit and one for a miss. In my experience, the GIF files should not be larger than 10K and the au files should be at least 6K to be playable. These are guidelines: your computer could possibly handle different sizes. Then we shall draw the image and let the user track it with the mouse. Hits will be rewarded by one sound, and misses by another. In order to reinforce the sounds, we shall also print out corresponding messages.

Algorithm The applet method for moving the image works like this. Once the image has been fetched and drawn, we can obtain its width and height. When the user clicks the mouse, a `mouseDown` event occurs and we can then check if the current mouse coordinates are within those of the image. After reacting with a win or lose sound and message, we repaint the screen, having moved the image. Moving the image is done by adding a random amount to the coordinates that we pass to `drawImage`. The message is displayed in a special browser area called the status bar with the `showStatus` method. As a result, the message does not appear if the program is run with a viewer.

Now consider carefully the dynamics of the system. When do things actually move? Well nothing happens in the applet, unless we activate an event. So the image will remain stationary until we start to move the mouse. Every time the applet detects a `mouseMove` event (as opposed to a `mouseDown` event) it can repaint the screen. Repainting includes changing the x, y coordinates, so the image will seem to move randomly as we move the mouse, and we shall have to 'chase' it. In order to make the game realistic, we move the image only if a current position coordinate is a multiple of 3. Thus the x can change without the y coordinate changing.

Program The program follows the algorithm and forms described above.

```
import java.awt.*;
import java.applet.*;
import java.awt.event.*;

public class CatchM extends Applet {

   /* Catching the Duke program by J M Bishop Dec 1996
    * =========================    Java 1.1 Jan 1998
    *
    * Try to catch the duke and hit it by pressing the left
    * mouse button.
```

```
* Illustrates sound, images and movement
* and mouse handling events. */

 int mx, my, limitx, limity ;
 int wins;
 int boardSize;
 Image duke;

 public void init() {
   wins = 0;
   boardSize = getSize().width - 1;
   duke = getImage(getCodeBase(),"duke.gif");
   this.addMouseListener (new mousePressHandler());
   this.addMouseMotionListener (new mouseMotionHandler());
 }

 class mousePressHandler extends MouseAdapter {

   public void mousePressed (MouseEvent e) {
     int x = e.getX();
     int y = e.getY();
     requestFocus();
     if (mx < x && x < mx+limitx &&
         my < y && y < my+limity) {
       wins++;
       getAppletContext().showStatus("Caught it!  Total " + wins);
       play(getCodeBase(), "sounds/ouch.au");
     }
     else {
       getAppletContext().showStatus("Missed again.");
       play(getCodeBase(), "sounds/haha.au");
     }
     repaint();
   }
 }

public class mouseMotionHandler extends MouseMotionAdapter {
  public void mouseMoved(MouseEvent e) {
    if (e.getX() % 3 == 0 && e.getY() % 3 == 0)
      repaint();
  }
}

public void paint(Graphics g) {
  // wait till the image is in before getting the
  // size. Can't put these statements in init
  limitx = duke.getWidth(this);
  limity = duke.getHeight(this);
  int change = boardSize-limitx;

  // draw a boundary
  g.drawRect(0, 0, boardSize, boardSize);

   // calculate a new place for the duke
   // and draw it.
```

```
        mx = (int)(Math.random()*1000) % change;
        my = (int)(Math.random()*1000) % change;
        g.drawImage(duke, mx, my, this);
    }
}
```

Testing Unfortunately, it is very difficult to show a test of the program in the book. Figure 12.8 shows a snapshot of the duke and a message, running in the HotJava browser, but this is one case where the you are going to have to get on to the web to see and hear it! The program can be found on the *Java Gently* site.

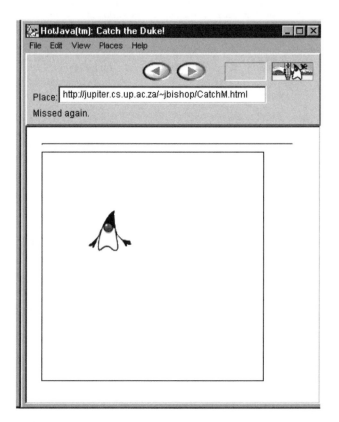

Figure 12.8 *Catching the Duke in the HotJava browser.*

Sound, images and the future

The worlds of graphics and audio have produced a great variety of file formats. One needs only bring to mind a few graphics file formats to see this: GIF87, GIF89a, JFIF (often called JPEG), PNG, PBM/PGM/PPM, TIFF, TARGA, PDS/VICAR Sun Rasterfile, BMP, ILBM, PCX, PICT, at almost at any colour depth from 1 to 32 bits. To support every file format is clearly not feasible and Sun made an obvious statement in favour of portability in its decision to support only a few formats in Java.

The essence is that if you want to support exotic formats of whatever nature, then it is incumbent upon you to make the necessary conversions to and from the formats that Java supports. As network bandwidth becomes more freely available, so the formats used for graphics and sound will evolve.

Sound uses far less resources than does graphics. Compare a 72 minute music CD with 650MB of 800×600, 32-bit colour, 55-frames-per-second animation. In the case of the sound, the human ear cannot discern the fact that the music is stored discretely, whereas given a 22 inch monitor, the pixels are visible at a normal viewing distance to most people. This brings home the fact that in order to store sound and especially high-quality graphics, we need high compression ratios if we are not to exhaust even the highest density storage media at our disposal. These high compression ratios, in turn, imply complicated code (with attendant bloat in program size) and, depending on the algorithms, even some loss in data (as in JFIF).

As if the above were not enough, the law has been an impediment to progress. Reflect upon the amount of time, energy and money poured into creating new formats, merely in order to obviate the need for licensing fees to some patent holder. A case in point is the GIF (Graphics Interchange File) format. It had been used free of charge by developers since its inception in 1987. It appears that CompuServe developed the format, but used LZW (Lempel-Ziv-Welch) compression, which is covered by US patent 4,558,302, held by Unisys Corporation. Unisys decided to enforce this patent, thus forcing all developers of code which use GIF in any way to pay royalties to Unisys or sublicensing fees to CompuServe. That this happened on 29 December 1994, once GIF had become a *de facto* standard, is food for thought. Since then, a new format, called the PNG (Portable Network Graphic) format, has appeared. PNG is essentially a better GIF, but is free and portable.[5]

From the above it should be clear that in order to keep the code small, Java supports few formats. This begs the question of how to convert existing files. There are free and shareware utilities for almost every conceivable format available. A good place to start would be at ftp://sunsite.unc.edu or one of its mirrors, as well as the Usenet newgroups and their FAQs (Frequently Asked Questions), the canonical site of which is ftp://rtfm.mit.edu.[6]

12.4 Case Study 6: The Nature Conservation Project

The project to create a web site to show the animals, birds and trees of Savanna was postulated and described in Chapter 1. Now we have sufficient knowledge to examine how such a system is put together, and what the relationships are among the HTML scripts, the Java applets and the images that will illustrate the site.

---

[5] Refer to Dr. Dobb's Journal of July 1995 for in-depth information on PNG.
[6] I am grateful to John Botha for researching and contributing this subsection.

Web pages

Referring to Figure 1.3 or Plate 1, which is the first page of the site, we see that it is a simple display consisting of a heading, some text, an image and two links – to animals and trees. A third link – to birds – is promised but not yet implemented. To create such a page, one can use the interactive editor in a browser such as Netscape, or one can write the HTML directly. Either way, there will be an HTML document which in its simplest form looks like this:

```
<HTML>
<BODY>

<CENTER><P><FONT COLOR="#0000FF"><FONT SIZE=+3>
Savanna Nature Conservation
</FONT></FONT></P></CENTER>

<P></P>

<CENTER><P><IMG SRC="Elephant.jpg" HSPACE=20 HEIGHT=117 WIDTH=178
ALIGN=LEFT></P></CENTER>

<P><FONT COLOR="#000000">Savanna's Nature Conservation Department aims
to help you find out about animals that inhabit the Grasslands of Africa.
</P>

<P>You can also interact with us, register sightings
and add to our data interactively.</P>

<P>Version 1 of our homepage has sections on
<A HREF="Animals.html">animals</A>,
birds and
<A HREF="Trees.html">trees</A>.
</FONT></P>

</BODY>
</HTML>
```

The document starts off with some header information. Thereafter the heading is printed in a larger than normal font. The image of the elephant is expected to be in the same directory as the HTML file itself, and it is in JPG format. Various dimensions are specified, and it is indicated that the image will go to the left of any text that follows. The next three paragraphs have the text with the last one including two links to other pages with file names Animals.html and Trees.html.

Animals.html follows a similar pattern, except that it has six images to display. At this stage, a schematic diagram of the system can be built up, as in Figure 12.9. The arrows indicate HTML links and the plain lines indicate images and applets that are included.

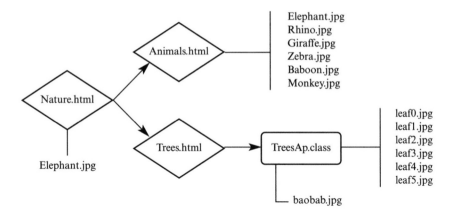

Figure 12.9 *Schematic of the Nature Conservation System.*

Including an applet

The Trees.html document presents the web page shown in Figure 1.5 and Plate 3. An abbreviated version of the html code for it is:

```
>HTML>

<BODY>
<CENTER><P><FONT COLOR="#008000"><FONT SIZE=+2>
Trees of Savanna</FONT></FONT></P></CENTER>

<P>With a twig in hand, find out what your tree is by selecting the
leaf type and giving the leaf measurements in millimetres. Some of the
trees we can identify so far are:</P>

<TABLE BORDER=1 WIDTH="100%">

<TR>

<TD><APPLET CODE="TreesAp.class" WIDTH=350 HEIGHT=300>
<PARAM NAME="entries" VALUE="19">
<PARAM NAME="tree-1" VALUE="Protea">
<PARAM NAME="codes-1" VALUE="165 175 176">
<PARAM NAME="tree-2" VALUE="Milkplum">
<PARAM NAME="codes-2" VALUE="156 166">

... and more parameters

NAME="tree-19" VALUE="Candle acacia">
<PARAM NAME="codes-19" VALUE="666">

</APPLET>

</TD>

<TD ALIGN=RIGHT><FONT COLOR="#0080FF"><FONT SIZE=-1>
Protea<BR>
```

```
Milkplum <BR>
Wild fig<BR>
... and more trees

Fever tree<BR>
Camel thorn<BR>
Umbrella thorn<BR>
Candle acacia
</FONT></FONT>
</TD>
</TR>
</TABLE>
<FONT COLOR="#0080FF"></FONT>
</BODY>
</HTML>
```

Once again, we start with a heading and a short piece of text. Then we want to have an applet next to a list of tree names. An easy way to accomplish this is to set up a table and put the applet in one of the cells and the text in the other. A side effect of using a table is that a nice border is drawn for free.

The applet tag specifies that the applet comes from `TreesAp.class`, and occupies a certain height and width. Thereafter there is a long list of names of trees and values. These are discussed below. The list of 19 trees is given as part of the HTML as well, and it is this list that is displayed in blue on the right of the table.

Getting data into an applet

Consider once again the Trees applet, the output of which was shown in Figure 1.5. The purpose of the applet is to receive three pieces of data – a leaf width, a leaf length and a matching leaf pattern – and to display an image of the tree that might have been found as a result. Figure 1.5 shows the entering of particulars related to the baobab tree, and Figure 1.6 and Plate 4 shows the result. This is the one way in which we pass data to an applet – by entering values in fields and clicking buttons.

However, this applet also needs to keep a complete list of trees and their associated particulars. How should this be done? There are three ways:

- Initialize an array with the data, as was done for the till example.

- Use the browser's PARAM facility.

- Read the data off a file using a remote connection.

The PARAM facility seems appropriate here. If we want to have parameters that form an array (such as our 19 trees) then there must be 19 different names for the parameters. If we call them by similar names, such as tree-1, tree-2 and so on, then we can use deft programming to pick off the parameters without listing each by name in the applet. The statement to get a tree parameter's value would be:

```
String tree = getParameter("tree-"+(i+1));
```

Tree codes

The applet constructs a three digit code from the data entered by the user. Each tree could have several (up to four, say) of these codes, since there is a range of leaf sizes that might apply. So for each tree we need its name, as described above, and we also need a set of codes that can be used to identify it. For example, the second tree (tree-2) called the Milkplum has alternate leaves of between 40 and 80 cm long and a width between 20 and 30 cm. This reduces to two codes (in a coding system adapted from Moll, Moll and Page[7]), namely 156 and 166. Therefore matching the tree-2 parameter shown above, we need to have a codes-2 parameter like this:

```
<PARAM NAME="codes-2" VALUE="156 166">
```

Of course, nature is notoriously difficult to code, and in reality there are possibly other trees that would fit a 156 or 166 code as well. But in the main, the Molls' system works and so we can proceed to choose a list of curious-sounding trees, enter them in the HTML with their codes, and activate the applet.

Inside the applet

In order to conclude this example, we should look at the details of the applet:

- how the layout is achieved;
- how the tree names and codes are stored and accessed in a hash table; and
- the event handling necessary to collect the user input and return an image.

These are all explained in the comments associated with the Java that follows.

Another aspect of this applet is that we react to user input by turning the fields green. When all the data has been entered and a tree has been sought, the user clicks the Again button and the fields revert to white. A similar technique could have been employed in the till and competition applets.

```
import java.applet.*;
import java.awt.*;
import java.awt.event.*;
import java.net.*;
import java.util.*;

public class TreesAp extends Applet implements ActionListener {

  /* The Trees applet    by J M Bishop   January 1997
   * =================    Java 1.1 Jan 1998

     Asks for information about the leaves of a tree.
     Codes the information and links to a URL where
```

[7] Eugene and Glen Moll and Nicci Page, *Common Trees*, Struik, 1989.

```
      further information about the tree is stored.
      Gets the tree names and codes from an HTML page.
      Illustrates interaction with a browser,
      button arrays, image tracking,
      nested panel layouts and string tokenizers.
*/

// A TextField, boolean and integer for each leaf part.
private TextField widthField, lengthField, messageField;
private Button againButton;
private boolean gotChoice = false;
private boolean gotWidth = false;
private boolean gotLength = false;
private int c, w, l;

private Hashtable table = new Hashtable ();

private String patterns [] = {
  "Alternate", "Opposite",
  "Whorled",   "Palmate",
  "Complex",   "Bipinnate"};

private Button patternButton [] = new Button[6];


public void init () {
//====================
  // First read in the parameters from the HTML page
    setUpTable();

  // Create the applet screen with two text fields above
  // and one below. In the centre is the grid of nine
  // leaf patterns, each a border panel in its own right
  // with a button in the south and a canvas occupying
  // the rest. The canvas is painted by the leafPattern
  // class. The font is set to 10pt.

  Font f = new Font ("SanSerif",Font.PLAIN,10);
  this.setFont (f);
  setLayout(new BorderLayout(0,0));
  Panel p = new Panel ();
    p.add (new Label ("Leaf width"));
    widthField = new TextField (8);
      p.add (widthField);
      widthField.addActionListener(this);
    p.add (new Label ("Leaf length"));
    lengthField = new TextField (8);
      p.add (lengthField);
      lengthField.addActionListener(this);
  add ("North",p);

  // Create a panel for the nine leaf patterns
  Panel q = new Panel ();
    q.setLayout(new GridLayout(2,3));
```

```
      for (int b = 0; b<patterns.length; b++) {
        Panel s = new Panel ();
          s.setLayout(new BorderLayout(0,0));
          s.add ("Center",new leafPattern (this,b));
          patternButton[b] = new Button(patterns[b]);
            patternButton[b].addActionListener(this);
            s.add ("South",patternButton[b]);
        q.add (s);
      }
    add ("Center",q);

    // Follow up with a message and again button
    // at the bottom of the applet.
    Panel r = new Panel();
      messageField = new TextField (30);
        r.add (messageField);
      againButton = new Button ("Again");
        r.add(againButton);
        againButton.addActionListener(this);
    add("South",r);
  }

  private void setUpTable() {
  //========================
      String s, item;
      StringTokenizer t;
      int code;
      s = getParameter("entries");
      int n = Integer.parseInt(s);
      for (int i = 0; i<n; i++) {
      // extract a tree name from the html
        String tree = getParameter("tree-"+(i+1));
      // read all its codes
        s = getParameter("codes-"+(i+1));
        t = new StringTokenizer (s);
      // store each code-tree pair in the table.
        while (true) {
          try {
            item = t.nextToken();
            code = Integer.parseInt(item.trim());
            table.put(new Integer(code),tree);
          }
          catch (NoSuchElementException e) {
            break;
          }
        }
      }
  }

  public void actionPerformed (ActionEvent e) {
  //==========================================
    Object source = e.getSource();
    String name = e.getActionCommand();

    if (source == widthField) {
      w = readValue(widthField);
      gotWidth = true;
```

```
    } else if (source == lengthField) {
      l = readValue(lengthField);
      gotLength = true;
    } else if (source == againButton) {
       resetFields();
    } else if (name instanceof String) {
      c = 0;
      while (!name.equals(patterns[c])) c++;
      gotChoice = true;
      patternButton[c].setBackground(Color.green);
    }
    if (gotChoice & gotLength & gotWidth)
      findTree ();
}

private void findTree () {
//========================
// Calculate the three-part code
  int part2=convertLength();
  int part3=convertWidth();
  int code = 100*(c+1)+10*part2+part3;
// Fetch the tree name from the table if it exists
  String tree = (String) table.get(new Integer (code));
  if (tree == null)
    setMessage("No information on code "+code+" yet.");
  else
    fetchTree (tree);
}

private void fetchTree (String treeName) {
//====================================
// Try to get a web page of information on
// the tree.
  try {
   AppletContext context = getAppletContext ();
    String s = treeName+".html";
    setMessage("Looking for "+s);
    URL u = new URL (getCodeBase(),s);
    context.showDocument(u,"_self");
  }
  catch (MalformedURLException e) {
    setMessage("No information for that tree yet");
  }
}

// Code conversion methods
//========================

private int convertLength () {
// returns a code based on the leaf length supplied
  if (l<=25) return 4; else
  if (l<=50) return 5; else
  if (l<=100) return 6; else
```

```
    if (l<=200) return 7; else
              return 8;
}
private int convertWidth () {
// returns a code based on the leaf width supplied
  if (w<=10) return 4; else
  if (w<=20) return 5; else
  if (w<=40) return 6; else
  if (w<=80) return 7; else
              return 8;
}

// Utility methods
// ===============
private int readValue (TextField t) {
    int x = Integer.parseInt(t.getText());
    t.setEditable(false);
    t.setBackground(Color.green);
    return x;
}

private void clearField(TextField t) {
  t.setEditable(true);
  t.setBackground(Color.white);
  t.setText("");
}

private void resetFields () {
  gotChoice = false;
  patternButton[c].setBackground(Color.lightGray);
  gotWidth = false;
  clearField(widthField);
  gotLength = false;
  clearField(lengthField);
  clearField(messageField);
  messageField.setEditable(false);
}

private void setMessage(String s) {
  messageField.setText(s);
  messageField.setBackground(Color.green);
}

class leafPattern extends Canvas {
//================================
  Image im;

  leafPattern(Applet a, int b) {
    weAre = a;
  // Construct the URL name
    pattern = "leaf"+Integer.toString(b)+".jpg";
  // Get the image
    im = weAre.getImage(weAre.getCodeBase(),pattern);
  // Ensure that the image has been received before
  // the constructor returns.
```

```
        MediaTracker tracker = new MediaTracker(weAre);
        tracker.addImage(im, 0);
        try { tracker.waitForID(0);}
        catch (InterruptedException e) {}
    }

    public void paint (Graphics g) {
        g.drawImage(im,0,0,this);
    }

    private Applet weAre;
    private String pattern;
    }
}
```

Testing

The applet's output is shown again in Figure 12.10 and Plate 3. Look at the HTML if you want to be sure of hitting trees. The figure shows the results of the correct values for the baobab tree (as shown in Plate 4).

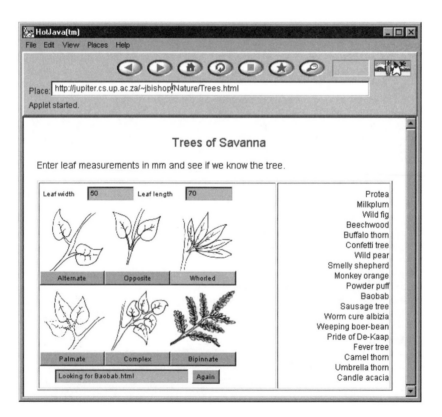

Figure 12.10 *The Trees applet running under HotJava. (See Plate 3.)*

Legal considerations

While writing applets that pull in images seems a great idea, there is a serious consideration: other people's pictures are usually copyrighted. The implication is that we cannot use them freely in our own web pages, even in experimental ones. We must use our own pictures, ones that we own. For this reason, the photographs in Chapter 1 were taken by myself, and the diagrams drawn especially for this book.

The infrastructure provided by Java's multimedia facilities is so powerful and easy to use that one tends to forget that the content required to fill an applet or web page also has to be created. Look out for shareware images, and when in doubt, ask permission from the author, artist, originator or publisher.

SUMMARY

Applets are similar to applications, but because they run within the context of the `Applet` class and a browser or viewer, they do not need a main method, and all input–output must be through the awt. An applet must have an accompanying HTML file which calls it. This HTML file can be supplied to an applet viewer or to a browser, or can be called from within a web page. Applets run in browsers stop only when the page they are in is discarded. Applets can get data from a web page through the `PARAM` facility. Java provides a considerable amount of security surrounding applets so that they cannot cause damage after coming over the network.

Applets, as well as applications, can make use of sound and images. Both can be simply set up in Java using objects to connect to au and GIF or JPEG files respectively. The images can be made to move on the screen by repainting the screen with new coordinates. Watching and waiting for images to be loaded require additional programming.

QUIZ

12.1   What is the method to be used instead of `println` in applets?

12.2   Compared with awt applications, why do applets not have `main` methods?

12.3   Applets usually have an `init` method: what is its counterpart in an application?

12.4   Give the HTML tag for running an applet in `Orange.class` with a width and length of 200 pixels.

12.5   What does the `getCodeBase` method do?

12.6   What are the two image formats supported by Java?

12.7   What does the `getAppletContext` method do?

12.8   Given the HTML parameter tag

```
<PARAM NAME = "yenexchange" VALUE = "6.578">
```

what would be the corresponding Java statement to assign the yen exchange rate to a double variable called rate?

12.9   In Example 12.4, what happens each time we call `repaint()` from the mouseMove method?

12.10   What is the name of the method used to read parameters from a web page into an applet?

PROBLEMS

12.1 **Your trees**. The Nature Project is in its infancy and still needs to be considerably extended to fulfil its mandate of allowing visitors to the site the ability to add new specimens that they identify. If you watch the *Java Gently* web site, you may see new versions of the system as they become available. One improvement you could make on your own is to change the list of trees to reflect your own environment. You should be able to do this by altering only the HTML.

12.2 **Till user's guide**. How to use the till applet is not really intuitive. Set up an HTML page that has some instructions on the left and includes the till applet on the right.

12.3 **Savanna News Banner**. If you have a scanner, scan in the masthead from your local newspaper and embed it in an HTML page which surrounds the competition applet. Otherwise create a big heading with a new and interesting font. Include the rules in small print below the competition.

12.4 **Lots of dukes**. Add more dukes to the catching applet. Have each move at a different rate.

12.5 **Letter value update**. Create a separate applet with a password which can be selected by a menu or button from the Competition HTML page and will enable one of the newspaper employees to change the letter values interactively.

12.6 **Nelson's applet**. Referring to Problem 11.6, put the GUI version of Nelson's coffee shop in an applet and HTML document.

12.7 **Student marks**. Consider Example 6.6 on student marks. Create an applet and HTML document to provide an interactive version of the program for students to access their marks.

12.8 **Interactive exchange rates**. Following on from Problem 6.8, create an applet to interface to the Bureau de Change.

12.9 **Changing prices**. The prices for fruit and vegetables change often. In the place where the Close button used to be on the till program, add a button called Reset which will bring up a new window, listing the products and their current prices, and allow the user to type in new prices for any product that changes. The price change should be effective immediately after the window has been closed.

12.10 **Pets Lost and Found**. Based on the pet tag system devised for the Savanna Veterinary Association (Case Study 4 and Problem 9.1), the *Savanna News* wants to set up an online version of its popular Lost and Found column. The idea is that owners who have lost pets will enter details and also a photograph. Those who have found pets can type in tag details as usual and get back the other data. Design and implement such a system using applets and web pages. Images of pets are available for use on *Java Gently's* web page under Other Material.

CHAPTER 13

Multi-threading

13.1 Introduction to multi-threading

In operating system terms, a program that is running is known as a **process**. An operating system can be running several processes for different users at any one time. Not all of these need be active: they could be awaiting their share of processor time, or they could be waiting for some information, such as user input.

Now within a single process, the same division into separately runnable subprocesses can be made. In Java these are known as **threads** and a program with threads is called **multi-threaded**. Each thread looks like it is running on its own. It can communicate with other threads in the same process, though care must be taken when this is done through changing the value of shared variables.

In the same way that the operating system shares time between processes, so it must share time among threads. The fairest way to share is to give each thread a time slice, at the end of which it is suspended and the next thread that is ready to run is given a chance. A less attractive method is for a thread to run until it needs information from elsewhere (another thread, or the user, say), and only then to relinquish control of the processor. The problem with this approach is that a single thread can hog the processor. By now, most systems are using the first approach.

Why threads?

Why do we actually need threads? Two particular situations illustrate their value:

1. **User interfacing.** If an applet or graphics application is busy drawing or displaying text, the user may wish to stop this activity. If a cancel button is provided, we can press the button, *but* the program will only detect the button press once it has reached a passive state: that is, it has finished computing or outputting and is waiting for events. However, if the button is being handled by a separate thread, the opportunity to react will come around regularly, even while the other computation is proceeding. Figure 13.1 illustrates the time line associated with two such threads.
2. **Many instances.** Sometimes one wants identical copies of a picture, of multiple windows or of different versions of a computation to be available simultaneously. For example, the set of traffic lights of Example 10.4 could be duplicated and we could watch two or three sets working at once. Each would be handled by a separate thread. In the simple case, the threads will be straight copies of each other and will run independently. Java also allows the threads to communicate and synchronize their activities, as discussed in Section 13.3.

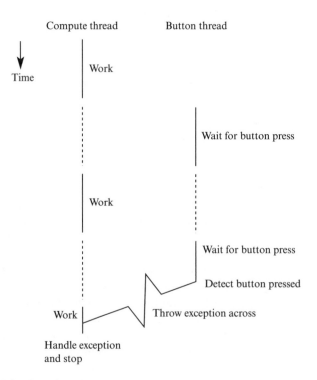

Figure 13.1 *Multi-threading for a user interface.*

From the user's point of view, the presence of multiple threads should be transparent. From the programmer's side, though, work has to be done to set up the threads in the first place, to keep them running and to detect when they should finish. During the lifetime of a process, threads can be created and destroyed at will. They are a cost-effective way of handling processor power and memory for non-trivial programs.

13.2 Setting up threads

To 'thread' a program, we first have to identify those methods that can run independently. Usually, these are already in a class and it is the class that becomes a thread, possibly in multiple instantiations.

Thread is a class in the java.lang package, which means that it is always available and no special import is needed. Any class that wishes to be a thread class, must inherit from Thread. In addition, Thread implements the Runnable interface, which has one method, run. Therefore the prospective thread class must implement run as well. Basically, we take the executable part of the class and put it in a run method (allowing run of course to call methods to assist it as usual).

The main method is by default a thread, and it is from there, or from another active method such as Applet's init, that the other threads are set in motion. As we shall see in later examples, threads can spawn their own threads as well.

Let us consider an example of changing a program to have threads. Take Example 11.2, the traffic light calibration. We would like the lights to rotate through their assigned sequence of red–yellow–green, while the buttons and other choices at the bottom of the screen are still active. In the original program, the main method sets up the headings and buttons, and then creates a canvas that has a paint method to draw the lights. Omitting the constructor and the event handling methods, the program looked like this:

```
import java.awt.*;
import java.awt.event.*;

public class Traffic1 extends Frame
                implements ActionListener, ItemListener {

    /*  The second Traffic Light program
     *                          by J M Bishop Oct 1996
     *           Java 1.1 version by T Abbott Oct 1997
     *        enhanced and revised by J M Bishop Oct 1997
     *  Adds options to set the duration for a light to
     *  be on, but choice is merely recorded, not
     *  acted upon at this stage.
     */

    private LightsCanvas lights;
    private TextField duration;
    private Choice colours;
```

```java
private Button walkButton;
private Button closeButton;

public Traffic1() {
   ... constructor code
}

public void actionPerformed(ActionEvent e) {
   ... event handling code
}

public void itemStateChanged(ItemEvent e) {
   ... event handling code
}

public static void main(String[] args) {
  Frame f = new Traffic1();
  f.setSize(350, 210);
  f.setVisible(true);
  f.addWindowListener(new WindowAdapter () {
    public void windowClosing(WindowEvent e) {
      System.exit(0);
    }
  });
}

private int light = 0;
String [ ] message = {"default","default","default","default"};

class LightsCanvas extends Canvas {
  public void paint(Graphics g) {
  g.drawOval(87, 10, 30, 68);
  g.setColor(Color.red);
  g.fillOval(95, 15, 15, 15);
  g.setColor(Color.yellow);
  g.fillOval(95, 35, 15, 15);
  g.setColor(Color.green);
  g.fillOval(95, 55, 15, 15);
    // walk light is also green
  g.fillOval(95, 85, 15, 15);
  g.setColor(Color.black);
  g.drawString("RED", 15 ,28);
  g.drawString("YELLOW", 15, 48);
  g.drawString("GREEN", 15, 68);
  g.drawString("WALK", 15, 98);
  g.drawString(message[0], 135 ,28);
  g.drawString(message[1], 135, 48);
  g.drawString(message[2], 135, 68);
  g.setColor(Color.black);
  g.drawString(message[3], 135, 98);
  }
}

}
```

Now we need to turn `LightsCanvas` into a thread. In other words, it must

- extend `Thread`, and
- have a `run` method which repeatedly executes.

But a class can inherit from only one other class, so we have to adopt the following strategy:

1. Let `LightsCanvas` extend `Thread`.
2. Pass an instance of the canvas to a new `LightsCanvas` constructor.
3. Store the reference to the canvas instance in the thread locally.
4. Call `getGraphics` to establish the canvas in the window with which the thread is dealing.

The `paint` method as it exists above is called automatically via the awt. Since we are now going to have independent drawing going on in a single window, we had better have it more under control. In other words, the `run` method should explicitly cause the drawing to be done.

The simplest run method is:

```
public void run () {
  while (true) {
    draw ();
    try {sleep (500);}  catch (InterruptedException e) {}
  }
}
```

Here we repeatedly draw the picture, waiting at least 500 milliseconds before doing it again. The `InterruptedException` can be thrown by the system to start the thread up if its turn has come round in the meantime.

Putting it all together, the new version of the `LightsCanvas`, with a new name, is:

```
class SetOfLights extends Thread {

  SetOfLights (Canvas c) {
    area = c;
  }

  public void run () {
    while (true) {
      draw ();
      try {sleep (500);}  catch (InterruptedException e) {}
    }
  }

  void draw ( ) {
    Graphics g = area.getGraphics();
    ... the contents of paint as before
    }
  }
private Canvas area;
```

To create the thread and set it running, we call its constructor and then call `start`:

```
SetOfLights lights = new SetOfLights (area);
lights.start();
```

In Example 13.1, the complete program for the new Traffic System is shown.

The `Thread` class

After the above informal introduction to threads, let us consider the `Thread` class more specifically. Among many others, it has the following important methods:

Thread creation and methods

*Threadclass threadname = **new** Threadclass (parameters);*
new *Threadclass (parameters)*

```
start ();
run ();
stop ();

sleep (milliseconds);
yield ();
```

A new thread is created in the same way as any other object declaration, as shown in the first line of the form. Alternatively, if there is no need to give the thread a name that its parent knows, we can use the second form, which simply creates a thread of the given class. Threads are dynamically created in Java: we do not need to state in advance how many of a certain kind of thread there will be. Every time a new thread declaration is executed, a new thread object comes into existence.

`start`, `run` and `stop` are the three important thread methods. After a thread has been created via its constructor, the creating method calls `start`, which is defined in the `Thread` class. `start` will cause `run` to be called, thus causing the thread to join the operating system's list of threads waiting to run. In a while, it will get its chance for the processor and start executing independently.

`run` will usually consist of a loop that continues until some condition is met, in which case the loop ends. At this point the `run` method meets a natural end and the thread dies as a result.

The `stop` method can be called from one thread to another and once received via the `Thread` class will cause the called thread to die. In most cases, the `stop` method is not used, and 'natural death' is more common.

`sleep` and `yield` are class methods. Both cause the thread to relinquish the processor. `sleep` will wait for the specified time, and then the thread will be ready to run again. `yield` is not needed if the operating system is sharing time among processors, but if it is not, then calling `yield` is a way for a thread to stand back and give others a chance.

Java also supports priorities for threads. These can be set as a value between 1 (low) and 10 (high) and direct the operating system as to which thread to run next, if there is a choice. Higher priority threads that are waiting to run will always go first.

It is now time to put this all together in a working example.

EXAMPLE 13.1 Traffic lights flashing

Problem The static representation of the lights in Example 11.2 needs to be improved to show the lights actually flashing. Furthermore, we would like to have more than one set of lights operational at any one time, so that we can compare changes.

Solution Implementing the flashing is a question of awt graphics programming. Displaying several lights can be done with threads. We create a new class for the lights as discussed above, have it extend `Thread`, and repeatedly draw the full set of lights when a New Set button is pressed. The time specified for the sleep will then represent the time that one of the lights is on and the others off. Using a switch-statement, we can implement the required green–yellow–red sequence.

Class design Because we are using threads, the relationship between the classes in awt and those we define is slightly altered. The new class diagram (refer back to Figure 11.3) is shown in Figure 13.2. It excludes some of the buttons and other components that are not necessary for this example.

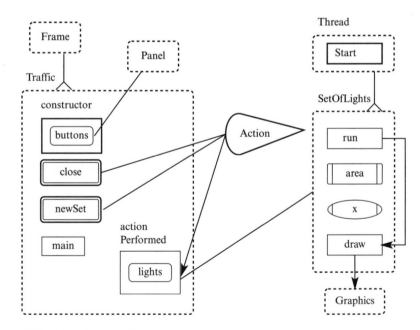

Figure 13.2 *Class diagram for the traffic lights flashing.*

The differences are those that we have already explained. `SetOfLights` inherits `Thread`, and so cannot also inherit `Canvas` as well. Instead, the canvas, called `area`, is passed as a parameter from `Traffic`'s `actionPerformed` method to `SetOfLights`' constructor. The lights objects are shown as being created inside the `actionPerformed` because this is where they are instantiated, on request from a New Set button. The reference to this canvas is used by the `draw` method to access the methods in the `Graphics` class successfully.

Program The `SetofLights` class is as follows:

```
class SetOfLights extends Thread {

  private int red = 0;
  private Canvas area;
  private int x;

  public SetOfLights(Canvas c, int x) {
    area = c;
    this.x = x;
  }
  public void run() {
    while (true) {
      for (int light = 0; light < 3; light++) {
        draw(light);
        try { sleep(500);}
        catch (InterruptedException e) { }
      }
    }
  }

  void draw(int light) {
    Graphics g = area.getGraphics();
    g.setColor(Color.black);
    g.drawOval(x-8, 10, 30, 68);
    g.drawOval(x,   85, 15, 15);
    g.drawString("RED",    x-90, 28);
    g.drawString("YELLOW", x-90, 48);
    g.drawString("GREEN",  x-90, 68);
    g.drawString("WALK",   x-90, 98);

    switch (light) {
      case 0:
        g.setColor(Color.red);
        g.fillOval(x, 15, 15, 15);
        g.setColor(Color.lightGray);
        g.fillOval(x, 35, 15, 15);
        g.fillOval(x, 55, 15, 15);
        break;
      case 1:
        g.setColor(Color.green);
        g.fillOval(x, 55, 15, 15);
        g.setColor(Color.lightGray);
        g.fillOval(x, 15, 15, 15);
```

```
        g.fillOval(x, 35, 15, 15);
        break;
      case 2:
        g.setColor(Color.yellow);
        g.fillOval(x, 35, 15, 15);
        g.setColor(Color.lightGray);
        g.fillOval(x, 15, 15, 15);
        g.fillOval(x, 55, 15, 15);
        break;
    }

  }
}
```

The run method has its own inner loop, going through the three light phases. Depending on which light has to be shown, the switch colours one circle in with the appropriate colour and renders the other two in gray. The program that activates these threads is:

```
import java.awt.*;
import java.awt.event.*;

public class Traffic2 extends Frame
      implements ActionListener {

  /* The third Traffic Light program
   *                               by J M Bishop Oct 1996
   *              Java 1.1 version by T Abbott Oct 1997
   *         enhanced and revised by J M Bishop Oct 1997
   * Enables several sets of lights to
   * operate simultaneously.
   *
   * Illustrates threads and graphics.
   */

  private Canvas area;
  private int lightsPosition = 105;
  private static final int lightsWidth = 150;
  private SetOfLights[] lights = new SetOfLights[3];
  private int nLights = 0, setWanted = 0;
  private Choice colours;
  private Button newSetButton;
  private Button walkButton;
  private Button closeButton;

  public Traffic2() {
    setTitle("Traffic Lights Version 2");
    add("North",new Label
      ("Savanna Traffic Light Simulation",Label.CENTER));

    area = new Canvas();
    area.addMouseListener(new MouseEvtHandler());
    add("Center",area);
```

```
      Panel buttons = new Panel();
        newSetButton = new Button("New Set");
          newSetButton.addActionListener(this);
          buttons.add(newSetButton);
        colours = new Choice ();
          colours.addItem("Red");
          colours.addItem("Green");
          colours.addItem("Yellow");
          colours.addItem("Walk");
          buttons.add(colours);

        buttons.add(new Label("Duration"));
        buttons.add(new TextField(""),3);
        buttons.add(new Button("Walk"));

        closeButton = new Button("Close");
          closeButton.addActionListener(this);
          buttons.add(closeButton);
      add("South",buttons);
    }

    class MouseEvtHandler extends MouseAdapter {
      public void mousePressed(MouseEvent e) {
        int n = e.getX() / lightsWidth;
        if (n < nLights)
        setWanted = n;
      }
    }

    public void actionPerformed(ActionEvent e) {
      Object event = e.getSource();
      if (event == newSetButton) {
        lights[nLights] = new SetOfLights(area, lightsPosition);
        lights[nLights].start();
        lightsPosition += lightsWidth;
        nLights++;
        if (nLights == 3)
        newSetButton.setEnabled(false);
      } else if (event == closeButton) {
        for (int i = 0; i<nLights; i++)
          lights[i].stop();
        setVisible(false);
        dispose();
        System.exit(0);
      }
    }

    public static void main(String[] args) {
      Frame f = new Traffic2();
      f.setSize(450, 210);
      f.setVisible(true);
      f.addWindowListener(new WindowAdapter () {
        public void windowClosing(WindowEvent e) {
          System.exit(0);
        }
      });
    }
}
```

The new addition to the button panel is a New Set button. When pressed, it will start up a new thread for another set of lights. In order to have the lights drawn across the window, we supply a new *x* starting position, which increases by 150 pixels for each light.

Testing Figure 13.3 shows the screen with three lights at different phases.

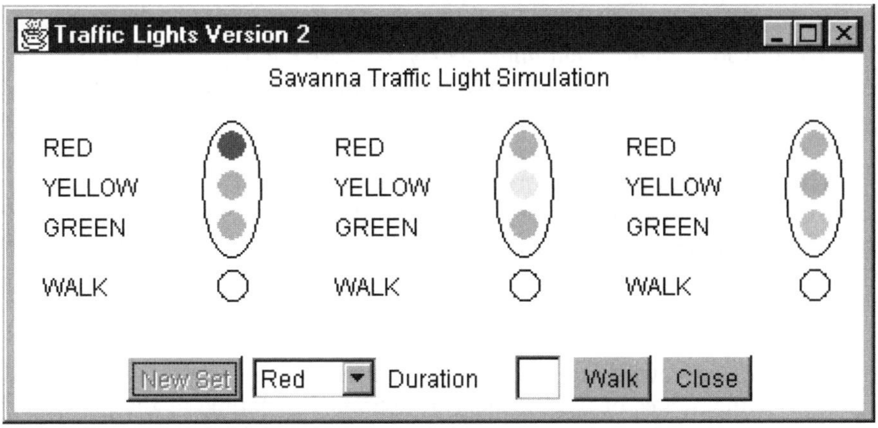

Figure 13.3 *The traffic lights flashing.*

Communication among threads

The threads in the above example are quite independent. However, it is often the case that threads need to pass information between each other – results of subcalculations, or signals to change to another mode of working, for example. Because threads are objects, such communication can use the normal object techniques, such as calling methods or updating non-private variables. On the face of it, there would seem to be no problem in threads communicating in either of these ways. However, conflicts can occur that would cause the program as a whole to give incorrect results. This is the subject of Section 13.3. Meanwhile, we can proceed with the traffic example, and show how simple, non-conflicting communication can be handled.

EXAMPLE 13.2 Traffic lights for walking

Problem Right at the beginning of the traffic light simulation (Example 10.4) we mentioned the objective of examining the effect of pedestrians pressing the walk button. The walk button is present in the control panel of the simulation as it stands. We would now like it to cause the walk light to flash as soon as a red light phase comes around again. Furthermore, we would like to reactivate the choice box and duration field, and pass this information to the flashing lights so that the simulation can become realistic.

Algorithm changes The first consideration is whether one leaves a single walk button for all sets of lights on the screen, or whether we alter the screen to have a walk button under each set. The latter seems more reasonable, but is more difficult to implement because we are using a very simple border layout to keep the lights in the centre panel and the buttons in the south. Therefore we elect to keep the one button, but we select the set of lights we want affected by clicking somewhere in that general area. A mouse listener with a `mousePressed` event is of assistance here.

The second point is what do we actually do once the walk button is pressed? Well, we must pass the information over to the particular thread running that set of lights. The thread need not react immediately, because the requirement is that it continues through its cycle until it reaches red, and then starts flashing the walk light. We can therefore achieve the communication by having a boolean variable called `walk` in the lights thread, and setting it to true once the walk button is pressed.

How do we know which thread to talk to? Well, each thread will need to be recorded in the main program with a name, and the simplest way is to have an array of threads. Depending on the mouse press on the central canvas, we deduce which set of lights is intended, and can make any subsequent press of walk refer to that thread in the array.

Previously, the lights objects were created inside `actionPerformed`, and the name, `lights`, was reused each time a new one was needed. Now because we need to keep track of the names of the threads throughout the lifetime of the program, we declare an array of threads as private. Each new thread of the array is activated via a call to `start`.

The final change is to use the choice box and duration field to alter the time that a light stays on. The change is quite simple. Instead of sleeping for 500 ms every time, we let a light sleep for `time[light]` milliseconds. In `actionPerformed`, the values of the `time` array are altered when required.

We do not give a class diagram this time, in order to encourage the reader to understand the program by drawing one.

Program The final simulation program removes the labels for the lights and replaces them with the current duration.

```
import java.awt.*;
import java.awt.event.*;

public class Traffic3 extends Frame
        implements ActionListener, ItemListener {

   /* The fourth Traffic Light program
    *                             by J M Bishop Oct 1996
    *              Java 1.1 version by T Abbott Oct 1997
    *           enhanced and revised by J M Bishop Oct 1997
    * Enables the different lengths of lights
    * entered as durations to be used in
    * practice.
    */
```

```
private Canvas area;
private int lightsPosition = 105;
private static final int lightsWidth = 150;
private SetOfLights[] lights = new SetOfLights[3];
private int nLights = 0, setWanted = 0;
private TextField duration;
private Choice colours;
private int light;
private Button newSetButton;
private Button walkButton;
private Button closeButton;

public Traffic3() {
  setTitle("Traffic Lights Version 3");

  add("North",new Label
     ("Savanna Traffic Light Simulation",Label.CENTER));

  area = new Canvas();
  area.addMouseListener(new MouseEvtHandler());
  add("Center",area);

  Panel buttons = new Panel();
    newSetButton = new Button("New Set");
      newSetButton.addActionListener(this);
      buttons.add(newSetButton);
    colours = new Choice ();
      colours.addItem("Red");
      colours.addItem("Green");
      colours.addItem("Yellow");
      colours.addItem("Walk");
      colours.addItemListener(this);
      light = 0;
      buttons.add(colours);

    buttons.add(new Label("Duration"));

    duration = new TextField("", 4);
      duration.addActionListener(this);
      buttons.add(duration);
    walkButton = new Button("Walk");
      walkButton.addActionListener(this);
      buttons.add(walkButton);
    closeButton = new Button("Close");
      closeButton.addActionListener(this);
      buttons.add(closeButton);
  add("South",buttons);
}

public void itemStateChanged(ItemEvent e) {
    String s = (String) e.getItem();
    if (s=="Red")    {light = 0;} else
    if (s=="Green")  {light = 1;} else
    if (s=="Yellow") {light = 2;} else
    if (s=="Walk")   {light = 3;}
}
```

```
class MouseEvtHandler extends MouseAdapter {
  public void mousePressed(MouseEvent e) {
    int n = e.getX() / lightsWidth;
    if (n < nLights)
    setWanted = n;
  }
}

public void actionPerformed(ActionEvent e) {
  Object event = e.getSource();
  if (event == newSetButton) {
    lights[nLights] = new SetOfLights(area, lightsPosition);
    lights[nLights].start();
    lightsPosition += lightsWidth;
    nLights++;
    if (nLights == 3)
    newSetButton.setEnabled(false);
  } else if (event == walkButton) {
    lights[setWanted].walk = true;
  } else if (event == duration) {
    lights[setWanted].time[light]=
      Integer.parseInt(duration.getText());
  } else if (event == closeButton) {
    for (int i = 0; i<nLights; i++)
      lights[i].stop();
    setVisible(false);
    dispose();
    System.exit(0);
  }
}

public static void main(String[] args) {
  Frame f = new Traffic3();
  f.setSize(450, 210);
  f.setVisible(true);
  f.addWindowListener(new WindowAdapter () {
    public void windowClosing(WindowEvent e) {
      System.exit(0);
    }
  });
}
```

The reaction to the walk button is to set the walk variable in the correct thread to true. The desired thread has been pre-selected by clicking the mouse somewhere on the screen and dividing by the width of a full set of lights, which we have set at 150 pixels.

The logic associated with the lights proceeds as follows. Each time the red light is about to come on, we need to check if the walk variable is set. If so, we go into a separate loop for 10 cycles which keeps the red light on, and alternates the walk light between green and gray. The run method is shown in the full class here:

```
class SetOfLights extends Thread {

  private int red = 0;
  private Canvas area;
```

```
private int x;
private int light;

// public variables
boolean walk = false;
boolean walkOn = false;
int time [] = {500, 500, 500, 500};

public SetOfLights(Canvas c, int x) {
  area = c;
  this.x = x;
}

public void run() {
  while (true) {
    for (int light = 0; light < 3; light++) {
      if (light == red & walk) {
        walkOn = false;
        for (int i = 0; i < 11; i++) {
          draw(light);
          try { sleep(time[3]);}
          catch (InterruptedException e) { }
          walkOn = !walkOn;
        }
        walk = false;
      } else {
        draw(light);
        try { sleep(time[light]); }
        catch (InterruptedException e) { }
      }
    }
  }
}

void draw(int light) {
  Graphics g = area.getGraphics();
  g.setColor(Color.black);
  g.drawOval(x-8, 10, 30, 68);
  g.setColor(Color.cyan);
  g.fillRect(x-90,10,70,100);
  g.setColor(Color.black);
  g.drawString(""+time[0], x-70, 28);
  g.drawString(""+time[2], x-70, 48);
  g.drawString(""+time[1], x-70, 68);
  g.drawString(""+time[3], x-70, 98);

  switch (light) {
    case 0:
      g.setColor(Color.red);
      g.fillOval(x, 15, 15, 15);
      g.setColor(Color.lightGray);
      g.fillOval(x, 35, 15, 15);
      g.fillOval(x, 55, 15, 15);
      break;
```

```
        case 1:
          g.setColor(Color.green);
          g.fillOval(x, 55, 15, 15);
          g.setColor(Color.lightGray);
          g.fillOval(x, 15, 15, 15);
          g.fillOval(x, 35, 15, 15);
          break;
        case 2:
          g.setColor(Color.yellow);
          g.fillOval(x, 35, 15, 15);
          g.setColor(Color.lightGray);
          g.fillOval(x, 15, 15, 15);
          g.fillOval(x, 55, 15, 15);
          break;
      }

    if (light == red & walk) {
      if (walkOn)
        g.setColor(Color.green);
      else
        g.setColor(Color.white);
      g.fillOval(x+1, 85, 14, 14);
    } else {
      g.setColor(Color.black);
      g.drawOval(x, 85, 15, 15);
    }
    }
  }
}
```

The walkOn variable is set and unset to control the flashing of the walk light. After ten iterations, walk is reset and the set of lights can proceed to the next normal phase, which would be green. The appropriate change is at the end of the in the draw method.

Testing The program can be run as before, and the walk button can be pressed for each of the sets of lights at different times, as shown in Figure 13.4 and Plate 9. Various durations have been entered, and the simulation is now actually quite useful.

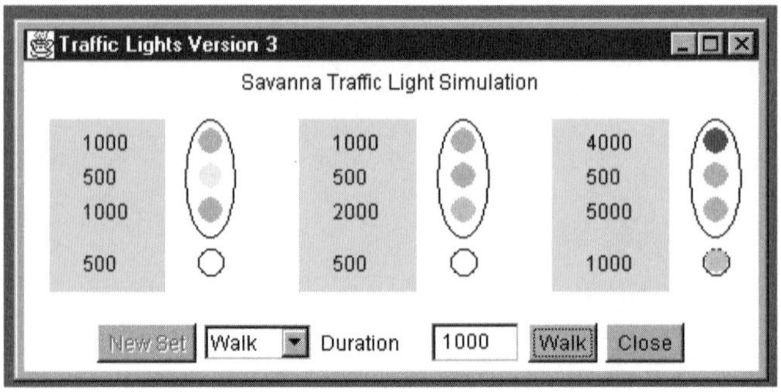

Figure 13.4 *The final traffic light simulation, with variable light duration. (see Plate 9.)*

13.3 Synchronization among threads

In the above example, the main program communicated with each thread individually. In other words, we had channels of communication as shown in Figure 13.5. There was no possibility that Traffic calling lights[0] could interfere with the communication between Traffic and lights[1], say. However, suppose for the sake of illustration that the lights threads have each to alter the same variable in Traffic (for example, a count of the number of times yellow lights come on). The calling diagram would be as shown in Figure 13.6.

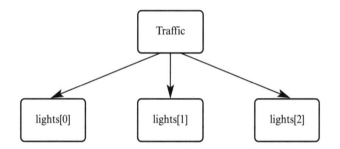

Figure 13.5 *Threads that cannot interfere with each other.*

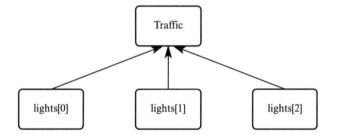

Figure 13.6 *Threads that could possible interfere with each other.*

Now there is a chance that the threads could interfere with each other's operation, leading to corrupted values. The corruption could happen like this. Thread 1 starts to increment a variable with value 52 to 53, say. It gets halfway through before it is interrupted by the operating system and Thread 2 is given the processor. Thread 2 reads the current value of the variable, which is still 52, updates it to 53 and continues. Control is eventually passed back to Thread 1 which is still in the middle of the update. It has already read the variable's value as 52 and so writes 53 back. The correct answer would have been 54 (after two updates), but the interference meant that Thread 1 overwrote the update made by Thread 2.

To avoid such a possibility, Java provides means for threads to **synchronize** their activities. There are two levels of synchronization provided:

- protection of shared resources;
- signalling changes in conditions between threads.

Protecting shared resources

In order to protect resources such as variables that could be accessed by several threads at once, we funnel updates through a method, and mark the method with a special modifier:

Synchronized method
`synchronized` *modifiers name* `(parameters)`

Java then guarantees that once a thread has gained access to a synchronized method, it will finish the method before any other thread gains access to that or any other synchronized method in that object. Such threads are placed in a queue, awaiting their turn. The thread therefore has exclusive access to the object from within the synchronized method. An object with one or more synchronized methods acts as a **monitor** on its data.[1]

In order not to delay the other threads unduly, synchronized methods should be kept to a minimum and only contain statements that are genuinely sensitive to interference.

EXAMPLE 13.3   Car-parks for a viewpoint

Problem   There is a famous viewpoint in the vinelands of Savanna that has two car-parks at its two access roads. We would like to keep track of how many cars enter each car-park and also how many cars in total visit the viewpoint.

Solution   Create an applet that shows a picture of the view as well as counters of the number of cars in the three places. At a later date, Savanna Conservation may decide to limit the number of cars at the viewpoint, in which case the car-parks will serve as buffers. We should bear this in mind when designing the system. The choice of an applet rather than application is made to show how threads interface with applets; we shall not be using the features of a browser, and the program can run in an appletviewer.

---

[1] **Monitors** are a very important operating system concept invented by Per Brinch Hansen and Tony Hoare in the early 1970s.

Design There are three different counters to consider. The main one, that of the viewpoint, 'belongs' to the applet itself. The other two are to operate independently and therefore reside in two separate additional threads. However the threads are identical in every respect except name (West and East car-parks), so we define one thread class and instantiate it twice.

Algorithm The main algorithm is the running of the car-parks. The sequence is as in Figure 13.7. Entering the viewpoint is done by calling a method that updates the total number of cars and displays it. Because the enter method can be called by two threads, potentially simultaneously, and because it updates a variable, we declare it as synchronized, thereby ensuring that the variable does not get corrupted.

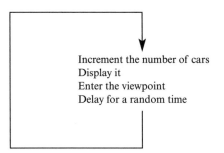

Figure 13.7 *Algorithm for a car-park.*

Program The program follows.

```
import java.io.*;
import java.applet.*;
import java.awt.*;
import java.util.*;

public class CarPark extends Applet {

   /*  The Car-Park applet     by J M Bishop  January 1998
    *  ====================     Java 1.1
    *
    * Simulates a viewpoint with two car-parks.
    * Reads and displays an image of the view.
    * Illustrates threads and a synchronized method.
    * Can be run simply in appletviewer.
    */

   Image im;
   ViewPoint view;
   Random delay = new Random();

   public void init () {

     // Get the image
       im = getImage(getCodeBase(),"reserve.jpg");
```

```
    // Ensure that the image has been received before
    // the constructor returns.
      MediaTracker tracker = new MediaTracker(this);
      tracker.addImage(im, 0);
      try { tracker.waitForID(0);}
      catch (InterruptedException e) {}
      Font f = new Font ("SanSerif",Font.PLAIN,24);
      setFont(f);

      view = new ViewPoint("View",150);
      new CarThread("West",0).start();
      new CarThread("East",300).start();
  }

class CarThread extends Thread {
//---------------------------

  int cars;
  int x;
  String pos;

  CarThread (String s,int n) {
    pos = s;
    x = n;
  }

  public void run () {
    while (true) {
      cars++;
      display(x,cars,pos);
      view.enter();
      try {sleep (factor(x));}
      catch (InterruptedException e) {}
    }
  }
}

class ViewPoint {
//-------------

  int x;
  int cars;
  String pos;

  ViewPoint (String s,int n) {
    x = n;
    pos = s;
  }

  synchronized void enter () {
    cars++;
    display (x,cars,pos);
  }
}
```

```
// Utilities
// ---------
  public void paint (Graphics g) {
    g.drawImage(im,0,0,this);
  }

  void display(int x, int cars, String s) {
    Graphics g = getGraphics();
    g.setColor(Color.orange);
    g.fillRect(x,300,120,50);
    g.setColor(Color.black);
    g.drawString(s+" "+cars,x+5,330);
  }

  int factor (int x) {
    return Math.abs(delay.nextInt()%5000+x);
  }

}
```

Should `display` also be synchronized? No, `display` is a passive method, merely taking parameters and displaying them. The displays are on different parts of the screen so no conflict is possible. Suppose `display` also had statements to print values. Would the output lines become entangled? Fortunately not, because `print` and all similar methods in the `PrintWriter` class are declared as `synchronized`. Therefore only one method can be using them to affect the `System.out` object at once.

Testing Figure 13.8 shows the output from the program, running under an applet viewer. The HTML contains only the applet tag, as the image is drawn by the applet, not by the HTML.

Signalling between threads

Protecting shared resources is one aspect of synchronization. The other is indicating to a thread when a condition that it is waiting for has been met. The methods involved are:

Synchronization methods
`wait ();` `notify ();`

If a thread finds that it cannot continue because the object it is busy with is not quite in the right state, it calls `wait` from within a synchronized method belonging to that object. The thread will then be placed on a queue associated with the object.

A thread that has altered some relevant data or conditions in an object should call `notify`. This will give all the waiting threads a chance to recheck their conditions

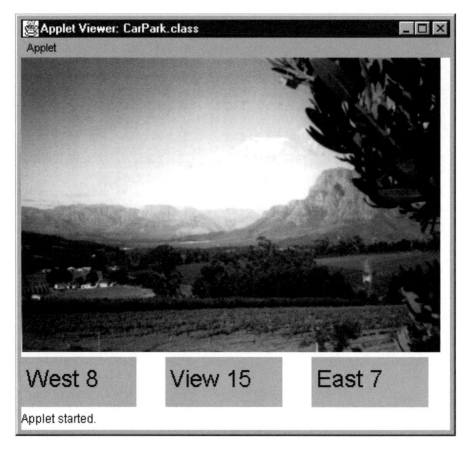

Figure 13.8 *The car-parks for the view site showing the counters. (See Plate 10.)*

for getting on the queue. Some of them may then be able to run at the next opportunity provided by the operating system.

In theory, threads that are waiting should eventually be notified that they can run. In practice, this depends on careful programming, considering all possible combinations. It is quite possible to construct a program where a certain condition does not get set and we find thread one waiting for thread two which is waiting for thread one. This situation is called **deadlock** and means of detecting and preventing it are covered in courses on operating systems and concurrency. Java can detect some logical errors, particularly if `wait` and `notify` are used with unsynchronized methods. In this case an `IllegalMonitorStateException` will be thrown.

The next, rather extensive, example shows how threads of different kinds can be started up at run-time and synchronized to achieve a common goal.

13.4 Case Study 7: Walkman hire

Savanna Museum is going to introduce a modern system of hiring out Walkman tape players which visitors can listen to instead of having guided tours of the exhibits on display. At the entrance to the museum, there is a counter where a variable number of volunteer helpers are on duty at any one time to hire out the Walkmen. The charge is one graz. Visitors arrive in groups of between 1 and 10 and wait until the correct number of Walkmen is available. We would like to simulate the system in advance, to see how many Walkmen will be needed for a given arrival rate of visitors.

Discussing the solution

How does one begin to tackle a simulation such as this? The stepping off point is to draw a diagram of the real-life set-up, and to use this to identify the objects and their interactions. Figure 13.9 gives a start.

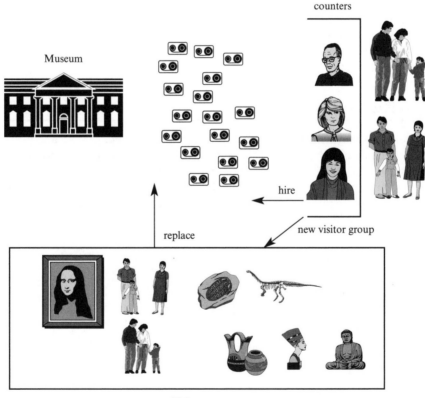

Figure 13.9 *Layout of the museum simulation.*

The day begins with the museum opening with a given number of Walkmen, and then counter threads being created, one for each helper available. The museum is a monitor class with two synchronized methods: hire and replace. The counter helpers call hire, and when their request for a given number of Walkmen is satisfied, they create a new visitor thread, simulating the idea of a visitor group wandering around the museum on their own. The visitors drop their Walkmen directly off at the museum exit, without joining counter queues again. This has the effect of replenishing the number of Walkmen for hire, and may enable a helper to satisfy a request.

For example, suppose there are only two Walkmen left. In the diagram, neither group at the counter can proceed, and must wait. Then suppose the group looking at the Mona Lisa decides to go home. They deposit their Walkmen and one or other of the groups will be satisfied, though not necessarily on a first come, first served basis. The pool will then be down to one or zero again.

Class design

This time we shall not draw a detailed class diagram, but rather indicate the interaction of the objects of the four classes at a high level. Figure 13.10 gives such a diagram. Synchronized methods are marked with an S in the corner. WalkmanHire instantiates the Museum class. It also starts up the counters as threads. The counters start up Visitor threads as needed. Counters hire Walkmen from the museum object, and visitors replace them.

Synchronized objects

Now consider the synchronization parts of the program in detail. hire and replace are the two methods that control the number of Walkmen and the amount of cash taken as deposits. Obviously, the sum of these two must always be equal to the initial amount. Here is what the class looks like. Read the comments to understand how the hire and replace interact. Museum provides some rudimentary commentary to the user as to how the hiring process is proceeding.

```java
import java.io.*;

class Museum {

  Museum (int w) {
    walkmen = w;
    cash = 0;
  }

  synchronized void hire (int c,int n) {
    // If there are not enough Walkmen left,
    // wait until someone at another counter returns
    // some and notifies us accordingly.
    // If the returns are not enough, we'll carry on
    // waiting.
```

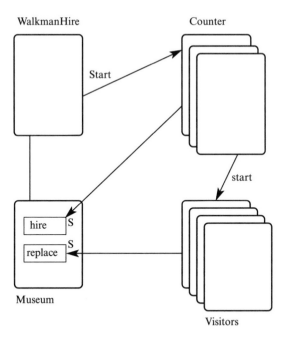

Figure 13.10 *High-level object diagram for the Walkman program.*

```
System.out.println("Counter "+c+" wants "+n);
while (walkmen < n) {
  try { wait(); }
  catch (InterruptedException e) {}
}

// Hire out the Walkmen and take the deposit.
// Let the customers at this counter "walk away"
// by relinquishing control of the monitor with
// a notify call.
walkmen -= n;
cash += n;
System.out.println("Counter "+c+" acquires "+n);
System.out.println("Pool status:"+
  " Deposits "+cash+" Total "+(walkmen+cash)
  + " Walkmen "+walkmen);
notify ();
}

synchronized void replace (int n) {

// Always accept replacements immediately.
// Once the pool and deposits have been updated,
// notify any other helper waiting for Walkmen.
System.out.println("Replacing "+n);
walkmen +=n;
```

```
      cash -= n;
      notify ();
   }

   private static int walkmen;
   private static int cash;
}
```

Calling the `hire` part of `Museum`, we have the `Counter` threads. Once their needs have been satisfied, they create a new `Visitor` thread and then sleep for a while before serving another batch of customers. Both the number of visitors in a group and the time between groups are based on random numbers.

```
class Counter extends Thread {

   Counter (Museum m, int q) {
      museum = m;
      queue = q;
   }

   public void run () {

      // Decide how many Walkmen are needed for a
      // group of visitors and attempt to hire them
      // (waiting until successful). The visitors are
      // sent off on their own to walk around (by
      // starting a new Visitors thread which runs
      // independently.)
      while (true) {
         int w = a(7);
         museum.hire(queue, w);
         new Visitors (museum, w).start();

         // Wait a bit before the next people arrive
         try {sleep(a(100));}  catch(InterruptedException e) {}
      }
   }

   Museum museum;
   int queue;
}
```

The `Visitors` threads simulate the groups walking around for a random time, viewing the exhibits and then returning the Walkmen directly to the `Museum` object. The `replace` method is synchronized so that there may be a small wait if a `Counter` thread is busy completing the hiring out of Walkmen at that precise moment, but otherwise, the visitors can get on their way without queueing.

```
class Visitors extends Thread {

   Visitors (Museum m, int w) {
      museum = m;
```

```
      groupSize = w;
  }

  public void run () {

    // The group walks around on its own for 50 time units.
    // You may need to alter this figure to suit your computer.
    // They then replace all their Walkmen and leave.
    // The thread dies with them.
    try {sleep((int) (Math.random()*1000)+1);}
        catch(InterruptedException e) {}
    museum.replace(groupSize);
  }

  Museum museum;
  int groupSize;
}
```

Finally, there is the main program itself. This is responsible for starting the `Museum` and `Counter` threads. In order to let the user change the size of the simulation, the numbers of Walkman and counters can be set from the command line. By default they are 50 and 3 respectively.

```
class WalkmanHire {

  /* The Museum Walkman Hire program      J M Bishop  Jan 1997
     simulates the hiring of Walkmen from a fixed pool for G1
     each. There are several helpers at different counters
     handling the hire and replacement of the Walkmen.

     The number of Walkmen in the original pool is 50
     and the number of helpers serving is 3,
     but these can be overridden by parameters at run time
     e.g. java WalkmanHire 100 8.
     The cash float starts at zero.

     Illustrates monitors, with synchronize, wait and notify.
     Shows a main program and two different kinds of threads
     running simultaneously.
  */

  public static void main (String [] args) {

    // Get the number of Walkmen in the pool
    // and open the museum for business.
    if (args.length >= 1)
      pool = Integer.parseInt(args[0]);
    else pool = 50;
    Museum m = new Museum (pool);
    // Get the number of helpers
    // and open the counters.
    if (args.length >= 2)
      helpers = Integer.parseInt(args[1]);
```

```
      else helpers = 3;
      for (int i=0; i<helpers; i++)
        new Counter (m,i).start();
    }
    static int pool;
    static int helpers;
  }
```

Testing

The program produces text output. Let us consider just a small part of it, at a point where the number of Walkmen is getting low. We number the lines for reference.

```
1.   Pool status: Deposits 15 Total 20 Walkmen 5
2.   Counter 1 wants 5
3.   Counter 1 acquires 5
4.       Pool status: Deposits 20 Total 20 Walkmen 0
5.   Counter 2 wants 7
6.   Counter 0 wants 2
7.   Counter 1 wants 4
8.   Replacing 1
9.   Replacing 2
10.  Counter 0 acquires 2
11.  Pool status: Deposits 19 Total 20 Walkmen 1
12.  Replacing 6
13.  Counter 2 acquires 7
14.  Pool status: Deposits 20 Total 20 Walkmen 0
15.  Counter 0 wants 5
16.  Counter 2 wants 1
17.  Replacing 1
18.  Replacing 5
19.  Counter 0 acquires 5
20.  Pool status: Deposits 19 Total 20 Walkmen 1
21.  Counter 2 acquires 1
22.  Pool status: Deposits 20 Total 20 Walkmen 0
23.  Counter 2 wants 2
24.  Counter 0 wants 7
25.  Replacing 7
26.  Counter 1 acquires 4
27.  Pool status: Deposits 17 Total 20 Walkmen 3
28.  Counter 2 acquires 2
29.  Pool status: Deposits 19 Total 20 Walkmen 1
```

The program was set running with a pool of 20 Walkmen and with three counters (0, 1 and 2). At the beginning of this extract, there are five Walkmen left. Counter 1 wants 5 and gets them, leaving none. At that point each of the counters puts in a request, and all are blocked until some groups start returning sets. On line 8, one set was returned to the pool, but this was not enough for any of the waiting threads, so they continue to wait. On line 9 another two come back. By line 10, there are three sets in the pool so the thread from counter 0 can continue. Notice that this was not the first one queued: counter 2 requested 7 on line 5, but still has to wait. Fortunately, on line 12, six more Walkmen come back, making seven in all, so that group can now continue. The pool, however, is back to zero again.

Study the rest of the output, and run the program yourself with different parameters to get a feel for the dynamics.

SUMMARY

In order to handle networks and user interaction better, Java provides for multi-threading. Classes can be turned into threads which run independently via their own run methods. Communication among threads is via method and variable access. If there is a chance that threads might interfere with each other, the methods they call are declared as synchronized. Java then guarantees that a thread in a synchronized method will finish before another is allowed into any synchronized method in the same object. To control threads so that one can wait for another, there are two thread calls, wait and notify.

QUIZ

13.1   In what units of time does the sleep method operate?

13.2   In which package is the Thread class declared?

13.3   Give a statement to create a new thread called x of class T.

13.4   In multi-threaded programs, does start call run or the other way round?

13.5   Do all methods in a monitor class have to be synchronized? Explain your answer.

13.6   Look at the output from the Walkman program in the Case Study. Which group had to wait a very long time to get their Walkmen?

13.7   Explain why the ViewPoint class in Example 13.3 was not made into a thread.

13.8   Give statements to create and start a new Car Park thread called North, with a counter to be displayed at position 450.

13.9   The following class is being turned into a thread:

```
class picture extends Canvas {
  public void paint (Graphics g) {
    g.drawImage (i,50,50,this);
    }
  }
```

Complete the transformation.

13.10   Suppose some Walkmen are being mended, and during the day a Curator thread is started up in the Museum program (Case Study 7) which will add in a number of Walkmen to the pool. Is this possible in the given system, and what method(s) would such a Curator thread call?

PROBLEMS

13.1   **British traffic lights**. In Great Britain, there is a fourth phase on every set of traffic lights. Between red and green, both the red and yellow lights come on. Alter the program in Example 13.2 to take this into account.

13.2   **Visible Walkmen**. The Walkman program (Case Study 7) could really do with a user interface that (a) shows how the Walkmen come and go; and (b) has a control panel so that the arrival of parties can be under the user's control, rather than generated automatically. Create such a user interface to run as an additional thread in the system.

13.3   **Broken Walkmen**. It could well happen that visitors find Walkmen that are no longer working when they finish. Instead of handing them back directly, we ask them to go back to the counter and hand them in specially. How would the class diagram have to change if we did this, and what methods would be needed? Implement this change and also add a Curator class which comes round periodically and collects broken Walkmen, returning them later.

13.4   **VIP visitors**. Some visitors are VIPs and should not have to queue long for Walkmen. Add another function to the Curator class to bring in such VIP groups occasionally and let them get Walkmen with a higher priority. Show on comparative sample outputs the effect that they would have.

13.5   **Working watch**. In Problem 10.2, we designed the face of a digital watch. Now, using a thread, make it work, with the digits clicking over and the buttons for resetting and displaying being active at the same time.

13.6   **Viewpoint full!** Savanna Conservation is concerned about the number of cars going up to the viewpoint in Example 13.3. See if you can extend the program so that the viewpoint has a maximum number of places and cars can only enter from the car-parks if there is space. If not, they use the wait synchronization method to queue. When a car leaves (after a random time spend looking at the view), the car-parks are notified that another car can come in.

CHAPTER 14

Networking

14.1 Connecting via URLs

Java was built to access the network. It has extensive features for network programming at various levels from connecting via URLs or sockets to accessing remote methods (RMI) and database connecting (JDBC). Because Java makes such connectivity so easy, we can justify including it in an introductory text such as this one, especially since we shall examine these new ideas by using examples in the usual *Java Gently* way.

All four methods for connecting are part of the Java core APIs and are available in the standard JDK and any browser that supports Java 1.1. Specifically, we shall be using `java.net`, `java.rmi` and `java.jdbc`.

The URL class

Java has a class called URL which enables the data referred to by a URL on the Internet to be downloaded, and some interaction with the resource to be achieved. Given a string, Java will create an appropriate URL which can then be used to establish a

URLConnection. The connection enables interaction as defined by the resource's protocol, perhaps via I/O streams.

The form for creating a URL is

URL creation

```
URL name = new URL (String);
URL name = new URL (base, String);
getDocumentBase ();
getCodeBase ();
```

For example,

```
URL info = new info
        ("file:/u/jbishop/java/Book/chap13/Walkmen/Museum.java");
```

will find the resource indicated and set up a reference to it from the Java program. The second form of the URL constructor enables us to have relative URLs. The above declaration can be split into two as follows:

```
URL info = new URL
        ("file:/u/jbishop/java/Book/chap13/Walkmen/");
museumURL = new URL (info, "Museum.java");
```

URLs can also be relative to the applet that is running. getDocumentBase returns the URL of the page from where the applet was loaded. getCodeBase returns the URL of the applet itself. Examples of the use of getCodeBase were shown in Section 12.3 and Example 12.4. The catching the duke applet refers to its own location and to files and subdirectories to display its image and sound files:

```
duke = getImage (getCodeBase (), "duke.gif");
play (getCodeBase(), "sounds/ouch.au");
```

Both constructors make sure that you have the correct syntax for forming a URL. If not, a malformedURLException is thrown. It is therefore usual to put the declaration in a try-statement and catch the exception.

URL connections

To access the resource at the URL, we shall have to set up a connection. If the resource is a text file, then we can create an input stream to it. The relevant form for achieving this is:

Creating a URL connection

```
URLConnection connection = URLname.openConnection ();
BufferedReader streamname = new InputStreamReader
    (connection.getInputStream());
```

The stream now acts as any normal input source. Its use is illustrated in the following example. Note that the opening of the stream can also be done using the Text class, as follows:

```
BufferedReader conin = Text.open(con.getInputStream());
```

EXAMPLE 14.1 Listing a file

Problem It is useful to be able to list files together with line numbers. Assuming the information is coming over the Internet via a URL, how can we produce such a listing?

Solution Connect into the resource and read each line at a time, printing a line number with it.

Program The program uses a local static method, list, just to separate the two operations of making the connection and printing the file.

```
import java.io.*;
import java.net.*;
import java.util.*;
import javagently.*;

class Lister {
  /* Listing a file  by  J M Bishop   January 1997
   * ==============          Java 1.1
   *
   * Illustrates the URL conections.
   * Must be called with an argument which is a URL
   * e.g. file:/ ...    or file:\
   */

    static void list (URLConnection c, String s)
                    throws IOException {

    // print a heading of the file name and date
      System.out.println(s+" on "+new Date());

    // underline the file name and date (which takes 32 chars)
      for (int i=0; i<s.length()+32; i++) System.out.print('-');
      System.out.println("\n");

    // list each line with a line number
      BufferedReader in = Text.open(c.getInputStream());
      for (int i=1; ; i++) {
        String line = in.readLine ();
        if (line == null) break;
        System.out.println(Text.writeInt(i,2)+" "+line);
      }
    }
```

```
        public static void main(String[] args)
                throws MalformedURLException, IOException {
            URL resource = new URL(args[0]);
            URLConnection connection = resource.openConnection();
            list (connection, args[0]);
        }
    }
```

Testing If we ran the program thus:

```
java Lister file:/u/jbishop/Book/chap14/Lister.java
```

we would get the same file out as follows:

```
file:/u/jbishop/Book/chap14/Lister.java on Mon Jan 12 13:24:38 GMT 1998
------------------------------------------------------------------------

 1 import java.io.*;
 2 import java.net.*;
 3 import java.util.*;
 4 import javagently.*;
 5
 6 class Lister {
 7   /* Listing a file  by  J M Bishop  January 1997
 8    * ==============        Java 1.1
 9    *
10    * Illustrates the URL conections.
11    * Must be called with an argument which is a URL
12    * e.g. file:/ ...   or file:\
13    */
14
15     static void list (URLConnection c, String s)
16                       throws IOException {
17
18     // print a heading of the file name and date
19         System.out.println(s+" on "+new Date());
20
21     // underline the file name and date (which takes 32 chars)
22         for (int i=0; i<s.length()+32; i++) System.out.print('-');
23         System.out.println("\n");
24
25     // list each line with a line number
26         BufferedReader in = Text.open(c.getInputStream());
27         for (int i=1; ; i++) {
28           String line = in.readLine ();
29           if (line == null) break;
30           System.out.println(Text.writeInt(i,2)+" "+line);
31         }
32     }
33
34     public static void main(String[] args)
35             throws MalformedURLException, IOException {
36         URL resource = new URL(args[0]);
```

```
37          URLConnection connection = resource.openConnection();
38          list (connection, args[0]);
39      }
40 }
```

From the listing we can see that the connection is opened on line 37. It is then passed to the `list` method for processing, together with the original argument from the command line. `list` needs this string in order to print the name of the file, which is done on line 19. The input stream is set up on line 26 and thereafter the loop takes care of the printing. The loop ends when `readLine` returns a null object (line 29). Notice that a null object is quite different from an empty line: lines 5, 14, 17 and so on are empty, but exist as strings and therefore are printed.

URLs are useful when we are dealing with applets and web pages. The above examples show that Java can integrate well into this environment. In Section 14.2 we shall look at connections at one level lower down: that of ports and sockets. But first let us take a look at fetching images.

Fetching images

How do we fetch images? In fact, there is a very easy way using the services of the awt, and in particular of the `awt.image` package. The form is:

Fetching an image

```
f.createImage ((ImageProducer) imagename.getContent());
```

`getContent` returns the entire contents of the file. `ImageProducer` is an interface, so we type cast the contents of the file into a class that conforms to the requirements of this interface. In the `Component` class, which `Frame` inherits, we call the `createImage` method which will convert an `ImageProducer` interface object to an `Image` object.

Once all this is done, we pass the fetched image to a `paint` method to be drawn.

EXAMPLE 14.2 Fetching an image

Illustration The following program illustrates the fetching of an image from a URL.

```
import java.awt.*;
import java.awt.event.*;
import java.awt.image.*;
import java.net.*;

public class FetchImage extends Frame {

   /*  Fetch an image program  by  J M Bishop  Jan 1997
    *  =====================  Java 1.1
```

```
   *   Fetches a jpg or gif image into a window.
   *
   *   Illustrates use of awt.image. */

  private Image i;

  public void paint(Graphics g) {
    g.drawImage(i, 50, 50, this);
  }

  public static void main(String[] args) throws Exception {

    FetchImage f = new FetchImage();
    URL imagename = new URL(args[0]);
    f.i = f.createImage((ImageProducer) imagename.getContent());
    f.setSize(300, 300);
    f.setVisible(true);
    f.addWindowListener(new WindowAdapter () {
      public void windowClosing(WindowEvent e) {
        System.exit(0);
      }
    });
  }
}
```

Testing To test out the program, we run it with a known image file name, as in:

```
java FetchImage file:/u/jbishop/java/Book/chap1/elephant.jpg
```

A window will open up (as is usual with awt programs) and the elephant image will be displayed therein. The window can be closed by clicking the close box, because we have included a `windowClosing` method for this purpose.

14.2 Ports and sockets

In the previous section, we concentrated on connections via high-level URLs. Java provides another level of connection, that of ports and sockets. A **port** is an abstraction of a physical place through which communication can proceed between a server and a client. The server is said to provide the port, and the client links into it.

Operating systems have processes assigned to specific ports, with server software that runs continuously, listening for anticipated messages of particular kinds. Ports are generally known by numbers. For example, connecting to port 13 will return the date and time of the computer. Other ports provide for receiving and sending mail, checking the status of the computer, finding out who is logged on, and so on. Most of the time these ports will not be available to mere users, as security could be impaired. However, there are many vacant ports which we can use where we can create our own services.

Such a service will be a multi-threaded Java program which provides sockets on the given port. A **socket** is an abstraction of the network software that enables communication in and out of this program. A Java socket can be created if we have a valid computer Internet address and a valid port number. Several sockets can be created on a single port, enabling many clients to make use of the service provided, as shown in Figure 14.1.

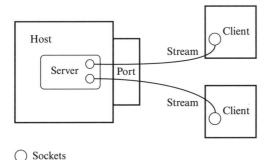

○ Sockets

Figure 14.1 *Diagrammatic view of ports and sockets.*

Once a socket has been created, the client and server communicate in whatever way has been arranged. In Java, the simplest method is to establish an ordinary stream from the server to the client. Thereafter, the server can use read and print methods to get and send data.

If the client is a Java program then it will also have a socket and streams that match those of the server. Alternatively, the client could be an existing program such as telnet, or the server could be an existing service such as the time of day. The forms associated with setting up a socket are:

Creating sockets

```
ServerSocket listener = new ServerSocket (port);
Socket name = listener.accept();
Socket name = new Socket (host, port);
```

---

and the forms for attaching input and output streams to it are:

Streams for sockets

```
BufferedReader instreamname =
    new InputStreamReader (name.getInputStream());
PrintWriter outstreamname = new
    PrintWriter(name.getOutputStream(),true);
```

If we are creating a socket on the server side, we first set up a permanent listening socket on that port, based on the `ServerSocket` class. Then for each client that accesses the port, a separate socket of the `Socket` class is set up via the `accept` method. From the client's side, to create such a socket we instantiate the `Socket` class directly and indicate the host to which it must connect.

The two stream connections follow the same pattern as any other stream connections. The one difference is that the output stream indicates to the `PrintWriter` class that it must flush each line (the `true` parameter).

EXAMPLE 14.3   Opening a port

Illustration A simple program to act as a client accessing an existing server on a host is the following. In this case, we use port 13 which returns the time of the computer. The program uses the second form for creating a socket.

```
import java.io.*;
import java.net.*;
import javagently.*;

class Ports {
  public static void main(String[] args) {

    String computer;
    int port;

    if (args.length > 0) computer = args[0];
    else computer = "jupiter.cs.up.ac.za";
    if (args.length > 1) port = Integer.parseInt(args[1]);
    else port = 13; // the clock port

    System.out.println("Accessing port "+port+" on "+ computer+"\n");
    try {

      // Create a socket to the given port.
      // Set up an input stream to read what the socket on that
      // side provides.

      Socket t = new Socket(computer, port);
      BufferedReader in = Text.open(t.getInputStream());

      // Read from the server until readLine
      // returns no more data
      while (true) {
        String s = in.readLine();
        if (s == null) break;
        else System.out.println(s);
      }
    }
    catch(IOException e) { System.out.println("Error" + e); }
  }
}
```

Testing If we ran this program without parameters, it would default to the computer called jupiter.cs.up.ac.za and to port 13. The result would be the date and time printed out, such as:

```
Accessing port 13 on jupiter.cs.up.ac.za

Sun Jan 19 15:57:14 1997
```

We now consider how to create our own server program on a spare port. Ports above 8000 are usually spare, so we can use one of those.

EXAMPLE 14.4 Creating an ATM server

Problem We would like to simulate the operation of ATMs (automated teller machines) connected to a bank, and handling the initial PIN (personal identification number) validation.

Solution We shall set up a server on a vacant port. The service should allow multiple connections from clients representing ATM machines. The protocol between the server and a client should go something like this:

Server	**Client**
Welcome to Savanna Bank	
Please type in your PIN number or type CANCEL	
	1234
Incorrect PIN. Try again.	
	5678
Please start your transactions	

We only have a simulation here, so there is no database of clients in this service, and the PIN will be 5678, for all clients!

Design If there are to be multiple clients then it is certain that they will be running at different speeds and will need their own threads within the server. This is no problem, as we have fully investigated how to set up threads in Chapter 13. The question is rather how to test the service. We could set up a Java client program similar to the one in Example 14.3, but actually there is an easier way: we can use another existing client, telnet. Telnet is a software program with a simple protocol which, in the absence of any other instructions, will read and write to a host, line by line. Thus we can telnet into our chosen port and type in lines one at a time.

Program The program makes use of a class called `InetAddress` which represents Internet addresses, as well as their string equivalents. The server follows (with comments to explain what is happening at each stage).

```java
import java.io.*;
import java.net.*;
import javagently.*;

class ATMServer {

  /* A simple server program    by J M Bishop December 1996
   * =======================
   *                                  Java 1.1 revised January 1998
   * Allows multiple simultaneous connections.
   * Illustrates sockets and networking.
   * /

  static final String magicPIN = "5678";

  public static void main(String[] args ) {

   // Set up the port address from the command line,
   // or default to 8190

     int port = 8190;
     InetAddress serverAddress=null;

     if (args.length > 0)
       port =Integer.parseInt(args[0]);
     try {
       serverAddress = InetAddress.getLocalHost();
     } catch (UnknownHostException e) {}

   // Initial printing on Server side only
   // using System.out

     System.out.println("******  SAVANNA BANK ********");
     System.out.println("Simulate an ATM session by "
           + "telnetting in to ");
     System.out.println(serverAddress.getHostName() +
           " on port "+port);
     System.out.println("from any number of different computers or");
     System.out.println("from different active Windows.");

   // Set up the server socket
     try {
       ServerSocket listener = new ServerSocket(port);

       int c = 0;
       while (!done) {

   // This is where the program waits for new clients
         Socket client = listener.accept( );
         c ++;
         System.out.println("Card inserted on " +
             client.getInetAddress().getHostName());
         System.out.println("Starting a new client, numbered "
             +c);
         new handler(client, c).start();
       }
```

```
        listener.close();
      }
      catch (IOException e) {
        System.out.println("Port "+port+
          " may be busy. Try another.");
      }
    }

  private static boolean done = false;

  static  void closeDown () {
    done = true;
  }
}
```

Notice that we do not keep track of the handlers by name or reference: they are simply spawned off to do their own thing. The handler threads look like this:

```
class handler extends Thread {

    private Socket toClient;
    private int id;

    handler(Socket s, int i) {
    // Remember the client socket number and client id number
      toClient = s;
      id = i;
    }

    public void run() {

      try {
        BufferedReader conin = Text.open
          (toClient.getInputStream());
        PrintWriter conout = new
          PrintWriter(toClient.getOutputStream(),true);

        conout.println( "Welcome to Savanna Bank");
        for (int tries = 0; tries < 3; tries++) {
          conout.println("Please type in your PIN "+
              "number or type CANCEL");
          String s = in.readLine();
          System.out.println("Client "+id+":"+s);

          if (s.equals("SHUTDOWN")) ATMServer.closeDown();
          else if (s.equals("CANCEL")) {
            out.println("Transactions halted. Goodbye.");
            break;
          }

          else if (s.equals(ATMServer.magicPIN)) {
            out.println("Please start your transactions");
            break;
          }
```

```
        else
           out.println("Incorrect PIN. Try again.");
      }
      System.out.println("Simulation complete. Thanks.");
   }
   catch (IOException e) {System.out.println("IO Error");}
 }
}
```

Each thread records its socket reference when constructed. It then asks for the input and output streams associated with that socket, which will give it access to the client that is on the other side. The handler sends an introductory message to the ATM and enters its loop, asking for a PIN three times. The client can also type CANCEL or there is a chance to stop the server (not generally advertised). When the loop ends, the socket to the client is closed and then the thread dies naturally.

Testing To run the server, we simply execute it as a normal Java program. If we want to telnet into the server as a client from the same machine (which is certainly possible) then we should run the server in the background using `java ATMServer &` or a separate window on a windowing environment. A typical session is shown in Figure 14.2. The kind of server represented in this example is taken further in Case Study 8.

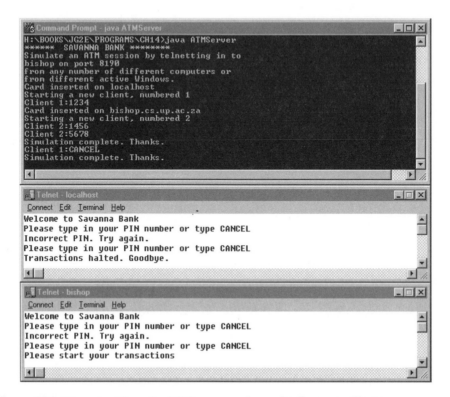

Figure 14.2 *The output from the ATM server and two simultaneous clients.*

14.3 Case Study 8: The Chatter system

In Example 14.4, each of the clients was completely independent. It would be nice to extend the system so that the messages typed in by one are relayed to each of the others by the server. Such a server is known as a 'Chat program'.

Keeping track of clients

The first issue is how to keep track of clients within the server. Clients can sign on and leave at will, and the number of clients could be very hard to control or predict. It thus makes sense to envisage a linked list of clients rather than an array, since we know that we can add and remove from such a list without worrying about the number of elements.

If we declare

```
private static List clientList = new List ();
```

where `List` is the class already in the `myutilities` package (defined in Section 8.4) then adding a new client thread's reference to the list is done by:

```
clientList.reset();
clientList.add(client);
```

We have to reset the list, because it may have been left in an unsatisfactory position by some other operation. This way, the new clients are added to the front of the list each time. These statements appear in the main program, just after the launching of a new handler for the client.

Now, how do we remove a client from the list? Clearly, the client must request such removal, once a BYE has been detected. The client knows what its socket reference is, and this is unique among the current clients. Therefore, the server can look through the list, comparing socket references, and when a match is found, delete that object from the list. The extract of code is:

```
Socket t;
for (clientList.reset(); !clientList.eol(); clientList.succ()) {
  t = (Socket) clientList.current();
  if (t.equals(s)) break;
}
clientList.remove();
```

Since this loop is in a method which has been called by a thread which 'owns' an existing socket, the loop will eventually detect a matching socket and reach the break-statement.

Broadcasting to all clients

Broadcasting a message to all clients is even easier than the above removal. Since the message has to be echoed to the originator as well, we do not have to differentiate between that client and the rest and we simply loop through all of them.

```
for (clientList.reset(); !clientList.eol(); clientList.succ()) {
  s = (Socket) clientList.current();
  p = new PrintStream(s.getOutputStream());
  p.println(name + ": "+message+"\r");
}
```

For each client on the list, we get the corresponding output stream and send the message there.

Synchronizing activities

The removal and broadcast operations both access the list of clients kept by the server. Given that the removal operation will make fairly drastic changes to the list, it would not be wise for both operations to be active simultaneously. Therefore they are declared as `synchronized` and Java will ensure that once one has begun, it will be finished before the other is attempted.

A class diagram

This time, let us record a class diagram for the server and its handlers, shown in Figure 14.3.

The server

The code for the chat server therefore looks like this in full:

```
import java.io.*;
import java.net.*;
import myutilities.*;

public class ChatServer {

   /* The Chatter program     by J M Bishop  January 1997
    * ===================     Java 1.1 January 1998
    * Sets up a server for multiple conversations.
    *
    * Join in by typing
    * telnet x y
```

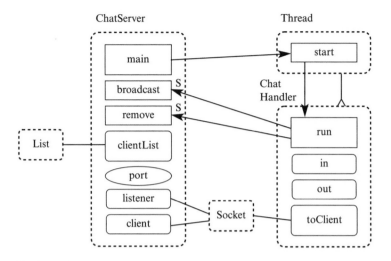

Figure 14.3 *Class diagram for the Chatter system.*

```
 * where x and y are the computer's name and port as
 * given when the Chatter starts.
 *
 * Illustrates sockets, streams on sockets,
 * threads, synchronization and the use of lists (again).
 */

private static List clientList = new List();
private static int id = 0;

public static void main(String[] args) throws IOException {
  // Get the port and created a socket there.
  int port = 8190;
  if (args.length > 0)
    port = Integer.parseInt(args[0]);
  ServerSocket listener = new ServerSocket(port);
  System.out.println("The Chat Server is running on port "+port);

  // Listen for clients. Start a new handler for each.
  // Add each client to the linked list.
  while (true) {
    Socket client = listener.accept();
    new ChatHandler(client).start();
    System.out.println("New client no."+id+
        " from "+ listener.getInetAddress()+
        " on client's port "+client.getPort());
    clientList.reset();
    clientList.add(client);
    id++;
  }
}

static synchronized void broadcast(String message, String name)
```

```
        throws IOException {
      // Sends the message to every client including the sender.
      Socket s;
      PrintWriter p;
      for (clientList.reset(); !clientList.eol(); clientList.succ()) {
        s = (Socket)clientList.current();
        p = new PrintWriter(s.getOutputStream(), true);
        p.println(name+": "+message);
      }
    }

    static synchronized void remove(Socket s) {
    /* Finds the client on the list (by comparing socket
     * references) and removes it.
     */
      Socket t;
      for (clientList.reset(); !clientList.eol(); clientList.succ()) {
        t = (Socket)clientList.current();
        if (t.equals(s))
        break;
      }
      clientList.remove();
      id--;
    }

}

class ChatHandler extends Thread {

  /* The Chat Handler class is called from the Chat Server:
   * one thread for each client coming in to chat.
   */

  private BufferedReader in;
  private PrintWriter out;
  private Socket toClient;
  private String name;

  ChatHandler(Socket s) {
    toClient = s;
  }

  public void run() {
    try {
      /* Create i-o streams through the socket we were
       * given when the thread was instantiated
       * and welcome the new client.
       */

      in = new BufferedReader(new InputStreamReader(
        toClient.getInputStream()));
      out = new PrintWriter(toClient.getOutputStream(), true);
      out.println("*** Welcome to the Chatter ***");
      out.println("Type BYE to end");
      out.print("What is your name? ");
```

```
        out.flush();
        String name = in.readLine();
        ChatServer.broadcast(name+" has joined the discussion.",
          "Chatter");

        // Read lines and send them off for broadcasting.
        while (true) {
          String s = in.readLine().trim();
          //Check first three characters for BYE.
          //Avoids problems with different line end characters.

          if (s.length() > 2 && s.charAt(0) == 'B' &&
              s.charAt(1) == 'Y' && s.charAt(2) == 'E') {
            ChatServer.broadcast(name+" has left the discussion.",
              "Chatter");
            break;
          }
          ChatServer.broadcast(s, name);
        }
        ChatServer.remove(toClient);
        toClient.close();
      }
      catch (Exception e) {
      System.out.println("Chatter error: "+e);
    }
    }
    }

  }
```

A sample chat session

Once again we use telnet for the clients. The following could be a sample chat session, as recorded on the server's display.

```
Chat/Chatter>java ChatServer 8191 &
[2] 5802
Chat/Chatter>The Chat Server is running on port 8191

Chat/Chatter>telnet jupiter 8191
Trying 137.215.18.16 ...
Connected to jupiter.cs.up.ac.za.
New client no.0 on client's port 57889
Escape character is '^]'.
*** Welcome to the Chatter ***
Type BYE to end
What is your name?
Nelson
Chatter: Nelson has joined the discussion.
Anyone out there?
Nelson: Anyone out there?
New client no.1 on client's port 1026
Chatter: Seagull has joined the discussion.
Hi Seagull
```

```
Nelson: Hi Seagull
Seagull: Hi Nelson, how's the coffee shop?
Great. Business is booming.
Nelson: Great. Business is booming.
Seagull: Oh well, bye for now
Seagull — you must type BYE to end
Nelson: Seagull — you must type BYE to end
Seagull: BYE
Try again
Nelson: Try again
Seagull: BYE
Chatter: Seagull has left the discussion.
BYE
Nelson: BYE
Chatter: Nelson has left the discussion.
Connection closed by foreign host.
```

Notice that we told telnet to look for the host called 'jupiter' and it translated this to a numeric Internet address, 137.215.18.16. The server, once it accepts the client, can get this Internet address and translate it back to its full string equivalent, in this case 'jupiter.cs.up.ac.za'. You can also use the special Internet address '127.0.0.1' to telnet into your own machine.

When running the chat server using telnet, some oddities may emerge when trying to say goodbye, or with the echoing or non-echoing of lines locally. It is worth experimenting to find out how your computers react.

14.4 Database connectivity

Databases are a cornerstone of computing in today's age. Java provides connectivity to databases via the JDBC (Java Database Connectivity). The JDBC allows a connection to be made to a database with no more fuss than connecting to a resource or image. However, Java also provides for SQL (Standard Query Language) statements to be sent, and the results of queries to be interpreted on return.

The form for connecting to a database is:

Connecting to a database

```
Connection con = DriverManager.getConnection (url, user, password);
```

The JDBC will look for an available driver for the type of database that the URL references. There are over 50 kinds of database supported in one way or another by JDBC.

Once the connection is successful, we can send SQL statements and get results back. The form is:

Querying a database

```
Statement stat = con.createStatement ();
ResultSet rs = stat.executeQuery("SQL query");
```

Then the result set can be processed in a loop, record by record.

EXAMPLE 14.5 Animals on a database

Problem Savanna Conservation has details of animals stored on a database, including pictures. They would like this data to be displayed on the web page in the Conservation system discussed in Chapters 1 and 12.

Solution The current Conservation system is merely a web page, so it cannot, without a major change, access the database. What we do instead is create a server-side database access program which gets the data and then turns it into HTML, for transmission back to the original system.

Design Figure 14.4 shows how such a system connects together. The client clicks on the <u>Animals</u> link as usual and is sent to the web server. The link here starts up a CGI (common gateway interface) script which runs the Java class. If we did not use CGI, then the class would have to be running continuously, which is not favoured by system administrators. The Java program accesses the database and gets the result sent back. It processes each record, turning it into a line of HTML and transmitting these lines back to the web page which can interpret them and display the animals found.

In this way, we can add more and more animals without touching the web page.

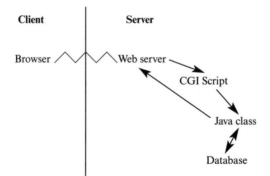

Figure 14.4 *Accessing a database.*

Program The program for the central server-side Java class which accesses the database is:

```java
import java.sql.*;
import java.io.*;
import java.util.*;

  public class Animals {

  /*  The Animals program    by L Botha  Sept 1997
   *  ==================     Java 1.1
   *
   * accesses a database of animals information.
   * Illustrates JDBC
   */

    public static void main(String args[])
     {
       System.out.println
         (" <HTML> <HEAD> <TITLE>Animals of Savanna</TITLE>");
       System.out.println(" </HEAD> <BODY>");
       System.out.println("<CENTER><P><B><FONT COLOR=\"#804000\">
         <FONT SIZE=+2>Animals of Savanna
         </FONT></FONT></B></P></CENTER>");

       try {
       // Link up to the database
         Driver pgd = (Driver) new postgres95.PGDriver();
         String sqlurl = "jdbc:postgres95:nature";
         Connection conn DriverManager.getConnection
            (sqlurl,"postgres","fLatLand");

       // Send over a query
         Statement stat = conn.createStatement();

       // Get the answer back
         ResultSet rs = stat.executeQuery("Select * from animals");
         boolean odd = false;

       // Process the records, turning each into HTML
         while ( rs.next() ) {
           String animal = rs.getString(1);
           String url = rs.getString(2);
           String descrip = rs.getString(3);
           System.out.print("<P><IMG SRC=\""+url+"\" HSPACE=20 ");
           System.out.print("HEIGHT=88 ");

       // Position animals to the left and right
           if (odd)
              System.out.println("ALIGN=LEFT>");
           else
              System.out.println("ALIGN=RIGHT>");
           System.out.println(descrip+"<BR>");
           odd = !odd;
         }
```

```
        } catch (SQLException ee) {
          System.out.println("Error reading database");
        }
      }
    }
```

Testing One needs a database to be able to test the program. The CGI script and web page (both very small) are on the web site. The resulting output is precisely that in Figure 1.4, if those same six animals were on the database.

14.5 Accessing remote objects

Sockets give us the ability to transmit raw data across machines, and database connectivity enables the transmission of structured relational data. In between these two ends of the spectrum is the very common case of transmitting data that is typed, and checked, but that is formatted to suit the programmer, rather than a database. In the Java model, such data would obviously be in the form of objects.

In addition to being able to send objects around a network, Java also allows us not to send them! What this means is that we can have objects situated on one computer and merely access them there, calling their methods to perform operations on them as required.

This description fits in exactly with the client–server model. The server holds an object that the clients want to fetch or access. Java requires that the server registers or **binds** the object in a central registry on that computer. Then the client must know which computer to go to, and the name by which the object was registered, whereupon it can **look up** the object and get a reference to it. Thereafter the object can be used as if it were local, and the Java Remote Method invocation system (or RMI) takes care of all the protocol, transporting and checking of data back and forth.

`java.rmi` is a core package in the JDK and is therefore available on all Java systems. The following forms show how binding and look up are achieved.

RMI binding

```
Naming.rebind ("Object name", remoteobject);
```

RMI look up

```
Classname localobject = (Classname)
        Naming.lookup (url + "Object name");
```

Once the look up has been successfully completed, `localobject` contains a reference to the `remoteobject`, but can be used just as any other local object.

EXAMPLE 14.6 RMI illustration

Problem Illustrate RMI with the simplest possible program.

Solution Have the server store a statement such as 'I am 46' and have the client fetch it.

Design The system consists of a server on one computer and a client on another. Both use the `java.rmi` package. The server binds an object in the registry and the client looks it up. The code is very simple, so we proceed directly to it.

Program The server looks like this:

```
import java.rmi.*;

public class ThingServer {
  public static void main (String [] args) throws RemoteException {

    ActualThing available = new ActualThing("I am 46");
    try {
      Naming.rebind ("Thing Service", available);
    }
    catch (Exception x) {
      System.out.println("Could not bind or no such host etc");
    }
  }
}
```

It sets up on the registry the following:

Name	Remote Object
Thing Service	I am 46

So anyone who asks for a 'Thing Service', gets the object containing the message 'I am 46'. The client to do so is:

```
import java.rmi.*;
import java.rmi.server.*;

public class ThingClient {
  public static void main (String args []) {
    String url = "rmi://jupiter.cs.up.ac.za/";
    try {
      Thing t = (Thing) Naming.lookup (url + "Thing Service");
      System.out.println(t.getThing());
    }
    catch (Exception e) {
      System.out.println("Error "+e);
    }
  }
}
```

t is the local object connected to the Thing Service. The class of t is:

```
import java.rmi.*;
import java.rmi.server.*;

  interface Thing extends Remote {
    String getThing () throws RemoteException;
  }

  class ActualThing extends UnicastRemoteObject implements Thing {

    ActualThing (String n) throws RemoteException {
      age = n;
    }

   public String getThing () throws RemoteException {
     return age;
   }

    private String age;

  }
```

Because Things are going to be dealt with across the network, they need special treatment, and Java wants to know about it. That is why Thing imports rmi and rmi.server and indicates in its methods and constructor that a RemoteException could be thrown, for example if the server goes down.

Testing The system can be tested on one computer with several windows or background jobs or on different computers, without change. However, rmi programs need special treatment. First of all, we start up the registry by executing

```
rmiregistry
```

Then we execute the server:

```
java ThingServer
```

Now clients can come in. If we type, in a new window,

```
java ThingClient
```

back will come the output:

```
I am 46
```

A realistic example of RMI is given in Case Study 9.

14.6 Case Study 9: The Airport Announcer system

The Savanna Airport Company has decided to computerize its announcements, rather than using an operator. Announcements come from two sources: airlines and the company itself. Airlines send out announcements as required regarding check-in, flight delays and so on. The airport is responsible for security messages which tend to be sent at regular intervals, automatically. We are therefore looking at a system with an initial model design as in Figure 14.5. The monitor handles the distribution of the messages, via loudspeakers as well as on the TV screens around the airport. To keep our example simple, we shall use a single monitor, operating as a scrolling line of text.

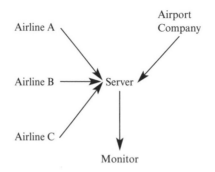

Figure 14.5 *Model for the Airport Announcer system.*

The airlines' applets

The system provides airlines with access to a set of applets. Each applet sets up a screen and asks for information which is then used to compose a message. For example, the check-in applet asks for a flight number and destination. It then dispatches the message such as:

> 'Will all passengers not yet in possession of boarding passes for flight SA567 to San Francisco please leave the queue and move directly to check-in 35 or 36.'

Other applets display messages for a boarding call, last call, flight delay and so. In each case, only the necessary information is called for. The Checkin applet with the result of its message is shown in Figure 14.6 and Plate 12.

The applet is put on the right side of a double frame, where the left side always has the menu of applets available. At start-up, the right side merely shows a background image, as in Figure 14.7 and Plate 11.

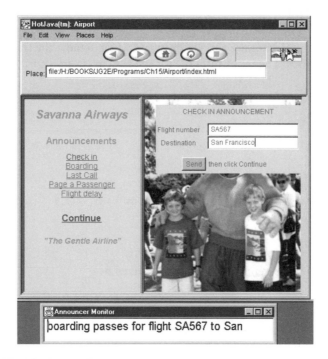

Figure 14.6 *The CheckIn applet for the Airport Announcer system with the Monitor below.*

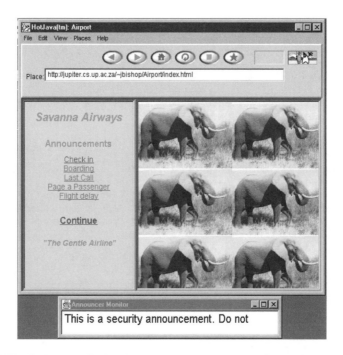

Figure 14.7 *The first screen for the Airport system, together with a security announcement.*

Airline-side HTML

The applets for the airlines are run via browsers which handle the frames, menu and background pictures. The index.html file for the system is very short:

```
<HTML>
<HEAD>
   <TITLE>Airport</TITLE>
</HEAD>


<FRAMESET COLS="215,*">
<FRAME SRC="Contents.html" NORESIZE SCROLLING="NO">
<FRAME SRC="Applets.html" NAME="Applets">
</FRAMESET>

</HTML>
```

The Contents frame presents the menu, and is given by:

```
<HTML>
  <HEAD>
     <META NAME="Author" CONTENT="JM Bishop">
     <TITLE>Contents</TITLE>
  </HEAD>
  <BODY TEXT="#CE5831" BGCOLOR="#F1D7BE" LINK="#EF5310"
        VLINK="#974D0F" ALINK="#EF5310" SCROLLING="NO">

  <CENTER>
  <H1>
  <I><FONT COLOR="#00CC00"><FONT SIZE=+3>Savanna Airways
     </FONT></FONT></I></H1>

  <H2>
  <FONT FACE="Arial, Helvetica"><FONT COLOR="#00CC00"><FONT SIZE=+1>
  Announcements</FONT></FONT>
  </H2>

  <FONT COLOR="#E17100">
  <A HREF="checkin.html" target="Applets">Check in</A>
  <A HREF="Board.html"   target="Applets">Boarding</A>
  <A HREF="Last.html"    target="Applets">Last Call</A>
  <A HREF="Page.html"    target="Applets">Page a Passenger</A>
  <A HREF="Delay.html"   target="Applets">Flight delay</A>
  </FONT><BR>
  <BR>

  <H2>
  <FONT COLOR="#00CC00"><FONT SIZE=+1>
  <A HREF="Applets.html" target="Applets">Continue</A>
  </FONT>

   <I><FONT SIZE=+0>"The Gentle Airline"
  </FONT></FONT></FONT></I></H2>
```

```
</CENTER>
  
 </BODY>
 </HTML>
```

The target tag in an HTML link indicates which frame the page should be loaded into. We declared two frames, Contents and Applets. So the above code indicates that each of the applets gets loaded into the right hand, or Applets, frame.

Notice that the Continue link pulls up the original right frame background, in so doing overwriting the applet that has just been used. Each of the HTML links points to another HTML file which is very simple, just setting up a background and calling in the appropriate applet. Checkin's looks like this:

```
<HTML>
  <HEAD>
     <TITLE>Check in</TITLE>
  </HEAD>

  <BODY TEXT="#CE5831" BGCOLOR="#F1D7BE" LINK="#A76330"
        VLINK="#974D0F" ALINK="#EF5310" BACKGROUND="Genishot.jpg"
        SCROLLING="NO">

  <APPLET CODE="Checkin.class" WIDTH=260 HEIGHT=120></APPLET>
  </BODY>
  </HTML>
```

The system is now ready to have the applets and servers added.

The applets

The applets are straightforward in that they have text boxes to be filled in. To get a better layout than provided by Grid layout (as shown in Figure 14.6) we use Grid Bag Layout. Although we have avoided it up to now, there is really nothing terribly difficult about Grid Bag. The position of the components in the grid is arranged so that the left ones get the space they need and the right ones get the rest. This arrangement is ideal for label–textfield pairs. The full text of the Checkin applet is:

```
import java.awt.*;
import java.applet.*;
import java.awt.event.*;

public class Checkin extends Applet implements ActionListener {

  /* The Check in Message Applet    by L Botha and J Bishop
   * =========================    Java 1.1 January 1998
   * receives the fields for the check in
   * message, constructs it and sends it
   * on to the rmi server which must be set
   * running first.
   */
```

```java
private Button sendButton;
private TextField flight, to;

public void init() {
  // the color is Java Gently's special orange, specified
  // as a hexadecimal number, taken from the HTML

  setBackground(new Color(0xF1D7BE));
  setLayout(new BorderLayout());

  add("North",new Label("CHECK IN ANNOUNCEMENT",Label.CENTER));

  Panel p = new Panel();
    // We use Grid Bag so that the labels and fields can be
    // be different sizes

    GridBagLayout layout = new GridBagLayout();
    p.setLayout(layout);
    GridBagConstraints c = new GridBagConstraints();
    c.gridwidth = 1; c.gridheight = 1;
    Label flightLabel = new Label("Flight number");
      c.gridx = 0; c.gridy = 0;
      layout.setConstraints(flightLabel, c);
      p.add(flightLabel);
    Label toLabel = new Label("Destination");
      c.gridx = 0; c.gridy = 1;
      layout.setConstraints(toLabel, c);
      p.add(toLabel);
    flight = new TextField("", 20);
      flight.addActionListener(this);
      c.gridx = 1; c.gridy = 0;
      layout.setConstraints(flight, c);
      p.add(flight);
    to = new TextField("", 20);
      to.addActionListener(this);
      c.gridx = 1; c.gridy = 1;
      layout.setConstraints(to, c);
      p.add(to);

    add("Center",p);

  Panel q = new Panel();
    sendButton = new Button("Send");
      sendButton.addActionListener(this);
      q.add(sendButton);
      q.add(new Label("then click Continue"));
    add("South",q);
}

public void actionPerformed(ActionEvent e) {
  Object source = e.getSource();
  if (source == sendButton) {
    String message =
      "Will all passengers not yet in possession of "
    + "boarding passes for flight " + flight.getText() + " to "
    + to.getText() + " please leave the queue and move "
```

```
        + "directly to check-in 35 or 36.";
        AnnouncerClient.sendMessage(message);
        flight.setText("");
        to.setText("");
     }
   }
 }
```

Connecting via RMI

Potentially, there could be many computers in this sytem. There are at least three – an airline, an announcer server plus monitor and the airport company – plus one more for each additional airline. The question is, how do the computers communicate? We could open sockets, but RMI is a more elegant solution, and surprisingly easy to set up and use.

Figure 14.8 gives a high-level diagram of the different classes that are required. The system is not symmetrical. The airline applets are coupled with a client that will dispatch a message to a local client on the same machine, but the airport company's client is based with the announcer because it is activated when the announcer wishes. It calls the company's server for an appropriate message.

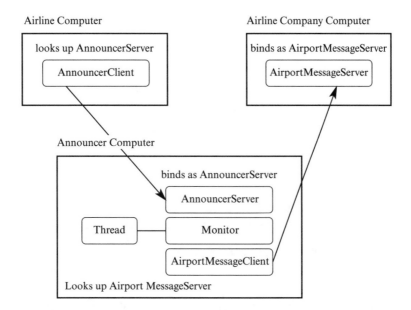

Figure 14.8 *Top level class diagram of the Airport system, showing the different computers.*

The applet calls its client as follows:

```
AnnouncerClient.sendMessage (message);
```

The client reacts by looking up a remote interface to the announcer server and passing the message on, as in:

```
Announcer an = (Announcer)Naming.lookup
                ("rmi://localhost/AnnouncerServer");
an.sendMessage(message);
```

The server's version of `sendMessage` stores the message in an array of messages. It is necessary to do so, since messages could be coming in thick and fast, certainly faster than the monitor can announce them. The server, though, is passive: it receives messages and then waits for the monitor to ask for them when it is ready to display them.

The monitor is a thread, and can therefore run at the same time as the server is accepting more messages. It gets a message from either one of the servers as appropriate. If the announcer has messages, it gets one, otherwise it waits a few seconds and asks the airport client for a message. The client connects up to the server and gets a message. The run method of the monitor is active, and looks like this:

```
public void run() {
  boolean startdelay;
  while (true) {
    startdelay = true;
    if (server.hasMessage()) {
      String msg = server.getMessage();
      while (msg.length() > 0) {
      String displaymsg = formatString(msg);
      message.setText("");
      message.setText(displaymsg);
      if (startdelay == true) {
      try { Thread.sleep(1000); } catch (Exception e) {}
        startdelay = false;
      }
      try { Thread.sleep(200); } catch (Exception e) {}
        msg = msg.substring(1);
      }
      message.setText("");
      server.removeMessage();
    }
    try { Thread.sleep(5000); } catch (Exception e) {}
    String newmsg = AirportMessageClient.getMessage();
    if (newmsg != null)
      server.sendMessage(newmsg);
  }
}
```

`Server` refers to the `AnnouncerServer`. `Monitor` asks if it has a message. If not, it waits a while and gets a message from its other source, the airport company using a local client and the remote server. The airport company running the remote server can add different messages at different times and change the timing for them. At present the system is set up to present one of the following messages in rotation:

'This is a security announcement. Do not leave baggage unattended at any time. Baggage left unattended will be removed and destroyed.'

'Children are not allowed to play on the escalators or in the lifts.'

'The Airports Company welcomes you and trusts you will have a safe and pleasant journey.'

The full code for the system is given on the web site, but Figure 14.9 summarizes the system with a full class diagram.

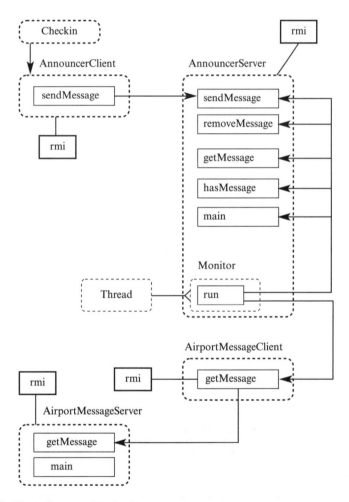

Figure 14.9 *Class diagram for the Airport server system.*

Running the system

To run the system, we need the equivalent of three background processes (or windows) and a browser. In the first window we set up the RMI registry by typing:

```
rmiregistry
```

In the next two windows, we activate the two servers, which bind themselves to the registry, i.e.

```
java AnnouncerServer
```

```
java AirportMessageServer
```

Then we enter the browser, opening index.html. The screen should give us Figure 14.7. If we click on <u>Check in</u> we will get Figure 14.6, and so on. The monitor window is started up by the AnnouncerServer, and is a small thin window through which the messages scroll. Try it out, and have fun!

SUMMARY

Java provides a variety of ways of connecting machines on the network, from URL connections to resources, to ports and sockets, database connectivity and remote objects. Each is supported by special classes and libraries and all are part of the standard Java language.

QUIZ

14.1 If elephant.jpg is an image file in the same directory as an applet which is currently running, give Java statements to access and display it.

14.2 In the statement

```
a.b = a.createImage((ImageProducer) imagename.getContent());
```

identify the class of each of the following objects:

```
a   b  ImageProducer  imagename
```

14.3 Can getInputStream and getOutputStream be used by both clients and servers?

14.4 In Example 11.7, the handler thread can call

```
server.closeDown()
```

if a special message is received. When will the server react to the message?

14.5 What is the difference between a socket and a server socket in Java's APIs?

14.6 What is the URL tag for displaying an image?

14.7 Why do you suppose the 'things' in Example 14.6 had to be declared together with an interface?

14.8 In the airport announcer system, could all three classes in the Announcer's Computer be active together?

14.9 What is the purpose of the 'target' tag in the HTML links (see the airline system for an example).

14.10 Write an RMI call to bind a thing (as defined in Example 14.6) under the name 'Secret'.

PROBLEMS

14.1 **Listing via HTML**. Experiment with the Lister program (Example 14.1) as an applet, with the name of the file coming in from a text field added to the applet's interface. Put the applet in an HTML page and have the HTML give a list of suggested files that can be fetched.

14.2 **Chatting clients**. The Chatter program (Case Study 8) provides a server only. Using the Ports program in Example 14.3 as a basis, create a Java program which can be started up on the client side and provide similar facilities to telnet.

14.3 **Chatting on the web**. Even after Problem 14.2, the user interface to the Chatter is pretty basic. Try making the server into an applet and embody it in an HTML page that provides instructions, displays the output, and has a separate line for typing in input.

14.4 **Knock knock!** Using the ATM server as a basis (Example 14.4) write a server to play Knock! Knock! The game goes like this:

Client	**Server**
Knock knock	
	Who's there?
Amos	
	Amos who?
Amos Quito.	

Use Telnet for the client again.

CHAPTER 15

Algorithms and data structures

15.1 About data structures

We conclude our study of Java by looking ahead to a more advanced computer science course, and the study of data structures.

> A **data structure** is a collection of **nodes** of the
> same class or type that is organized and accessed
> in a defined way.

A node would usually be an object, but could be as simple as an integer. The fact that the definition states that the nodes must be of the same class or type means that we can refer to a structure of that type, for example a list of coffees or a hash table of strings.

The linked list data structure that we built up in Section 8.4 was an *ad hoc* one, designed for the purpose. Another problem might require a very different data structure.

In computer science, though, there are several recognized data structures that crop up again and again in solutions to problems. They have names and defined properties, and in a sense can be regarded as an extension of the basic data types of a language.

Java has recognized the importance of data structures and has supplied classes in its standard packages for a good number of them. Just to provide a check list, Table 15.1 gives a canonical list of data structures, indicating those that are in Java and those that are covered in this edition of the book.

In this chapter we revisit linked lists in order to add some more features and give another example of their use. We also cover two more Java data structure classes – Stack and BitSet – and look at how queues can be implemented based on arrays or linked lists.

Data structure	Java class (if any)	*Java Gently* section
array	*built-in*	6.1, 6.2
extensible array	java.util.Vector	6.4
linked list		6.3, 8.4
stack	java.util.Stack	15.4
queue		15.4
tree		
hash table	java.util.Hashtable	6.4
set	java.util.BitSet	15.6
dictionary	java.util.Dictionary	
sequential file	java.io.File_Stream	4.2
random file	java.io.RandomAccessFile	

Table 15.1 *Table of data structures*

Properties

Each data structure has properties relating to the following:

- relationship to other nodes;
- composition of a header node;
- point of addition of nodes – front, back or anywhere;
- point of deletion of nodes – front, back or anywhere;
- direction of scanning – none, forwards, backwards or other.

As we get to each data structure, we shall address these issues.

Representation

Data structures can be represented as either **arrays** of objects or as nodes **linked** by their references, as already shown in Section 8.4. The decision as to which method to employ depends on two factors. A linked representation has the advantage that the number of nodes in the structure can be completely flexible: with an array representation, the maximum number would have to be fixed. On the other hand, linked-based structures require space for the links, and these increase the overall size of the structure.

There is no inherent complexity related to the programming in either case, and we shall present both representations, endeavouring to show the underlying algorithms as independent of the representation. In so doing, we create **abstract data types** which have recognizable forms and properties, and can be used only as specified.

Algorithms

Two of the operations we will often need for a data structure as a whole are sorting and searching. Before we start on looking at the inner details of data structures, therefore, we complete our study of the basic algorithms that should be part of a computer scientist's toolkit. The list includes:

- a linear search and a faster one;
- a straight sort and a faster one.

A linear search was shown in Section 6.3 for arrays, and Section 8.4 for linked lists, and straight sorting was covered in Section 6.3. Both the faster algorithms make use of a basic computing technique – **recursion** – without which no textbook on programming would be complete.

15.2 Linear and binary searching

We can define a **sequence** as a data structure that has the property that each element is reachable after the previous one. In other words, the structure can be accessed in sequence. Examples of such structures would be an array, a list or a file stream. A hash table is not a sequence, however, although a Java hash table can be accessed sequentially via an enumerator.

If we have a sequence of values then we can search for a particular value by starting at the beginning of the sequence and comparing each element in turn. This is called **linear** searching, because we scan the sequence in a linear way.

The linear searching algorithm is an example of a double-exit loop: either the value is found in the sequence, or the end of the sequence is reached before the value is found. These kinds of loop were examined extensively in Section 5.3, where the sequence was the input data stream, and again in Section 8.4 for a linked list. Let us now translate that logic to searching an array.

The advantage of searching an array is that we know its length. We can therefore use a for-loop, together with the extra control it provides for stopping if not found. A first attempt at the linear search is:

```
int i;
for (i = 0; i< a.length; i++)
  if (a[i] == x) break;
```

Though simple and neat, this loop has an unfortunate defect: at the end we do not know if we exited the loop because we found the item or not. Now, if we are certain of finding the item, this is fine. But in the general case, we cannot be so sure. Notice also that we deliberately declared i outside the loop so that we could access a[i] afterwards.

That means that the algorithm returns two values: a yes/no indicator (or boolean, say) and an index. This makes it very difficult to parcel the search up into a method, since we can return only one value from a method (unless we return a multi-valued object).

A possible technique is to return the index, but to set it to some out-of-range value if the item was not found. Possible values could be –1 or length. Instinctively this smacks of bad practice. An altogether better approach is to use a user-defined exception. Consider the following proposal:

```
class ItemNotFoundException extends Exception { }

item a [] = new item [n];

static int LinearSearch (item a [], item x)
                    throws ItemNotFoundException {
  for (int i = 0; i< a.length; i++)
    if (x.equals(a[i])) return i;
  // item not found: no normal return
  throw new ItemNotFoundException();
}

//Test the method
try {
  int found = LinearSearch (a, x);
  // do whatever is necessary with a[found]
    ...
}
catch (ItemNotFoundException e ) {
  // react to x not being there
    ...
}
```

The method is passed the array and the item being sought after. It loops through the array, using the array's own length as a stopping condition (which makes the method nicely general), comparing each item with x. The comparison is done via a call to equals, since we are assuming here that the items are objects. If the item is found, we return immediately. If the loop eventually ends, we throw the exception.

The calling method has a try–catch pair. If the search is successful, the next statement is executed, whatever it is. If not, control transfers to the handler in the catch-part and alternative arrangements must be made. There is a test program on the web site that shows this method in action. We do not include it here, because we want to press on to the next search algorithm – the binary search.

Binary searching

If the data to be searched is ordered, that is, sorted, then there are more efficient searching methods than linear search. The archetypal one is called **binary search**. It involves splitting the sequence in half, and searching only that part where the value must lie. One can be certain about which half the value is in, because the sequence is assumed to be sorted.

For example, suppose we have the sorted sequence:

23 45 61 65 67 70 82 89 90 99

and are searching for the value 90. Informally, we could divide the sequence in two between 67 and 70 and see that 90 must be in the right-hand side:

23 45 61 65 67   70 82 89 90 99

We divide this subsequence in two between 89 and 90 and move to the right again:

70 82 89   90 99

The sequence we are interested in is now two long, but we still divide and move to the left, where we find 90:

90   99

This took four divides and compares, compared with nine with a linear search.

Clearly, binary search is faster *on average*, but not every time. If the value being sought was 23 (the first in the sequence), binary search would still start in the centre and move gradually to the left to find it. The best way to formulate such a binary search is by using a technique called **recursion**:

> **Recursion** allows us to describe an operation in terms of itself, based on modified data and with a stopping condition.

Using this idea, an algorithm for binary search is:

Binary search a sequence for x
  If the sequence has one element,
    compare x with it and return found or not found.
  Otherwise consider the element in the middle of the sequence.
    If $x <$ middle element, then **binary search** left subsequence for x
    else **binary search** the right subsequence for x.

In many cases, the sequence or subsequence to be split will not have an even number of elements and so we adopt the convention that the extra element goes to the left subsequence. Looking at the algorithm, one can see that an improvement would be to add an additional condition in the second part, to consider whether the value being sought is in fact the middle element at the time.

Conditions for binary search

Binary searching relies on the values being ordered, but it also relies on being able to index the sequence. Thus, binary searching is not possible on files or lists. It works on arrays only.

EXAMPLE 15.1 Animated binary search

Problem In order to illustrate binary search, we shall develop a Java program to implement the algorithm above, and show the stages of the search as it develops.

Solution We start off with a sequence of numbers, and every time we split the sequence, we shall print out only those numbers left in the sequence. This begs the question of how we 'split a sequence'. The answer is that we do not! What we do is keep only one sequence and indicate the left and right limits each time.

Algorithm There is a slightly difficult part in splitting a sequence. If the sequence starts at 0, the midpoint is at $n/2$, where n is the last index. For example, for an array going from 0 to 9, $9/2 = 4$ is the midpoint. However, if a subsequence runs from j to k in a larger sequence, then the midpoint of the subsequence is at position $(j + k)/2$. You should verify that you understand why this is so.

Program The program to animate the binary search follows. We have chosen to use character data stored as objects, and to read it in. Remember to keep the data sorted, or the program will not function correctly. (Alternatively, slot in a sort procedure and sort the data first, just to make sure.)
    The important part of the binary search method is its use of recursion, and we therefore list it separately first, with line numbers.

```
1.    static int BinarySearch (item a [], item x, int left, int right)
2.        throws ItemNotFoundException {
3.      display(a,left,right);
4.      if (left==right)
5.        if (x.equals(a[left])) return left;
6.        else throw new ItemNotFoundException ();
7.      else {
8.        int mid = (int) ((left+right) / 2);
9.        if (x.equals(a[mid]))
10.          return mid;
```

```
11.        else
12.        if (x.less(a[mid]))
13.           return BinarySearch (a, x, left, mid);
14.       else
15.           return BinarySearch (a, x, mid+1, right);
16.        }
17.     }
```

BinarySearch will call itself with the left or right subsequence (lines 13 and 15) until the subsequence is of length one (detected on line 4). Then it either exits with an exception (line 6), or returns the index of this subsequence (line 5). The point of call was line 13 or 15, so the return comes back to one of these. Both result in the method reaching a natural end (line 17) and so a return to the previous point of call is made again. Once again, this could be line 13 or 15. Eventually, the very first call of BinarySearch, which was made with the full sequence, will reach its natural end, and control will go back to the main program. All along, the index value that was detected as holding the required item x is being passed back as the return value of the method.

The main program and associated classes look like this:

```
import javagently.*;
import java.io.*;

public class Animated {

   /* The animated binary search program  by J M Bishop   Jan 1997
    * ===================================   Java 1.1
    * searches a sorted sequence for a given value
    * and shows the workings of binary sort.
    *
    * Illustrates recursion and user defined exceptions
    */

   static item a [] = new item [10];
   static int counter;

   static int BinarySearch (item a [], item x, int left, int right){
   //---------------------
       ... as above
   }

   public static void main (String args [])
     throws IOException {

     BufferedReader in = Text.open(System.in);
     System.out.println("**** Testing the binary search ****");
     System.out.println("Type in 10 sorted characters "+
                                       "separated by spaces");
     for (int i=0; i<a.length;i++)
       a[i] = new item (Text.readChar(in));

     // Loop to try several searches
     while (true)
       try {
         counter = 0;
```

```
            Text.prompt("Find what value?");
            item x = new item(Text.readChar(in));
            System.out.println("The array is:");
            System.out.println("0  1  2  3  4  5  6  7  8  9");

            try {
              int found = BinarySearch (a, x, 0, a.length-1);
              // do what ever is necessary with a[found]
              System.out.println((char) x.data+
                      " was found at position "+found
                      +" in "+counter+" probes.");
            }
            catch (ItemNotFoundException e ) {
              // react to x not being there
              System.out.println((char) x.data+" was not found in "
                +counter+" probes.");
            }
          }
        }
      catch (EOFException e) {break;}
    }

    static void display (item [] a, int left, int right) {
      for (int j = 0; j < left; j++)
        System.out.print("   ");
      for (int j = left; j <= right; j++)
        System.out.print((char) a[j].data+"  ");
      System.out.println();
      counter++;
    }

  }

  class item {
  // ---------
  // the objects being sorted

    item (char i) {
      data = i;
    }

    boolean equals (item x) {
      return data==x.data;
    }

    boolean less (item x) {
      return data < x.data;
    }

    char data;
  }
  class ItemNotFoundException extends Exception { }
```

Testing Several tests are shown, including one when the number was found, and one
when it was not. Note that e and j were found in fewer probes than with a linear

search, but that finding b took slightly more. A real advantage of the binary search is that it can always establish that an item is not there in far fewer probes than a linear search can. The exact number of probes is given by a formula which we shall discuss in the next section.

```
**** Testing the binary search ****
Type in 10 characters separated by spaces
a b c d e f g h i j
Find what value? e
The array is:
0 1 2 3 4 5 6 7 8 9
a b c d e f g h i j
e was found at position 4 in 1 probes.
Find what value? b
The array is:
0 1 2 3 4 5 6 7 8 9
a b c d e f g h i j
a b c d e
a b c
b was found at position 1 in 3 probes.
Find what value? j
The array is:
0 1 2 3 4 5 6 7 8 9
a b c d e f g h i j
          f g h i j
                i j
                  j
j was found at position 9 in 4 probes.
Find what value? x
The array is:
0 1 2 3 4 5 6 7 8 9
a b c d e f g h i j
          f g h i j
                i j
                  j
x was not found in 4 probes.
```

15.3 Quicksort and performance

There are many different algorithms for sorting, but one that is a classic because of its overall good performance is known as **Quicksort**. Sorting is based on the twin operations of comparing and exchanging; Quicksort is based on the principle that any exchange must take place over the greatest distance possible. Thus, instead of exchanging adjacent elements, we select elements that are at virtually opposite ends of the sequence. To do this, we adopt the split-in-half idea used in binary search. Basically, we split the sequence at a certain point and move all the bigger items to the right and the smaller items to the left, using 'long exchanges'. This done, we concentrate on each subsequence in turn, doing the same until only one item remains in each. Quicksort does not split each subsequence exactly in half, as binary search did, but divides on the position around which the last exchange was made.

Put in algorithmic terms, Quicksort is:

Quicksort
   Provided the sequence has more than one item
      Choose an item as a pivot (e.g. the midpoint)
      Move all items less than it to the left
      Move all items more than it to the right
      Quicksort the left subsequence
      Quicksort the right subsequence

where the algorithm for the Move is given in Figure 15.1.

Move

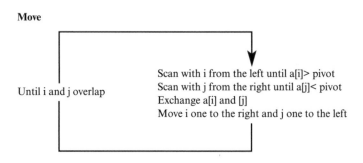

Figure 15.1 *Algorithm for a move in Quicksort.*

Quicksort is quite complicated and, strangely enough, animating it or performing an example in detail does not make it clearer. It is one of those algorithms that one has to understand in theory, and then accept as correct. It is, however, possible to program it quite concretely in Java.

In Java, a recursive Quicksort is:

```
1.      static item [] Quicksort (item [] a, int l, int r) {
2.        if (l < r) {
3.          display(a,l,r);
4.          int i = l;
5.          int j = r;
6.          int k = (int) ((l+r) / 2);
7.          item pivot = a[k];
8.          do {
9.            while (a[i].less(pivot)) i++;
10.           while (pivot.less(a[j])) j--;
11.            if (i<=j) {
12.               item t = (item) a[i].clone();
13.               a[i] = a[j];
14.               a[j] = t;
15.               i++; j--;
16.            }
17.         } while (i<j);
```

```
18.          a=Quicksort (a, l, j);
19.          a=Quicksort (a, i, r);
20.        }
21.      return a;
22.    }
```

Note some points about the programming. On line 7 we set up the pivot as a reference to the middle element using assignment, but on line 12, we use `clone` to make a copy of `a[i]`. Why the difference? The reason is that lines 12–14 are performing a swap of the two elements, `a[i]` and `a[j]`. Before we wipe out `a[i]` on line 13, we need to copy its contents.

Like `BinarySearch`, Quicksort is a typed method returning an array. Therefore when it is called, it takes `a` as a parameter and returns the new version as its result.

There is a test program for Quicksort on the web. Here is some typical output:

```
**** Testing Quicksort ****
27 91 42 23 40 74 96 28 31 59
27 31 28 23
27 23 28
    27 28
      28 31
                74 96 42 91 59
                42 96
                  96 74 91 59
                    91 96
23 27 28 31 40 42 59 74 91 96
```

On each line, the method displays the subsequence it has been given to sort. The initial pivot, 40, is not considered after the first line, because we had shifted everything greater than it to the right and everything less than it to its left. That means that 91 and 42, which were originally on its left, would have swapped with 31 and 28 respectively. You can see the result on lines 2 and 6, which show the first two subsequences.

A look at performance

The need to look for different algorithms to solve the same problem stems from a desire for speed: newer algorithms may be faster and therefore, in everyone's eyes, better. What differences in speed are found? With searching and sorting algorithms, they can be quite considerable. Moreover, the speed of the algorithms is proportional to the number of items involved, and therefore can become quite significant once there are thousands or millions of items.

There are two ways of comparing performance: theoretical and experimental. Let us look first at the theoretical performance. We calculate the speed of an algorithm based on the number of 'basic operations' it has to perform. These basic operations are rationalized to include only comparisons and exchanges, and assessing the performance boils down to counting the occurrence of these inside loops.

Comparison of sorts

Consider selection sort which we dealt with in Section 6.3. The outer loop goes for $n-1$, and includes $n-1$ exchanges. The inner loop runs from *leftmost* to $n-1$ and so reduces by one at each iteration. The number of comparisons is therefore:

$$(n-1) + (n-2) + (n-3) + \ldots + 1 = n(n-1)/2$$
$$= (n^2 - n)/2$$

To simplify matters, we ignore the coefficients in the number of exchanges and simply say that they are of the order n^2. If we add in the number of exchanges, the whole process is still dominated by the n^2 term.

Quicksort, on the other hand, uses a partitioning algorithm, which in rough terms involves $\log_2$ iterations. On each iteration, n comparisons are done, and roughly $n/6$ exchanges. Quicksort is therefore considered to operate at a speed proportional to $n \log_2 n$. In real terms, how does this compare with the order of performance of selection sort? Table 15.2 evaluates both formulae for various values of n. The difference is phenomenal. Suppose the unit of time for one iteration is 1 microsecond (10^{-6} s). Then for a million items, Quicksort will take 20 seconds, whereas selection sort will take around $11\frac{1}{2}$ days! It is interesting, though, that at this rate of 1 μs, the difference between the two sorts would not really be noticeable until n exceeds 1000. At this point, selection sort will take a full second, whereas Quicksort will take only 1/100 of a second. In an interactive environment, the difference may not even be noticed.

Table 15.2 *Comparison of the speed of selection sort and Quicksort*

n	Selection sort order n^2	Quicksort order $n \log_2 n$
10	100	30
50	2 500	300
100	10 000	700
1 000	1 000 000	10 000
10 000	100 000 000	130 000
100 000	10 000 000 000	1 600 000
1 000 000	1 000 000 000 000	20 000 000

So why do we not use Quicksort all the time? The answer is provided by the other performance indicator we have: space. Java methods occupy space in memory for their instructions, as well as for their data. Both the algorithms have roughly the same number of statements, so there is not much to choose on the instruction side. However, there is a big difference in data space used. Selection sort declares four local variables and uses them throughout. Quicksort declares eight local variables and parameters for each recursive call. Since recursive calls are stacked up, it may be in the worst case that for a million items, there are 160 items stacked up by Quicksort.

Yet even this is not a lot, and therefore we can probably conclude that the slight wariness with which ordinary programmers regard Quicksort is probably due to an unfamiliarity with recursion. Of course, Quicksort does not have to be programmed recursively, but the non-recursive version is even more awkward.

Comparison of searches

The two searches we looked at can easily be seen to have performances related to n (linear) and $log_2 n$ (binary). Here, the difference in speed is even more dramatic than sorting (Table 15.3). Put in real terms, this means that to search a telephone directory of a million entries by means of binary search, we should be able find any entry in no more than 20 goes. Very much better than an entry-by-entry linear slog!

Table 15.3 *Comparison of the speed of linear and binary search*

n	Linear search order n	Binary search order $log_2 n$
10	10	3
50	50	6
100	100	7
1 000	1 000	10
10 000	10 000	13
100 000	100 000	16
1 000 000	1 000 000	20

Where is this leading?

The study of algorithms, and their analysis of performance, is a cornerstone of computer science, and a major part of a second computer science course. In addition to the two sorting algorithms mentioned here, you will learn other sorts such as bubble sort (very slow), merge sort and tree sort (very fast), and pigeonhole sort (extremely fast, but fussy). You will learn how to choose an algorithm for a given solution, and look at the limits of algorithms: how fast can they really get? It is a fascinating study, and we have merely touched on it here.

15.4 Stacks and queues

We now start on the first of our data structures – the humble **stack**. Informally, a stack is defined as its name suggests: it is a pile of items which gets added to and removed from its top. A stack is often drawn upright, as in Figure 15.2(a), although it can be drawn on its side as in Figure 15.2(b).

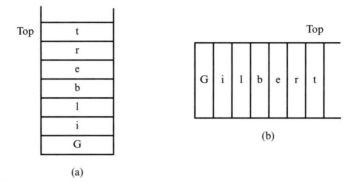

Figure 15.2 *Diagrams of stacks.*

Stack properties

Formally, we can detail the properties of a stack according to the criteria stated in Section 15.1 as:

- Nodes are arranged in sequence.
- There is one end, the **top**.
- Nodes are added to the **top**.
- Nodes are removed from the **top**.
- The stack cannot be scanned: only the **top** node is visible.[1]

A stack can also be known as a LIFO or Last-In First-Out list.

The `Stack` Class

We are now in a position to define the stack as a class. Fortunately, Java provides such a class in its `util` package, with the following methods:

Stack class

```
public class Stack extends Vector {
  public Object push (Object item);
  public Object pop () throws EmptyStackException;
  public Object peek () throws EmptyStackException;
  public boolean empty ();
```

---

[1]Actually Java cheats: it provides a method for searching through a stack (called search), but we shall ignore it here.

The Push method takes the item and pushes it on to the top of the stack. The Pop method returns the top item, 'popping' the stack at the same time, while the Peek procedure returns just the top item, without popping the stack. The Empty method determines whether there are any items on the stack. The Stack class is based on Vector, which means that a stack would be efficiently implemented as an array, but would not be restricted to a specific size.

The stack methods are defined for the superclass Object, so that we can put any other class's objects onto a stack, and remove them, provided we provide the correct type cast. Although Java will not enforce it, we should restrict each stack to items of the same class.

The next example is a simple one, but serves to illustrate the effect of using a stack.

EXAMPLE 15.2   Reversing a sentence

Problem Reverse a sentence of any length, word by word.

Solution Stacks have the property that they can be used to reverse a sequence. Each word is put on the stack as it is read. Eventually when the sentence ends, the words will be stacked up, one on top of each other. We can then go through the stack again, popping the words off.

Program

```java
import java.io.*;
import javagently.*;
import java.util.Stack;

public class Reverser {

  /* Testing the stack class  by J M Bishop  Jan 1997
   * ---------------------  Java 1.1
   * Reads a sentence and reverses it using a stack.
   *Illustrates push, pop and empty in Java's Stack class.
   */

  public static void main (String args [])
    throws IOException {

    BufferedReader in = Text.open (System.in);

    Stack S = new Stack();
    System.out.println("**** Testing the Stack class ****");
    System.out.println("Type in a sentence and end the input "+
      "(cntrl-D or cntrl-Z)");
    System.out.println("The original sentence is: ");

    while (true) {
```

```
        try {
          String word = Text.readString(in);
          S.push(word);
        }
        catch (EOFException e) {break;}
    }

    System.out.println("The reversed sentence is:");
    while (!S.empty())
      System.out.print (S.pop()+" ");
    System.out.println();
  }
}
```

Testing Expected input and output would be:

```
**** Testing the Stack class ****
Type in a sentence and end the input (cntrl-D or cntrl-Z)
The original sentence is:
The curfew tolls the knell of parting day,
The reversed sentence is:
day, parting of knell the tolls curfew The
```

Uses of stacks

Stacks are useful for recording the state of a computation as it unfolds. A typical example is the evaluation of expressions that involve precedence and nesting. A stack is also the data structure that implements recursion. In a language such as Java, it is usually possible to use recursion with its implicit stack rather than an explicit stack. The next data structure is probably more useful in practice.

Queues

Although stacks are the simplest structures we have, their property of reversibility is not always useful. A more common data structure is one where the items can be removed in the same order in which they were inserted. Such a structure is known as a **queue** or FIFO list (First-In First-Out).

In order to implement this property, a queue has to have two ends, indicating the front and back. New items are added on to the back, and items are removed from the front. Queues are usually drawn sideways, as in Figure 15.3(a). However, an innate property of queues is that they move forward: as an item is removed from the front, so all the other items behind it move up one. We can see immediately that such moving in an array implementation would be inefficient, and so we can already consider an alternative depiction of a queue as a circle. Here there is a fixed number of slots in the circle and the queue moves around it, as in Figure 15.3(b).

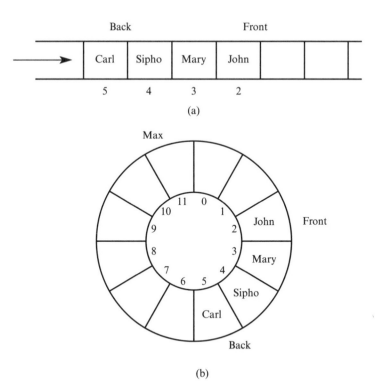

Figure 15.3 *Flat and circular queues.*

Queue properties

Formally, we can detail the properties of a queue as:

1. Nodes are arranged in sequence.
2. There are two ends, the **front** and **back**.
3. Nodes are added to the **front**.
4. Nodes are removed from the **back**.
5. The queue can be scanned from the front to the back.

The queue abstract data type

We are now in a position to define the queue as a data type. As for stacks, we define it in terms of the superclass Object. However, Java does not have a predefined queue class, so we need to implement one. On what should it be based? The choices are an array, the Vector class or the List class. The last two will allow the queue to be of variable size. The List is probably more powerful than we need, since we do not need to remove elements anywhere in it, only at the front. Vector provides complete extensibility, but we actually want to control the queue by reusing elements that have been vacated, in a circular manner, as in Figure 15.3(b). In fact, a simple array is a good choice.

What should we do if the queue gets full or if an attempt is made to remove an element when it is empty? The correct response is to throw an exception. This we do, using one exception with a parameter for full or empty. As was done with the Java Stack class, we define Queue based on the Object superclass.

Bounded Queue

```
public class Queue {
  Queue(int n);
  void       add (Object x);
  Object     remove ();
  boolean    empty ();
  boolean    full ();

  void       reset ();
  void       succ ();
  boolean    eol ();
  Object     current ();
}
```

A property of a circular queue is that it is bounded, and we can specify the bound in the constructor. In an array implementation, any bound specified would have to be less than the maximum size of the array declared within the queue class itself. The Add method (sometimes known as enqueue) adds an item to the back. Remove takes the item off the front (providing such an item exists). Remove is sometimes known as dequeue. Empty checks for an empty queue, and full checks if all the spaces allocated to the queue have been used up.

Property 5 above indicated that we should be able to scan the queue, perhaps doing something to each item. For example, we may wish to print the queue out, or search for a particular item. Without more sophisticated language features, it is difficult to generalize the scanning operation. We therefore have to allow the user access to the queue itself. This can be done in a controlled way by insisting that all scanning operations use the four iterator methods, which are the familiar ones defined before for the List class.

We now consider an example of the use of the above definition of a queue, *before* looking at how the queue itself is implemented.

EXAMPLE 15.3   Doctor's waiting room

Problem   A doctor has a small waiting room with a small number of chairs – say seven or so. Patients can come in and wait there, but once the seats are full, they tend to go away and come back later. Simulate this behaviour, so that the doctor can decide if it is essential to build a bigger waiting room.

Solution We can set up a queue with a maximum size and randomly let patients arrive and be seen by the doctor. The state of the queue can be continuously displayed and when it is full, a signal can be made, and arrivals ignored until there is space again.

Algorithm We can simulate what is happening with the algorithm of Figure 15.4. There is a 1 in 2 chance at each iteration that a patient will arrive (signified by checking whether the dice throw is even) and there is a 1 in 3 chance that the doctor will be ready to see another patient (dice is 1 or 2). There is also a 1 in 3 chance that nothing will happen (dice is 3 or 5). We run the simulation for a set number of times and watch what happens.

Simulation

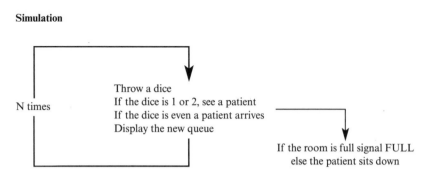

Figure 15.4 *The simulation of a doctor's waiting room.*

Program The contents of the queue are the same simple integer items we used for the `Stack` example. The class item is taken from that example (15.2), and not repeated here.

```
class WaitingRoom {
    /*  Simulation the Waiting Room    by J M Bishop    Jan 1997
     *  --------------------------      Java 1.1
     *  Shows a queue growing and shrinking in response to
     * random events.

     * Illustrates queues and queue iterators.
     */

    public static void main (String args []) throws QueueException {

        Queue chairs = new Queue (7);
        item patient;
        int choice;

        System.out.println("*** Doctor's Waiting Room Simulation ***");
        System.out.println("There are 7 chairs");
        System.out.println("Arrivals on 2,4,6; patients seen on 1,2");
        System.out.println();
        System.out.println("Time\tChoice\tPatient numbers");
```

```
     for (int i = 2; i<30; i++) {
       choice = (int) (Math.random()*6+1);
       System.out.print(i+"\t"+choice+"\t");
       display(chairs);
       try {
         if (choice == 1 || choice == 2)
           if (!chairs.empty())
             patient = (item) chairs.remove();
         if (choice == 2 || choice == 4 || choice == 6)
           chairs.add(new item(i));
       }
       catch (QueueException e) {
         System.out.println("\t\t\tWaiting room "+e.getMessage());
       }
     }
   }

  static void display (Queue q) {
    if (q.empty()) System.out.print("Empty"); else
    for (q.reset(); !q.eol(); q.succ())
      System.out.print(((item)q.current()).data+"  ");
    System.out.println();
  }
}
```

Testing A run could look like this:

```
*** Doctor's Waiting Room Simulation ***
There are 7 chairs
Arrivals on 2,4,6; patients seen on 1,2
```

Time	Choice	Patient numbers					
2	4	Empty					
3	3	2					
4	5	2					
5	3	2					
6	4	2					
7	3	2	6				
8	3	2	6				
9	4	2	6				
10	2	2	6	9			
11	5	6	9	10			
12	6	6	9	10			
13	1	6	9	10	12		
14	4	9	10	12			
15	5	9	10	12	14		
16	4	9	10	12	14		
17	4	9	10	12	14	16	
18	5	9	10	12	14	16	17
19	1	9	10	12	14	16	17
20	5	10	12	14	16	17	
21	1	10	12	14	16	17	
22	5	12	14	16	17		
23	3	12	14	16	17		

24	6		12	14	16	17			
25	4		12	14	16	17	24		
26	6		12	14	16	17	24	25	
27	4		12	14	16	17	24	25	26
					Waiting	room	Full		
28	3		12	14	16	17	24	25	26
29	3		12	14	16	17	24	25	26

The room got full only once in this short run, but given the random nature of the 'dice' throwing, completely different runs could be obtained. Notice that when we have a 2, the queue is both added to and removed from in one iteration. This circumstance occurs on lines 10–11.

Queues using arrays

The best array implementation for a queue is a circular one. The back of the queue starts at 0, and gradually moves up to the maximum size. Once there, the next position considered for adding is 0 again, provided a remove has taken place and there is no live data there. Because of this, the conditions for full and empty are not based on whether the indicators are 0 or max, but on a count of the number of live items. The full class definition for a queue is:

```
public class Queue {
   /* Queue abstract data type  by J M Bishop  Jan 1997
    * Implements a queue as a bounded circular array.
    * Has a set maximum of 100 elements. */

   Queue (int m) {
     if (m <= maxQueue) size = m; else size = maxQueue;
     front = 0;
     back = -1;
     live = 0;
     reset();
   }

   void add (item x) throws QueueException {
     // throws an exception if the queue is full
     if (live < size) {
       back = (back + 1) % maxQueue;
       Q[back] = x;
       live++;
     }
     else throw new QueueException("Full");
   }

   Object remove () throws QueueException {
     // throws an exception if the queue is empty
     if (live >=1) {
       Object x = Q[front];
       front = (front + 1) % maxQueue;
```

```
        live--;
        return x;
     }
     else throw new QueueException("Empty");
  }

  boolean empty () {return live == 0;}
  boolean full () {return live == size;}

  // Iterator methods
  void reset () {now = front;}
  void succ () {now = (now+1) % maxQueue;}
  boolean eol () {if (back==maxQueue)
                     return now == 0;
                  else return now > back;}
  Object current () {return Q[now];}

  private
  int size,        // total vector capacity;
      front, back, // indicators
      live,        // number of used spaces in the circular queue
      now;         // position for displaying the queue
  private Object Q [] = new Object [maxQueue];
  static private int maxQueue = 100;

}

class QueueException extends Exception {
  QueueException (String s) {super(s);}
}
```

Notice that all the data items are declared private in the queue, and are instance variables, to be replicated for each object.

Queues using lists

As with stacks, queues cannot be altered except at the ends, so the only advantage of
using a list as a base for the queue is to obtain complete flexibility of the size. Notice
that we would still provide a border facility, so that a queue can stop growing. The
above class definition can be very simply translated into a version based on lists and
is left as an exercise for the reader. The WaitingRoom program should run without
change if the one class is replaced by the other.

15.5 Linked lists again

The list discussed in Chapter 8 was very simple, and had the odd property that by
adding new items to the front, it stored data backwards. What we were really creating
was a stack – a very neat data structure because it has only one indicator. If we would

prefer to store the data in the correct order, then we need two indicators – one for the front and one for the back, as in a queue.

In fact, linked lists can be more general than either a stack or queue and can permit operations to occur not just at the ends, but anywhere in between.

Linked list properties

Formally, we can define the properties of a list as:

- Nodes are linked together linearly in both directions, forwards and backwards.

- There are two ends to the list – the front and the back.

- Nodes can be added anywhere in the list.

- Nodes can be deleted anywhere in the list.

- The list can be scanned forwards or backwards.

The new List class

The formal definition of the full-blown DLList class using DLNodes is given below. It gives more control to the programmer, and makes the DLNode class and two indicators visible so that positions within the list can be discovered, retained and used later. DL stands for doubly-linked, which is how the list is stored, and which gives it its power.

```
DLList

void       addBefore (Object x, DLNode pos);
void       addAfter (Object x, DLNode pos);
Object     remove (Node pos);
DLNode     search (Comparable x, int comp);
boolean    isempty ();

Object     current ();
void       reset ();
boolean    eol ();
void       succ ();

DLNode front, back;
int size;
```

The add method is replaced by addBefore and addAfter. Remove is augmented by a parameter, indicating which node should be removed. A search method based on the linear search of Section 15.2 has been added. It has the option to search either for equality, in which case the constant SAME must be supplied as a second parameter, or for ascending or descending order (LESS and MORE). That is why the item that is being searched for is not an `Object`, but is of the interface class `Comparable`. `Comparable` is defined as follows:

Comparable interface

```
interface Comparable {
  boolean less (Object x);
  boolean same (Object x);
  booelan more (Object x);

  final static int LESS = 0;
  final static int SAME = 1;
  final static int MORE = 2;
}
```

By using `Comparable` in the `DLList` class, we can leave the actual implementation of the comparison methods to the data types themselves. For example, a typical type that could be stored in a list would be:

```
class Student implements Comparable {

  double height;
  String name;

  Student(double h, String s) {
    height = h;
    name = s;
  }

  public boolean same (Object x) {
    return (name == ((Student) x).name);
   }

  public boolean less (Object x) {
    return (height < ((Student) x).height);
  }

  public String toString () {
    return ("\t"+height+"\t"+name);
  }
}
```

The constants are there so that users can select which order they require. If they select SAME and the item is not found, then an `ItemNotFoundException` is thrown.

A call to `DLList`'s constructor will initialize the list, setting the front and back indicators to null, and the size to zero. Unlike the other data structures, we allow the user of the object to have access to the list indicators. If we really wanted to protect them, we could make them private and provide equivalent access methods. The class DLNode is used to indicate a single node in the list. We do not, however, reveal exactly what class this is, and so maintain a degree of protection.

The following example makes excellent use of the new facilities of the DLList class. It is followed by a look at the implementation of the class.

EXAMPLE 15.4 Photograph line-up

Problem A photographer is going to photograph a class of students, and wants them neatly arranged by height. The idea is to have the taller people in the back rows, and for each row to slope downward from the centre. Given a class of students and their heights, we would like a plan of where each should stand.

Example Each row should be lined up as shown in Figure 15.5.

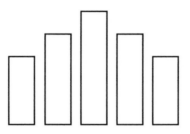

Figure 15.5

Solution We start by creating a single line of everyone in height order. Then, starting at the tallest, we peel off however many we want per row, and create a new list starting in the middle and adding alternately to the right and left. Suppose we label the people A, B, . . . where A is the tallest. Then a row of seven people would be arranged thus:

  G E C A B D F

Algorithm The algorithms make very good use of the list methods defined above. First, we consider how to create a list in height order (Figure 15.6). The result will be a list with the front pointing to the tallest person.

Now we consider how to peel off a row and create the left–right effect (Figure 15.7). For ease of computation, we assume that the row will have an odd number of people. Adding to the back equates to addAfter(back) and adding to the front becomes addBefore(front). We can print out or display the line, by calling the iterator methods. Then, we can erase the line and start with a new one. Erasing a list in Java is as simple as setting it to null, as then all the nodes that were associated with it will be garbage collected in a short while.

Program As before, the program is surprisingly clean and short, since all the work is done in the well-defined list methods.

Create an ordered list

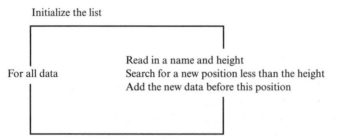

Figure 15.6

Create a left–right sorted list

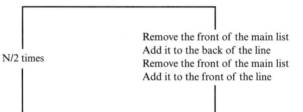

Figure 15.7

```
import java.io.*;
import javagently.*;

class Photo {

  /* The class photo program    by J M Bishop  January 1997
   * ========================    revised January 1998
   *
   * Uses doubly linked lists to set up the rows
   * for a class photo, based on height.
   * Illustrates List handling.
   */

  static DLList studentList = new DLList();

  static void lineUp () throws IOException, ItemNotFoundException {

    BufferedReader in = Text.open("students.dat");
    System.out.println("The students as read in are:");
    while (true) {
      try {
```

```
        double h = Text.readDouble(in);
        String n = Text.readString(in);
        Student s = new Student (h,n);
        System.out.println(s);
        DLNode higher = studentList.search(s,Comparable.MORE);
        studentList.addBefore(s,higher);
      }
      catch (EOFException e) {break;}
  }
  System.out.println("The students in height order are:");

  for (studentList.reset(); !studentList.eol();
       studentList.succ())
    System.out.println(studentList.current());
}

public static void pickOff (int row) {
  System.out.println("Row "+row+"\t");
  DLList line = new DLList ();
  Student s;
  s = (Student) studentList.remove(studentList.front);
  line.addAfter(s,line.back);
  for (int i = 0; i<rowSize/2; i++) {
    s = (Student) studentList.remove(studentList.front);
    line.addAfter(s, line.back);
    s = (Student) studentList.remove(studentList.front);
    line.addBefore(s, line.front);
  }
  for (line.reset(); !line.eol(); line.succ())
    System.out.println(line.current());
  line = null;
}

public static void main (String args [])
    throws IOException, ItemNotFoundException {
  System.out.println("**** The class Photo ****");
  lineUp();
  for (int row = 1; studentList.size > 0; row++)
    pickOff (row);
}

static final int rowSize = 7;
}

class Student implements Comparable {
  double height;
  String name;
  Student(double h, String s) {
    height = h;
    name = s;
  }

  public boolean same (Object x) {
    return (name == ((Student) x).name);
  }
```

```
public boolean less (Object x) {
  return (height < ((Student) x).height);
}

public String toString () {
  return ("\t"+height+"\t"+name);
}


}
```

Testing The program would process this and produce the following arrangement:

```
**** The Class Photo ****
The students as read in are:
        1.8     Danie
        1.58    Petra
        1.9     John
        1.55    Harry
        1.81    Mary
        1.75    Craig
        1.71    Sipho
        1.77    Diamond
        1.4     Tiny
        1.79    Michael
        1.76    Robert
        1.69    Elizabeth
        1.68    Lucy
        1.5     Sarah
The students in height order are:
        1.9     John
        1.81    Mary
        1.8     Danie
        1.79    Michael
        1.77    Diamond
        1.76    Robert
        1.75    Craig
        1.71    Sipho
        1.69    Elizabeth
        1.68    Lucy
        1.58    Petra
        1.55    Harry
        1.5     Sarah
        1.4     Tiny
Row 1
        1.75    Craig
        1.77    Diamond
        1.8     Danie
        1.9     John
        1.81    Mary
        1.79    Michael
        1.76    Robert
Row 2
        1.4     Tiny
        1.55    Harry
        1.68    Lucy
```

```
1.71    Sipho
1.69    Elizabeth
1.58    Petra
1.5     Sarah
```

The program has the restriction that the number of students must be a multiple of the row size, but this is a minor detail.

Implementing linked lists

We have assumed that the lists will be implemented using references and the DLNode class. Since insertion and deletion are allowed anywhere, it would be messy to use an array. We have also committed ourselves to supplying a front and back indicator, and to maintaining the size of the list.

There are still, however, several choices to be made in the implementation. The first issue is whether we go for a **singly-linked list** or a **doubly-linked list**. A singly-linked list will have links going from the front indicator to the last node, where the link will be null. The list's back indicator will refer to the last node. This is shown graphically in Figure 15.8.

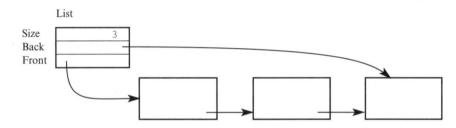

Figure 15.8 *A singly-linked list.*

The advantage of this implementation is that it uses up the minimum of extra space (one reference per node). However, it is not so easy to insert nodes before another node, and scanning the list backwards will require recursion.

An alternative is to spend an extra reference per node and to link the list in both directions. This gives us Figure 15.9. Doubly-linking a list is the most flexible

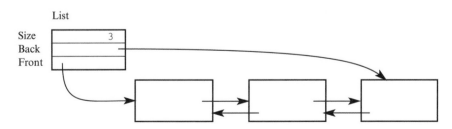

Figure 15.9 *A doubly-linked list.*

arrangement, and is not all that difficult to maintain. First of all, we need to augment the DLNode class with the extra reference:

```
class DLNode {
  /* The Node class version 2  by  J M Bishop   Jan 1997
     for storing objects in doubly linked lists
  */

  DLNode (Object d, DLNode f, DLNode b) {
    data = d;
    forward = f;
    backward = b;
  }

  DLNode forward, backward;
  Object data;
}
```

The implementation of such a DLList class is:

```
public class DLList {

  /* A doubly linked list class    by J M Bishop Jan 1997
   * -------------------------
   * allows storage of data in nodes which are linked
   * and can be traversed in either direction.
   *
   */

  DLList ()
    {now=null; front=null; back=null; size = 0;}

  void addBefore (Object x, DLNode pos) {
    if (size == 0) {
      // add to front (special)
      front = new DLNode (x,null,null);
      back = front;
    }
    else if (pos==null) {
      // add to front
      DLNode T = new DLNode (x,null,back);
      back.forward = T;;
      back = T;
    }
    else if (pos==front) {
      // add before front
      DLNode T = new DLNode (x,front,null);
      front.backward = T;
      front = T;
    }
    else {
      // add in the middle
      DLNode T = new DLNode (x,pos,pos.backward);
      pos.backward.forward = T;
      pos.backward = T;
```

```
    }
    size ++;
  }
  void addAfter (Object x, DLNode pos) {
    if (size == 0) {
      // add to front (special)
      front = new DLNode (x,null,null);
      back = front;
    }
    else if ((pos==null)||(pos==back)) {
      // add to back
      DLNode T = new DLNode (x,null,back);
      back.forward = T;
      back = T;
    }
    else {
      // add in the middle
      DLNode T = new DLNode (x,pos.forward,pos);
      pos.forward.backward = T;
      pos.forward = T;
    }
    size ++;
  }

  Object remove (DLNode pos) {
    Object T = pos.data;
    if (front == back) {
      front = null;
      back = null;
    } else
    if (pos == front) {
      front.forward.backward = null;
      front = front.forward;
    } else
    if (pos == back) {
      back.backward.forward = null;
      back = back.backward;
    } else {
      pos.backward.forward = pos.forward;
      pos.forward.backward = pos.backward;
    }
    size--;
    return T;
  }

  DLNode search (Comparable x, int comp)
    throws ItemNotFoundException {
    if (front == null) return front;
    for (reset(); !eol(); succ())
      switch (comp) {
      case Comparable.LESS :
        if (x.less((Comparable) current())) return now;
        break;
      case Comparable.SAME :
        if (x.same((Comparable) current())) return now;
        break;
```

```
        case Comparable.MORE :
          if (!x.less((Comparable) current())) return now;
          break;
      }
    if (comp == Comparable.LESS) return null;
    if (comp == Comparable.MORE) return null;
    else throw new ItemNotFoundException();
  }

  boolean isempty ()   {return front == null;}

  Object   current ()  {return now.data; }
  void     reset ()    {now = front;}
  boolean eol ()       {return now == null;}
  void     succ ()     {now = now.forward;}

  DLNode front, back;
  int size;
  private DLNode now;
}

class ItemNotFoundException extends Exception { }
```

In the add and remove procedures, we consider four different cases, depending on whether the list is empty or we are dealing with an end, whereupon the front and back pointers need special attention. In the general case, the insertion of a new node before another one, referred to by pos, follows the symmetric pattern:

```
newnode.backward = pos.backward;
newnode.forward = pos;
pos.backward.forward = newnode;
pos.backward = newnode;
```

and removal is done by:

```
pos.backward.forward = pos.forward;
pos.forward.backward = pos.backward;
```

15.6 Bit sets

The last data structure that we shall consider in this edition of *Java Gently* is the bit set. As we know from mathematics, a set is an unordered collection of items of the same type on which operations such as union, intersection and membership are defined. A bit set is different in that it is envisaged as a sequence of bits, each of which is known by number and can be turned on and off. Sets and bit sets are very similar in effect, but differ in the way they are used. In a set of integers, one could check whether it contained 8; in a bit set, one would check whether the 8th bit was on.

Some of the methods provided for Java's bit sets are given in the following form:

```
Bit sets

BitSet ();
BitSet (int n);

public boolean get (int b);
public void set (int b);
public void clear (int b);
public void and (BitSet s);
public void or  (BitSet s);
public void xor (BitSet s);
```

After having created a bit set with a given size or by using the default, we can set, get and clear individual bits. Then we can also combine two sets using the three operations shown. For an explanation of the results of bit operations, go back to Section 3.2 on booleans.

Bit sets are fairly restrictive in that they can record only integer numbers. That is, we cannot have sets of characters, for example. We can now consider an example of the use of sets, in fact of arrays of bit sets in this case.

EXAMPLE 15.5 Training schedules

Problem Employees at Savanna Inc. attend training courses, and a record of each course attended or planned to attend is kept on a file. We wish to discover which employees are signed up for which courses, and which courses overall have been used. We would also like to know which employees need computer user codes, given a list of courses that will be using the computer.

Solution One could construct arrays with the name of each employee who has done a course. Alternatively, if both the employees and courses are identified by number, then sets can be used.

Algorithm Assume that the data has employee numbers followed by a list of course numbers. A typical file would look like this:

```
50      1 2 3
44      3 8 7
99      1
61      1 7
```

meaning that employee 50 is meant to attend courses 1, 2 and 3; employee 99 is meant to attend 1 only, and so on. We need to keep a set of employee numbers for each course, and a set of all courses taken. This is done with the data structures:

```
static BitSet courses [];
static BitSet schedules [];
```

The algorithm then consists of reading in a number followed by its courses. For each course, we add the employee number to the set in the `courses` array indexed by that course. Then we also add the course to the employee's record in the `schedules` array. The important statements are:

```
// Put employee n on course c
    courses[c].set(n);
// Put course c in employee n's schedule
      schedules [n].set(c);
```

Before we can set bits in a bit set, though, we must take care that the object has been created. For example, creating a new course set would be done like this:

```
// Create course c if not yet started
    if (courses[c] == null)
       courses[c] = new BitSet (employeeMax);
```

Program The program is arranged in three sections, each its own method, namely: `readIn`, `display` and `userCodes`. One aspect of this program, unrelated to bit sets, is how to read data that has a terminator such as the end of a line. The `Text` class will not work in this case because it is oblivious to ends of line. Never mind: by now we are able to write our own input routines, picking off numbers from a `StringTokenizer` as we want them.

Reading in starts by getting a whole line, then tokenizing it and counting the number of tokens (using a predefined method). After getting the employee number, a for-loop can be used to process each course as described above.

```
static void readIn () throws IOException {
    // Uses its own StringTokenizer since data is read a line
    // at a time. A blank line signifies zero tokens and
    // ends the reading of data.

    String s;
    StringTokenizer T;
    int n, c, ntokens;

    while(true) {
      s = in.readLine();
      T = new StringTokenizer (s);
      ntokens = T.countTokens ();
      if (ntokens == 0) break; // no more employees
      n = getInt(T);

      //Create a schedule for employee n
      schedules [n] = new BitSet (courseMax);
      for (int i=0; i<ntokens-1; i++) {
        c = getInt(T);
```

```
      // Create course c if not yet started
      if (courses[c] == null)
        courses[c] = new BitSet (employeeMax);

      // Put employee n on course c
      courses[c].set(n);

      // Put course c in employee n's schedule
      schedules [n].set(c);
    }
  }
  System.out.println("Data read in successfully.");
}
```

Getting in the list of courses that use the computer follows a similar pattern, and the students enrolled for that course are added into another bit set as follows:

```
codesNeeded.or(courses[c]);
```

The rest of the program is concerned with printing out the sets neatly.

```
import java.util.*;
import java.io.*;
import javagently.*;

public class Training {

  /* Training schedules program     by J M Bishop   Jan 1997
   * ==========================     Java 1.1
   * Creates class lists and schedules for employees,
   * including a list of those who are taking special courses.

   * Uses bit sets and its own StringTokenizers rather than
   * javagently's Text class.
   */

  static BitSet courses [];
  static BitSet schedules [];
  static BufferedReader in = Text.open (System.in);
  static int employeeMax, courseMax;

  public static void main (String arg []) throws IOException {

    // The main program declares two arrays of sets and then
    // calls the three static methods to read and print out
    // the data.

    System.out.println ("*** Training Schedules ****");
    Text.prompt("What is the highest course number?");
    courseMax = Text.readInt(in);
    Text.prompt("What is the highest employee number?");
    employeeMax = Text.readInt(in);
```

```java
      // Create an array of sets, one for each course
      // Each set will be EmployeeMax big
      // but is created later as the data is read in
      courses = new BitSet [courseMax];

      // Create an array of sets, one for each employee
      // Each set will be CourseMax big
      // but is created later as the data is read in
      schedules = new BitSet [employeeMax];

      System.out.println("Enter each employee's schedule as follows:");
      System.out.println("Employee number  course numbers");
      System.out.println("Example 100  12  7  4  15");
      System.out.println("End with a blank line");
      readIn();
      display();
      userCodes();
   }

   static void readIn () throws IOException {
       _ as above
   }

   static void display () {
     // prints each of the set arrays slightly differently.
     // calls printSet for printing a single set

     System.out.println("The course lists");
     System.out.println("================");
     for (int c =0; c<courseMax; c++) {
       System.out.print(c+": ");
       if (courses[c]==null) System.out.println("No students");
       else
         printSet(courses[c]);
     }
     System.out.println("The schedules");
     System.out.println("=============");
     for (int n = 0; n < employeeMax; n++) {
       if (schedules[n] != null) {
         System.out.print(n+": ");
         printSet(schedules[n]);
       }
     }
   }

   static void userCodes () throws IOException {
     // A method to illustrate a bit set operation.
     // given a subset of the course numbers,
     // create the union (or) of all the employees
     // signed up for them and print that set.

     Text.prompt("Which are the computer-related courses?");
     BitSet codesNeeded = new BitSet(employeeMax);
```

```
    String s;
    StringTokenizer T;
    int c, ntokens;

    s = in.readLine();
    T = new StringTokenizer (s);
    ntokens = T.countTokens ();
    for (int i=0; i<ntokens; i++) {
      c = getInt(T);
      codesNeeded.or(courses[c]);
    }
    System.out.println("Employees needing usercodes");
    System.out.println("===========================");
    printSet(codesNeeded);
  }
  static void printSet (BitSet b) {
    // Prints the members of a single bit set

    for (int i = 0; i < b.size(); i++)
      if (b.get(i)) System.out.print(i+"  ");
    System.out.println();
  }

  static int getInt (StringTokenizer T) {
    String item = T.nextToken();
    return Integer.valueOf (item.trim()).intValue();
  }
}
```

Testing   A sample run would give:

```
*** Training Schedules ****
What is the highest course number? 10
What is the highest employee number? 100
Enter each employee's schedule as follows:
Employee number course numbers
Example 100 12 7 4 15
End with a blank line
50 1 2 3
44 3 8 7
99 1
61 1 7

Data read in successfully.
The course lists
================
0: No students
1: 50 61 99
2: 50
3: 44 50
4: No students
5: No students
6: No students
7: 44 61
```

```
8: 44
9: No students
The schedules
=============
44: 3 7 8
50: 1 2 3
61: 1 7
99: 1
Which are the computer-related courses? 2 3
Employees needing usercodes
==========================
44 50
```

SUMMARY

This quick tour through algorithms and data structures emphasized that there is always more than one way of approaching the solution to a problem. In sorting and searching, we had linear or binary methods (with vastly differing performances). Recursion was also introduced as a means of expressing solutions in a simple and elegant way.

In data structures, we can implement via arrays or linked lists, with different effects. However, what we did manage to achieve is a defined set of properties for each data structure, which are adhered to no matter what the implementation chosen.

Four data structures were discussed — stacks, queues, linked lists and bit sets. The two Java-implemented ones — stacks and bit sets — served as guides for the definition of the other two. In the examples associated with illustrating the data structures, some of the lesser-used Java features cropped up again: interfaces, tokenizers and user-defined exceptions.

QUIZ

15.1   If the linear search in Section 15.2 was to be used to search an array of integers, what line would you change?

15.2   Give the phases that would be printed by the animated binary search looking for 10 in the following list of numbers:

2 5 7 8 10 13 16 20

15.3   Under what condition is binary search always faster than linear search?

15.4   If we pushed the numbers one to ten onto two stacks, S1 and S2, alternately, and then took all of S1 followed by all of S2 off, what would be printed out? The code is:

```
Stack S1 = new Stack(5);
Stack S2 = new Stack(6);
for (int i = 1; i<=10; i+=2) {
  S1.push(i);
  S2.push(i+1);
}
while (!S1.empty())
  System.out.print(S1.pop()+" ");
while (!S2.empty())
  System.out.print(S2.pop()+" ");
```

15.5   In the doctor's waiting room example (15.3), assume that each time period is 2 minutes. In the run shown here, how long has the patient now first in the queue been waiting when the simulation ends?

15.6 Given a list defined as

```
DLList L = new DLList ();
```

write a call to the search method of the `DLList` class to check whether the object C is in the list or not, and to print out the result.

15.7 Given the doubly-linked list shown in Figure 15.9, show all the statements that would be executed to add a node containing W after the O, making HOWN.

15.8 Show the steps to then add a node containing S before the front of the list, making SHOWN.

15.9 Give a definition of a new bit set that will keep track of all courses taken by anyone in the Training Schedules Example 15.5.

15.10 Write the statement that can be added to the `readIn` method to update the set of all courses each time a student's particulars have been processed.

PROBLEMS

15.1 **Speedier concordance**. How could the concordance of Problem 7.5 be speeded up with faster sorting and searching?

15.2 **Stack spy**. Suppose we wanted to print out the contents of a stack, without destroying them, and without using anything other than push and pop operations. Write a program to do this.

15.3 **Waiting statistics**. It is clear that some patients in Example 15.3 could wait a long time before being seen by the doctor. At each display, compute the total time waited by all the patients in the queue and print this out on the right hand side.

15.4 **Queues with lists**. Implement a queue class based on linked lists. Could it be done by inheriting from the new `List` class?

15.5 **Palindrome with a stack**. Solve the palindrome problem (7.4) using a stack rather than an array.

15.6 **Winning a raffle**. At a party, everyone is given a numbered raffle ticket. After supper, a number is drawn and the person with the number wins the prize, and so does that person's family. Write a program to read in people in families into lists, to organize a draw, and to print out the winning person and his/her family.

15.7 **Sorting lists**. Linked lists can be sorted as follows: Create a new list of the same kind. Add each element into it with a LESS or MORE comparison as required. Then the new list is a sorted version of the old. Add such a sort method to the `List` class and test that it works.

15.8 **Electronic diary**. Students at Savanna University have to undertake a group project in their third year. The number of groups and the number of students in a group vary from year to year. One of the difficult tasks at the beginning of the year is establishing when members of a particular group can meet and discuss their project, since they may be taking different courses and have different timetables. They would like to get computer assistance in arranging meetings. Make use of bit sets and linked lists to set up such an electronic diary program.

Answers to quizzes

Chapter 1

1.1 A compiler translates a program written in a human-readable computer language into a computer-executable machine language.

1.2 A compilation error occurs if the language is used incorrectly, e.g. with incorrect spelling or grammar. A logic error results from a program that is asked to perform an invalid action, such as division by zero, or to take a sequence of steps that do not produce the desired result.

1.3 Clock speeds are going up all the time, but you could have a 150 megaHertz processor.

1.4 Computers running Java would start at 32 megabytes.

1.5 Removable diskettes are fairly standard at 1.44Mbytes. Hard disk drives start from 1 gigabyte upwards.

1.6 This textbook certainly fits on two 1.44Mbyte diskettes on my computer.

Chapter 2

2.1 The call for a completely symmetrically placed circle may need slightly different pixel coordinates on different computers. The following works on a Sun:

```
g.setColor (Color.blue);
g.drawOval (20,30,260,260);
```

2.2
```
Tree marula = new Tree ();
```

2.3 Instance variables, because we need a name for each instance of a tree.

2.4
```
System.out.println
   ("-------------------\n" +
   "|   Jane Bramley    |\n" +
   "|   104 Cane Street |\n" +
   "|   Freetown        |\n" +
   "-------------------");
```

```
System.out.println ("-------------------");
System.out.println ("|    Jane Bramley   |");
System.out.println ("|    104 Cane Street|");
System.out.println ("|    Freetown       |");
System.out.println ("-------------------");
```

In the first example, the five lines of the address would not fit on one program line, and so will need to be split into separate strings, concatenated together.

2.5   2
       900009
       64
       3
       3
       2

2.6   `x = Math.sqrt ((b*b-4*a*c)/(2*a))`

2.7   `getDefault` is used to get the default locale that a program is running in. We put this in the object `here`. Then we create an artificial locale for Germany and superimpose it on `here`. The information for Germany is stored in `there` and is set into the computer using `setDefault`.

2.8   ```
       int distance;
       double flour;
       int age;
       int minutes;
       double balance;
       ```

2.9    | | |
       |---|---|
       | `main` | method |
       | `final` | keyword |
       | `System` | class |
       | `newArrive` | variable |
       | `NewFleet` | class |
       | `out` | object |
       | `Math` | class |
       | `class` | keyword |
       | `println` | method |
       | `round` | method |
       | `100` | constant |
       | `arrive` | variable |

2.10   ```
       quiz2.java:3: Identifier expected.
       max = 10;
          ^

       quiz2.java:5: Identifier expected.
          double K =1,1000;
                       ^

       quiz2.java:7: Identifier expected.
          static int 2ndPrize = G25;
                     ^
       ```

```
quiz2.java:7: Invalid character in number.
  static int 2ndPrize = G25;
              ^
quiz2.java:9: Duplicate variable declaration: double x was double x
  static double x = 6;
              ^
5 errors
```

Line 2 did not have a type. Line 4 used a comma instead of a full stop in a number. Two reasons for rejecting an identifier starting with a digit caused line 6 to fail. Line 8 redefined the variable x.

Chapter 3

3.1   None.

3.2   The output from the loops as given would be:

```
1
2
3
4
1
2
3
4
+
```

```
        for (int number=1; number < 6; number++) {
          System.out.print(number);
          for (int sign = 0; sign < number; sign++)
            System.out.print("=");
          System.out.println('+');
        }
```

```
1=+
2==+
3===+
4====+
5=====+
```

3.3   If there is no data to be copied into an object when it is created, and no other initializing to be done, then we do not have to supply a constructor explicitly.

3.4
```
for (int century = 1900; century < 2000; century +=10)
   System.out.print(century+" ");
System.out.println();
```

3.5
```
boolean scoreok, mathsok, csok, qualified;
scoreok = score >= 20;
mathsok = maths <= 'C';
csok = cs <= 'D'
mathsok = mathsok | (maths >= 'D' & csok);
qualified = scoreok & mathsok;
```

3.6　`Tickets blank ('=', '|', 7, 15);`
　　　`varyBox (' ');`

3.7　The reason for declaring `price` as a character is quite convoluted. Start at the last method called, namely `aLine`. It has three parameters, and the middle one is called `centre`. When `aLine` is called for the top and bottom lines of a ticket, the character in `hori` is supplied as the actual parameter. `hori` is initialized in the constructor, and is usually '=' or '-'. Thus if `hori` is a character, so must `centre` be, and therefore so must `price` be a character. In terms of what is printed out, it would not matter whether `price` is character or integer, but the former makes more sense, as well as being compatible with the rest of the class.

3.8　`taxrate -= 0.5;`

3.9　`mountain (0, 0)  invalid because second parameter must be char`
　　　`mountain (8,'8') fine`
　　　`mountain (6)     invalid because only one parameter`

3.10　No, because `aLine` has been declared as private.

Chapter 4

4.1　Firstly, there are no curly brackets around the three statements involved in the swap, so that copying `x` into `temp` is the only statement that depends on the `if`. The others are done in either case. Secondly, once `x` has been changed via `x=y`, it is no use to say `y=x` if we want the old value of `x`. The corrected version is:

```
if (x > y) {
  int temp = x;
  x = y;
  y = temp;
}
```

4.2　`BufferedReader marksIn = new BufferedReader`
　　　`(new FileReader ("marks"));`

　　　or simply

　　　`BufferedReader marksIn = Text.open("marks");`

4.3　It will print out

　　　Error in number. Try again.

4.4　`4  10  9  8   7  or`
　　　`4   7  8  9  10`

4.5　`EOFException` could occur while reading (it will get thrown out by the `Text` class) and `DivideByZeroException` could occur during the division.

4.6　The `readString` method of the `Text` class expects words to end with white space, i.e. a blank or end of line or tab. Therefore a call to read a country name will only give United, unless we fool `readString` by joining the two words somehow.

4.7 Unix uses control-D. Windows uses control-Z.

4.8 `569833`

Ha! Remember to put explicit strings of a couple of spaces, or a string containing a tab escape character, between numbers when they are written in one `println` call. Thus the following would be better:

```
System.out.println(i+" "+j+" "+k);
```

4.9 `pre` can have only one of the values listed. So once it has been established which it is, checking for the others can be skipped. The answer is to put in else-parts or even better to use a switch-statement as discussed in the next chapter.

```
if      (pre == 'm') System.out.print("milli");
else if(pre == 'c') System.out.print("centi");
else if(pre == 'K') System.out.print("kilo");
System.out.println("metre");
```

4.10 We would have to separate the numbers and the units, as in 65 kg and 7 and then read the number followed by the string. `readString` will read everything after the number, including the space. If we do not want the space, we can trim the string as follows:

```
n = Text.readInt (in);
unit = Text.readString(in).trim();
```

Chapter 5

5.1 The last one looks like it may be different but in fact it relies on the default value of `ch` to get it going. Thereafter it works the same as the others.

5.2
```
switch (i) {
   case 0: System.out.println("Sunday"); break;
   case 1: System.out.println("Monday"); break;
   case 2: System.out.println("Tuesday"); break;
   case 3: System.out.println("Wednesday"); break;
   case 4: System.out.println("Thursday"); break;
   case 5: System.out.println("Friday"); break;
   case 6: System.out.println("Saturday"); break;
}
```

5.3 In every case we need an impossible value. For ages, maybe 999 or –1. For air temperatures in Celsius, 999 would also work. For years, we really cannot predict a finishing year, so –1 would be best.

5.4 Over to you!

5.5 If the value is not specified, none of the cases is executed, and the switch 'drops through' to the next statement.

5.6 `while (true)`

5.7　The do-try will enable an exception to the operation to be caught and handled, and then the loop can repeat again.

5.8
```
int n = 0;
while (n<=20) {
  System.out.print(n+" ");
  n+=2;
}
```

5.9

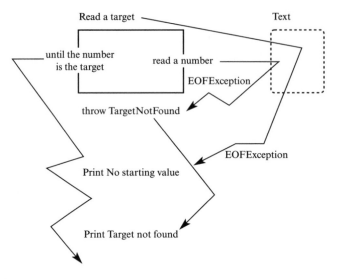

5.10　The calling statement would become:

```
if (mygame.getYourChoice(in)) break;
```

Chapter 6

6.1

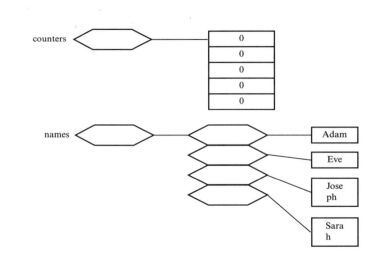

6.2 **Array**   a sequence of values of the same type of fixed size indexed by integers starting at 0 and accessed using [ ], e.g. a[4]

Table   a grid of values arranged in rows and columns, in Java also indexed by integers and of fixed size, accessed using [ ], e.g. t[i][j]

Matrix   a multi-dimensional table

Vector   a special Java class for storing array elements that has no fixed size, and elements are accessed using methods such as `getElement`

Dictionary an association between two kinds of data, one known as the key and the other as the value. Implemented in Java as a hash table with access methods such as `get` and `put`.

6.3   Its own class, which is `Judge`, gives it a length in the constructor, i.e.

```
score = new int [noofJudges];
```

6.4   There are several errors:

(a) The declaration of A should only have A mentioned once, on the left side, i.e.

```
int A [] = new int [10];
```

(b) The length of an array is given by the property `length`, not a method, so there should be no brackets.

(c) `A.length` returns 10, but the last index for A is 9, so `A[A.length]` does not exist.

6.5   Yes.

```
monthlyAverage (B, 100);
```

6.6
```
exchangeRates.put ("yen", new Double (167.9));
Double rate = (Double) exchangeRates.get("yen");
System.out.println(rate.doubleValue());
```

6.7   The rows come first.

6.8   `Hashtable` is in `java.util`

6.9   The last line returns an `Object` which has to be converted into `Dates` before it can be assigned. The correct line is:

```
Dates d = (Dates) holidays.get ("Foundation Day");
```

6.10   `java.lang.ArrayIndexOutOfBoundsException:`

Chapter 7

7.1
```
for (int i = 0; i<3; i++)
    System.out.println(names[i]+" e at "+names.indexOf('e'));
```

7.2   a positive number

7.3
```
word = word.toLowerCase();
word = word.charAt[0] + word.subString[1];
```

7.4   (a) `int i = Integer.parseInt(s);`

(b) `System.out.println(s);`

7.5   (a) The default for printing numbers larger than 999 arranges them with commas, e.g. 1,000.

(b) Numbers are truncated if the space allowed is not sufficient, e.g. printing 1000 in a space of 3 will give 0. (*Java Gently* Text class will rather expand the space in this case.)

7.6   Suppose our default locale is US and we want the salary in yen.

```
System.out.println("Salary is "+
    Number.Format.getCurrencyInstance(Locale.JAPAN).format(salary));
```

7.7
```
tragic.set (Calendar.YEAR, 1997);
tragic.set (Calendar.MONTH, Calendar.AUGUST);
tragic.set (Calendar.DAY, 31);
```

7.8   The answer depends on your locale, of course. For a UK locale it would be

Wednesday, 7 October 1998

but for a US locale it would be

Wednesday, October 7, 1998

7.9   No, the date format depends on the locale. As we change the locale in the main method, we want this change to be reflected each time in the way in which the dates are printed. Thus the statements must be executed over and over again.

7.10   `setMonths` is an instance method: it acts on a particular `DateFormatSymbols` instance.

Chapter 8

8.1   `name` is declared as private.

8.2   Yes. In the `CoffeeShop` class, a new object is created for each new coffee, referred to by an array item `C[blend]`. If we pass this reference to a class method `prepareToStock` in the `Coffee` class, then its data items can be accessed and updated, even though the reference itself will not be changed. The `prepareToStock` method would become:

```
static void prepareToStock (BufferedReader in, Coffee c)
  throws IOException {
  c.name = Text.readString(in);
  // and so on, using c. to access each member
  c.newBatchIn(in);
```

8.3 The reference to display inside sell refers to the display method visible at the time, i.e. Coffee's one. b is a batch, so that inside display itself, the reference to b.display() is to the display method of the Batch class.

8.4
```
public Object clone () {
  // clones a Coffee object
  Coffee c = new Coffee ( );
  c.name = new String (name);
  c.price = price;
  c.stock = stock;
  c.reorder = reorder;
  c.BatchStock = BatchStock.clone ();
  return c;
}
```

Of course, the List class does not have a clone method, and so one will have to be created before the above will compile.

8.5 C is in the same packages as E so package accessibility is possible. Declare e as:

```
int e;
```

8.6

8.7 The 90 kg of the Thu Jan 16 1997 batch would be sold first, then 10 kg from the Feb 05 batch to complete the sale. 2.25 kg would be left.

8.8 Comparing s with null with == does not tell us whether s is an empty string or not. It tells us whether s is a null object or not. The statement should be

```
System.out.println("s is an empty string is " + s.equals(""));
```

8.9 Nested classes can be accessed outside of their enclosing class; member classes may not.

8.10 The class diagram for the `Coffee2` class is

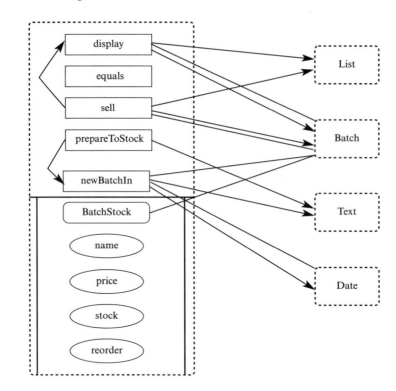

Chapter 9

9.1
```
class Giraffe extends Herbivores {
   Giraffe (String n, int w, double k) {
      name = n;
      grassneeded = w;
      neck = k;
   }
   private double neck; // its length
   // and more about giraffes
}
```

9.2 car must implement at least the five methods defined in the `Movable` interface.

9.3 `Sortable`.

9.4
```
public boolean lessThan (Sortable a) {
   Giraffe g = (Giraffe) a;
   return (neck < g.neck);
}
```

9.5 No. There is only one constructor for `Elephant` and it needs three parameters.

9.6

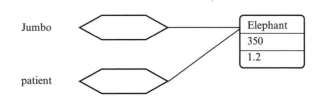

9.7   In the XTags class, the previous version of toString, defined in the inherited class Tags, is overridden.

9.8   Depending on whether the object stored in register[i] is a Tag or an XTag, different versions of toString (as explained in 9.7 above) will be called. The one returns a string made up of two values, the other a string made up of three values.

9.9   checkTag is a static method in the main Vet2 class. The whole method is bracketed by a try-catch pair. In the try-part, a lost pet's name is read in. If instead a control-D or control-Z (signalling end of data) is typed, the catch-part is executed. It throws the EOFException back at the caller, which is the main method.

9.10   a = n; cannot assign an object of a superclass without a cast. Needs

```
a = (Animals) n
```

e = r; e and r are not related by inheritance.

Chapter 10

10.1   Component is an abstract class and therefore cannot be directly instantiated as an object.

10.2   Once the frame f has been declared and set visible, the awt looks for a paint method for f and calls it.

10.3   BorderLayout

10.4
```
Choice c = new Choice ();
c.addItem ("Monday");
c.addItem ("Tuesday");
c.addItem ("Wednesday");
c.addItem ("Thursday");
c.addItem ("Friday");
c.addItem ("Saturday");
c.addItem ("Sunday");
```

10.5   The lights are drawn with coordinates relative to a top-left corner of (0, 0) on a canvas. This canvas is then inserted in the centre of the window so that its origin coincides with the origin of the centre of the border layout (see Figure 10.10). The contents of the canvas are not adjusted by the border layout in any way.

10.6   `Font mine = new Font("Serif",Font.BOLD,24);`

10.7
```
setLayout(new BorderLayout());
add ("North", new Label message[0]); // the WARNING title
Panel p = new Panel();
  p.setFlowLayout .. etc
  for (int i = 1; i<n; i++)
    p.add(new Label(message[i]));
add ("Center", p);
add ("South", new Button("Wait"));
```

10.8   `Traffic0` declares buttons that have to be watched and handled. The handling is done in the `actionPerformed` method, which is the required method of the `ActionListener` interface. By implementing this interface, `Traffic0` is linked to the event processing for buttons.

10.9   In the constructor, which has a default `BorderLayout`, we can add the button to the South as follows:
```
closeButton = new Button("Close");
closeButton.addActionListener(this);
add("South", closebutton);
```

The button must be declared in the class, and the class must inplement `ActionListener`. Then we add an `ActionPerformed` method as follows:

```
public void actionPerformed (Actionvent e) {
  if e.getSource() = closeButton {
    setVisible(false);
    dispose();
    System.exit(0);
  }
}
```

10.10 `p` is a Panel declared as part of the frame that `ButtonTest` extends. We add the `Reboot` button to this panel, then add the panel to the South of the frame. The second `add` refers to the current object which is the frame itself hence the different indents.

Chapter 11

11.1   `int i = Integer.parseInt(t.getText());`

11.2
```
TextField name = new TextField(8);
p.add(new Label ("NAME"));
p.add(name);
```

11.3   `TextArea` specifies an area in which text can be displayed and scrolled. Text can be selected and a cut-and-paste effect obtained. `ScrollPane` creates a viewing area for graphics and text with horizontal and vertical scrollbars.

11.4   Typing into a `TextField` does give a normal `ActionEvent` which is the same as for a Button. There is another event called `TextEvent` which can also be used, since a `TextField` is a `TextComponent` by inheritance. (Refer to Table 11.1.)

11.5 *event*`.getSource()`

11.6
```
double getDouble (TextField t) {
    return Double.valueOf(t.getText)).doubleValue();
}

// called by

kg = getDouble(weighField);
```

11.7 Adding three more products is simple: there are three gaps at the end of the `items` 'and corresponding' `unitcosts` arrays. If we add more than three more items to these arrays (which can be done without formality) these will not be displayed unless we increase the arrangement of the grid of buttons as well. This is set up in Till's constructor, which at the moment refers to 12 buttons precisely. It could be altered to refer to `items.length` as the ending for the for-loop. We may then also need to increase the height of the frame, as set out in the main program.

11.8 It will colour the field in on the screen (from white to light gray usually) and data cannot be entered into it until a `setEditable(true)` is called.

11.9 The sequence which handles the pressing of the Weigh button would become:
```
if (arg.equals ("WEIGH")) {
  weightField.setText("");
    if (chosen)
      weighField.setEditable(true);
}
```

11.10 The `message` array is used by both the `Traffic1` class (in `actionPer-formed`) and the `LightsCanvas` class. Therefore it assumes package level accessibility and is not declared private.

Chapter 12

12.1 `drawString`

12.2 The applet takes over the function of setting up the program and its size.

12.3 A constructor.

12.4
```
<APPLET code="Orange.class" width=200 height=200>
</APPLET>
```

12.5 `getCodeBase` finds out where the applet came from so that it can fetch other information from the same source.

12.6 GIF and JPG.

12.7 `getAppletContext` finds out where the applet is running so that the applet can perform operations on that machine. An example is writing in the status bar.

12.8
```
String s = getParameter ("yenexchange");
double yen = Double.parseDouble(s);
```

12.9 The `paint` method is called. It has new coordinates for the duke, who therefore seems to have moved.

12.10 `value = getParameter(name);`

Chapter 13

13.1 Milliseconds.

13.2 `java.lang`

13.3 `T x = new T();`

13.4 `start` does indeed call `run`.

13.5 No, only those methods that access data items at potentially the same time as other methods must be declared as synchronized.

13.6 Counter 1 asked for four Walkmen at time 7. It only got them at time 26.

13.7 The `ViewPoint` class is an inner class of the main program and therefore runs with its thread of control. As there are no buttons to watch or other actions for the main program to attend to, it can provide all the necessary computing power that `ViewPoint` needs.

13.8 `new CarThread ("North",450).start();`

13.9
```
class picture extends Thread {
   private Canvas a;
   picture (Canvas a) {
      area = a;
   }
   public void paint (Canvas a) {
      Graphics g = area.getGraphics ();
      g.drawImage (i, 50, 50, this);
   }
}
```

13.10 The `Curator` could call the `replace` method in the `Museum` class. This would have the effect of adding more Walkmen, but it would also take money out of the till, which is not what would be intended. A version of `replace` is needed which adds Walkmen but does not affect the deposits.

Chapter 14

14.1
```
Image e = getImage(getCodeBase(), "elephant.jpg");
g.drawImage (e,0,0,this);
```

14.2
a	any class extended from `Frame` and `Component`
b	class `Image`
`ImageProducer`	is an interface
`imagename`	class `URL`

14.3 Yes.

14.4 A handler that detects a SHUTDOWN message calls the `closeDown` method in the server. This causes the Boolean `done` to be set to true. However, the server will not detect that `done` is true until it comes around the loop to start a new client. So it needs another new client to start up before it can shut down! It is, however, polite enough to keep going with this new client until they both close together.

14.5 A `ServerSocket` object resides on the server and its function is to listen for new clients. A `Socket` object also resides on the server, but there is one created for each client, to handle its traffic.

14.6
```
<IMG SRC=\file:\... name ... >
```

14.7 A remote access system has objects on one computer, and access to them from another. The object class is defined on the server computer and access to some of its methods is needed on the client. These methods are grouped in an interface which the client refers to. The server has the actual implementation of the interface in a class which may be more elaborate.

14.8 Only two would be active together. The monitor could be displaying a message while a new one comes in, or it could ask the client to fetch an airport message. It would not be displaying or checking airline messages while this happens. However, new airline messages could come in.

14.9 If a web page has been set up in frames, then each frame can be given a name and one frame can load fresh information in another by specifying its name.

14.10
```
try {
    Naming.rebind ("Secret", secretThing);
}
catch (Exception x) {}
```

Chapter 15

15.1 The if-return statement would become

```
if (x == a[i]) return i;
```

15.2

```
2   5   7   8   10   13   16   20
                10   13   16   20
                10   13
                10
```

15.3 If the item being sought is not present, binary search will detect this fact in $\log_2 n$ probes, whereas linear search will require the full n.

15.4 The stacks after the pushing part look like this:

```
S1     1 3 5 7 9
S2     2 4 6 8 10
```

The resulting printout is:

```
9 7 5 3 1 10 8 6 4 2
```

15.5 Patient numbered 12 was added to the queue at time 12. At time 29 he or she had been in the waiting room for (29–12+1)*2 minutes, i.e. 36 minutes.

15.6
```
try {
   // X will be the place in the list where C is found
   Object X = L.search(C,Comparable.SAME);
   System.out.println("C is in the list");
}
catch (ItemNotFoundException) {
   System.out.println("C is not in the list");
}
```

15.7 The question is not well specified. First of all, we assume that Wobj, Oobj and so on are the names of objects with the corresponding data (separate to the copies in the list). Then we have to find the position of O. This can be done with:

```
try {
   // Opos will be the place in the list where O is found
   Object Opos = L.search(Oobj,Comparable.SAME);
}
catch (ItemNotFoundException) {
   System.out.println("O is not in the list");
}
```

Now we call

```
L.addAfter (Wobj, Opos);
```

Inside addAfter the following statements are executed:

```
if (size == 0)
else if ((Opos==null)
else {
Node T = new Node (W,Opos.forward,Opos)
Opos.forward.backward = T
Opos.forward = T
```

15.8   The call would be

```
L.addBefore (Sobj, Hobj);
```

Inside addBefore the following statements would be executed:

```
if (size == 0)
else if (Hpos == null)
else if (Hpos == front)
Node T = new Node (Sobj, front, null)
front.backward = T
front = T;
```

15.9   `allcourses = new BitSet (courseMax);`

15.10 `allcourses.set(c);`

List of syntax forms for Java

Index